P9-AFI-422

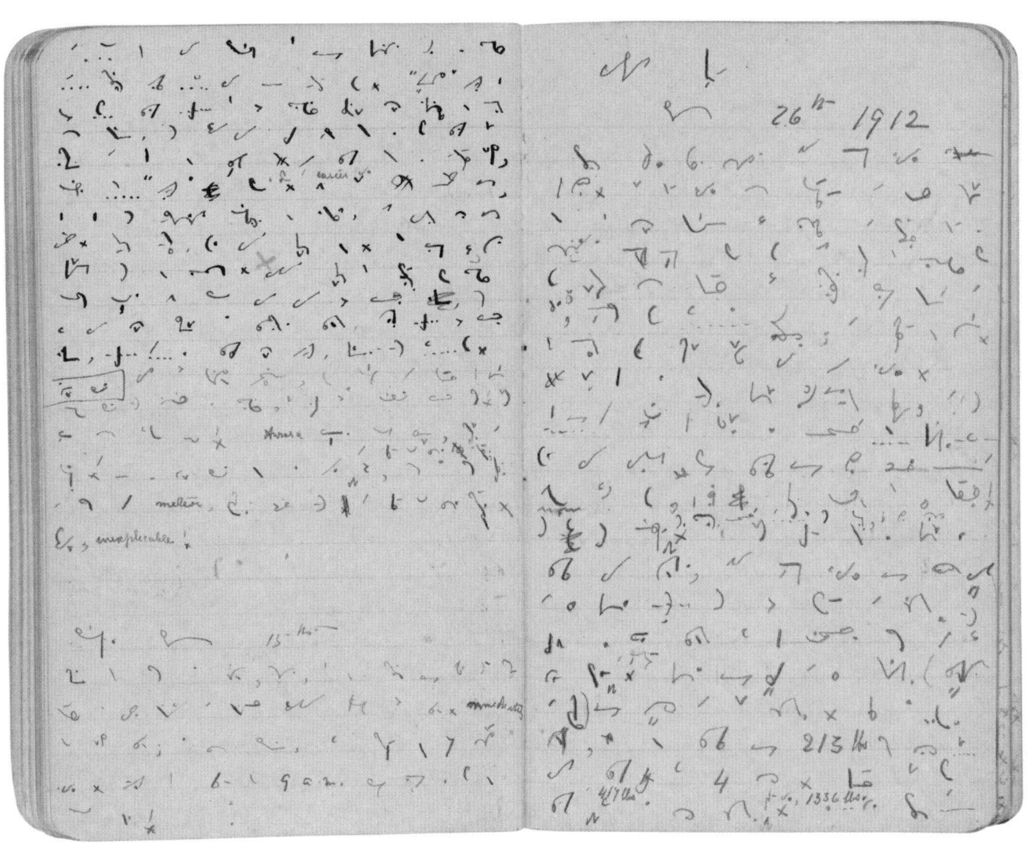

EXPLORERS’ SKETCHBOOKS

Fu-zag-ta.
Zoo. Jo-wei-xa.
No. 30.
MAP
showing the country
between Minindie & the Depôt
with the Darling as boundary.
Surveyed & drawn
by
Ludwig Becker.
Decbr. 15th 1860.
N
Mag.
Depôt
Camel's Feeding Ground
Dry Lake.
River
Darling
Minindie
Mile

Darling Depôt, Decb. 17.-60.

I shot this bird to-day, believing it to be the builder of such nests of which I found one on a Gum-tree at the Darling Depôt. The nest is 7 inches high and 9 inches in diameter. it is build of Darling-clay with bits of grass mixed with it & is lined with the fibres of bark, grass, and a few feathers. It looks somewhat like a bee-hive, and appears to have taken seven days to build it if each ring counts for one days work. — The bird is of the size of a small crow, black over all, with the exception of 10 featheas of the under-side of each wing, these feathers are white; then the point of the beak is pale flesh colored, and the conjunctiva near the cornea of the eyes is pink, while the iris is dark brown. The native name for this bird is Curali. — Having no books with me, in reference to birds I do not know its scientific name, but it will be found in Gould's work, and for that purpose I sketched the bird, but I believe the nest is not figured by Gould. L. Becker.

Draught of the Falls and Portage.

Lewis and Clark Codices.

Codex A.—Clark.

Journal

May 13, 1804—Aug. 14, 1804.

(complete.)

Clark's No. 1.

Biddle's No 1

Coues' A.

Folios 92 — pages 184

Codex Aa

American Philosophical Society,

(FOUNDED 1743.)

104 SOUTH FIFTH STREET.

PHILADELPHIA.

May 1804 to Sept. 1805

EXPLORERS' SKETCHBOOKS

THE ART OF DISCOVERY & ADVENTURE

Huw Lewis-Jones ↘↗ Kari Herbert
Foreword by Robert Macfarlane

CHRONICLE BOOKS
SAN FRANCISCO

Front cover (clockwise from top left): Henry Walter Bates: © The Trustees of the Natural History Museum, London; Howard Carter: © Griffith Institute, University of Oxford; Abel Tasman: Dutch National Archives, The Hague; Margaret Mee: Royal Botanic Gardens, Kew; Edward Norton: © Norton Everest Archive.

Back cover: A collection of Sir Ghillean Prance's notebooks, photographs, equipment, and specimens: Photography Martin Hartley/Art Direction Huw Lewis-Jones, Prance Collection.
Half-title: Charles Harrisson's Antarctic sledging journal written in phonetic shorthand.

Pages 2-3 (clockwise from top left): Philip Georg von Reck's journal, 1730s; Edward Norton, sketch of a fellow climber on the Everest expedition, 1924; Hector Horeau, 'Temple view of Sphinx Avenue and Pylon', el-Sebua, 1838; Ludwig Becker, white-winged chough, 1860; von Reck's journal, 1730s; Titian Ramsay Peale, polar bear, 1830, probably from a museum specimen; sketch map by Ludwig Becker, the country between Minendie and the Depot with the Darling River in 1860.

Frontispiece: Journals from Lewis and Clark's 'Corps of Discovery' expedition.

page 10: A page of sea birds by Dutch scholar and pastor Jan Brandes.

Page 20: Page from the sketchbook of Philip Georg von Reck; page 21: sketches by William Heaton Cooper.

First published in the United Kingdom in 2016 by Thames & Hudson Ltd.

First published in the United States in 2017 by Chronicle Books LLC.

Library of Congress Cataloging-in-Publication Data is available.
ISBN: 978-1-4521-5827-3
Manufactured in China

10 9 8 7 6 5 4 3 2 1

Chronicle Books LLC
680 Second Street
San Francisco, CA 94107
www.chroniclebooks.com

Chronicle books and gifts are available at special quantity discounts to corporations, professional associations, literacy programs, and other organizations. For details and discount information, please contact our premiums department at corporatesales@chroniclebooks.com or at 1-800-759-0190.

CONTENTS

FOREWORD

Robert Macfarlane

One of the most remarkable stories in this remarkable book concerns the explorer-missionary David Livingstone. On the morning of 15 July 1871, Livingstone was in the Congolese town of Nyangwe. Suddenly, Arab slave-traders opened fire on the local inhabitants. As the shooting started, Livingstone took cover – and watched, appalled, as hundreds of Congolese were gunned down.

Desperate to record the massacre, but lacking either fresh paper or ink, Livingstone improvised. He crushed berries to make coloured juice, tore pages from a copy of the London *Evening Standard*, and scribbled his description of the atrocity in berry-ink perpendicular to the dense columns of newsprint. When finally published, Livingstone's eyewitness account caused such outrage that it led to the closure of the Zanzibar slave-market. But the original document itself was so fragile, and the ink so weak, that his handwriting soon became illegible and then all but invisible. It is only recently that 'spectral imaging technology' has made his original script decipherable again – a ghostly account of a distant moment brought shimmering back into modern view.

Again and again in *Explorers' Sketchbooks*, versions of this shimmering-back – this 'spectral' retrieval – occur. These pages teem with visions and encounters that are startling for their immediacy, despite being separated from us by great gulfs of geography and history. A crane fly buzzes across Linnaeus's Lapland journals. A colourful Sarawakian tree-frog squats on Alfred Wallace's, its wide webbed feet gripping each corner of the page onto which it has been painted. The exquisite pencil draughtsmanship of William Burchell records the head of a South African white rhino as vividly as if it has just pushed its horns through the paper. Sydney Parkinson draws the swirled tattoos on the buttocks of Māori men who visited James Cook's ship the *Endeavour* in November 1769 (those buttocks themselves constituting a very different kind of sketchbook, and the tattoos another form of pen-and-ink record), and his drawings cause a moment to leap back to life: Māori and mariners communicating cautiously, Parkinson closely observing these bare-skinned, black-inked men as they move around the deck of the ship, the waves foaming on the cliffs of the Cape Brett peninsula, Parkinson's pencil scratching on the page...

I had thought myself reasonably familiar with the history of exploration, having researched the subject, written on it and been inspired by it for the past twenty years or so. But in this book Huw Lewis-Jones and Kari Herbert have shown me the considerable limits of my knowledge – and opened up dazzling new horizons and vistas to me. They have made a rich realm in which to wander, an archive into which to dive, a *wunderkammer* of *wunderkammers* – beautifully collected and curated, and magnificently produced. It stands as testimony to its authors' deep love of their subject, and also to their great erudition as cultural historians.

There are famous documents and legendary names here (Speke, Shackleton, Humboldt, Scott, Stark, Audubon), but they are joined by a host of lesser-known remarkable figures. John Auldjo, for instance, an early ascensionist of Mont Blanc, who went on to make exquisite plan-view maps of the lava-flows of Vesuvius: a sort of deep-time-lapse image of the volcano's successive eruptions. I was fascinated to meet the brandy-drinking, bandit-loving lepidopterist, Margaret Fountaine – who stored her sketchbooks within silk sleeves – and the oceanographer William Beebe, who took a bathysphere down into the abyssal depths of the Caribbean Sea, and brought back images of creatures so fabulously toothsome and contorted that they seemed to have writhed straight from the imagination of Hieronymus Bosch. Most surprising of all to me, perhaps, are Maria Sibylla Merian's surrealist seventeenth-century assemblages, derived from her travels in South America: a black monkey holding a Surinam cherry next to a European forget-me-not, all painted on the skin of an unborn lamb carried from Amsterdam.

Repeatedly in *Explorers' Sketchbooks*, I was reminded of the eerie durability of paper and ink: its ability to survive across centuries, and to preserve not just data but also textures of feeling and imagination. 'He was always thinking on paper and clarifying his mind', observed Elizabeth Chatwin of her husband, Bruce Chatwin, perhaps the most influential of recent journal-keepers. Notebooks and sketchbooks are never only receptacles for finished thought. Their materiality shapes the nature of record. So it is that – reading them back – we can catch glimpses of perception in action, awe as it strikes, or fear at its frost-point.

I end with an image that I cannot get out of my mind. In the summer of 1883 a young German geographer called Franz Boas set sail for Cumberland Sound in the Canadian High Arctic. The time Boas subsequently spent among the Inuit of that region would shape his future work as an anthropologist, which would in turn shape the modern disciplines of anthropology and ethnography. On the approach to Cumberland Sound, Boas's ship was stuck for several weeks among the ice-floes. He passed the time with characteristic curiosity, sketching and painting the environment around him. One of those paintings is reproduced here, with a scribbled caption dating it to 28 July 1883. It shows a jagged iceberg floating in a dark sea. The centre of the iceberg has been hollowed out by wave-action, leaving a blue arch narrowing away to a distant point of pale light. The iceberg is startling – but the arch is *mesmerizing*. Its eye-beckoning blueness, the promise it offers of vision, the dangers and hardships that will attend the pursuit of that vision ... it stands for me as a strange emblem of the drives, dreams and desires that are on display in the extraordinary pages you are about to read.

INTRODUCTION

THESE ROUGH NOTES

Huw Lewis-Jones ↘↗ Kari Herbert

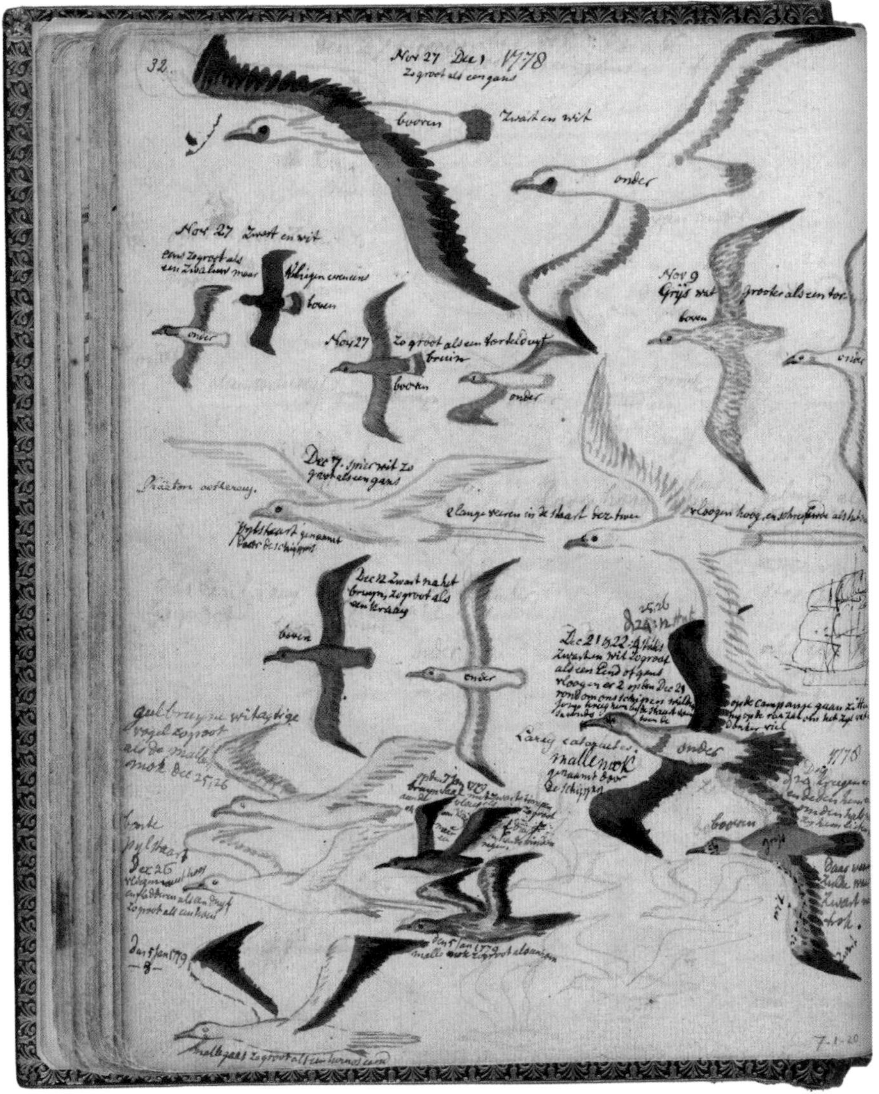

Odysseus made his journeys and then Homer wrote about them. To discover and to reveal – that is the way every artist sets about his business. All art is, I suppose, a kind of exploring.

ROBERT J. FLAHERTY, 1949

Three billion miles from Earth, a robotic spacecraft offers the first glimpse of an icy world at the edge of the solar system. It is 14 July 2015 and the craft has travelled for almost ten years to make a flyby of the dwarf planet Pluto. Back at mission control in Maryland, the first images begin to arrive and the world's press has gathered. It's a historic moment for the *New Horizons* team – their nuclear-fuelled probe has exceeded everyone's expectations. Likened in size by its creators to a 'grand piano fused to a satellite dish', it manages to capture about 150 observations of Pluto and one of its moons, Charon, though it has taken sixteen months for all the data to be transmitted back by radio waves to Earth. The results of this incredible feat of exploration exist as small pulses of energy launched home across the black void of space.

New worlds are revealed in images. These electronic sketches, if you like, present a vision of things never before seen. We learn that Pluto has immense ice mountain ranges as high as the Alps, and deep canyons and ridges carved by volcanic processes as yet unknown. And the exploration continues. The little craft speeds onwards towards the Kuiper Belt, a vast disc of asteroids and ancient lumps of frozen gas. And all the while, the probe takes photographs. We await more results that might never come. Stephen Hawking, the Cambridge cosmologist, sends a message to the team. 'The revelations ... may help us to understand better how our solar system was formed. We explore because we are human and we long to know.'

A little over a century ago, an explorer of a different age, Captain Robert Scott, trudged across a frozen wasteland that was also little known and uncharted, a terrain akin to the surface of another planet. No radio-wave data transfer, television feeds or satellite uploads for Scott and his companions. Rescue is unlikely and the odds overwhelming. But he has a job to do, to gather information and wrestle some meaning from the chaos of the void before him. He drafts reports in his hut, isolated from the rest of the world during the long Antarctic winter, jotting notes into his journal at night as he and his team inch their way south off the edges of their maps. At home, a generation inspired by their efforts waits eagerly for news.

But the Norwegian Roald Amundsen is the first to reach, describe and photograph the great emptiness at the South Pole. For Scott it would be over a year before the world hears his story. As Amundsen fills the headlines, Scott and his companions are still struggling north in a bid to reach safety. Scott's sledging journals are written in borrowed sketchbooks, small and light to carry, fitting snugly in the pocket, their pages perforated near the spine, thin unlined sheets, bound in leather. A blizzard envelops his team and they are confined to their tent. Eventually, Scott is alone. Each of his companions has died. He knows that help will not come; this was a risk he was willing to take. He waits for death. 'Had we lived, I should have had a tale to tell of the hardihood, endurance, and courage of my companions which would have stirred the heart of every Englishman,' he writes, shortly before he can write no more. 'These rough notes and our dead bodies must tell the tale.'

Eight months later they were found. At midday, 12 November 1912, some 11 miles to the south of a stash of food that would surely have kept them alive, the top of a tent is just discernible, its sides covered by the drifting snow. After they had dug out the tent, the search party saw outlines. Three men were inside. On the floor cloth was a small pile of letters. A chronometer, a flag, some socks, a few books. A lamp formed from a tin and some wick fashioned

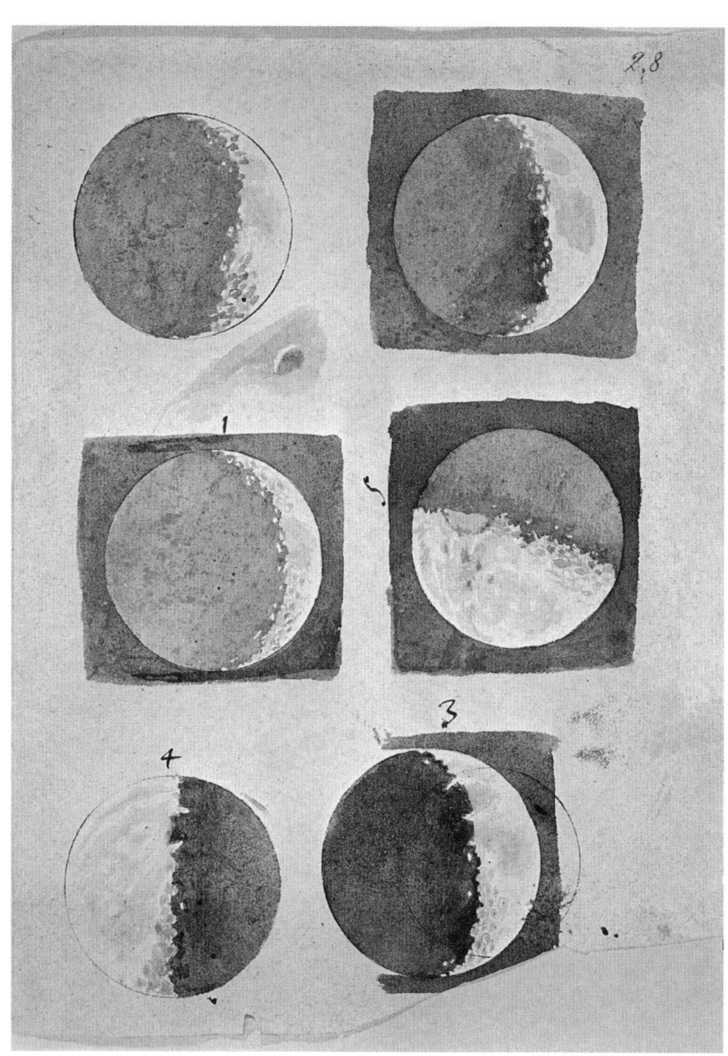

Galileo's observations of the Moon with a newly invented telescope in 1610 changed the way the whole Earth system was understood. Human curiosity is the heartbeat of exploration. The desire to look to the heavens, or over the next hill, is an impulse shared by explorers throughout the centuries.

This composite of enhanced colour images of Charon and Pluto was taken by NASA's *New Horizons* probe as it passed through the Pluto system on 14 July 2015. They are shown with approximately correct relative sizes, but their true separation is not to scale.

from the hair of a finnesko boot had been used to burn the little methylated spirit that remained before the light went out completely. Later, the tent poles were taken away, so the tent covered the bodies. And over them they built a cairn and erected a cross made with a ski.

Beneath a sleeping bag they had found a wallet, and within it a small brown notebook. It contained simple instructions. The finder was to read what was inside and then take it home. Read in hushed tones, this was the first time the terrible tragedy that had befallen Captain Scott and his companions was heard. The eleven men of the search party gathered on the ice and listened to the story. Amundsen's achievement was confirmed. Here was the proof, from the men who had the misfortune to see his victory with their own eyes. Here, scribbled in pencil, was a message from the dead for those who might dare to follow.

A distant planet and a tent in a storm. Two echoes of exploration. Perhaps this is a strange way to begin? And yet, they tell a story of trying to discover a world outside our own. It is a history of tremendous courage and often thankless endeavour; a succession of advances and setbacks, of knowledge hard won at great expense and risk; a tale of technological ingenuity and human effort. Travel back another two hundred years, say, long before the invention of photography and film, to a time when all the observations from the field were carried home in journals, charts and artworks; then, crammed within small notebooks, the whole success of an endeavour might lie in the marks made with pencil and ink. In the form of accounts of scientific discoveries, descriptions of distant lands and new species, or experiences that could lead to greater understanding, the lines contained in these little journals had the power to change the world. And despite the dramatic advances in technology and equipment over the centuries, there is one vital piece of kit in most explorers' pockets that hasn't changed much at all – and that is the journal. Here is the means to provide a lasting record; within the notebook lies the opportunity to recount a story in case the traveller never made it back alive.

From the earliest sea voyages, explorers were encouraged to make careful records. 'Take with you paper and ynke', ran such advice in the 1580s, 'and keepe a continuall journal or remembrance day by day, of all things as shall fall out worth the knowledge, not forgetting or omitting to write it, and note it, that it may be shewed and read at your returne.' To *discover* and to *reveal*, to observe and then show, therein lie the principles for a voyager on a distant journey; little has changed in these most basic of impulses. When John White was hired as artist for Walter Ralegh's expedition to the New World in 1585, he too sailed with a host of instructions. His drawings of what is now North Carolina are the earliest surviving record of the flora and indigenous life of North America. They are priceless as a result. Other intrepid artists of this age were encouraged to sketch 'all strange birds, beastes, fishes, plantes, hearbes, trees and fruites'. The world was expanding before their eyes.

Many followed through the years, gradually pulling back the boundaries of what was fearsome and unknown, and yet danger attended almost every step. James Cook was butchered to death on a beach. David Livingstone was beset by dysentery and malaria, and Knud Rasmussen died from eating fermented auk. Alexandrine Tinne was hacked down and left to bleed in the desert; her body was never found. But their journals live on. In the case of Sydney Parkinson's sketches, Naomi Uemura's climbing diary or Scott's 'rough notes', these marks on paper survived their lives cut short.

Though some were swallowed up, as Joseph Conrad had it, by the mystery their hearts were set on unveiling, most survived against the odds. Often for them the far greater risk would be not leaving home to begin with. Ernest Shackleton's justification for his wayward life, it has been said, was simple: 'I chose life over death for myself and my friends. I believe it is in our nature to explore, to reach out into the unknown. The only true failure would be not to explore at all.' And for many, rather than being a record of despair or distress, writing in a notebook was a moment of pure happiness: a chance to describe a beautiful view, or sketch something memorable, like taking a photograph, an image to last, a discovery to be visualized and shared. Obviously many of the journals here were kept in the good times, when weather was favourable, perhaps painting under clear skies, when the day's march was done and water boils in the billy for tea, or, in the case of William Burchell, as the

sun sets and hippo steaks sizzle on the fire. These notebooks can also speak of delight and enjoyment.

This is a visual compendium celebrating many adventurous and inquisitive travellers and our choices are deliberately eclectic. We feature famous names as well as many that deserve to be better known. Much of what is included has never been published before. From history through to the present day, we explore with remarkable and intrepid individuals who spent their lives journeying deep into barren desert and rich rainforest: pioneering explorers and map-makers, botanists and artists, plant-hunters, ecologists and anthropologists, eccentrics and visionaries, men and women, all curious to see and record what might lie beyond the horizon.

From the banks of the Amazon to the heart of Africa, from Maya ruins to great mountain ranges, from the Mongolian plateau to the sublime icescapes of the Far North – all these lie between the pages of small notebooks, field diaries and cloth-bound sketchbooks. We meet Victorian scientists with their obsession to collect and name every organism, and dashing adventurers who were free to roam unencumbered by the demands of precision. Amateurs and professionals, veteran and novice, all clearly used notebooks in different ways. For some the writing of a journal was a lifelong habit, a pleasure and a comfort, and a treasury of memories for a life after adventuring; for others keeping a journal was a daily chore to be endured. Yet most persisted, for without it what was there to show for their efforts?

From coastal profiles to drawings of first contact, detailed observations and idle imaginings, things significant and insignificant, indecipherable scribblings and important discoveries – they are all here. We have notebooks from the summit of Everest, the first sight of the South Pole, the initial accounts of Victoria Falls, from the heart of great deserts and inside Tutankhamun's

Captain Scott in his 'den' on 7 October 1911, photographed by Herbert Ponting. Scott spent much of his time in the evenings in the hut at Cape Evans reading, making entries in his diaries, writing reports, planning the next stages of their journeys, and penning letters to family and supporters back at home. His journals are central to his memory.

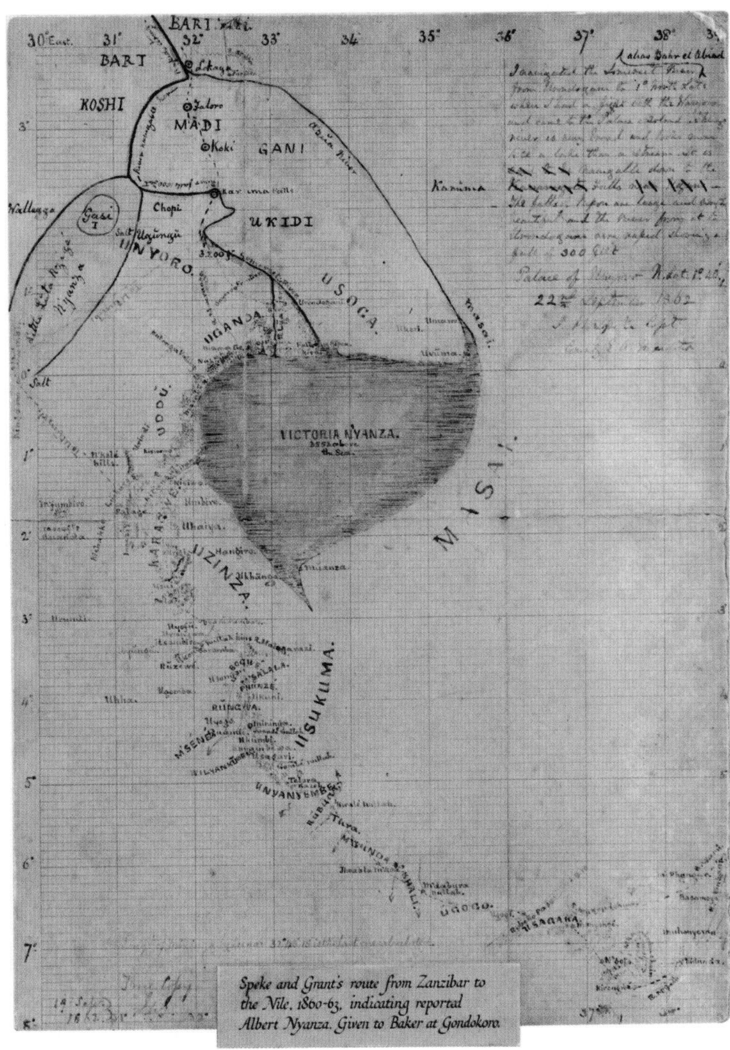

John Speke and James Grant's route from Zanzibar to the Nile. Speke pinpointed the place where the Nile issues from Lake Victoria on 28 July 1862. This hand-drawn map was essential in proving his claim.

tomb. We see the first drawings of icebergs, of rare butterflies and bugs, sacred monuments and ancient inscriptions, and the earliest Western depictions of Native Americans, Inuit hunters, Māori warriors and African kings. We cross mountain ranges, sail unknown coastlines and trek into virgin rainforests in search of birds of paradise. This is exploration at first-hand, the edges of the world at first sight. At its simplest, this is a book of what people saw and what they thought others might like to see. It is an album of journeys. Sketchbooks and journals are usually private, often never intended to be seen in public, intentionally informal, yet they are where insights are treasured and stored,

A record of a different kind: a sketchbook in material form. Titian Peale, avid collector, created mementoes from his time in the field to inspire future artworks. Treating his specimens with camphor and heat, he hermetically sealed them in shallow glass-faced wooden boxes.

ideas developed, immediate experiences set down. In a sense they are working documents, and the process is often as fascinating as the end result. For some explorer-artists, creating images in the field was a considerable investment of time and effort, often in trying situations, and accuracy of observation was paramount. Through these notebooks we have the opportunity to eavesdrop on moments of exploratory inspiration. Sketches mark the process of creating, and journals the very act of discovering.

The process of creating this book has itself been an exploration, a treasure hunt, trying to track these special rare objects down. In obscure libraries, private collections, dusty attics, sometimes passed down through families, perhaps even abandoned in the field or presumed lost, journals are nomadic objects. These were the books that explorers kept close to their hearts, carried in the jacket pocket, to bear witness to the wonders of the world. Even the smallest notebooks can reveal environments to defy the imagination. Yet, beauty is in the eye of the beholder and some journals, worn and frayed, have been overlooked in the passage of the years. Battered and neglected, stored away and long forgotten perhaps, they have awaited rediscovery. Now is the chance to open them again.

We have arranged this collection alphabetically to offer a serendipitous and sometimes surprising juxtaposition of explorers, ranging widely over time and space. Everyone is equal and we find wonderful contrasts in content. No single volume could ever hope to capture the vast array of images that have been, and continue to be made in remote areas, but we hope to have touched the spirit of the whole. This book of notebooks not only refers to artists' sketchbooks in the traditional sense, but also takes in the range of mark-making in the field – on charts, in journals and letters, on objects even – and back at home, considering the various ways in which a region is reported or understood.

Exploration can be an act of storytelling. But have we lost the narrative art of travel? It is often said that the skill of letter writing is dead. In a world of email and instant communication, it would be fair to think that the practice of keeping a journal has disappeared too. This is an age of travel blogs and

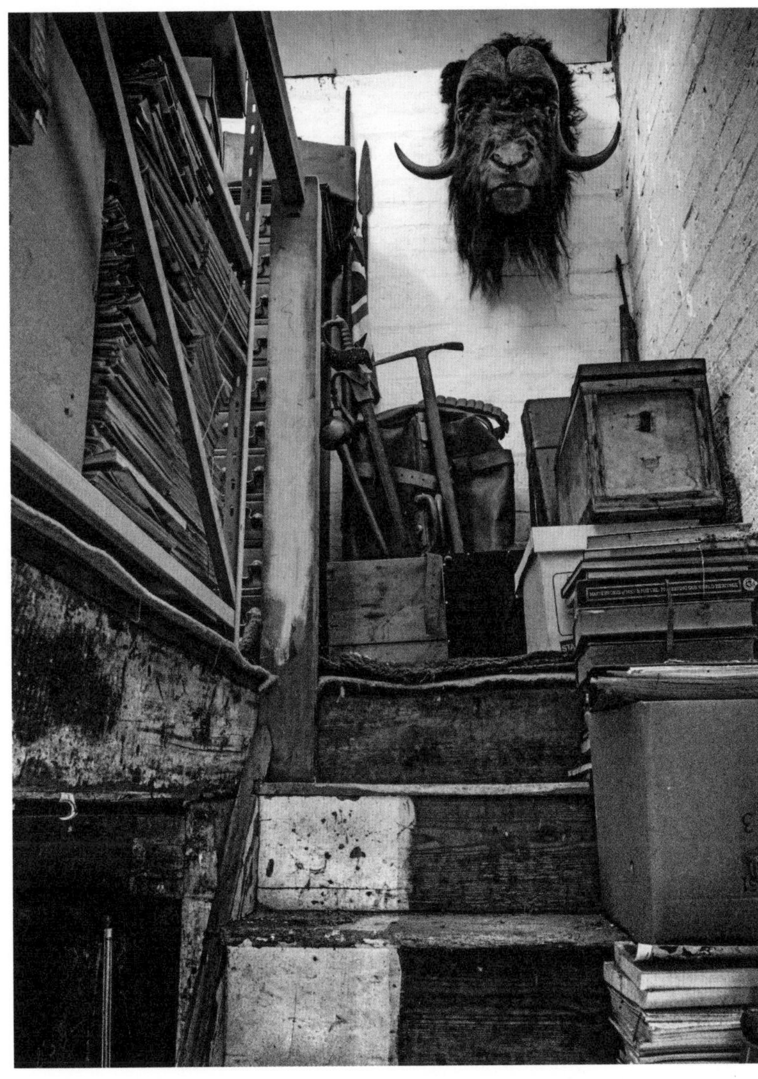

Standing at the threshold of an explorer's archive. Creating this book was an exploration in itself, travelling to many private collections to uncover their secrets.

endless twitter feeds, a new kind of daily note-making perhaps. Information is shared as never before. Digital information is uploaded by satellite in even the most inaccessible environments, relegating pencil marks to the past, some say. Pixels have replaced paintings. Can this be true?

We asked a small team of explorers to provide insights into the art of discovery, reflecting on what their sketchbooks and journals mean to them and exploring how these precious notebooks relate to the journeys that shaped their past and future paths. We are given tantalizing glances, snapshots, into the very soul of the life less ordinary. Here are the thoughts of a wilderness artist, an Amazonian plant-collector, a penguin ecologist, a bestselling ethnobotanist, even a NASA astronaut. What may have been most significant about the lunar voyage, for example, was not that men set foot on the Moon, but that they had at last looked back on the Earth. A shift in perspective – something that all true exploration provides – may be the ultimate prize to be won when the urge to make bold journeys still runs deep. As fellow astronaut Michael Collins has said: 'It's human nature to stretch, to go, to see, to understand. Exploration is not a choice, it's an imperative.'

What really makes an 'explorer'? You might conjure a mental image of a figure dressed in tweed or khaki, telescope under one arm, chart or rifle in another; and you'd be close to the truth for a typical kind of Victorian traveller in Africa. But appearances, of course, are as varied as motives. Most nonetheless were driven to make contributions to knowledge. That was usually the first justification, but it is well to be wary of this word 'exploration'. Cook spoke of making 'voyages of discovery', John Hanning Speke aimed for 'geographical discoveries', others talked of 'journeys', 'travels', even mere 'wanderings'. As men of science came to the fore, new species were valued as much as new territories. Yet, the more that was discovered it seemed the less we came to know. For those at home, filling in the blank spaces of foreign lands was true exploring, but foreign to whom? And what place in this narrative for those local guides and porters who made such discoveries possible? What of those people who knew these lands before the Westerners came with their over-stuffed expeditions, and who had, in many cases, seen most of these wonders before?

Their histories are mostly lost to time. They left few records, scarce trace. But by taking as inclusive a definition of exploration as possible we can broaden this story, at least a little. We can meet all manner of pioneers and travellers, but also artists, adventurers, missionaries, surveyors, scholars, geographers, whalers, mariners, geologists, biologists, fossil-hunters and engineers, diplomats and mercenaries, administrators and colonists, entrepreneurs and photographers, through to some modern-day travel writers. All have captured something of their first sight of a land in a memorable or meaningful way – immediate and unmediated.

The celebrated travel writer Colin Thubron is a master of reducing a journey to its essentials, and he refuses to forgo his notebooks. They are essential to his literary explorations. 'My notebooks are crucial and they become sacred to me. The vitality of a landscape or a journey is in its detail. You might start with difficulty but you end up being engulfed by it. Whether it's the texture of a rock, or an expression of a person. Notebooks, like alternative books, can be read, and re-explored at journey's end. The main problem is this overwhelming worry that builds. I have fear toward the end of a journey that I'd lose them. The loss would be irreparable.'

What unites everyone in this book is that they all, at some stage in their varied lives, took a risk; they chose to defy the conventional, to brave a difficult voyage, to leave the comforts of home and explore. They all let the promise of the unimaginable lead them over the horizon and they were willing to embrace the unknown. And they all set down a record of what they'd seen for others following after them. By opening the notebooks of others we are able to join them on significant historic journeys.

Notebooks clearly matter. They are invested with intricate practical and personal value, and many layers of meaning. Yet we need not think too hard. In this simple celebration of travel told though special journals, we can also enjoy the pictures. Here is art for its own sake, images that speak of the thrill and the boredom of the field, and the joys and frustrations that are encountered.

There must always be room for the old-fashioned habit of writing on paper. If this book can inspire someone to sit awhile, to watch and listen, and to draw or jot some thoughts down, then the effort in making it has its reward. Next time you go on a journey, pack a little notebook in your rucksack alongside all that electronic gear, or better still, leave all that stuff at home. Fill the pages of your notebooks with adventure and experience. Follow your curiosity. Just make sure you come home to share your story.

Consider oceanographer William Beebe, who ranged widely on land before plunging half a mile into the deep. Though his exploits brought him attention, the aim for Beebe was not fame, but life: 'The supreme joy of learning, of discovering, of adding tiny facts to the foundation of the everlasting *why* of the universe; all this makes life one never-ending delight.' The essential truth that he found was that happiness lay in keeping his mind, and his eyes, open. 'Boredom is immoral', he would declare. 'All a man has to do is see. All about us nature puts on the most thrilling adventure stories ever created, but we have to use our eyes. I was walking across our compound last month when a queen termite began building her miraculous city. I saw it because I was looking down. One night three giant fruit bats flew over the face of the moon. I saw them because I was looking up. To some men the jungle is a tangled place of heat and danger. But, to the man who can see, its vines and plants form a beautiful and carefully ordered tapestry.'

In this echo of a rich life, among the many offered in this book, you can find the simplest definition of the exploring impulse: the continuing desire to look up and look down. There is so much still to be discovered right here on Earth. Listen to the wisdom found in these notebooks. All you really need is good preparation, some good companions and, certainly, a good pencil. Go and get lost. You might then find what you were looking for.

REYKJAVIK, 2015

From Mongolia to the South Pole, sketchbooks have proved indispensable for explorers through the ages. Here are Hedin sketching in Central Asia; Nansen on board his ship *Fram*; Breton drawing in Chamber E, Chichén Itzá; Stark on horseback; and Wilson working up a sketch during the long polar night inside the base hut at Cape Evans.

THE SKETCHBOOKS

ROALD AMUNDSEN 1872-1928

We go on with our lives in our hands each day.
But it is pleasant to hear – nobody wants to turn back.

As a child in Norway, Roald Amundsen had been fascinated by the story of Sir John Franklin's disappearance in the Arctic ice while trying to discover the Northwest Passage. He read Franklin's books time and again, and later confessed that they 'thrilled me as nothing I had ever read before ... A strange ambition burned within me, to endure the same privations ... I decided to be an explorer.'

Amundsen was initially destined for a career in medicine. But having failed his exams, and with both parents dead, he was free to decide his future. Aged 25, he joined the 1897-99 *Belgica* Expedition, under the Belgian Adrien de Gerlache, the first to overwinter in the Antarctic. Amundsen thrived in this environment. On returning home he earned a master mariner's certificate and set his sights on achieving what Franklin and countless other explorers had been unable to.

In 1903, Amundsen set sail from Oslofjord in his sloop *Gjøa* and headed north until the ice-choked straits forced him to anchor. For nearly two years he lived with the local Netsilik Inuit, learning to hunt, dress and travel as they did. This knowledge would prove vital for success in future expeditions. Finally, in September 1906, Amundsen and his small crew reached Nome, Alaska, becoming the first to traverse the Northwest Passage.

Although celebrated for his achievement, Amundsen soon looked to another great first in exploration – the North Pole. He had already departed on *Fram*, a ship used previously by Fridtjof Nansen, when he heard news that American explorers Robert Peary and Frederick Cook were both claiming they had discovered the Pole. Amundsen turned his ship and headed south instead, knowing that Robert Falcon Scott was also aiming for the South Pole.

On 14 December 1911, Amundsen opened his journal and scribbled 'Thanks be to God!'. By dead reckoning they had arrived at the South Pole, and it was clear that they were the first to do so. After taking a series of observations, the five men, with their dog teams, planted the Norwegian flag in the polar plateau. Three months later *Fram* quietly dropped anchor off Hobart, Tasmania. Wearing a modest sailor cap and sweater, Amundsen checked into a hotel before sending three coded telegrams: the first to the King of Norway, the second to his mentor Nansen, the third to his brother. The following morning his victory was announced. 'The reporters almost broke down the door to my bedroom', Amundsen noted in his diary.

Amundsen went on to fly over the North Pole in an airship, the first to do so. He died in the Arctic, when his aircraft was lost while searching for his friend, Italian pilot Umberto Nobile. The achievement for which he is best known, however, was tainted. With Scott's death, Amundsen lost all sense of glory. The South Pole had never been his life's goal. As he wrote in his journal on reaching that desolate spot: 'I had better be honest and admit straight out that I have never known any man to be placed in such a diametrically opposite position to the goal of his desires ... The regions around the North Pole – well, yes, the North Pole itself – had attracted me from childhood, and here I was at the South Pole. Can anything more topsy-turvy be imagined?'

Amundsen's entry for the day he reached the South Pole, 14 December 1911 (as he had crossed the date line it was the 14th, not the 15th; he corrected this in his later writings). The entry begins: 'So we arrived, and were able to raise our flag at the Geographical South Pole.'

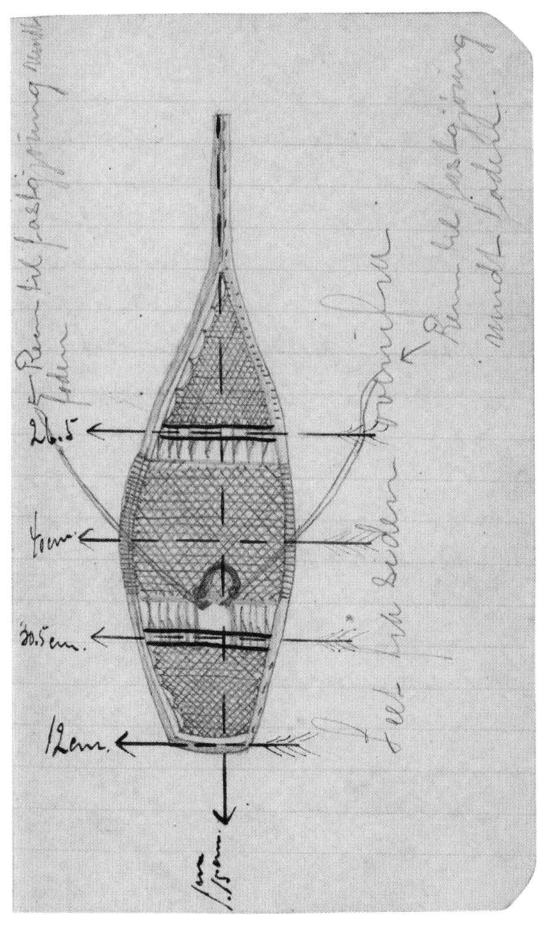

de, der har en aa ski, manövrerer disse
med lethed.

1 Januar 1899.

Hvad jeg finder at være absolut nödvendigt for et
polarekit:

Slæder af bedste konstruktion.
Lange, solide isfile.
Sterke, solide arbeidsslæder – som vore
fra Langesundsfabrikken.
Jordhakker af denne facon:

Disse egner sig meget godt for isarbeide.
Rigelig forsyning af snebriller.
Sprængstof, man med sikkerhed kjender virkningen og fungangsmaaden med.
Reservematerialer for slæder, truger, ski og

1

Söndag 8. Jan 1899.

Brak for et par dage siden min ene
egeski – gjort paa Langesundsfabrikken. Dette
kan ingenlunde lægges hverken materiale eller
arbeide tillast. Mine ski er for lange, som jeg
har omtalt saa ofte og ei praktiske for isen.
At et par ski – specielt lange – maa slide meget
her, vil forstaaes af fölgende tegning, der vil
at klargjöre den ofte for skien indtagen stilling.

Skruing Isen Skruing

Skien hviler med det forreste parti paa en skruing
og med det agterste ligeledes. Hele tyngden kommer
altsaa til at hvile paa midtpartiet, der ligger frit
uden underliggende stötte. Dette er en stil-

Sketches from the *Belgica* Expedition, 1897-99. Amundsen's journals were not intended as guides for future travellers, but more as a straightforward log of his daily activities, neatly written and highly factual. He would generally only include a small sketch in his journal when he was excited by technical observations on equipment.

JOHN JAMES AUDUBON 1785-1851

Rough as it is ... America will always be my land. I never close my eyes without travelling thousands of miles along our noble streams; and traversing our noble forests.

Appearing as the intrepid woodsman, Audubon sent this little sketch of himself to an admirer in 1826.

Opposite: The Gray Catbird, with its egg, was drawn on the banks of the Ohio River in June 1810. The Carolina Parakeet was drawn in June 1811; the last known bird in the wild was killed in 1904, and though some were kept in captivity the species was soon declared extinct.

With a rifle in one hand and his paint-box in the other, John James Audubon devoted his life to capturing the beauties of the natural world. Though he died worn out and neglected, he is now often described as America's most significant naturalist-artist. His monumental book, *Birds of America*, printed on the largest sheets of paper then available – the double-elephant-sized folio – was an extraordinary undertaking. Portrayed in the 435 plates are 1,065 birds, representing 489 species, all life-sized and in their natural habitats.

In his quest to observe and paint, Audubon spent years travelling on foot and horseback, and by canoe, skiff, schooner and steamboat. He explored dense forest and mighty rivers, from the sweltering Florida Keys to northern Labrador. The excitement and joy of the wilderness outweighed the considerable discomforts. For Audubon the process of faithfully recording a new species of bird was as important as charting an unknown land. As he said: 'Seldom have I experienced greater pleasures than when ... under a burning sun, after pushing my bark for miles over a soapy flat, I have striven all day long, tormented by myriads of insects, to procure a heron new to me, and have at last succeeded in my efforts.'

Born Jean Jacques Laforest Audubon in Santo Domingo, he was the son of an affluent French sea captain and plantation owner and his mistress, Jeanne Rabin, a French chambermaid. He grew up in France, raised by his stepmother to take a keen interest in nature, art and music. Almost every day, instead of going to school he made for nearby fields and riverbanks. By the time he returned home in the evenings his picnic basket was filled with birds' nests, eggs, lichens, flowers and pebbles.

In 1803, the year that Lewis and Clark were preparing to leave on their journey across the American continent, Audubon was eighteen years old and fearful of being drafted into the Napoleonic Wars. To escape conscription he was sent to America to oversee the family-owned farm near Philadelphia. Here, he would instead spend most of his time walking in the woods, hunting, preserving and drawing birds. With various business ventures ending in bankruptcy, he dedicated himself to his 'grand idea': creating a colossal book of all the birds of America. His friends believed this aim impossible, and urged him to abandon his plans, sell his drawings and return home to France. But he stuck to his task.

The watercolours here are some of Audubon's earliest. None made before 1803 survive, and he regularly destroyed his drafts. In these precious early works we can glimpse the makings of the man as an artist, their vibrant colours hinting at his growing mastery of his skills, as well as an eye attentive to intricate detail. In later life, Audubon would feel compelled to record the beauty of the wilderness before it vanished. He saw the country's trend towards urbanization and, despite being a prolific hunter himself, as a wanderer and woodsman, he sensed the increasing fragility of the environment. Though his reputation as an artist has soared since his death, renown certainly eluded him in life. Scribbled in one of many journals is his motto: 'Time will uncover the truth.'

Turdus Lividus
Cat Bird
Red Banks Ohio River
No. 41.

Juglans oliveformis
Carolina Parrot
Psittacus Carolinensis

And then how amply are the labours of the naturalist compensated, when, after observing the wildest and most distrustful birds, in their remote and almost inaccessible breeding places, he returns from his journeys, and relates his adventures to an interested and friendly audience.

List of drawings of Birds from Nature and of the Size of life by J. J. Audubon, in the possession of Edward Harris.

No. 1. Head of a Cassowary
2. Chuck-wills-widow
3. Night Hawk
4. Whip-poor-will
5. Osprey or Fish Hawk
6. Red Shouldered Hawk
7. Passenger Pigeon
8. House Wren
9. Belted King Fisher
10. Yellow Bird or Gold Finch
11. Meadow Lark
12. Blue Jay
13. Copy do.
14. Carolina Parrot
15. Copy - do - -
16. Cedar Bird Male
17. — do — Female
18 Orchard Oriole, Male
19 — do — Female
20 Yellow Billed Cuckoo
21 Summer Red-bird Male
22 — do — Female
23. Scarlet Tanager male
24 — do — Female
25. Great American Shrike or Butcher Bird
26. Bank Swallow
27. Green Backed Swallow
28. Black and White Creeper
29. Chimney Swallow
30. Brown Creeper
31. Blackcapt Titmouse
32. Crested Titmouse
33. Blackcapt Nuthatch
34. Red Winged Starling
35.
36. Indigo Bunting
37. Rice Bunting or Reed Bird
38. Rose Breasted Gros Beak
39. Red crowned Black Woodpecker, Male
40. Ivory Billed Woodpecker female
41. — do — male & female
42.
43. Gold winged Woodpecker
44.
45.
46. White-throated Sparrow
47. Fox-coloured Sparrow
48. Black-throated Bunting
49.
50. Great-crested Fly-catcher
51.
52. Hooded Flycatcher
53. Red eyed Flycatcher
54. Small green crested Flyc.r & Pewit Flycatcher
55. Red eyed Flycatcher
56. Small Blue-Grey Flycatcher
57.
58. Kentucky Warbler
59.
60. Maryland Yellow-Throat
61. Caution Warbler
62. Blue Yellow-Back Warbler
63. Robin
64. Cat-Bird
65. Ferruginous Thrush
66. Water Thrush
67. Yellow Crown Thrush
68. Hermit Thrush
69. Wood Thrush
70. Rail
71. Tell-Tale Godwit
72. Snipe
73. Killdeer
74. Solitary Sand-piper
75. Bartram's Sandpiper
76. Spotted Sandpiper
77. Willet
78. Green Heron
79. American Widgeon
80. Canvass Back Duck
81. Sprig-tail Duck
82. — do — female
83. Spoon-billed Teal
84. Long-tail Duck
85. Shell Drake
86. Blue Winged Teal
87. Golden-eyed Duck female
88.
89. Black Surf Duck
90. Golden-eyed Duck

Audubon kept lists of the drawings he made of birds from nature, and also precisely recorded their size. Such measurements would be essential when creating his masterpiece, *Birds of America*.

These sketches by Audubon, some of the earliest that survive, show his developing skill; he would later become known as America's most significant naturalist-artist. The Pied Avocet, was drawn near Nantes in France, possibly in 1806. The female Belted Kingfisher, with details of feathers (opposite), is from the falls of the Ohio River, July 1808.

L'Alcion de l'Amerique septentrionale Buffon
King Fisher
Chute de l'Ohio July 15. 1808.
drawn by J. J. Audubon
Belted King Fisher
Alcedo Alcion
No. 110

JOHN AULDJO 1805-1886

My own face was scorched, my lips much swollen, and my eyes inflamed; but this was the sole inconvenience I experienced.

Auldjo's dramatic watercolour of his party during their ascent of Mont Blanc, sheltering during a storm on the edge of a yawning chasm. His was a new approach to depicting and writing about adventure and mountaineering, bringing them vividly to life. Opposite is his sketch of a panoramic view of Alpine peaks, glaciers and other features, all numbered and labelled (Mont Blanc is number 1).

Having struggled to the top of Europe's highest mountain in 1827, John Auldjo promptly fell asleep. Roused later with some champagne, he drank in the glorious view that stretched out beneath him and penned a quick letter to his sister. He had every reason to celebrate – he was among the few who had stood on Mont Blanc's broad summit.

It was only the fourteenth successful ascent since that by the Chamonix men Jacques Balmat and Michel-Gabriel Paccard in 1786, and it was undoubtedly the first to bring the mountain to the attention of a wider public. This was due partly to Auldjo's ability to convey in words the perils and pleasures of climbing, but also – long before photography – to illustrate them in his lively sketches, which enabled those at home to experience the climb for themselves.

John Auldjo, a Scot born in Montreal, Canada, was schooled as a boy in London, became a student in Cambridge and lived much of his life in Europe. His father's death in 1821 left him financially free to pursue his passions of painting and geology, and he travelled to the Continent in the spring of 1827 to enjoy a tour. Seeing Mont Blanc – 'the monarch of the Alps' – sitting in 'dazzling splendour enrobed by clouds', he was immediately compelled to sketch it, and the same day he set about finding someone to help him scale it.

It was too early in the season and no guide was willing, so Auldjo waited until August, when his chance came. In his knapsack went 'some warm clothing, a telescope, and thermometer', his drawing materials, a leather mask with green eye glasses to protect against snow blindness, and a handful of double-headed screws that he later fixed on the heels of his boots for extra grip. Most important of all, he made sure that his guides hauled up an ample supply of provisions: twenty bottles of red wine, two bottles of brandy, champagne, eighteen chickens, two joints of veal and mutton, six sausages, six lemons, sugar, French plums, and 'a large quantity of cheese'. They would take no chances of going hungry on the mountain.

Summit secured, Auldjo returned to safety and was later persuaded to publish an account of the climb. Illustrated with numerous engravings based on his vivid drawings, it was an instant bestseller and was reprinted to meet demand. A few precious original watercolours depicting the ascent survive in the collections of the Alpine Club in London.

Auldjo lived for a while in Naples, where he enjoyed the social scene with his new friend, archaeologist Sir William Gell, also a gifted artist. He made his first foray on to the slopes of Vesuvius in 1831 and published another book detailing his explorations. His sketches at the crater's edge, coupled with his attractive visualizations of the sequence of principal eruptions, ensured it a wide audience as a pioneering guidebook. Eventually running out of funds, Auldjo was forced to live abroad in the 1850s, finally settling in Geneva, where he served as the British Consul until his death. 'A clever man and a good fellow', Auldjo was modest too, and his early adventures have been largely forgotten. Few sketches or paintings remain from the final period of his life, but his letters reveal his warmth and enthusiasm for his friends and the natural world.

BREVEN
1 Mt Blanc.
2 Dome de Goûtè
3 aiguille de Goûtè
4 le grand rocher Rouge
5 le grand Plateau.
6 le grands et petits mulêts
7 glacier de Bossons.
8 Montagne de la côte
9 glacier de Taconnaz
10 Montagne des Feaux
11 l'aiguille sans nom.
12 le Mt. Blanc du Tacul
13 aiguille du Midi
14 aiguille du plan
15 aiguille du grepond
16 aiguille du charmoz
17 & 18 aiguilles du Lechand
19 aiguille Verte
20 glacier de Bois et mer de glace
21 Hospice du Mont en vert.
22 aiguille d'argentière
23 aiguille du Tour
24 aiguilles Rouges.
25 Chamonix le Bourg.
26 Lac du Breven
27 aiguille du Roussette au Col de Bonhomme
28 Mt Blanc St Gervais
29 aiguille du Bionnassy.

I stopped for an instant and looked down into the abyss beneath me: the blood curdled in my veins, for never did I behold anything so terrific. I have endeavoured, in a sketch which the singularity and peril of our position induced me to take … to represent the scaling of this wall. The great beauty of the immense crevices around us, so deep, so bright, that the imagination could hardly measure them, excited not only my admiration, but even that of the guides, accustomed as they were to such scenes.

Auldjo's sketch showing the approach to Mont Blanc, on which he 'endeavoured to mark, as correctly as the nature of the sketch will allow, the line pursued in the ascent'.

Opposite: In his published account of another climb, Auldjo described his and his companions' method of sliding or *glissading* down slopes, using their staffs as a kind of rudder to steer, which both shortened the time taken and caused great merriment - unless a crevasse opened up at the bottom.

A series of lithographs from Auldjo's sketches of his first-hand observation of eruptions of Vesuvius, often made at such close quarters that he described the intense heat; he includes himself sketching or looking on.

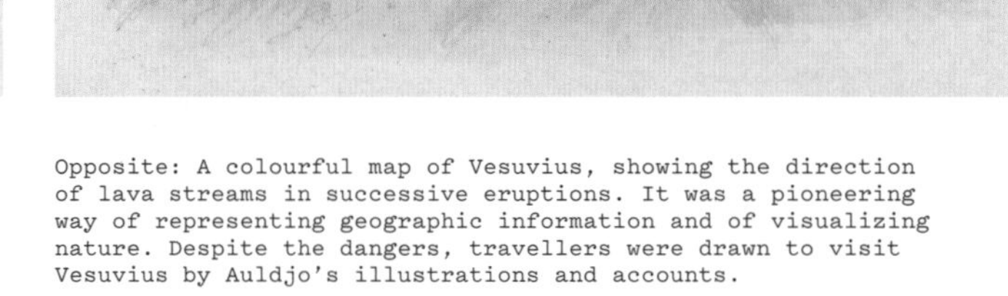

Opposite: A colourful map of Vesuvius, showing the direction of lava streams in successive eruptions. It was a pioneering way of representing geographic information and of visualizing nature. Despite the dangers, travellers were drawn to visit Vesuvius by Auldjo's illustrations and accounts.

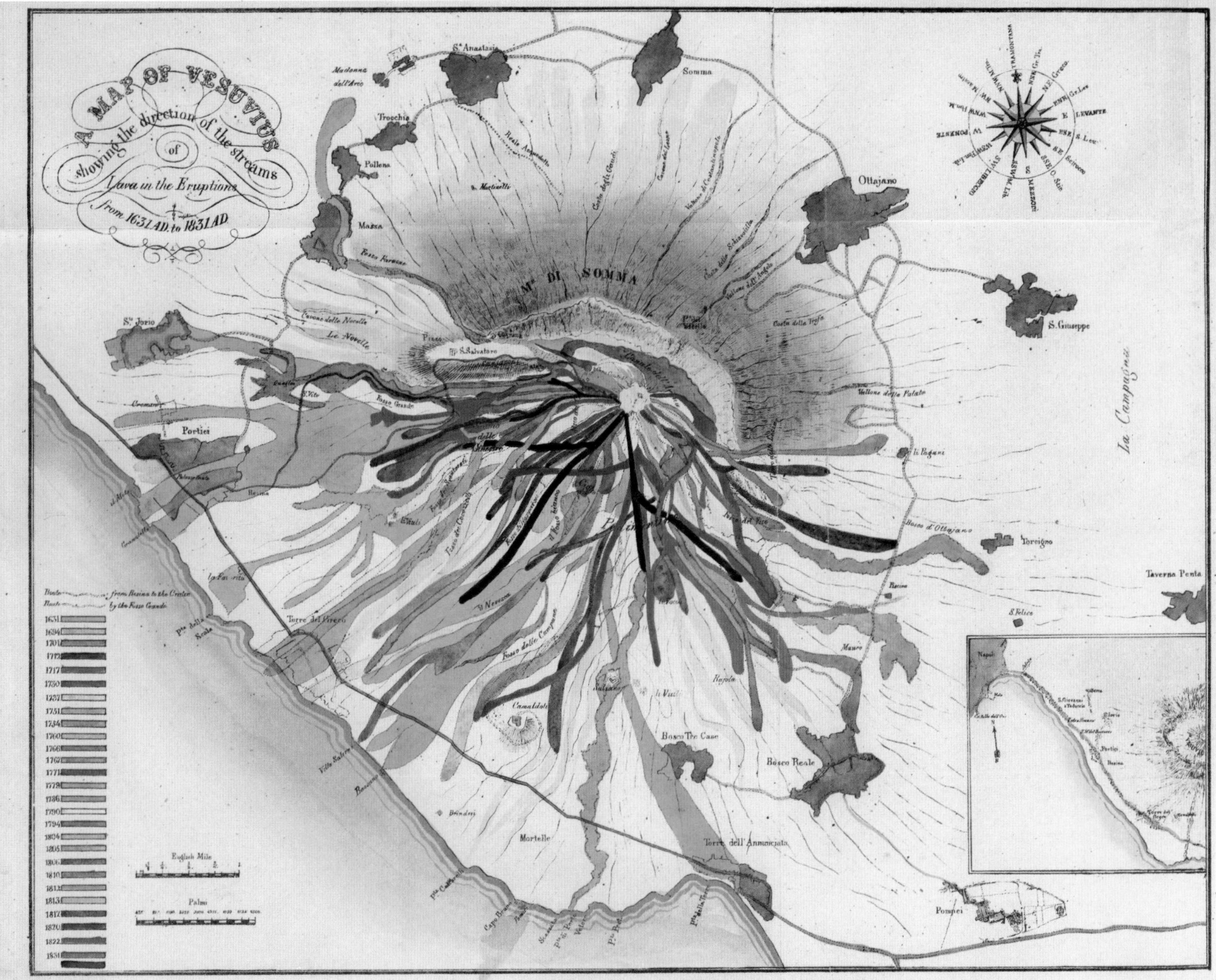

A MAP OF VESUVIUS
showing the direction of the streams
of
Lava in the Eruptions
from 1631 A.D. to 1831 A.D.
Mt. DI SOMMA
Somma
Ottajano
S. Giuseppe
Portici
Resina
Torre del Greco
Torre dell' Annunziata
Pompei
Bosco Tre Case
Bosco Reale
La Campagna
Taverna Penta
English Mile
Palmi
V. Marzoli f. in Lit.

THOMAS BAINES 1820-1875

Artists have always some odd fancy that sensible people would never dream of …

Rarely without pencil and sketchbook to hand, Thomas Baines was untiring in capturing the world around him. England-born, he spent most of his adult life exploring in southern Africa. Though slightly built and with a limp – the result of a poorly reset fractured femur, which earned him the nickname 'Cripple Thigh' – he was a daring traveller, a natural observer and a master of camp craft. He seems a most likeable fellow, considerate of those he met and with an infectious zest for life.

The son of a master mariner and grandson of a whaling captain, it's perhaps no surprise that young Baines was drawn to distant horizons. His appetite for adventure took him to Cape Colony in 1842, where he later served as an official artist during the Frontier Wars. He worked as painter for a cabinet maker, then set himself up as a portrait artist, but his wanderlust meant he could not stay confined to his studio. His first journey into the interior was beyond the Orange River in 1848, followed by two other expeditions, including an attempt to reach the swamps of the Okavango.

His talents led to his being invited on Augustus Gregory's expedition to the tropical coasts of northern Australia in 1855. The aim was to explore the Victoria River and evaluate the region for settlement. Baines made many paintings and sketches, and took part in an audacious attempt in an open longboat with two companions to link up with Gregory at the Albert River at the southern end of the Gulf of Carpentaria, which almost cost him his life. Undeterred, and with his reputation again preceding him, in 1858 he was asked to join David Livingstone's expedition to the Zambezi, doubling as artist and storekeeper.

Sadly, Baines quarrelled with Livingstone and was unfairly dismissed for theft. He had used some canvas from expedition stores to paint a portrait while recovering from malaria, which displeased Livingstone's brother. But it was not long before Baines set off again, accompanying the dashing hunter-explorer James Chapman in his cattle-trading travels through Namibia in 1862. They reached the Victoria Falls on 23 July and spent many weeks exploring. Baines hoped to find Livingstone there, and clear his name, but the elusive explorer had already moved on. Interestingly, Chapman was a keen photographer, one of the first to make full use of the new technology on an African expedition. Times were changing, and art would no longer be the main tool for recording in the field. Baines continued to sketch and paint, as well as surveying and collecting specimens.

The expedition ruined Baines's health and exhausted his finances, so he returned to Cape Town and set to work. He developed many of his field sketches into desirable oil paintings, and a fashionable album of Victoria Falls prints was published in London in 1865. Later, he led an expedition to explore the goldfields of Matabeleland and managed to win a mining concession from its chief, Lobengula. He was busy writing an account of this expedition and preparing to return to the goldfields when he fell ill with dysentery and died at his cousin's house in Durban. His paintings were sent to Windsor Castle, where, it is said, Queen Victoria took great pleasure in showing them to her children, and they were later exhibited at the Alexandra Palace. Baines's work is still admired today and forms an invaluable first-hand record of places that were about to change irrevocably.

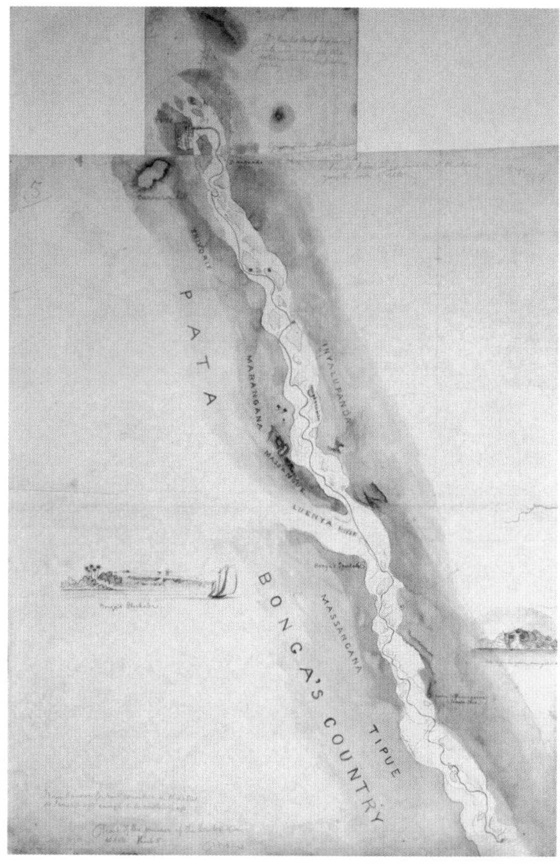

A hand-drawn map by Baines showing the route that Livingstone took down the Zambezi in the steam launch *Ma Roberts*.

Opposite: Baines's watercolour sketches of wildebeest and baobab trees near the Mtwetwe salt pan, 1862, and a mangrove swamp at low water, near the mouth of the Kongone River, Zambezi, 22 November 1859. His written notes say: 'The light tree is Doacenna. The long drops are the seeds of the mangrove, which pierce the soft mud when they fall.'

Kongone

Lo Bengulu King of Matabeli land reviewing his army on their return from a successful raid among the Mashonas -
T Baines Tuesday Nov 15 1870

'Bengulu, King of Matabeliland reviewing his army on their return from a successful raid among the Mashonas.' Baines inserts himself into the picture, sketching at the back.

Opposite: The village of Tabooka Mashona, east of the Bembisi River, 20 October 1870. Baines would make rapid sketches on the spot and work up watercolours later.

Village of Tabooka mashona petty chief East of the Bembisi River and about 21 miles South East of the Road - Octr 20th 1870 -
T Baines

Opposite: The people seated are rubbing a skin to make it pliable, while the women are carrying rhino intestines as water bags. Among the trees strips of meat are drying in the sun.

A meteor and a comet streak across the night sky over Baines's wagon; one of his annotations also notes 'Damara carrying fire'. Both sketches here are from 1862.

HENRY WALTER BATES 1825-1892

I led here a solitary but not unpleasant life; there was a great charm in the loneliness of the place.

On 26 May 1848 two young British naturalists, Henry Walter Bates and Alfred Russel Wallace, stood aboard a trading vessel moored at the mouth of the Amazon and gazed out across the land they were about to explore. To their west rose the frontier of a great primeval forest, which blanketed the country for some two thousand miles to the foot of the Andes.

Neither Bates nor Wallace had family wealth or connections. Bates had left school at thirteen, continuing his education at the local Mechanics' Institute. In 1844 he met Wallace, who shared his interest in natural history. Both men were so impressed by *A Voyage up the Amazon* by W. H. Edwards that they decided to undertake their own expedition to the region to 'gather facts towards solving the problem of the origin of species' and to collect insects. After a year together, they realized more could be achieved by going it alone.

Bates would spend eleven years collecting within a vast network of unexplored rivers and tropical rainforest. He sailed on the Rio Tocantins then moved up the Amazon, eventually making camp at Tefé. He lived simply, surviving on a small income from selling specimens to dealers in Europe. Though suffering from frequent attacks of fever, he distracted himself from illness and loneliness by focusing entirely on his work. He filled his journals with careful observations and intricate, life-size watercolour studies of beetles and butterflies, and collected over 14,000 species, of which some 8,000 were new to science.

Only once did he confess to homesickness. With his base-camp located deep in the jungle, it had been years since he had received news or parcels from his family. His clothing was worn to rags, he was barefoot ('a great inconvenience in tropical forests') and he had been robbed. He had also run out of things to read: 'I was obliged at last to come to the conclusion that the contemplation of Nature alone is not sufficient to fill the human heart and mind.' It was time to pack up and return home.

Back in England, Bates penned his now famous paper: 'Contributions to an insect fauna of the Amazon valley'. He proposed the theory of insect mimicry, now known as Batesian mimicry, whereby harmless butterflies adopt the characteristics of an unpalatable or noxious species to avoid attack from insectivorous birds. Such mimicry vastly improved their chances of survival. His discovery immediately confirmed his standing as a brilliant naturalist. Darwin wrote that it was 'one of the most remarkable and admirable papers I ever read in my life' and he urged Bates to write a memoir. In 1863 *The Naturalist on the River Amazons* was published. It quickly achieved classic status as a fine example of literary scientific writing.

Today, Bates's sketchbooks and narrative provide a stark reminder of the precarious future for the Amazonian rainforest. Bates witnessed early on the precursors of the destruction to come. After years of travelling upriver, he had returned to Pará to find his favourite forests cleared. 'The noble forest trees had been cut down, and their naked half-burnt stems remained in the midst of ashes, muddy puddles, and heaps of broken branches.' In place of the forest, chimneys would rise up. 'It was natural', Bates poignantly concluded, 'to feel a little dismayed at the prospect of so great a change.'

Bates encountering curl-crested aracaris or toucans. Having shot one for his collection, he retrieved it and was suddenly surrounded by its companions: 'They descended towards me ... some of them swinging on the loops and cables of woody lianas, and all croaking and fluttering their wings like so many furies.'

Opposite and overleaf: Bates was passionate in his study of insects, and in his eleven years in the Amazon jungle he filled pages with watercolour and pencil sketches of beetles and butterflies. He realized that some harmless butterflies adopted the characteristics of unpalatable species to avoid attack, a discovery that would become known as Batesian mimicry.

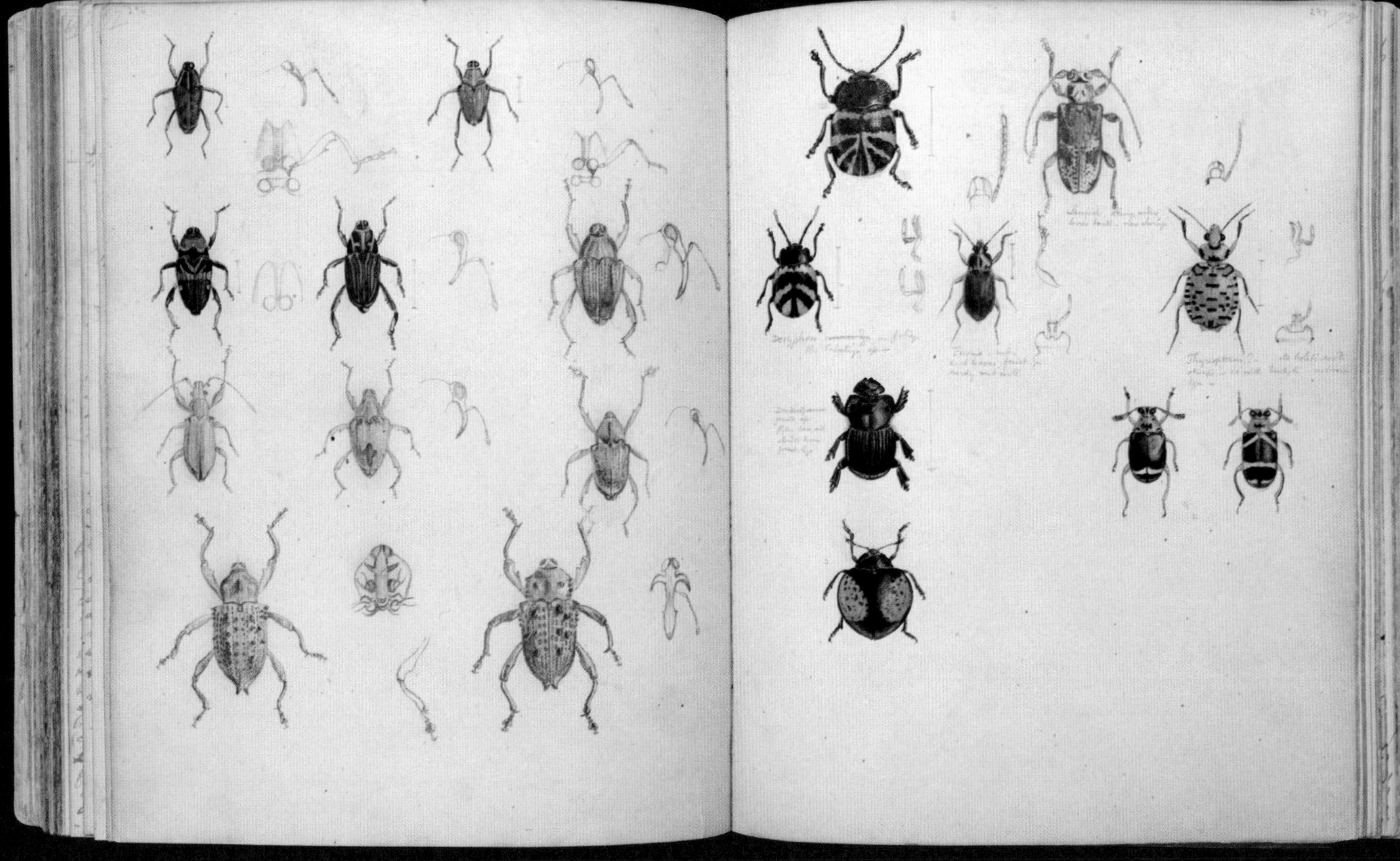

4th Section — Species of bluish or metallic colours with blk spots & marks above — **Tharops** Doubleday

143 ♂
144 ♀
(yell.)

Underside blue dull steel colour — moist woods, Pará, Santarem, rare

145 ♂
yell.

Pará, unique

3
439 ♂

Ega, rare — & I think same sp. at Pará — prefers upper side of leaves &c

4
440 ♂

Villa Nova at flowers, believe same sp. at Pará

5
285 ♂

This sp. rather different in habits from the above, it does not frequent the shade of the woods, nor is ever seen about foliage — it prefers the muddy or sandy shores of rivers & sometimes is seen in open places in forest: in all these places it settles on ground, at ordure or moist chips of wood — delights also to settle on passing canoes it is not common anywhere, I have seen it in the Cupari, at Villa Nova & at Ega —

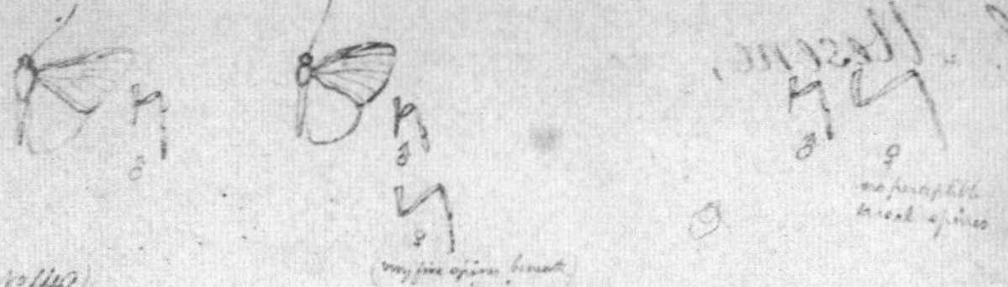

(No149)

(No 154)

(No156 & 157)

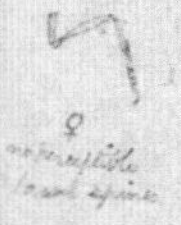

♀ no perceptible basal spines

very fine spine basal [illegible]

(No153)

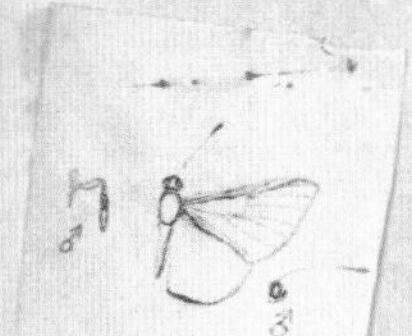

No160

Mesene Pharea

scarlet species, [illegible]

Common throughout Amazons, [illegible] leaves [illegible]

Mes. Leucophrys Bat.

151 ♂ Aveyros
470 ♀ ? Villa Nova –
scarlet, [illegible]
471 ♂ – Ega –
Common at Aveyros [illegible]

Mes. Hya[illegible]

152 ♂
153 ♀

Smaller than 1 – [illegible]

[illegible]

The ♂ of this has the palpi long, visible from above, [illegible]

Santarem, common

MESENE 1

LUDWIG BECKER 1808-1861

I fear I shall leave for the Interior with only an outfit consisting of a few colours and sketchbooks, and two small geological hammers.

At the age of 52, German artist Ludwig Becker was considered by some to be too old for a strenuous overland journey. Becker, however, disagreed. He had the skills and experience to be a valuable asset, and with impressive connections within the scientific and artistic circles of Melbourne, his place on the Victorian Exploring Expedition of 1860-61 was assured.

Becker had been trained in the sciences and painting in Darmstadt, Germany, before moving to Frankfurt, where he worked as portrait artist and court painter to the Archduke of Hesse. Craving adventure, in his early 40s he arrived in Van Diemen's Land, as Tasmania was then known. There he studied the flora and fauna, and painted miniatures. Lady Denison, wife of Tasmania's governor, summed him up as 'a most amusing person, talks English badly, but very energetically – he is one of those universal geniuses who can do anything ... a very good naturalist, geologist.'

In 1852, lured by the gold-rush, Becker moved to Victoria and settled in Melbourne, soon becoming a key figure in the city. By the time the Victorian Exploring Expedition was announced, later known as the Burke and Wills expedition, Becker believed he was the best candidate for the position of naturalist and artist. On 20 August 1860 the large caravan of camels, horses and wagons slowly moved out of Royal Park in Melbourne to the cheers of ten thousand people. It was a grand enterprise: the first coast-to-coast crossing of Australia from Melbourne to the Gulf of Carpentaria. Traversing the unexplored interior, the expedition would seek out areas suitable for colonization, and map a route for the construction of an overland telegraph line.

Soon, however, the expedition was in disarray. Aware that rival explorer John Stuart was also attempting a similar crossing, expedition leader Robert Burke became impatient and careless, frequently leaving provisions behind in his haste to make progress and veering away from their planned route. He regarded the scientific programme as an impediment, ordering Becker to write and sketch only when everyone else was asleep. Unlike many other explorer artists who sketched in the field and created paintings in the studio later, Becker tried to complete his watercolours on site. This was not always easy. Hermann Beckler, the medical officer and botanist, observed that the flies 'sucked the colours and inks from [Becker's] quills and brushes and threw themselves recklessly on to every damp spot on his painting'.

Within six months, irreparable rifts had developed between Burke and several expedition members, many of whom were suffering from scurvy. In April 1861, Beckler wrote that Becker was beyond recovery: 'I shall have to bury him here, and then what an outcry there will be for me in Melbourne!' Seven men from the expedition died, including Becker, Burke and third-in-command William Wills.

Becker was mourned by colleagues at the Royal Society of Victoria as one of its 'most gifted and unassuming members', and tributes appeared in newspapers throughout the Australian colonies as well as in Germany. Despite the harsh conditions and privations, Becker had managed to create a meticulous record of flora and fauna, geology and hydrography, and had completed 70 watercolours, drawings and maps. He had displayed an extraordinary commitment to his art and science.

Becker was fascinated by all aspects of the new country he passed through and whenever possible he spent time with the Aborigines, recording and drawing their daily life. Above is the artist's and doctor's tent at 'Bilwaka', Darling, October 1860. Opposite: The huge caravan crossing the Terrick-Terrick Plains.

No. 2.
Crossing the Terrick - Terrick Plains, Aug. 29. 60 - L. Becker.

Hard work in the camp, want of vegetables and of fresh meat, great heat with flies & moskitos – are not apt to support one whose greatest desire is to try to unveil some of the mysteries of this country.

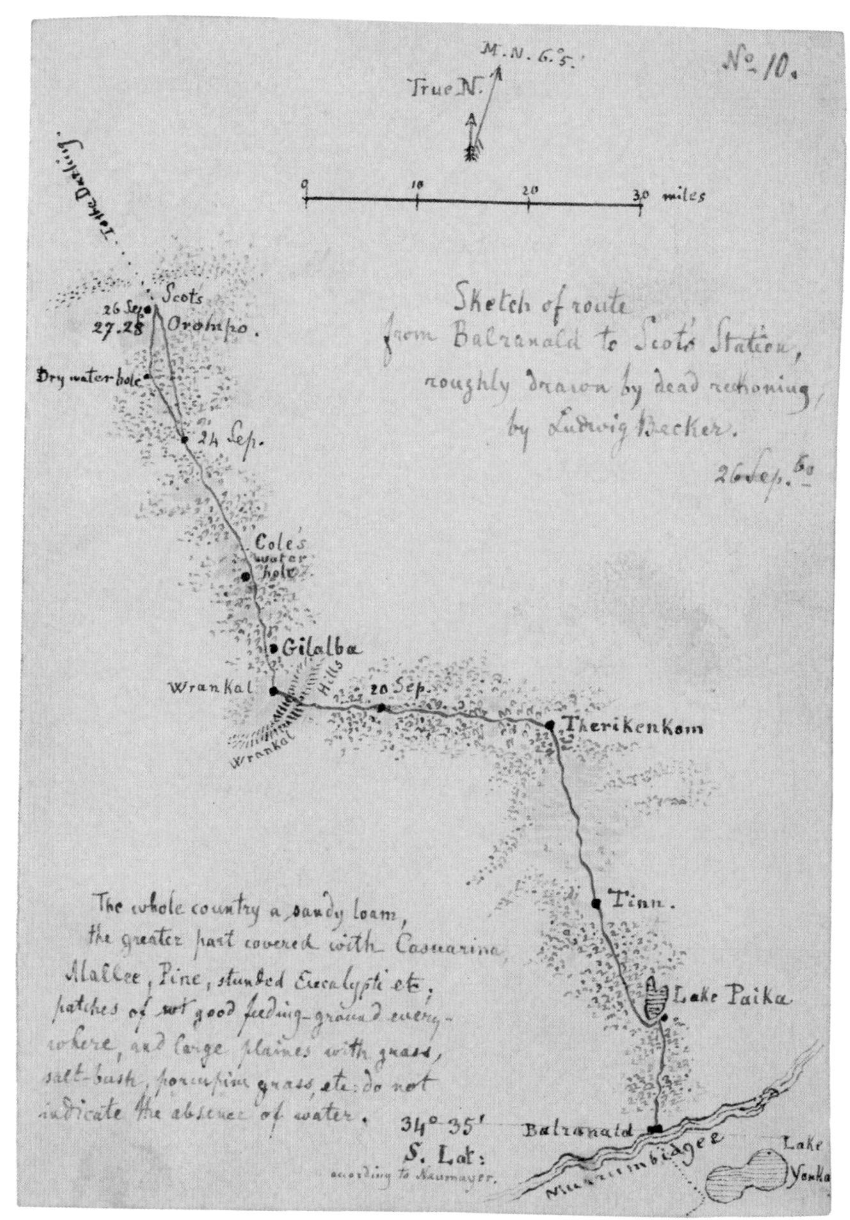

A hand-drawn sketch-map by Becker of the route taken from Balranald to Scot's Station, September 1860. Becker was charged with creating daily expedition reports and maps, as well as sketching and recording flora, fauna, geology, anthropology, meteorology and astronomy.

Opposite: Becker despaired that he hadn't the reference books or tools to do his work properly, and was tormented by the heat, dust and insects, but he created a significant scientific record, sketching until he was too weak to continue. He drew the Purple-backed Wren or 'fly-catcher' (left) in February 1861 and the Stimson's Python (right) in March 1861, the month before he died.

This species of a fly-catcher I caught near my tent, which was pitched on the border of an extensive mud-plain; there was no water near, not for many miles. – Color: upper part of head blueish-grey with a brownish tint; back: grey, with a brownish hue; wings: brown; tail: steel-blue with black bands across; neck and belly: yellowish-white; eyes: brown, and in the midst of a cinnamon-colored spot; bill: dark-fleesh-colored. legs: pale-yellowish-brown. The inner half of the white feathers is black. Four large bristles – half white, half black – are behind the nostrils. The specimen figured here in its natural size was a male. The colors of the female are more uniform-greyish-brown, the brown spot round the eyes is wanting. – The flower belongs to a parasitical plant, of which two species – loranthus – are growing near the camp.

Feb. 25-1861, camp on the border of the mud-desert. Ludwig Becker.

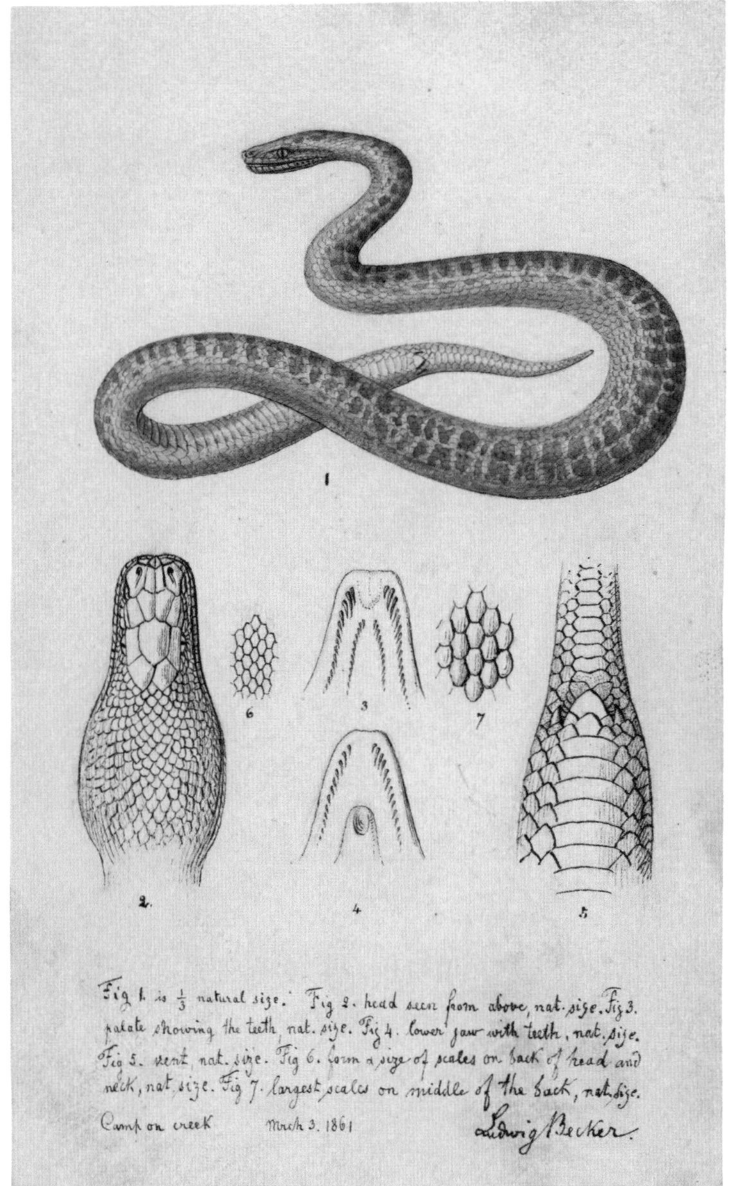

1
2.
6
3
7
4
5
Fig 1. is $\frac{1}{3}$ natural size. Fig 2. head seen from above, nat. size. Fig 3. palate showing the teeth, nat. size. Fig 4. lower jaw with teeth, nat. size. Fig 5. vent, nat. size. Fig 6. form a size of scales on back of head and neck, nat. size. Fig 7. largest scales on middle of the back, nat. size.
Camp on creek
March 3. 1861
Ludwig Becker.

WILLIAM BEEBE 1877-1962

I can only think of one experience which might exceed in interest a few hours spent under water, and that would be a journey to Mars.

By the time he was sixteen, ever-curious William Beebe already knew his life's calling. Writing in his journal on New Year's Eve, he decided that 'to be a Naturalist is better than to be a King', and for the next seven decades he would follow this insight. As an explorer he shared his wide discoveries with millions of people, as they eagerly listened to the radio or enjoyed his books, safe in their armchairs at home. Exploring then explaining, finding and educating, Beebe's gift was in opening the eyes of a generation to the intricate beauties of the natural world.

Already well known as an adventurous ornithologist and director of tropical research at the New York Zoological Society, Beebe became internationally famous in 1931 when he embarked on an underwater voyage into the unknown. He joined forces with Harvard graduate Otis Barton, a young engineer and sometime-actor with the wealth to finance his dream of observing deep-sea creatures in their natural habitat. Their craft was a bathysphere, which the press dubbed the 'Barton Tank'. Essentially a hollow steel ball with walls an inch thick, its three tiny windows were made of fused quartz, and it carried a high-pressure cylinder of oxygen. 'The longer we were in it', Beebe recalled, 'the smaller it seemed to get.'

In waters off Bermuda, they began the bathysphere's first manned dive and reached a depth of almost 245 m (800 ft). With a telephone linked to the surface, Beebe could dictate his observations to listeners above. Their thrilling descents in 1932 were relayed in live broadcasts over radio, making them both household names. On 15 August 1934 they made a dive to 923 m (3,028 ft) – over half a mile deep, and beyond the reach of sunlight – a record that remained unbeaten for fifteen years. They only stopped when their cable was about to run out. Their descriptions of the strange undersea creatures they encountered caught in the bathysphere's spotlight enthralled the public. Below them, the ocean disappeared into darkness. There, said Beebe, 'lay a world that looked like the black pit-mouth of hell itself'.

For Beebe, the dives were about the potential to discover and describe all manner of species never before seen. He also came to cherish the freedom of descending below the surface wearing just a copper diving helmet and investigating shallower waters with his collecting net. From Baja in California to the Pacific coasts of Central America, Beebe explored widely in the name of science: the first well-known, and well-trained, scientist to dive as part of his field research, opening up the secrets of the world's richest faunal communities, the coral reefs, long before the likes of Jacques Cousteau. In later years he returned to dry land, buying acres of tropical forest in Trinidad and establishing a research station there.

Beebe's sense of wonder was endless. Whether vast underwater mountain chains or the evolution of a single feather in a pheasant's tail, all things captured his interest. And yet, he came to realize that such beauty could not be endless. Beebe's vision of the interdependence of ecosystems would draw attention to their increasing fragility. His childhood wish would lead him to pioneer conservation, now so essential to the survival of wildlife on this shrinking planet.

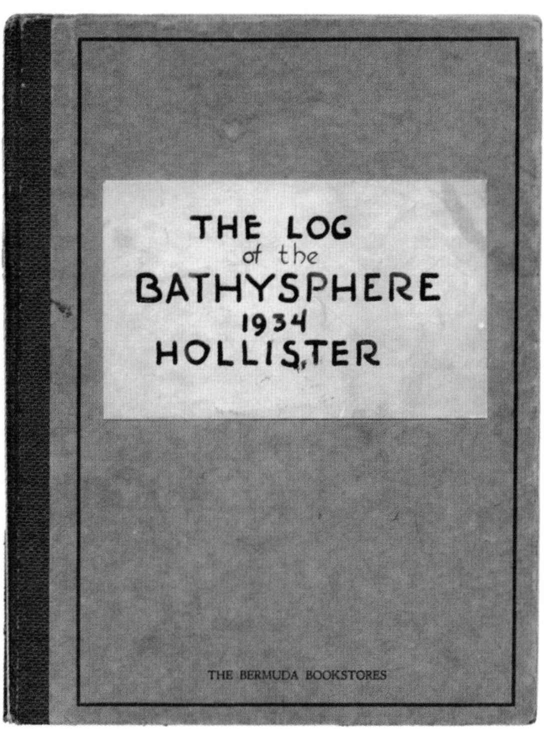

The cover of a logbook of notes dictated by Beebe to Gloria Hollister via telephone from his bathysphere. This log includes an entry for 15 August 1934, a record-setting dive to 923 m (3,028 ft). When safely back on the surface, Beebe would work closely with his artist Else Bostelmann to create accurate depictions of the species he had seen in the depths. Opposite is *Chiasmodon niger* – the black swallower – plus the contents of its stomach.

Else M. Bostelmann

B-843

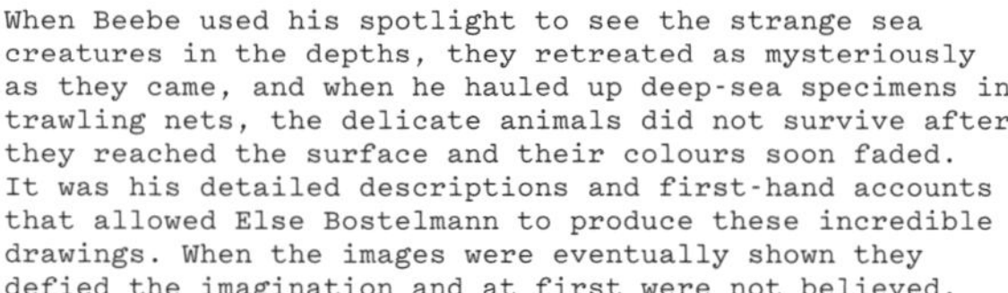

When Beebe used his spotlight to see the strange sea creatures in the depths, they retreated as mysteriously as they came, and when he hauled up deep-sea specimens in trawling nets, the delicate animals did not survive after they reached the surface and their colours soon faded. It was his detailed descriptions and first-hand accounts that allowed Else Bostelmann to produce these incredible drawings. When the images were eventually shown they defied the imagination and at first were not believed.

All the images here are of specimens from expeditions in the waters off Bermuda. These creatures boggled the mind. Above left, *Gastrostomus* pursuing *Dolopichthys*; above right, *Lamprotoxus flagellibarba*; and opposite, *Lasiognathus piscatorius*, a type of angler fish, hunting its prey.

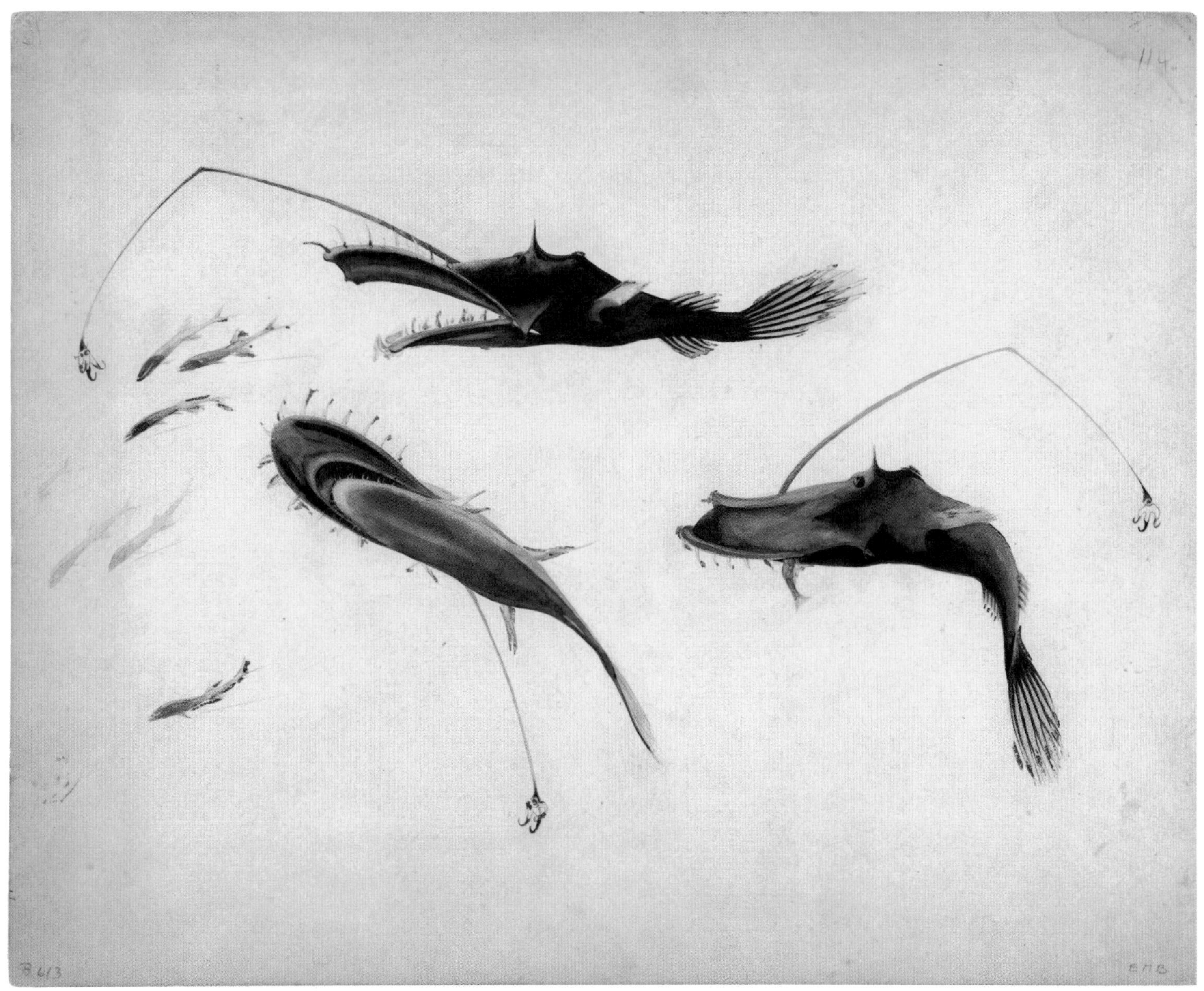

GERTRUDE BELL 1868–1926

How big the world is, how big and how wonderful. It comes to me as ridiculously presumptuous that I should dare to carry my little personality half across it.

After the SS *Ortona* docked in Beirut in 1905, Gertrude Bell headed towards the customs house, a revolver in her pocket and a faithful servant by her side. With impeccable charm, she engaged the customs officer in conversation as her servant proclaimed how grand a lady his mistress was; both hoped that her firearms and maps, carefully wrapped in 'aggressively feminine' petticoats and lace-edged undergarments, would not be discovered. Flattered by the Englishwoman's attention, the officer waved her equipment through, and Bell headed into the Syrian Desert.

Granddaughter of the formidable northern industrialist and politician, Sir Isaac Lowthian Bell, Gertrude was a force to reckon with. By the time of her first visit to Persia at the age of 23, she had already achieved a First in Modern History at Oxford and made several new ascents in the Alps. She would go on to become the first female political officer in British military intelligence and make several extraordinary journeys into areas no Western traveller had ventured. Perhaps most notable was her journey to Ha'il in central Arabia, in 1913–14. A scholar, writer, poet, historian, archaeologist, linguist, mountaineer, explorer, political officer and king-maker, Bell had the ear of the Prime Minister and moved as an equal among sheikhs and imams.

She rode on horseback through the Arabian and Syrian deserts, her saddlebags bulging with sketchbooks, journals, maps and cameras. She travelled conspicuously, with up to twenty camels or mules laden with tents, her folding bed and canvas bath, rugs and tables, china, crystal glasses and silver cutlery for fine dining, accompanied only by Arab guides. She was fearless, intrepid and erudite, a lone Englishwoman in the male, Muslim world of the Middle East, whose aristocratic bearing invariably impressed the lords of the desert. The great sheikh Fahad Bey said of her, 'she is only a woman, but she is a mighty and valiant one'.

A keen observer and note-taker, Bell created maps that would become highly influential in British imperial policy-making. Daily she wrote letters home, then filled her journals. Just as others might collect butterflies or rare plants, Bell collected people. She made friends easily and nurtured her contacts. She excelled in diplomacy, even so far as breaking bread and smoking with bandit chiefs after her caravan had been robbed at knife-point, ensuring the return of all her equipment and a safe onward passage. These skills combined made her a perfect spy.

Fluent in eight languages and with an unmatched knowledge of the tribes, geography and politics of the area, Bell worked at the Arab Bureau in Egypt with T. E. Lawrence during the First World War, helping to secure British interests in the Middle East. Earning the trust of Winston Churchill, she assisted in drawing up the borders of the new nation of Iraq and recommended that King Faisal should be its first ruler. Bell came to be known as *Khatun*, or the 'Uncrowned Queen of Iraq'.

Two days before her 58th birthday Bell died of a sleeping pill overdose. She was buried with full honours in Baghdad. Although not universally popular among her contemporaries in British intelligence, there was no denying she was remarkable. She had the gift, as author Vita Sackville-West wrote, 'of making everyone feel suddenly eager; of making you feel that life was full and rich and exciting ... Whatever subject she touched, she lit up; such vitality was irresistible.'

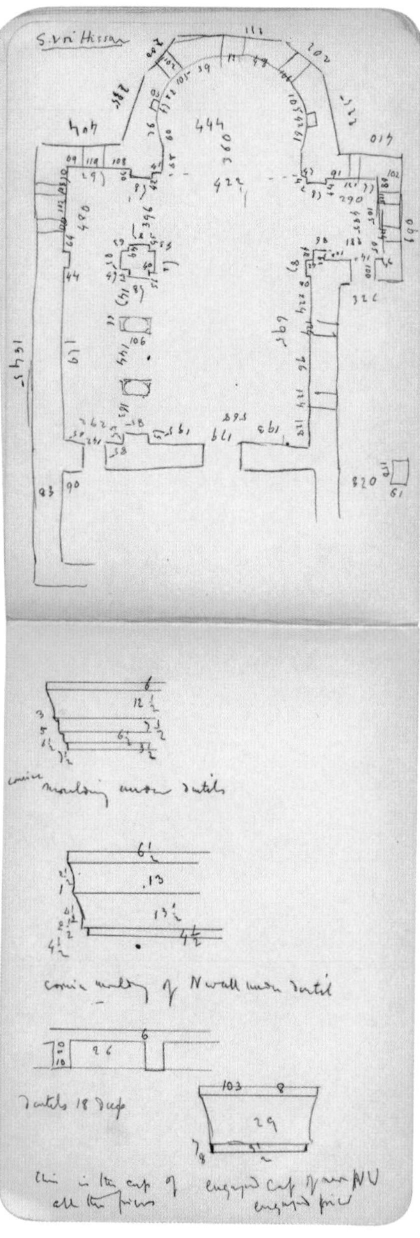

I want to go out east to a wild country called the Safah and under the protection of the Druzes I can go, but the Turks ... spend their time telling me how horribly dangerous it is, not a word of all which talk I believe.

Opposite: Bell wrote and made detailed drawings no matter how tired she was, or how difficult the circumstances. The pages of this notebook from her travels in Syria and Iraq in 1905-14 contain a sketch of a temple floor plan and details of cornice mouldings.

Bell was a highly skilled linguist. This is a page of her notes in Arabic and English. 'I shall not forget the misery of copying a Syrian inscription in the drenching rain, holding my cloak around my [sketch] book to keep the paper dry. The devil take all Syrian inscriptions, they are so horribly difficult to copy.' Bell had travelled to Persia at the age of 23 to visit her uncle, Sir Frank Lascelles, who was British minister at Tehran. Almost immediately her lifelong fascination with the East began.

This water [belongs] to the chief (?)...
ʿAli b. Rāzā (?)
He was present at this water

and he watered the camels in the year 11 (?)
and he brought back goats (?)

and there was present Saʿd .... b. ʿĀda
b. ʿAli (or ʿĪsa?) b. ʿAwākir (?) of Hijaz
and he wrote the wusūm 99

There is a moment, too, when one is newly arrived in the East, when one is conscious of the world shrinking at one end and growing at the other till all the perspective of life is changed.

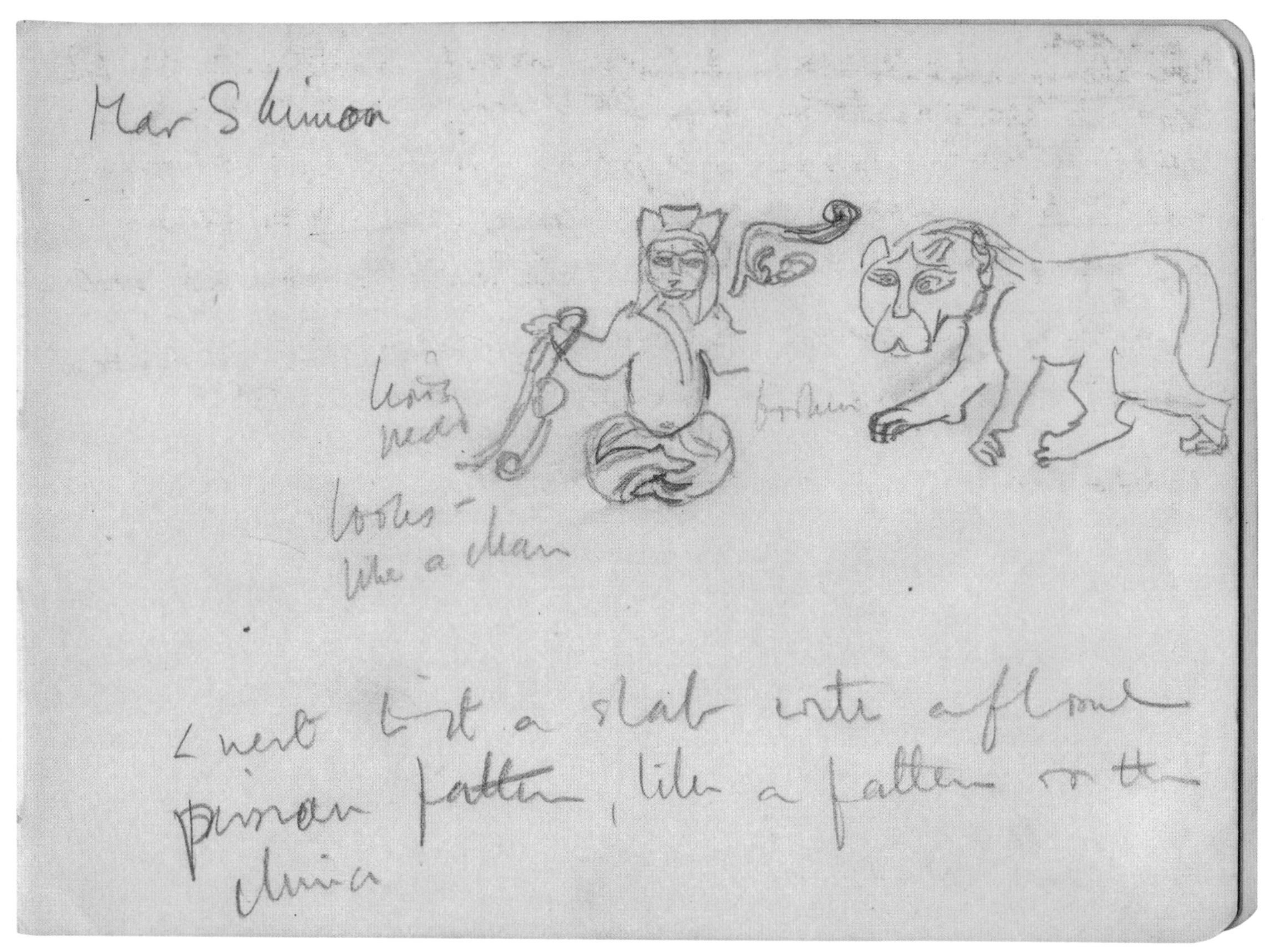

Pages from Bell's notebooks from her travels to Syria and Iraq, with sketches of pottery fragments from Samarra and details of decoration.

FRANZ BOAS 1858-1942

I went out today exactly like an Eskimo with my harpoon and all the accessories and sat by the water as patiently as they ... as you can see, I am now truly just like an Eskimo.

It was among the Inuit of Cumberland Sound, Baffin Bay, that 25-year-old German geographer Franz Boas would have an epiphany that would not only shape his own career, but would also ultimately have far-reaching impacts on a whole field of science.

Boas arrived in late August 1883 and established his base at a Scottish whaling station on the island of Kekerten. From there he made extensive journeys with the Inuit by dog sled and boat, mapping the coastline and recording native place-names. For a year he immersed himself in Inuit culture. He wore their clothes, ate their food and lived in snow houses; he learned their language and their ways of doing things, and listened closely to their stories, beliefs and legends.

By the time Boas left Cumberland Sound, he had concluded that an entirely new approach to anthropology was needed. He would go on to become a distinguished and hugely influential figure, pioneering the 'four field approach' – a discipline of methodology combining archaeology, linguistics, physical anthropology and cultural anthropology – while also championing the values of exhaustive research, fieldwork and folklore scholarship.

An ardent opponent of racism and fascism, Boas emigrated to the United States and became professor of anthropology at Columbia University. Although he would subsequently conduct impressive fieldwork with the Kwakiutl Indians of the Pacific Northwest, he would never immerse himself as intensively with any culture again. Nevertheless, his holistic approach to the study of human behaviour led him to become known as the 'Father of Modern Anthropology'.

Above and opposite: Boas travelled around 4,000 km (2,485 miles) by boat and dog sled with the Inuit, mapping the coastline and recording indigenous life and place-names. The map represents the spread of indigenous peoples across the Arctic.

Overleaf: While he was stuck on board ship for weeks among the ice floes attempting to reach Cumberland Sound, Boas spent his time drawing and sketching, including these icebergs, becoming absorbed in this strange new world.

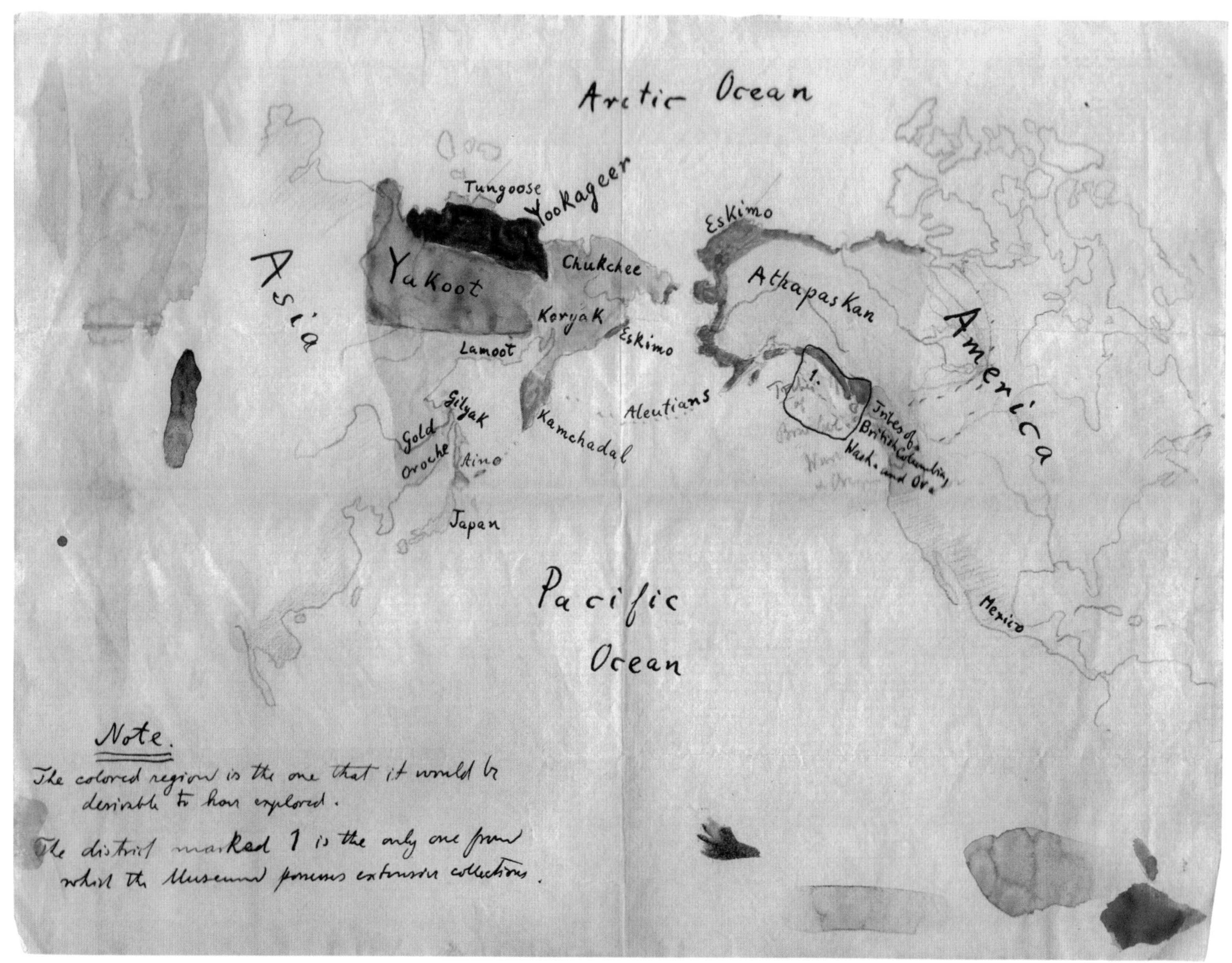

Arctic Ocean
Tungoose
Yookageer
Eskimo
Asia
Yakoot
Chukchee
Atkapaskan
America
Koryak
Eskimo
Lamoot
1.
Gilyak
Aleutians
Tribes of British Columbia, Wash. and Or.
Gold
Kamchadal
Oroche
Aino
Japan
Pacific Ocean
Mexico
Note.
The colored region is the one that it would be desirable to have explored.
The district marked 1 is the only one from which the Museum possesses extensive collections.

8
Eisberg. 28 Juli 1883.

No 13
Eisberg. 28t Juli. 1883

Challenge
DUPLICATE BOOK
FEINT
100 LEAVES DUPLICATE
REF 6565 : 44
summit
NOTE BOOK
Ruled Feint
NAME
SUBJECT
WHSMITH
55p
Note Book
GREENLAND DIARY
1991
BRITISH MADE
WHSMITH
Duplicate Book
Feint 100 Numbered
Duplicate Sets
Chris
Sepu Kangri
Diary
SEPU KANGRI
97
+
SEPU KANGRI
98
OLYMPIC
Carbon
Book

CHRIS BONINGTON 1934-

I look at climbing not so much as standing on the top as seeing the other side. There are always other horizons before you.

For many years the famous face of British mountaineering, Sir Chris Bonington's first taste of climbing came when, as a sixteen-year-old, he hitchhiked from his home in London to tackle Snowdon, armed with a pair of hobnailed boots and his old school coat. Though he was swept off the mountain in heavy snow, the seeds of adventure were sown.

A series of impressive early routes in the Alps forged Bonington's reputation, including the first British ascent of the southwest pillar of the Aiguille du Dru in 1958 and, teaming up with Don Whillans, Ian Clough and the Polish climber Jan Dlugosz, the celebrated first ascent of the Frêney Central Pillar on Mont Blanc in 1961. Later that year he also achieved the long-sought first British ascent of the north face of the Eiger. After a successful expedition to Patagonia, where he overcame the difficult granite spire of the Central Tower of Paine, he also developed a career as an adventure photojournalist. He would always carry a small notebook on his climbs, but increasingly his cameras became the important tool for recording his exploits. Photographs served as vital visual shorthand when writing the books and giving the countless lectures that 'built the foundations for a new freedom': earning enough money for the next expedition.

Having resigned his commission in the army, Bonington joined a team to the Himalaya, and happily turned down a job with Unilever to head to South America. 'I had to choose between selling margarine and adventure. I chose adventure.' In 1970 he masterminded the ascent of the south face of Annapurna, which marked the start of a new era of climbing in the Greater Ranges; never had such a difficult route been tackled at such altitudes. He would subsequently lead two high-profile attempts on Everest's southwest face, in 1972 and 1975. The 1972 attempt failed, but the 1975 expedition was a resounding success, albeit marred by the death of charismatic climbing cameraman Mick Burke.

The climb hastened the passing of an era of large-scale expeditions and, as with most elite mountaineers of the period, Bonington instead chose to pursue 'alpine-style' ascents of big peaks from then on. Among the highlights are his 1977 first ascent of the fearsome Ogre in the Karakorum with Doug Scott, which involved a nightmare retreat after Scott broke both legs and Bonington several ribs. In the spring of 1985, at the age of 50, Bonington finally reached the summit of Everest himself. 'Though we'd used oxygen and followed the classic route', he says, 'it was still one of the great moments of my life, as much for the friends made as for the achievement of standing on the top and enjoying the vista of mountains falling away beneath my feet. It was a perfect day.'

Other expeditions followed: to Greenland, Antarctica, the Caucasus, and the Himalaya, as well as writing many books. To mark his 80th birthday, in 2014, he returned to the Orkney Islands to climb the Old Man of Hoy. He had made the first ascent of this sea stack back in 1966. 'The ideal kind of expedition for me now though', he confides, 'is to a remote valley deep in the Himalaya, with an unnamed 5,000-m mountain at its head. A few weeks of exploring, tackling new lines on unclimbed rock with a handful of friends, then returning to camp for a good game of bridge.'

The mountains have been a lifelong passion for Bonington, as witnessed by the impressive accumulation of notebooks recording his many expeditions and this photograph of him on one of his early climbs, in England in 1955.

JAN BRANDES 1743-1808

I witnessed that game from start to finish because I was in the good graces of the Honourable Governor and was allowed to walk around freely ... I have made rough sketches.

Dutch scholar and pastor Jan Brandes and his pregnant wife Anna stepped ashore for the first time on the island of Java in Indonesia in 1778. It was an exciting opportunity – in the employ of the Dutch East India Company (VOC), Brandes was taking up a post as minister at a new Lutheran parish in Batavia (Jakarta), the heart of Asiatic trade. Soon after their arrival, their son was born, but a year later Anna died. Brandes raised the child alone, with the help of servants, and buried his grief in his art, filling large sketchbooks with drawings and paintings. Batavia, founded as an administrative centre for the VOC, had a multicultural but dislocated society in which Brandes never felt at ease. He resigned after six years and travelled with his son to Ceylon (Sri Lanka) and then South Africa, before eventually settling in Sweden.

In contrast to Batavia, both Ceylon and South Africa had thriving Dutch communities, and Brandes was warmly welcomed. He met the Governor of Ceylon, Willem Jacob de Graaf, witnessing his audience with the envoys of the King of Kandy, and went on an expedition in the jungle near Colombo, which resulted in a unique set of drawings of the capture, taming and guarding of 25 elephants.

Competent in several languages and with a keen interest in science and religion, Brandes was also a prolific amateur artist, with an eye for detail and enthusiasm for a wide range of subjects: ornithology, entomology and botany; portraits, still lives and topography; biblical scenes, architecture, even the cosmos. Hidden in private family archives for over two centuries, his extraordinary collection of documentary-style drawings and watercolours are only now being appreciated for the wealth of information they provide on eighteenth-century colonial life.

Brandes had an unusual documentary style to his drawings, and captured the multicultural society of Java. In his paintings of family life at home in Batavia, his son Jaantje is often seen playing or learning alongside Bietja, an Indonesian slave girl.

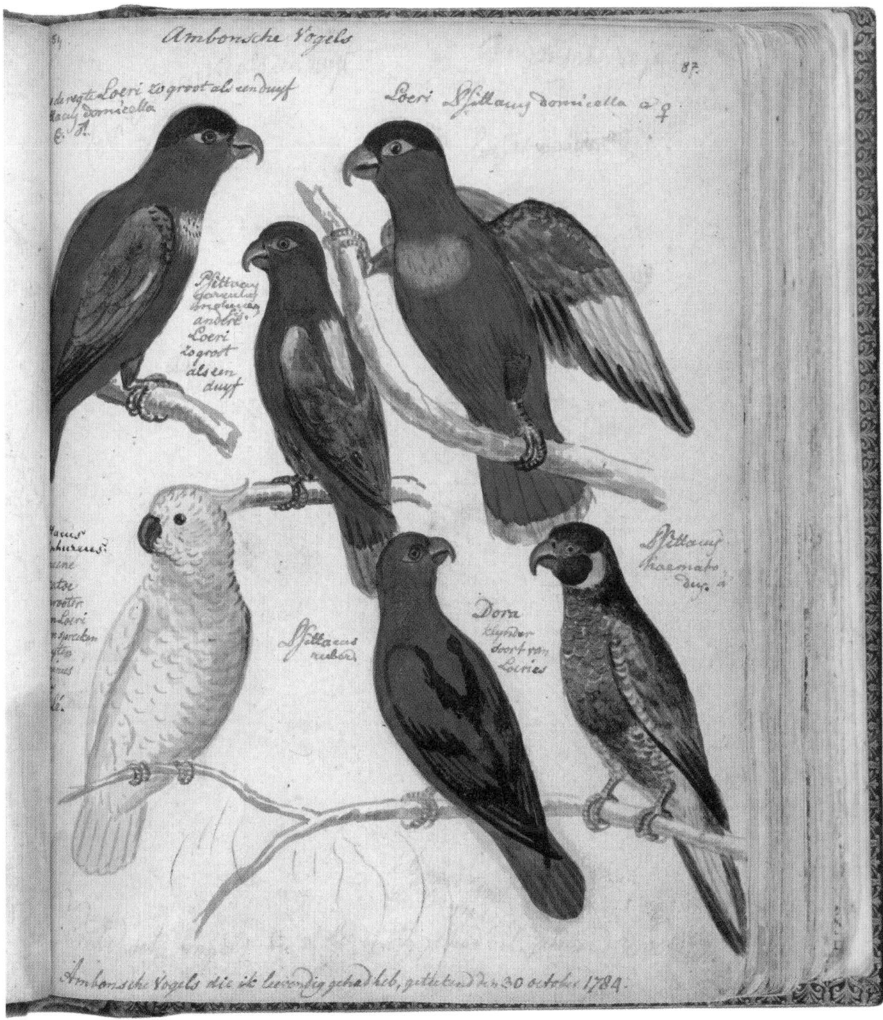

Above and overleaf: Brandes filled his sketchbooks with beautifully observed drawings of everything he found of interest, from flowers and parakeets, to marine life, temples and portraits. Despite the passage of time, his sketches still retain their vivid colours.

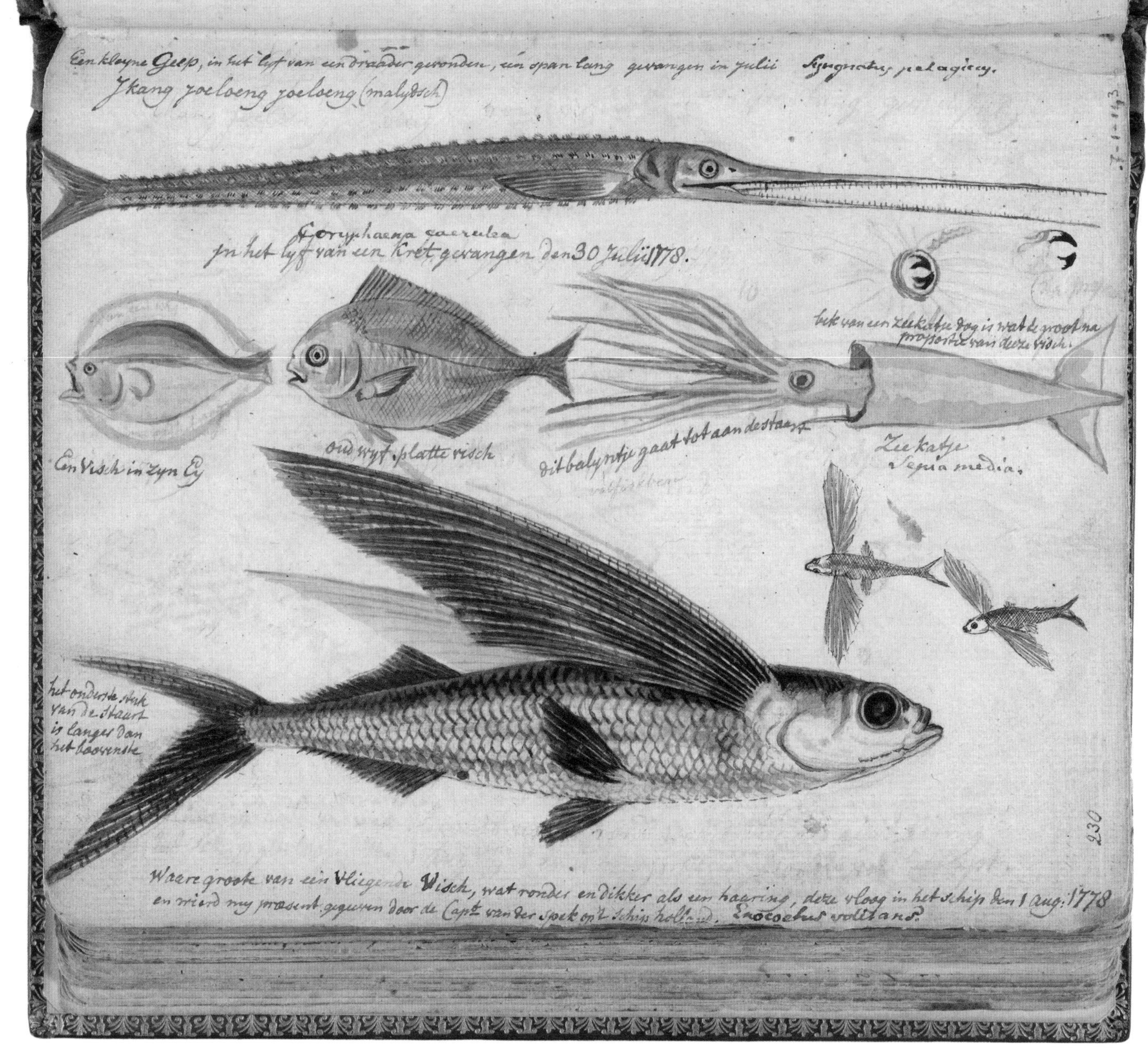
Een kleyne Geep, in het lyf van een draader gevonden, een span lang gevangen in julii Syngnatus pelagicus.
Jkang joeloeng joeloeng (malydsch)
Coryphaena caerulea
in het lyf van een Kret gevangen den 30 Julii 1778.
bek van een Zeekatje dog is wat te groot na proportie van deeze visch.
Een Visch in zyn Ey
oud wyf platte visch
dit balyntje gaat tot aan de staart
Zee katje
Sepia media.
het onderste stuk van de staart is langer dan het boovenste
Waere groote van een Vliegende Visch, wat ronder en dikker als een haaring, deze vloog in het schip den 1 aug: 1778
en wierd my present gegeven door de Capt. van der Spek op 't schip holland. Exocoetus volitans.
230

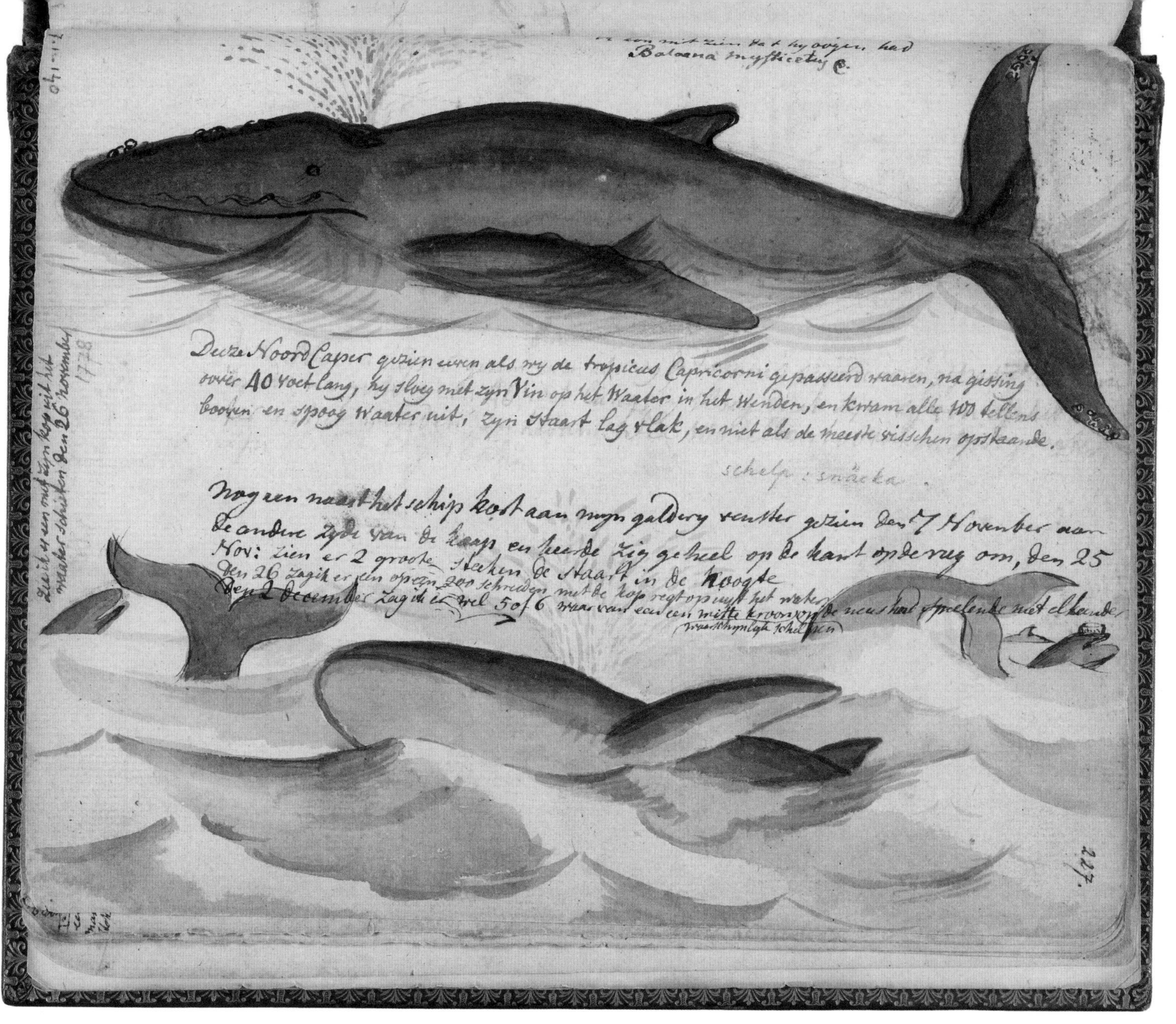
Balaena mysticetus
Deeze Noord Caper gezien even als wy de tropicus Capricorni gepasseerd waaren, na gissing
over 40 voet lang, hy sloeg met zyn Vin op het Waater in het Wenden, en kwam alle 100 tellens
booven en spoog Waater uit, zyn Staart lag plat, en niet als de meeste visschen opstaande.
1778
schelp : snäcka
Nog een naast het schip kort aan myn galdery venster gezien den 7 November aan
de andere zyde van de kaap en keerde zig geheel op de kant op de rug om, den 25
Nov: zien er 2 groote steken de Staart in de hoogte
den 26 zag ik er een op een 200 schreden met de kop regt op uyt het water
den 2 December zag ik er wel 50 of 6 waar van een een witte kroon op de neus had speelende met elkaander
227.

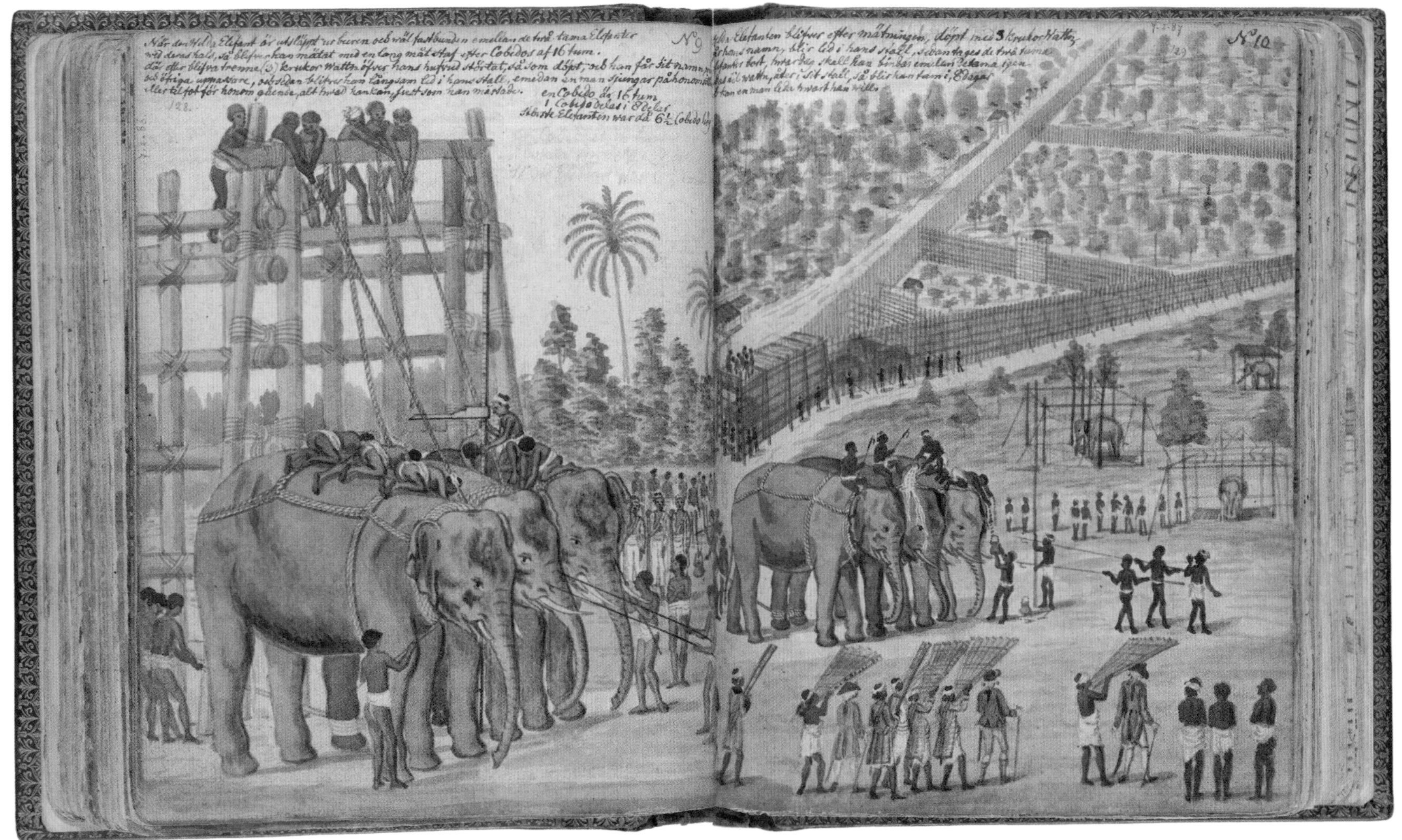

As a friend of the Governor of Ceylon, now Sri Lanka, Brandes enjoyed the privilege of witnessing special events and being taken on some fascinating excursions. He captured the drama of a wild elephant hunt in the jungle and the harnessing and training of the elephants in an elephant kraal near Colombo.

GLORIOUS FOREST

Ghillean Prance

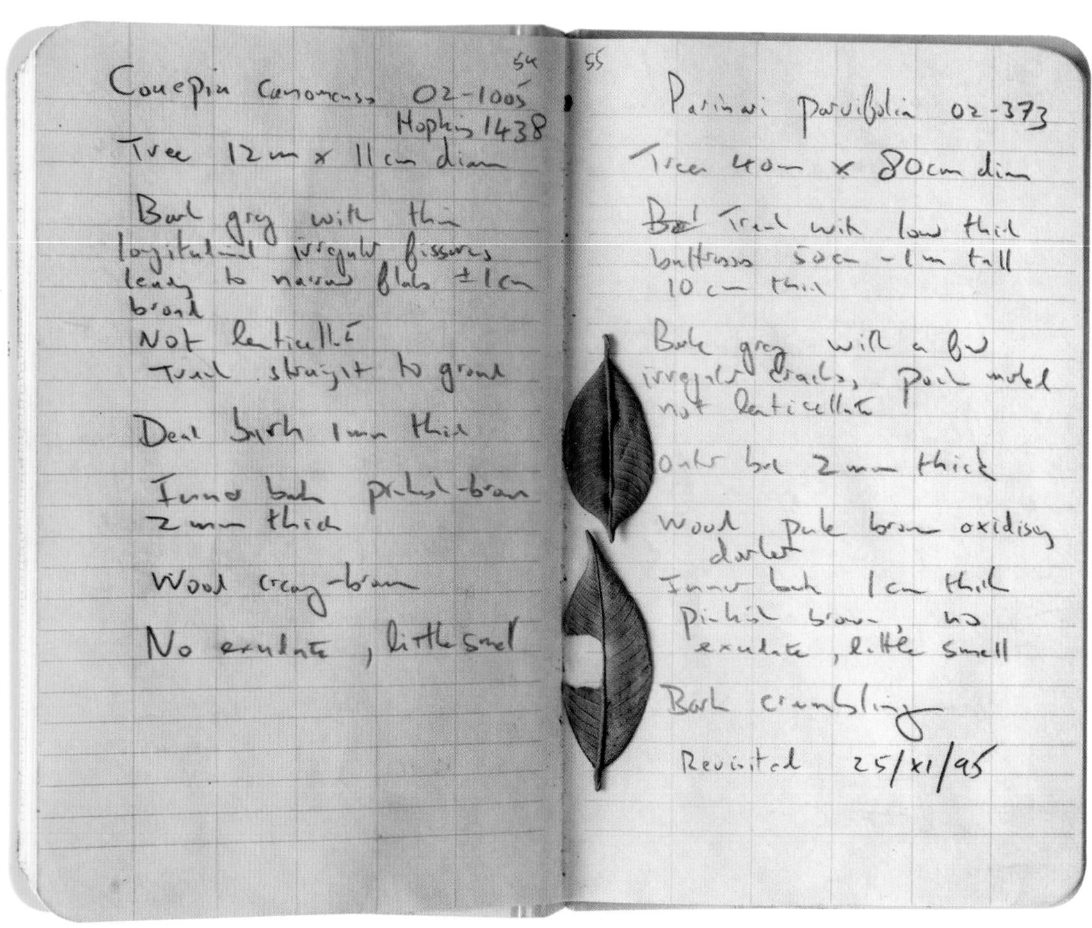

A notebook containing descriptions of trees encountered in the field by Prance, including details of height, the colour and texture of the bark and the wood, and smell, with samples of pressed leaves.

Notebooks are an essential part of my exploring kit. Other things of course are important in a practical sense ... and each might mean the difference between life and death in the jungle. But, in terms of making a genuine contribution to knowledge, the careful marks that you make in a journal will be the things that outlive you.

You could say that my whole exploring life began with a Brazil nut. It's a tree that towers above the rainforest canopy, and you often can't find another for hundreds of metres. I wanted to understand more about their cycle of life. And so I packed my rucksack and went. As young botanists we delved into the unknown, carrying our notebooks and a clear motive: to document, to observe and to bring back new knowledge for the benefit of others. Curiosity sustained us at every step. My journals were filled with every conceivable bit of observational data, and yet there was always so much more that could be found.

Plants and fungi are one of the last great frontiers for exploration in the modern day – a fragile world close to human activity and yet still so little understood. Our planet is home to over eight million different kinds of animals and plants, each locked in their own fight for survival. Yet ever since we humans emerged as a species, we've done our best to use and abuse the plants around us. We've dug them up, cut them down, damaged and degraded them. We're doing so now on a greater scale than ever, but neither we, nor any other animal, can survive without plants. Our green inheritance is being squandered. This seems like madness to me.

How did I learn this? Well, I've always loved nature; I can't really remember a time when it wasn't part of my life. Increasingly my interests were aimed towards tropical botany and I studied for my doctorate in the Forestry Department of Oxford University. So, in a lifetime of journeying in the jungles, my first steps were made by growing seeds in a greenhouse there. I joined an expedition to the Wilhelmina Mountains, in the deeply forested interior of Suriname. This was the start of my work for the New York Botanical Garden, and that first journey in 1963 changed my life forever. 'Undisturbed rainforest' – those are two of the most beautiful words I can think of. It's like walking into a cathedral. I was just overwhelmed by the diversity and the magnificent size and shape of the towering trees. Each day brought a new treat for me, a novice in the forest.

A one-year position as a post-doctoral researcher turned into a 25-year career in New York, during which time I eventually ran the *Projecto Flora Amazonica,* a joint Brazilian-American exploration programme to survey the flora of the region. In 1971, on one memorable journey, my team trekked through 275 km (170 miles) of forest, sleeping in hammocks, encountering anacondas, collecting and documenting how indigenous peoples used the local plants for food, hallucinogens and poisons for their arrows. On that trip alone we collected 700 plant and fungi specimens, many new to science.

Decades on, I've now discovered and classified hundreds of new species, but what is much more rewarding is seeing a new generation of students emerge from our programmes in tropical botany at Manaus, a city in the heart of the forest basin. I helped to establish the first graduate programme in the Amazon there, and our scholars are now leading their own expeditions into the field, taking forward the conservation work we started, with passion, curiosity, excitement and local knowledge.

Exploring in the Amazon of course presents hazard and hardship. You need tenacity and a willingness to put up with some pretty unpleasant and

THE
FIELD BOTANIST'S BOOK
SAFESPORT
NEW AMERICAN STANDARD BIBLE
Pen-Tab
NOTE BOOK
60 SHEETS
5 IN. x 8 IN.
K-8529 - OPEN END
K-5829 - OPEN SIDE
29¢
1973-4

exhausting work. It's not all glorious days in the field; there are long hours in the library and lab too. People do tend to think of the rainforest as a very dangerous place – rivers full of piranhas, poisonous snakes, clouds of mosquitoes, scorpions and spiders that fall from the trees – but actually the most annoying injury was when I snapped my Achilles tendon while dancing the samba. I was in Brazil leading a group of wealthy eco-tourists, an unusual situation for me. But in the forest I feel at home. I've lived with sixteen different Indian tribes and nothing really troubles me, although I will admit that biting swarms of fire ants can be intensely painful.

To survive here you have to be determined and resourceful. Once when we reached the end of a river and were planning to cross one watershed into another, I came down with malaria and had to walk for three days through uncharted forest to get help. Early on I also made sure to learn how to fix the motors on my boats. You don't want to go over the top of a waterfall in your canoe because your motor has failed to start. But there is sheer joy to be found here too. Perhaps it is seeing a new type of animal behaviour or discovering an undescribed species of plant. For me, one of the most precious recent experiences was to be able to take my young grandsons to the rainforest and observe the spark of wonder in their eyes when they saw a jaguar.

If we are to pass on this planet in good shape for future generations, we must act quickly, and carefully. We are losing species because of human activity, and yet the magnitude of this loss is still unappreciated. Recent studies suggest that an astonishing 86 per cent of all plants and animals on land and 91 per cent of those in the seas have yet to be named. During the first ten years of my exploration in Amazonia I was privileged to travel widely and had the opportunity to carry out research untroubled by environmental issues. But the more I understood complicated pollination mechanisms by bats, beetles, birds and butterflies, and the ways in which plants defend themselves against the hordes of leaf-eating predators, the more I sensed the fragile web of life here. By the 1970s the situation in the Amazon was changing drastically, and large-scale development, accompanied by massive destruction of the forest, had begun. The Trans-Amazon Highway was under construction.

Now the rainforest reaches us all – from the tyres on your car, the chocolate we enjoy so much, to the coffee we drink every day or the medicines we use – so it's vital that we gain a better knowledge of the delicate balance of this ecosystem. Almost everywhere you look, intricate interrelationships can be discovered, whether it's scarab beetles pollinating giant water lilies, or, in the case of Brazil nuts, in seeing how the tree propagates. An orchid, a bee, an agouti rodent and indigenous nut gatherers are all connected in a nexus of interdependence. Sever a link and the system breaks down. We have also lost our spiritual connection with the Earth and the sense of valuing the forest for its own sake. Conservation is an issue of justice and equity as much as the environment.

I can't really describe any better than this why I've devoted my life to studying plants. We must all strive in our own ways to protect the Amazon and the wonderful people who depend on the forest for their future. And it can even come from something as seemingly simple as making small marks in a notebook, as it is from these field observations that discoveries emerge. On every expedition, I took time to fill my journals with observations: colours, contexts, encounters, sights and sounds, and list upon list of data. When deep in the rainforest the challenge is keeping them safe and dry. Back at home, working on a collection, writing a paper or later a book, I would be lost without them. With new discoveries comes a greater understanding and appreciation. There are so many things to explore close at hand. We look beyond the Moon to Mars, and yet have still not nearly catalogued all the species of animals, plants and fungi with whom we share this beautiful planet Earth.

A collection of Prance's early notebooks, photographs, equipment, dried plant specimens and objects, representing a lifetime of research.

ADELA BRETON 1849-1923

In the gilded cage of English civilization, I think longingly of American wilds and anything that reminds me of them is a pleasure.

'You look at Miss Breton and set her down as a weak, frail and delicate person who goes into convulsions at the sight of the slightest unconventionality in the way of living,' wrote American archaeologist Alfred Tozzer in 1902, 'but I assure you, her appearance is utterly at variance with her real self.'

Adela Breton, English Victorian gentlewoman, artist and self-styled intrepid archaeologist and anthropologist, only really embarked on her career in earnest aged 50. Unmarried, wealthy and with no immediate family to care for, Breton set her sights on the ruins and pyramids of Chichén Itzá, hidden in the dense undergrowth of the Yucatán jungle of Mexico. By the time of her first encounter with Tozzer, Breton had already spent ten winters in Central America, sketchbook always in hand, painstakingly copying and drawing ancient glyphs and sculptures.

Few talented architectural copyists, however daring they imagined themselves, were willing to endure the privations of jungle exploration. Breton was more than up to the task, travelling with her trusted Mexican servant on horseback over a country that was more often than not roadless, and camping among remote Maya ruins for weeks, sometimes months at a time. She devoted the final 23 years of her life to recording the subtle nuances of colour found in the frescoes of Chichén Itzá and other important sites before they faded or eroded.

Breton's timing was perfect. The ruins were only just being uncovered and had not yet been fully exposed to the elements. They were ancient and crumbling, but still could be appreciated in all their vibrant colour. Breton's genius was her ability to capture every tone, every detail with such precision. Today, her copies are the only record in colour of these irreplaceable elements of 'lost' cultures, long before the invention of colour photography.

'The remarkable thing about those ancient [Yucatec] painters', Breton wrote, is 'their understanding of tone is wonderful and this makes it so difficult to do justice to them in copies. Every tint must be in exact harmony with its neighbours, *in tune* like chords in music.' Accurately representing these tones was something she strove for.

Independent and outspoken, she may not always have been a comfortable companion, but the quality of her work would be highly respected. In time, Mexico became more like home than England, and no matter how often she fell sick when travelling there, she was drawn back again and again.

Breton continued to travel extensively, including to Australia, Japan and Fiji, but her heart was always in Chichén Itzá. Towards the end of her life, during a spell in New Brunswick, she wrote: 'The mornings here are so like tierra caliente that I often sigh and think of Chichen, and of the wide green ways between the forests of Northern Vera Cruz, with the big blue butterflies ... like bits of sky fallen here and there. I, too, have been in Arcadia.'

Breton's watercolour sketches of the House of the Magician, Chichén Itzá (above) and the ruins at Mitla, Oaxaca (opposite). In several of her sketches she included one of her travelling companions to provide a sense of scale.

Overleaf: Drawings of three figures from Tantoyuca, Vera Cruz, and various views of a jamb from an inner doorway of Temple A at Chichén Itzá. Breton filled her leather-bound sketchbooks with landscapes and architectural details. Her accurate tracings and drawings of ancient sites now provide an invaluable record as so much has since faded or disappeared.

Tantoyuca
Tantoyuca
S. Andres Tuxtla
[in Southern Vera Cruz]
at Escuela Normal
At Escuela Normal. Jalapa
[Tantoyuca, in northern Vera Cruz]
Ea 82-99

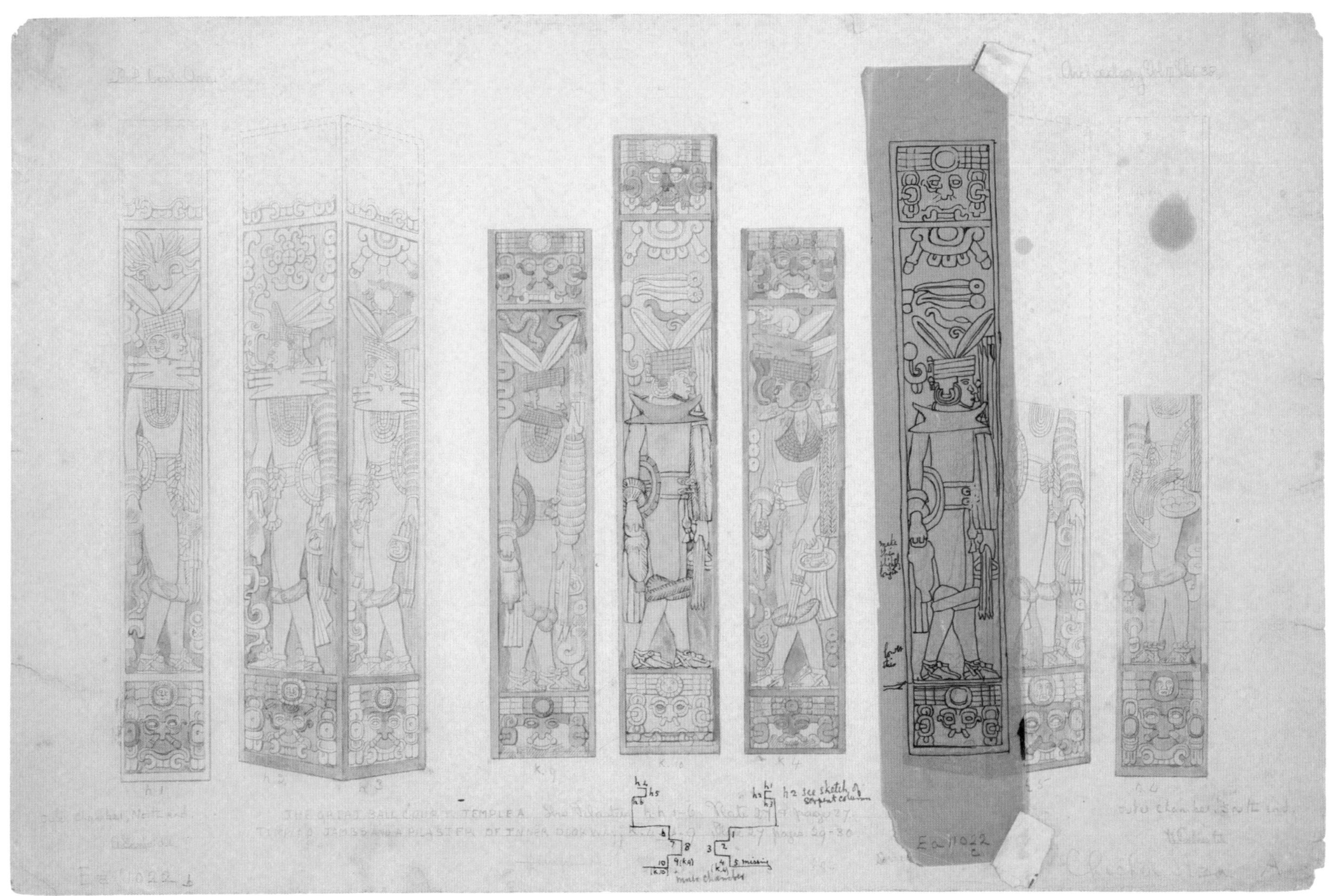

WILLIAM BURCHELL 1781-1863

The travels ... were undertaken solely for the purpose of acquiring knowledge.

For William Burchell, true happiness was to be found in travelling alone, stretching out on a grassy bank under an African sky to sketch in his journal while a hippo steak sizzled over the fire. Though now little known, Burchell was a remarkable botanical polymath: an independent naturalist and pioneer ecologist, he was also an able surveyor, author and artist, an amateur musician, a linguist and ethnographer, and a prolific collector. He won some fame in the early nineteenth century for his expeditions in St Helena, South Africa and Brazil, amassing significant collections of plants and describing many new species. His wealthy family were the owners of a London nursery, so it's perhaps no surprise that he would be drawn into the plant-hunting business.

Born in London, Burchell was a trader turned schoolmaster in St Helena when he began experimenting with the introduction of exotic plants brought there by ships returning from the Orient. His fiancée had set out to join him in 1807, but on arrival she announced a change of heart: she had decided to marry the captain of the ship that had brought her there. Burchell was unfazed – exploring was to become his passion, and he remained a bachelor until his death in 1863.

In 1810 he sailed to Cape Town with his collections and began his travels deep into the surrounding country, through Cape Province to the remote Karoo plains. By 1815 it is said he had covered 7,250 km (4,500 miles), studying and gathering new plants, and faithfully sketching his discoveries, all from the relative comfort of his custom-designed collecting wagon. It was a combination of mobile home, laboratory, library and art studio, and crammed full with supplies and packing cases, a brandy barrel, painting materials, rifles and ammunition, a sextant and telescope, charts and trading goods, and a natural history library of 50 volumes. It is little wonder that he had to secure an extra ox wagon en route to accommodate the treasures he collected. He returned to England with over 60,000 specimens, many new to science: seeds and bulbs, skins and bones, and other curiosities such as zebra and white rhinoceros. As important perhaps were also his numerous sketches, drawings and writings.

While in England, Burchell published two volumes of an account of his travels in South Africa, but in 1825 he set out for Brazil. He first spent time collecting around Rio de Janeiro, before sailing down the coast to São Paulo, where he led a party into the interior jungles in the rainy season. He continued on to Pôrto Nacional, collecting and sketching at every step, descending the Rio Tocantins and the Amazon to reach the coast at Belém in 1829. It was a mammoth journey, and it is reflected in the abundant collections he took home: over 16,000 insects, 817 bird skins of 362 species, and countless plants. By this time, it is said his London herbarium had grown to about 140,000 specimens.

Burchell would be awarded an honorary doctorate by Oxford University, but his travels had exhausted his personal fortune and, much to his annoyance, many of his specimens were irreparably damaged while in storage at the British Museum. While his South African sojourn inspired settlers to make their own journeys to the Cape, he never published his Brazilian findings. Increasingly disillusioned and reclusive, he withdrew from society to catalogue his collections in private. He ended up taking his own life, his work unfinished, by hanging himself in his garden shed.

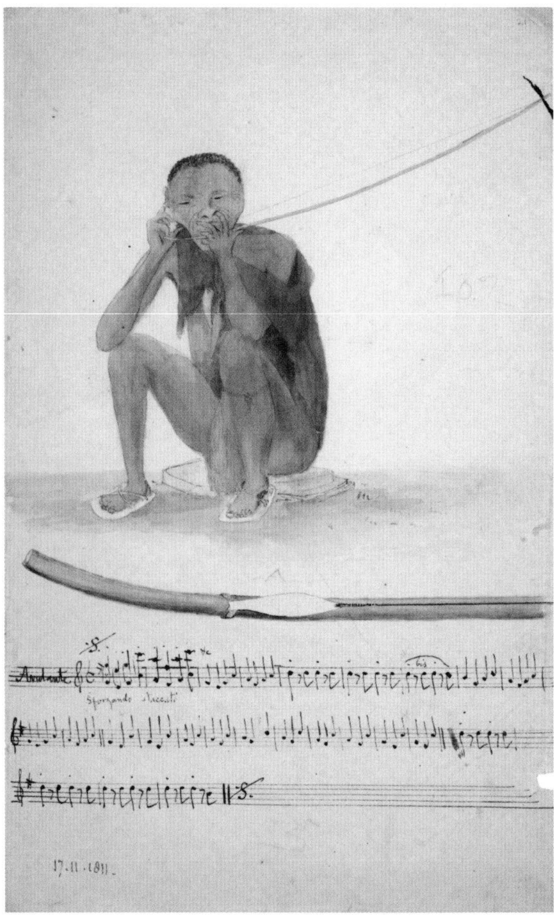

Watercolour drawing of a Bushman playing a *Goráh*, which Burchell described as a combination of a stringed and a wind instrument. In his published memoirs he recounts how the old musician, having been invited to play for him, sat himself down and rested his elbows on his knees. Putting a finger into one ear, he then began his solo, while Burchell himself was occupied not only in drawing the figure and the instrument, but also in listening to the notes and trying to remember them so that he could later transcribe them accurately.

Top: A view of Cape Town, Table Bay and Tygerberg, 26 December 1810. In the foreground, under the shade of his umbrella as protection from the great heat, Burchell has shown himself at work. He recorded the temperature that day as 102°F (39°C).

In 1825 Burchell sailed to Brazil as a member of a British diplomatic mission, and spent several years there amassing a vast collection of specimens of plants and animals, and sketching. Above is a view of Santos, a coastal town in the province of São Paulo.

Burchell travelled widely in South Africa, recording and collecting obsessively. Above is a scene of stalking a herd of elephants and opposite sketches, with descriptions and measurements, of a tortoise and rhinoceros. The White Rhino, *Rhinoceros simus*, sometimes called 'Burchell's rhinoceros', was identified as a separate species in 1812.

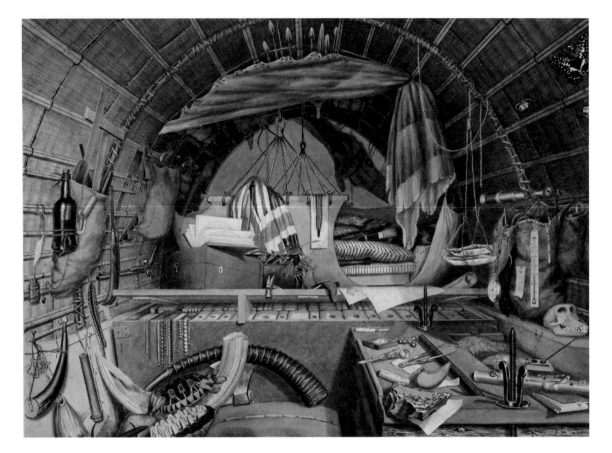

A blazing fire of dry acacia wood, enabled me to write my journal and arrange the memoranda of the day. As we had brought neither gridiron nor plates, a forked stick, about two feet long, supplied the place of both. On this fork a steak of our hippopotamus was stuck … the luxuries … of the dining-room were here reduced to their simplest forms; the grassy bank, the forked stick, and a small pocket-knife, supplied the place of all the costly furniture of a palace.

But to me, every spot on which my wagon stood, was home: there was my resting-place; there was my abode … Whenever I view my drawing of its interior, a thousand agreeable reflections are brought to mind: in an instant I am transported back again to African scenes … In the contemplation of past dangers, there is a pleasure and satisfaction.

'Inside of My African Wagon', a watercolour by Burchell; ever detailed, he noted that sketching this scene took him four days and the painting some 120 hours in total. He started on 12 February 1820 drawing the tortoise, elephant tooth and hippopotamus tusk, and two days later, the press screws, memorandum book, flute and shell. His collecting wagon, pulled by a team of oxen, was his home and also a mobile laboratory, in which he could simultaneously travel and write, read and sketch, measure and dissect.

Opposite: Burchell's field sketches covered a huge variety of subjects, reflecting his range of interests, including botany, zoology and ethnography. He also sketched scenes of camp life (including himself next to the camp fire, bottom left) and the indigenous peoples who guided and helped him on his expeditions.

Philip
Stuurman
Andries
Philip
Philip
Gerrit
a girl of Klaarwater
Lina
610
11.1.13.

532
22.8.12
b
9.9.12

321
321
321. 18.1811.

HOWARD CARTER 1874-1939

The exhilaration of discovery, the fever of suspense, the almost over-mastering impulse, born of curiosity, to break down seals and lift the lids of boxes, the thought - pure joy to the investigator - that you are about to add a page to history.

On 4 November 1922, British archaeologist Howard Carter opened his field diary and wrote five words diagonally across the page: 'first steps of tomb found'. He was on the threshold of what would prove to be the greatest discovery in modern Egyptology. Carter was about to unearth the tomb of the boy-king Tutankhamun.

For over two centuries, teams of archaeologists had descended on the Valley of the Kings and meticulously scraped away at the sand and rubble, uncovering over 60 tombs. By 1922, the area had been declared exhausted. Carter was undeterred. He was adamant the Valley held one more secret.

Trained in drawing and painting by his father, artist Samuel John Carter, seventeen-year-old Howard Carter had set sail for Egypt and gained employment with the Egyptian Exploration Fund under the tutelage of the eminent archaeologist Flinders Petrie at Amarna. He made superb drawings of the reliefs in Hatshepsut's temple at Deir el-Bahri. At Beni Hasan he faithfully copied ancient drawings and hieroglyphs during the day, and slept with the bats in the tombs at night.

It would be three decades before he would make his grand discovery. In the meantime he worked for the Egyptian Antiquities Service, before an argument at Saqqara with tourists led to his resignation. In 1909 he began work under the patronage of the wealthy Egypt enthusiast, the fifth Earl of Carnarvon, though not all his excavations proved fruitful. There were also times he found he had to defend sites from local looters: 'Shinning down a rope at midnight into a nestful of industrious tomb-robbers is a pastime which at least does not lack excitement,' he later remarked.

By 1922, Carter's team had worked a full six seasons in the Valley of the Kings, with little to show for their labours, and this was to be the last season. 'We had almost made up our minds we were beaten,' Carter later admitted. As he was about to down tools, a local boy bringing water stumbled upon a rock. With further investigation, steps were discovered leading to a doorway with unmistakable royal seals. 'It needed all my self control to keep from breaking down the doorway, and investigating then and there,' Carter wrote.

On 26 November 1922, with Carnarvon in attendance, Carter made a small hole in a second door and held a candle to it. In his journal he wrote: 'It was sometime before one could see, the hot air escaping caused the candle to flicker, but as soon as one's eyes became accustomed to the glimmer of light, the interior of the chamber gradually loomed before one, with its strange and wonderful medley of extraordinary and beautiful objects heaped upon one another.' On the other side of the door was an unparalleled ancient Egyptian royal burial, unseen for three millennia.

The public were enthralled by the exquisite treasures, and fascinated by the image of the mummified boy-king with his fabulous gold mask. This was more than an archaeological find – it was a riveting human story, as well as a unique insight into an ancient people. It took Carter ten years to meticulously examine and catalogue the treasures. He died in London, aged 64. On his gravestone is the quotation from the alabaster 'Wishing Cup' Carter retrieved from Tutankhamun's tomb: 'May your spirit live, may you spend millions of years, you who love Thebes, sitting with your face to the north wind, your eyes beholding happiness.'

A year after he first discovered Tutankhamun's tomb, Carter came upon the pharaoh's sarcophagus behind an immense gold wall - the side of an enormous shrine. He made painstaking sketches of the nested coffins and all the burial objects in situ.

Opposite: Harry Burton, Egyptologist and archaeological photographer, created records of every item in Tutankhamun's tomb, a task that took eight years. This image of a throne was annotated by Carter and Burton, including precise colour information.

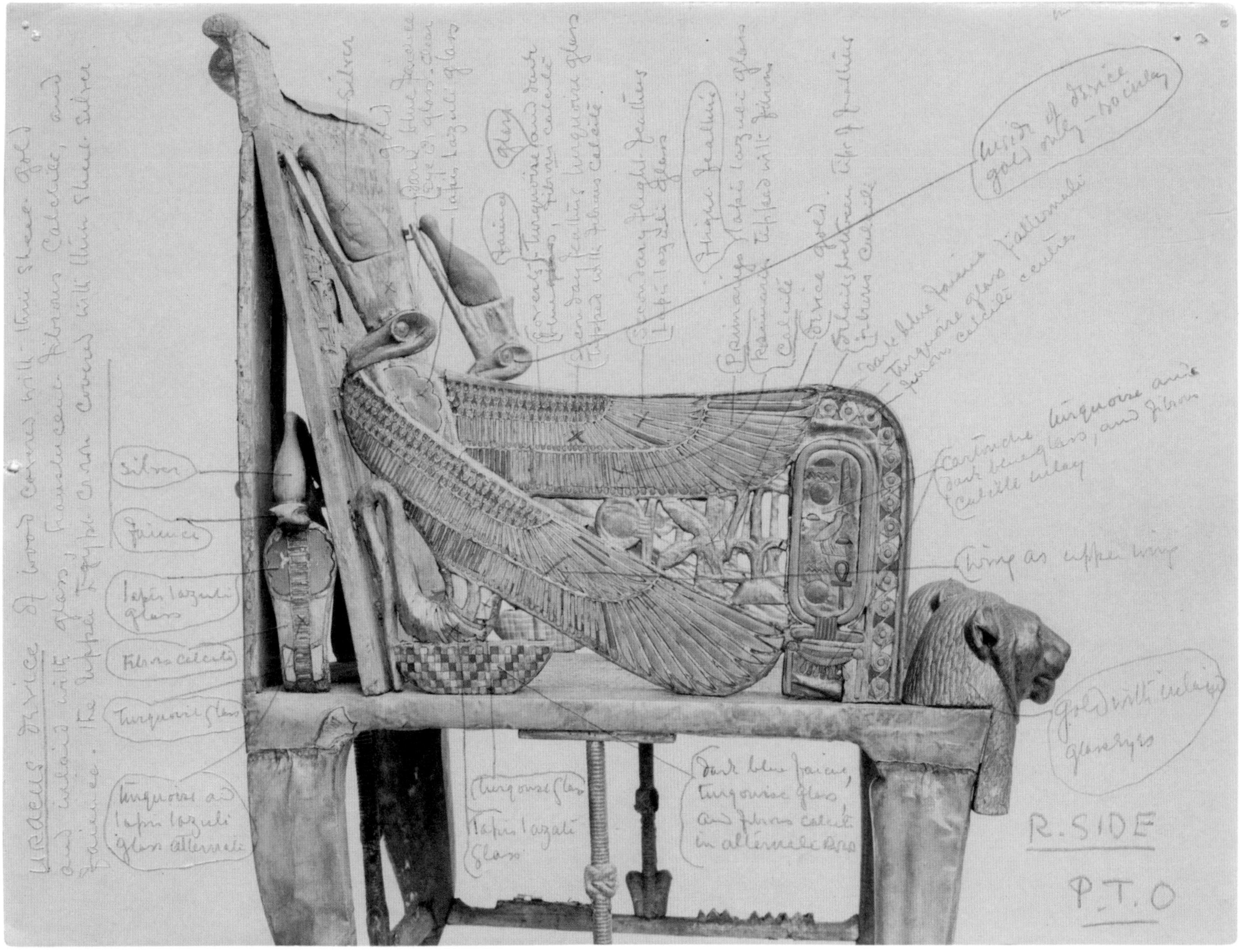

Uraeus frieze of wood covered with thin sheet gold and inlaid with glass, translucent fibrous calcite, and faience. The upper Egypt crown covered with thin sheet silver

Silver

Dark blue faience
Eye of glass, clear
Lapis lazuli glass

Glass

Faience

Coverts: Turquoise and dark blue faience, fibrous calcite

Secondary feathers turquoise glass tipped with fibrous calcite

Secondary flight feathers lapis lazuli glass

Upper feathers

Primaries lapis lazuli glass
Remainder tipped with fibrous calcite

Calcite

Frieze gold

Scales between tips of feathers fibrous calcite

Disc of frieze gold only – no inlay

Dark blue faience alternately
Turquoise glass
fibrous calcite centre

Cartouche turquoise and dark blue glass, and fibrous calcite inlay

Wing as upper wing

Silver

Faience

Lapis lazuli glass

Fibrous calcite

Turquoise glass

Turquoise and lapis lazuli glass alternate

Turquoise glass

Lapis lazuli glass

Dark blue faience, turquoise glass and fibrous calcite in alternate rows

Gold with inlaid glass eyes

R. SIDE

P.T.O

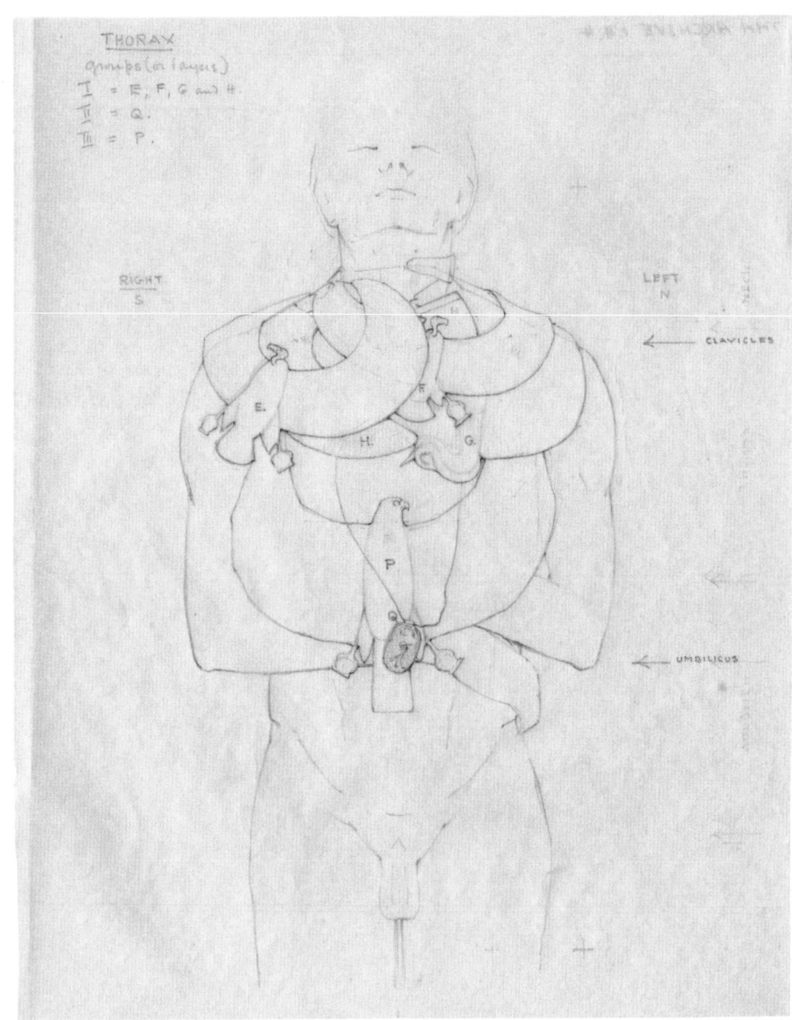

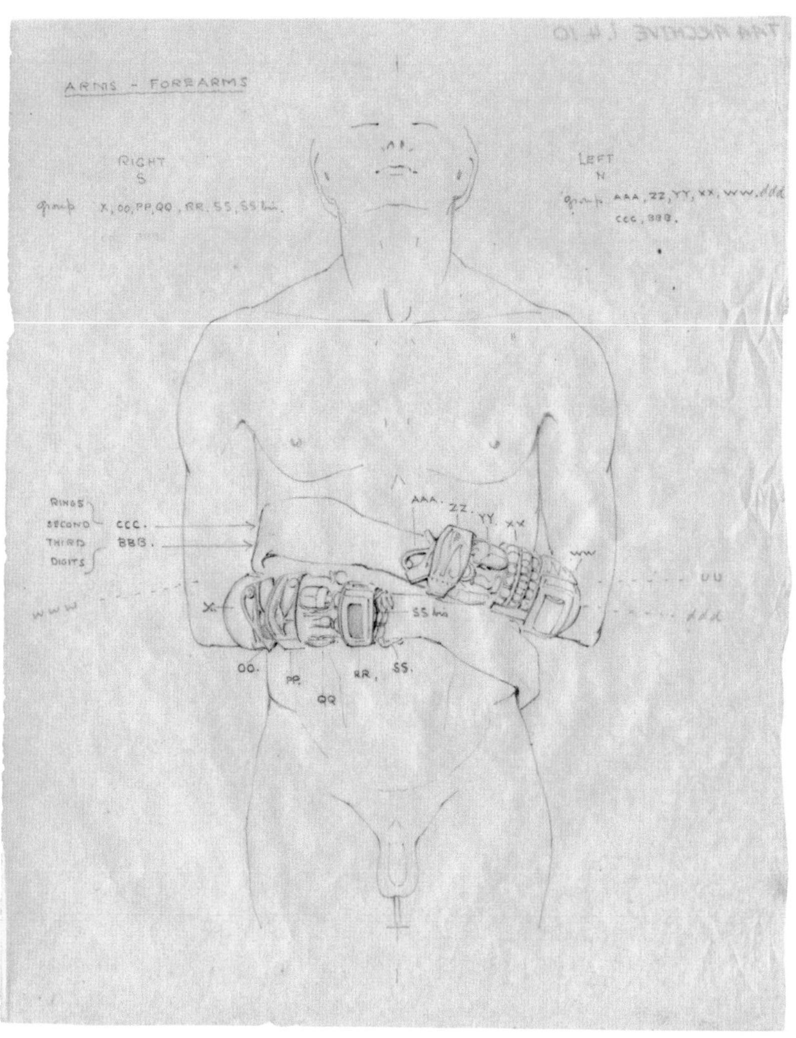

Two of Carter's precise drawings of the young king's body as it was unwrapped, revealing a wealth of jewellery, including collars, necklaces and armlets. On 28 October 1925 he wrote: 'The penultimate scene was disclosed - a very neatly wrapped mummy of the young king, with golden mask of sad but tranquil expression.'

Opposite: This watercolour by Carter displays his artistic skills in the task of accurately copying a Horus falcon of Lower Egypt from the mortuary temple of Queen Hatshepsut at Deir el-Bahri, 1895.

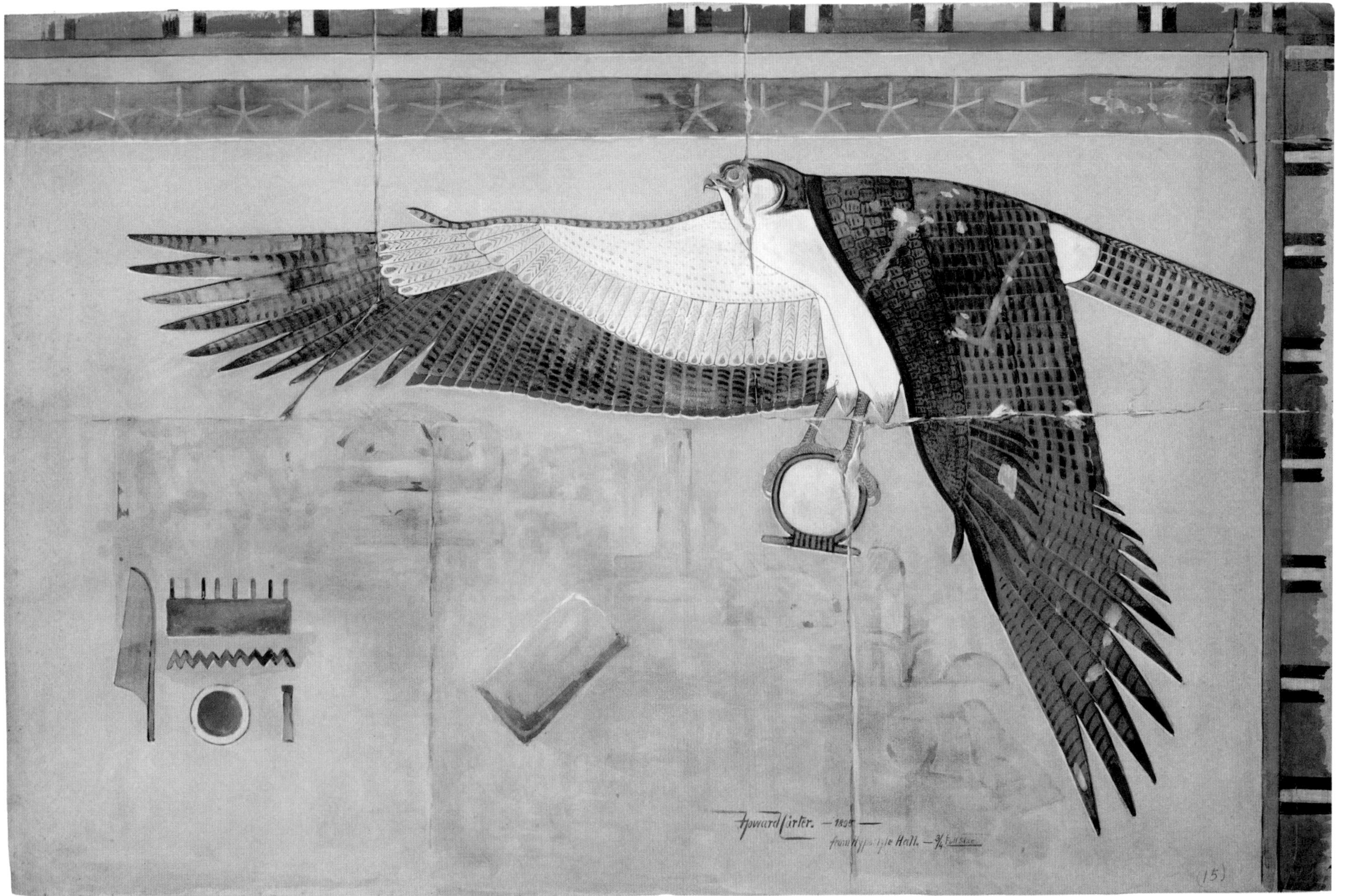
Howard Carter.
(15)

BRUCE CHATWIN 1940-1989

In school I was an addict of atlases and was always being ostracized for telling tall stories.

It all began with a piece of 'brontosaurus'. Or so Bruce Chatwin would have us believe. Perhaps it all started with arguably his most famous sentence, a telegram sent to his editor at the *Sunday Times* which read: 'Gone to Patagonia for six months.' In December 1974, the 34-year-old Chatwin left Buenos Aires on the night bus, heading south in search of the scandalous, the bizarre, the terrible, the sublime, beginning a journey that would transform him into one of the most original writers of his generation.

Under-appreciated for most of his life – despite the success of *In Patagonia* in 1977, or *The Songlines* in 1987 – since his death Chatwin's reputation has soared, assuming cult-like status. Yet he has been accused of being a fraud, of making things up, but that mistakes his craft: he was a writer in love with the *world*, piecing together experiences with sensitivity and insight, exploring the mind as much as a landscape. But it is fair to say he rarely let the truth get in the way of a good story.

In his passport, Chatwin put 'farmer' as his profession, but his life was spent almost constantly travelling, a large proportion of it in the study of nomads. He preferred to journey alone: 'two people have a defence, but a single person is approachable'. Mystery became a central part of his character as dashing author. His agent, publishers – not to mention his wife – rarely knew exactly where he was, save for occasional phone calls and letters. Scribbled inside one of his notebooks is this telling line from Montaigne: 'I ordinarily reply to those who ask me the reason for my travels, that I know well what I am fleeing from, but not what I am looking for.' In another, a simple quote from Rimbaud: 'I was forced to travel.'

Chatwin described his journey through Patagonia as 'a Quest or Wonder Voyage', a meditation on wandering for its own sake. At a time when maps and guidebooks were beginning to obliterate the unexpected in the landscape, Chatwin encouraged his readers to do the opposite – to move off the beaten track, to go slow, to observe, to write things down. His prose was honed to bare essentials and it has been much imitated, though rarely equalled.

His travels in Patagonia formed an exploration through an imaginary terrain as much as the real, a verbal journey of interesting encounters. His journals give little clue as to where, or indeed when, he went, but they are filled with glimpses of those things that caught his gaze. He traces the story of Butch Cassidy; describes a sect of witches; tracks down mad pretenders to non-existent thrones; all the while pursuing the remains of that brontosaurus, which turned out, inevitably, to be no dinosaur at all, but a ragged remnant of skin from a giant sloth.

His works have become modern-day classics that defy categorization; and the man himself remains an enigma. *In Patagonia* is a masterpiece of travel, history, poetry and adventure combined, but we learn very little of Chatwin himself. Yet for most people, he is now a man defined by his journals. His black moleskine notebooks have become his signature, but in the early days he used almost anything that came to hand; most were cheap and easily available: spiral-bound red school books; yellow-paged 'Evidence' legal pads; blue Azmat journals carried on journeys in Afghanistan; or obscure notebooks purchased at train stations in Russia or Peru. All are absolutely crammed with jottings about people, snapshots of a place – a treasury of useful detail when later crafting his prose, 'zigzagging among texts and through time'.

In black biro, green ink, pencil and pen, even pink felt-tip, all manner of precious marks and observations spread across the page. It is a shifting stream of mental process. 'He was always thinking on paper and clarifying his mind, like a conversation', his wife Elizabeth recalls. Briefly home from his travels, he mostly wrote by hand on the yellow legal pads, correcting and deleting, discarding sheet after sheet, typing up with large margins, then changing more. He hated the thought of writing on a computer and never owned or wanted one. His notebooks were always piled close to hand. He once said that to lose his passport would be inconvenient, but to lose a notebook would be a disaster.

The black-bound notebooks that Chatwin regularly bought in Paris have now become legendary. They are filled with jottings, draft paragraphs, lines of poetry, fleeting descriptions of people, chance encounters, and are hard to unscramble. When he set off on a journey he often just grabbed whichever notebook lay to hand. It's not unusual for a single moleskine to include parts of many journeys - South America, Australia, Russia, Africa - all in one, and he rarely dated his entries.

Chatwin often said he became a writer 'to explain his own restlessness'. He laboured in obscurity under the pressure of his first book, a work provisionally entitled 'The Nomadic Alternative'. It took him all over the world in its research, and though the project was abandoned, it undoubtedly informed much of his later writing. Here is a page featuring idle doodles and some possible titles: 'Life is a journey'.

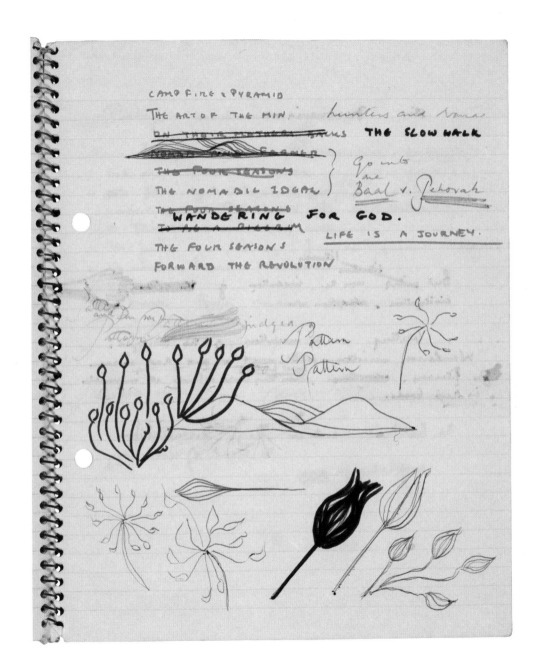

CAMP FIRE & PYRAMID

THE ART OF THE MIN

THE SLOW WALK

THE NOMADIC IDEAL

Baal v. Jehovah

WANDERING FOR GOD.

LIFE IS A JOURNEY.

THE FOUR SEASONS

FORWARD THE REVOLUTION

Pattern

Pattern

JAMES COOK 1728–1779

I, whose ambition leads me not only farther than any other man has been before me, but as far as I think it is possible for man to go.

Captain James Cook was the greatest explorer of his age. This is a simple statement of fact. It is impossible to do justice to a man of such determination, so this can only offer a glimpse of his skills. In navigation, cartography and hydrography he was peerless. In having the courage to sail beyond the horizon of what was known, he essentially redrew the map of the world.

Cook's three main voyages between 1768 and 1779 provided his European masters with unrivalled information about the Pacific Ocean, and about those who lived on its coasts. He filled swathes of the blank chart with new knowledge. During his lifetime his exploits were widely admired, but after he was killed on a remote Hawaiian shore his supporters turned him into a hero of the Enlightenment, a man who had made the ultimate sacrifice in the pursuit of science.

His achievements are all the more incredible considering his humble origins in a family of farm labourers from Marton, North Yorkshire. He first went to sea at the age of eighteen, and rose from the lowest ranks of the merchant marine to the Royal Navy. His talent for surveying was born in North American waters during the Seven Years War. He then refined his techniques, tackling the fog-cloaked coastlines of Newfoundland with characteristic accuracy and persistence. In time he would discover and chart new coastlines from Antarctica to the Arctic, from New Zealand and the east coast of Australia to the west coast of North America, and many hundreds of islands in between.

He sailed into the Pacific 250 years after Ferdinand Magellan, but it was Cook and his crews that detailed the shores of this vast ocean and made its geography and people visible to a Western audience. He dispelled the myth of a temperate southern continent, crossed the Antarctic Circle for the first time and described seas rich with seal and whale life. His voyages enabled the collecting, identification and drawing of thousands of new plants, mammals and birds, and the ambitious men of science he took with him, notably Joseph Banks, added immeasurably to the new fields of botany, astronomy and oceanography – in short, widening the realm of human understanding. This was exploration in every sense of the word.

For some, the most remarkable of Cook's discoveries was not a new continent, but that scurvy, so long the scourge of distant sea voyages, could be overcome by an appropriate diet that included cress, sauerkraut and a daily issue of lemon juice. Though his voyages had their geopolitical motives, and the lasting legacy of cultural encounters in the Pacific is a difficult one, Cook was no colonist, and in reading his journals his humanity shines through.

Energized by his overwhelming scientific impulse, his voyages were well-equipped and fully committed explorations, with the only modern equal perhaps being NASA missions. As an explorer he was willing to challenge conventional wisdom, to dare what most thought impossible, to make his own path, unconcerned with fame. 'The man who wants to lead the orchestra', he once wrote, 'must turn his back on the crowd.' His greatest happiness was in creating maps, and his curiosity would change the world forever.

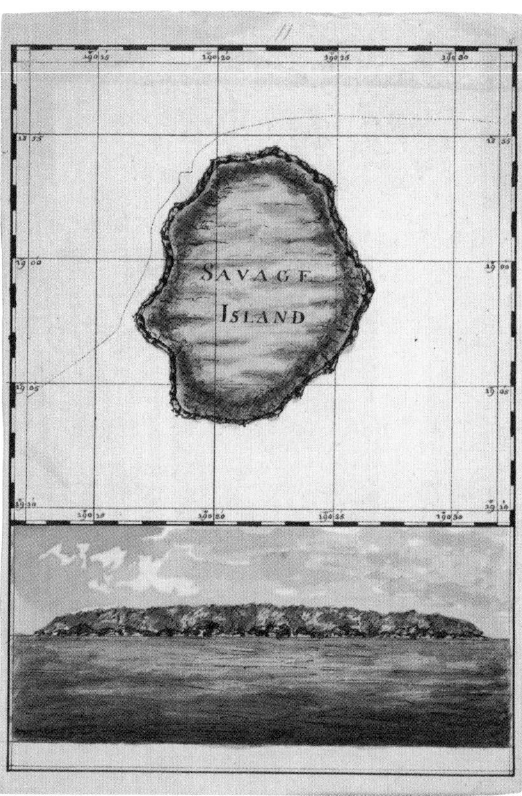

In 1774, Cook was the first European to sight the coral atoll of Niue in the Pacific. He named it 'Savage Island' after the locals gave his men trouble landing. Opposite is an illustrated chart of the southern hemisphere showing the route of the *Resolution* on Cook's second voyage of discovery.

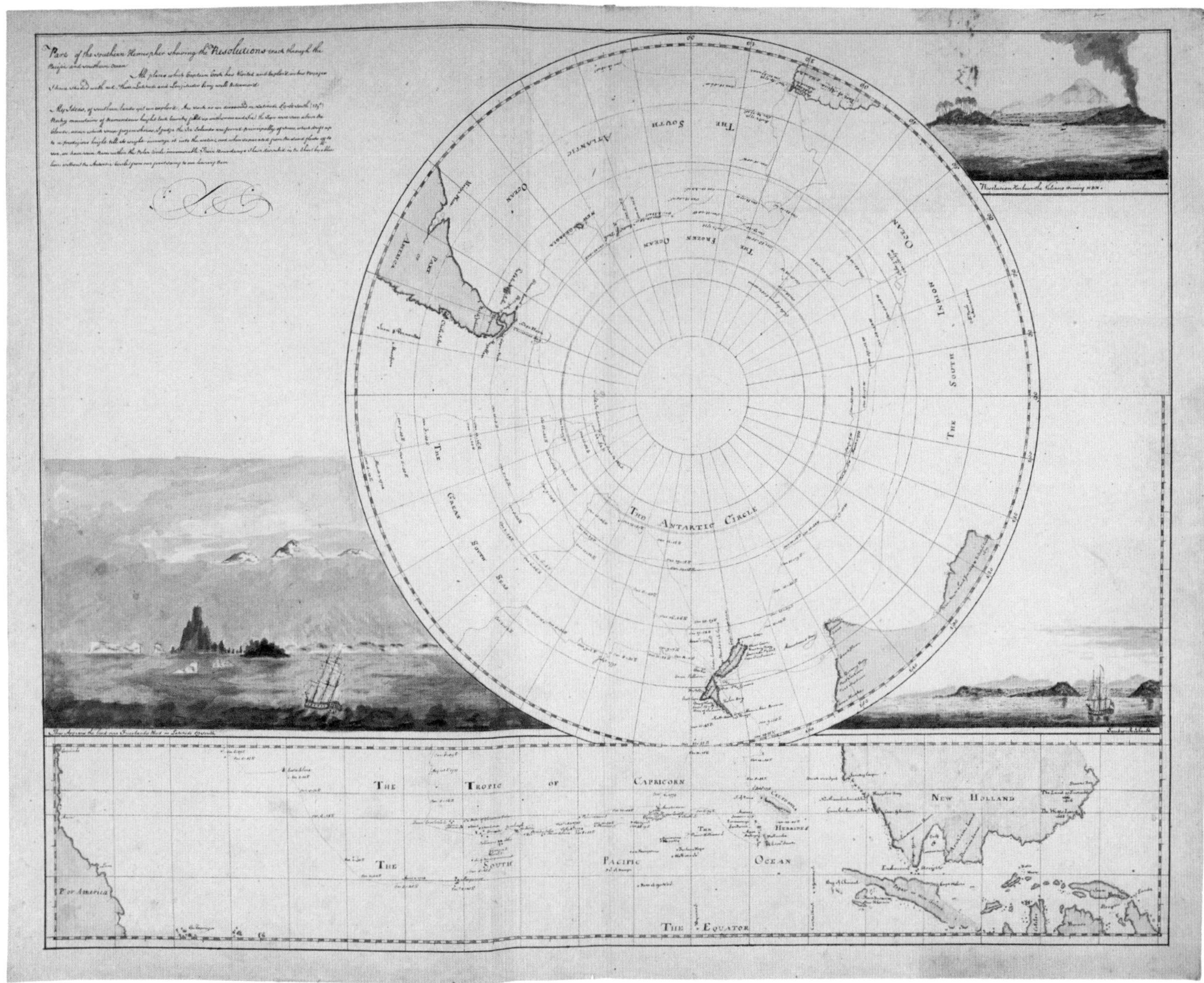

Part of the southern Hemispher showing the Resolutions track through the Pacific and southern Ocean
All places which Captain Cook has Visited and Explor'd in this Voyage I have shaded with ink. Their Latitude and Longitude being well determin'd.
The South Atlantic Ocean
The Frozen Ocean
The South Indian Ocean
Part of America
The Antartic Circle
The Great South Sea
The Tropic of Capricorn
New Holland
The South Pacific Ocean
The Equator

A plan of the harbour of St Johns, Newfoundland. In 1762 the young Cook was master of the *Northumberland* under Captain Alexander, Lord Colville. The ship was involved in a campaign to recapture St Johns from the French, enabling Cook to carry out a number of surveys which so impressed Colville that he wrote to the Lords of the Admiralty: ‘that from my Experience of Mr Cook’s Genius and Capacity, I think him well qualified for the Work he has performed, and for greater Undertakings of the same kind’. This was the letter that really launched Cook’s career. The Governor of Newfoundland was equally impressed, and when he needed a marine surveyor to chart its coasts, he specifically asked for Cook. Elevated to the rank of King’s Surveyor, Cook would spend the next five years engaged in this work, cruising the coasts of Newfoundland and returning to London to spend the winter working on his charts.

Opposite: Cook’s journal from his second voyage as the *Resolution* is searching for the fabled Great Southern Continent. This page of observations opens with ‘Weather and Remarkable Occurrences’. They crossed the Antarctic Circle for a third time on 26 January 1774, later reaching 71°10'S on 30 January when they could go no further because of the solid sea ice.

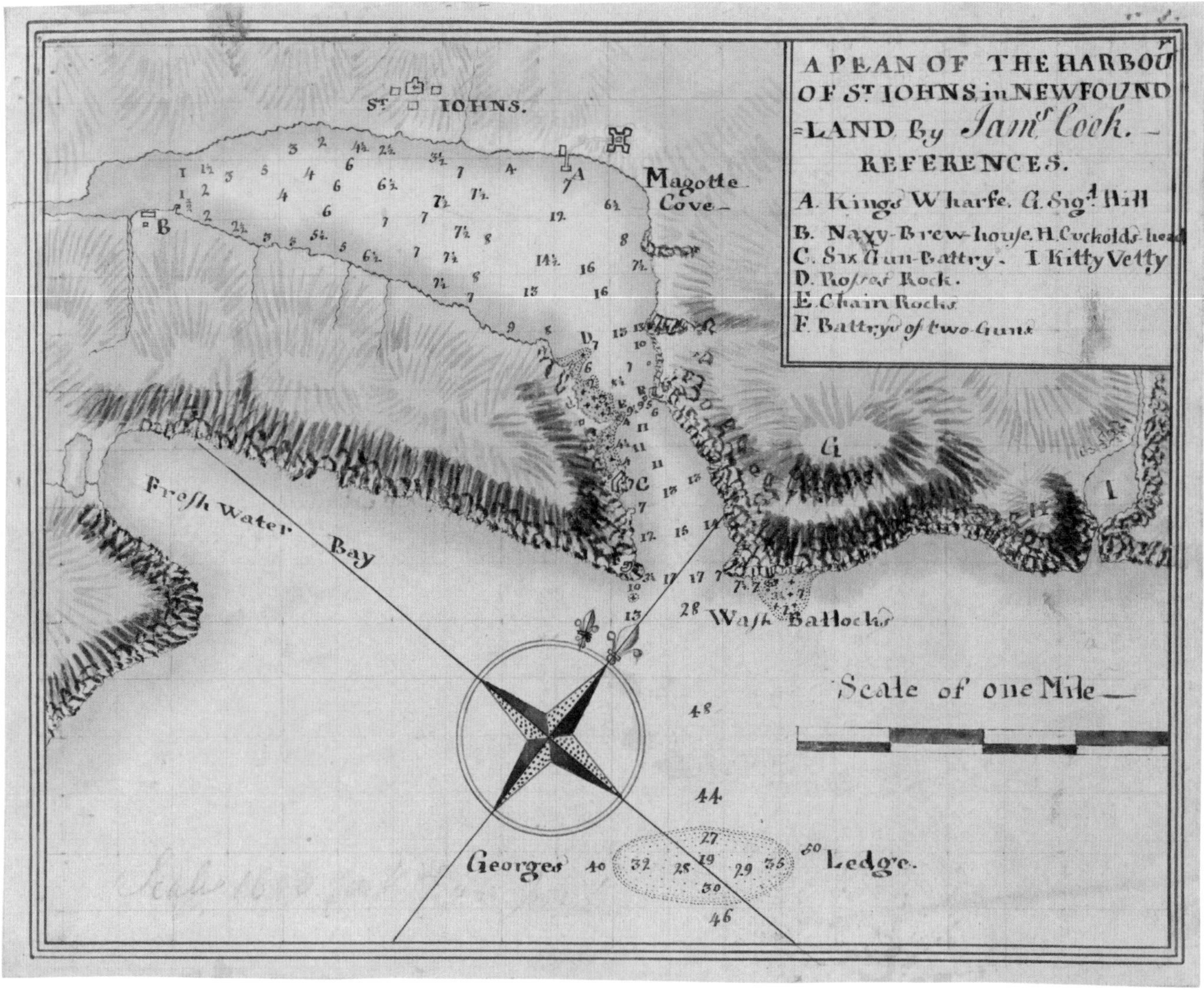

Time	Therm. Noon	Winds	Course	Dist. Sailed Miles	Lat. in South ° '	Long. in West Reck. ° '	Long. in West Watch ° '	Long. made C. Pallisser ° '	Var. ° '
Mond. 27	35	SW NW & NE	N. 36° E	27	65..53	133..42	133..22	50..57	—
Tues. 28	33¼	Easterly	N. 5°30' W	94	64..20	134..4	----	50..35	
Wed. 29		SE	N. 6° E	116	62..24	133..37	---	51..2	13..46
Thurs. 30	33¾	South & West	N. 30° E	85	61..5	134..12	---	50..27	
Frid. 31	34½	Westerly	N. 19° W	90	59..40	135..11	135..11	49..28	13..9
Jan.ry Sat. 1	36½	NW to East & SSE	N. 16° W	32	59..9	135..29	----	49..10	
Sund. 2	38¼	SW Westerly Calm East	N. 23 W	78	57..58	136..27	---	48..12	11..12
Mon 3	36	NE round by the East to SW	NWbW	130	56..46	139..45	139..40	44..54	—

Weather and Remarkable Occurrences —

We continued to steer to the north with light airs from the West till 6 o'clock in the am when meeting with a quantity of small Ice we hoisted out two Boats and took on board sufficient to fill all our empty Casks and for several days present expence; this done we hoisted in the Boats again and made sail to the NW with a gentle breeze at NE clear pleasant frosty weather —

The same Weather continued till the AM when the wind increased to a fresh gale attended with thick snow Showers and sharp frosty weather. Ice islands, not half so thick or so many as before —

Continual snow and sleet and a fresh gale at SE and SSE with which we steered North Easterly till Noon then NWbN —

The same weather continued till 3 pm when the wind abated and the weather cleared up and became fair: soon after found the variation to be 13°..46' E. Lat. 62°..12', Long.de 133..52 W. In the am had little wind at SW and dark Cloudy weather — Several Whales seen, but few birds, a swell from WNW — Passed several islands of ice —

PM little wind with showers of snow and sleet; Middle fresh gales, latter gentle breeze and clear pleasant weather; this gave us an opportunity to air the spare sails and to clean and smoak the ships betwixt decks. At noon we found our selves 20 Miles north of account having had no observation the three preceding days; it is natural to suppose there must be a Current from the South which brings along with it, tho' with a slow motion the many ice islands we daily see —

In the PM had a few hours calm which was succeeded by a breeze from the East and enabled us to reassume our NW BN Course, but have little hopes of meeting with land in that quarter as we have had a long hallow swell from WNW and NW the three preceding days. Piercing cold weather, frequent snow showers — many ice islands —

The wind increased to a fresh breeze and veered to the SW and West attended with some snow showers. At 5 o'clock in the am it fell calm, being then in Lat. 58°..2' S. Long.de 136..12 W. the variation was 11°..12' East. At 9 a breeze sprung up at East with which steered NWBW. The swell still continues to come from this quarter, notwithstanding the wind has not blown from thence for some time past, one cannot have a better sign than this of there being no land in that direction. At 8 o'clock in the PM past three ice island in the Lat. of 58°39' and have seen none since. Fresh gales with snow and sleet, till towards noon when the weather became fair and the wind veered to SW. About this time saw two small Divers of the Petrel Tribe, such as are usally seen near land and two pieces of sea weed. A great number of Blue Petrels and Sev.l Albatrosses of the large white or grey kind —

32

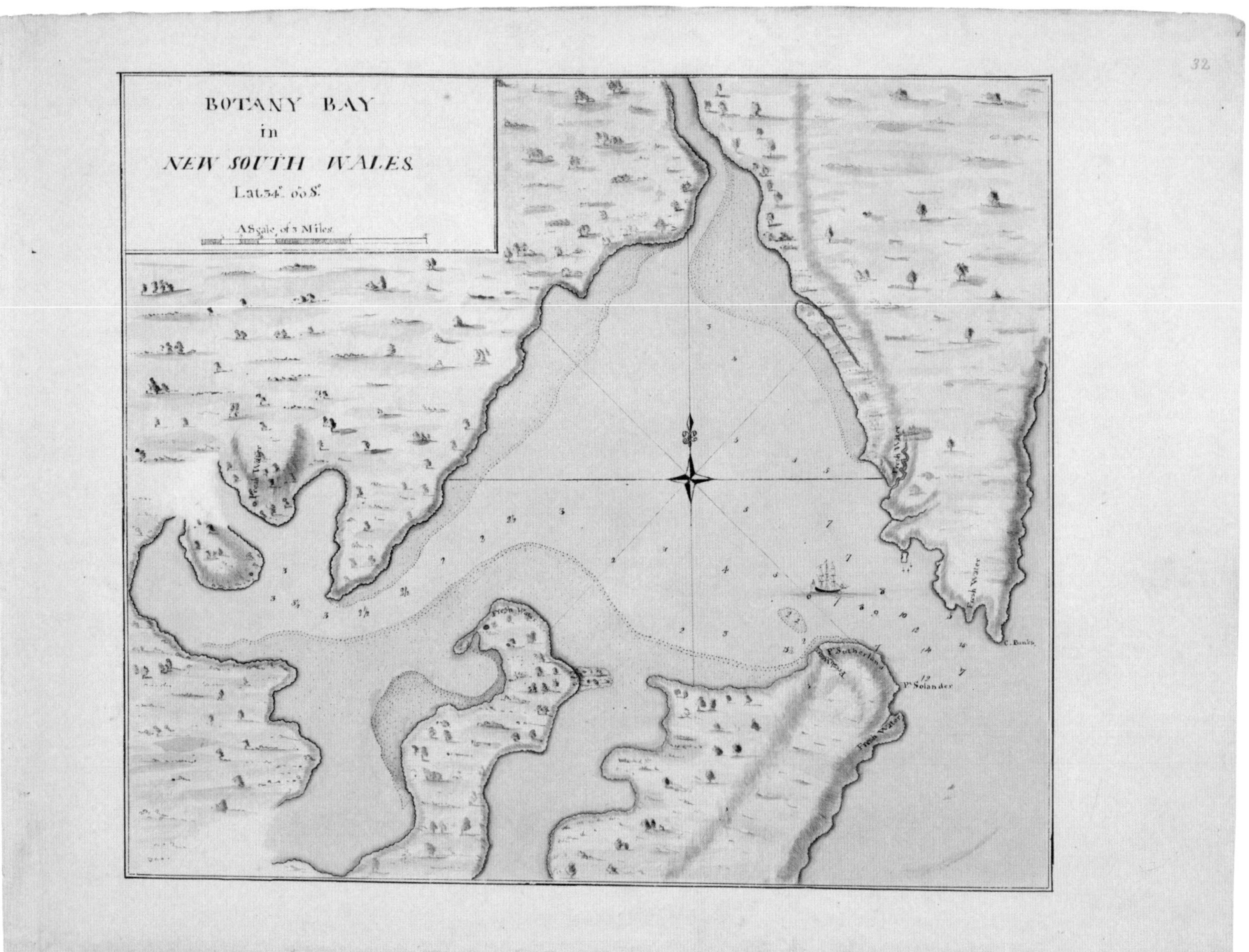

BOTANY BAY
in
NEW SOUTH WALES
Lat.34°. 0'0 S°.
A Scale of 3 Miles
Fresh Water
Fresh Water
Fresh Water
Fresh Water
Pt. Sutherland
Pt. Solander
C. Banks

Such are the vicissitudes attending this kind of service, and must always attend an unknown navigation, was it not for the pleasure which naturally results to a man from being the first discoverer, even was it nothing more than sand and shoals, this service would be insupportable.

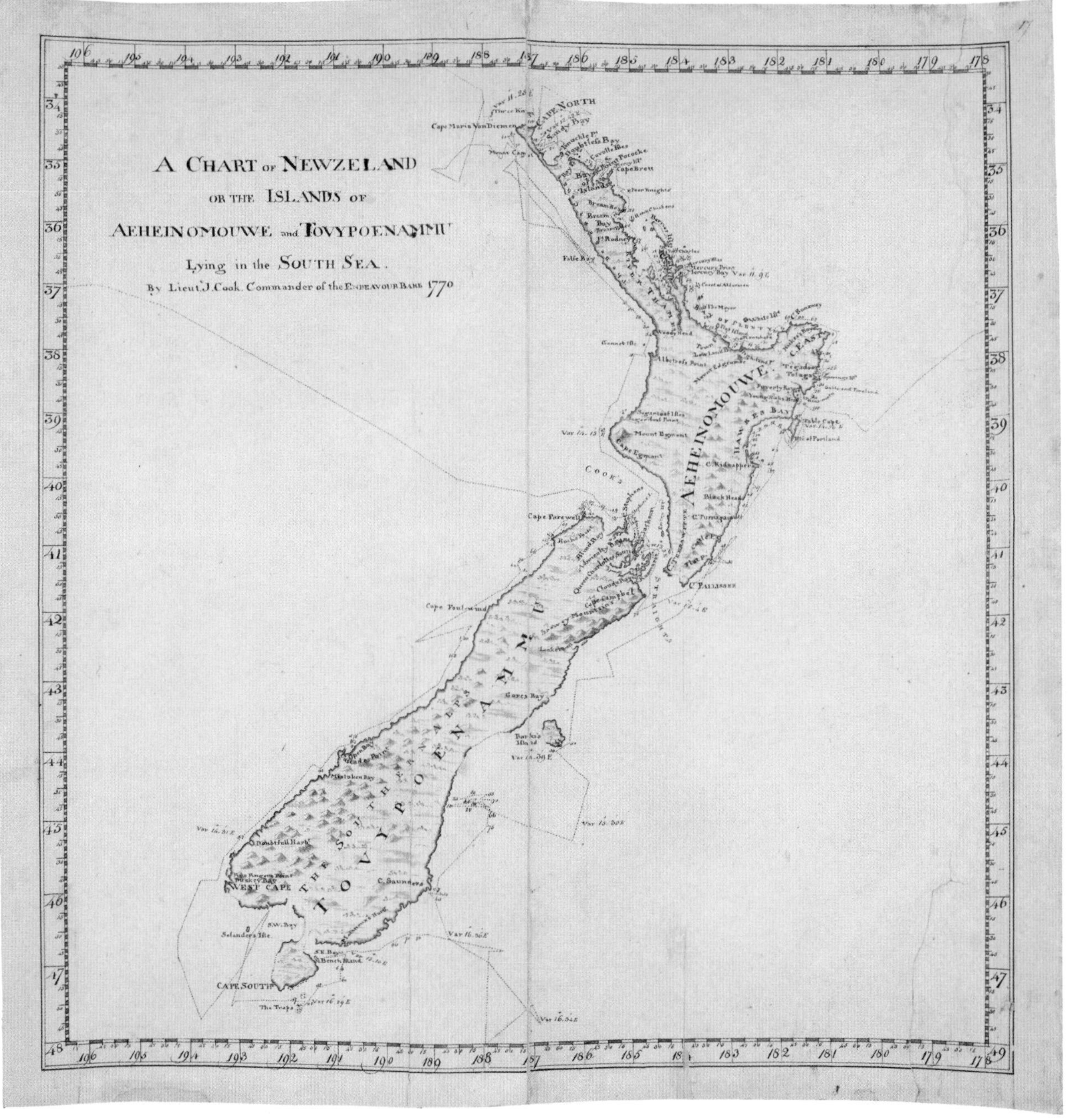

Opposite: A chart of Botany Bay in New South Wales, after April 1770. Cook was a brilliant map-maker and his charts had an immediate impact and ongoing influence. Such was their accuracy that many were still being used decades after his death.

Chart of New Zealand 'or the Islands of Aeheinomouwe and Tovypoenammu lying in the South Sea', made on board *Endeavour*. Exploring many river mouths and bays from October 1769 to March 1770, Cook was the first to chart the coastline accurately.

WILLIAM HEATON COOPER 1903-1995

The painting of mountain country has always brought me a sense of wonder and delight intermingled with humility.

A lifetime of walking, climbing and painting in the Lake District can be expressed in a single pencil line or brushstroke within a treasured sketchbook. Fell, lake, tarn and crag, each inscribed with their own lore and love. Born at the foot of the Coniston fells, in the heart of the English region that would nourish his soul, William Heaton Cooper was the third child of celebrated Victorian landscape artist Alfred Heaton Cooper. Young Heaton would join his father in the hills, learning to enjoy sketching *en plein air* and roaming through unexplored valleys. He won a scholarship to study painting at the Royal Academy Schools in London, but was overwhelmed by the confinement and jostle of the busy city. On his father's death he returned to the Lake District and his art flourished.

Cooper met and climbed with many of the pioneers of British rock climbing in the 'classic period' between the Wars. He was first asked to take some friends climbing in 1923, and although he had done a great deal of scrambling, he had never actually used a rope. He borrowed a length of cart rope from a local farmer and took on Gimmer Crag in Langdale. The route they achieved was 'Chimney Buttress', and it would lead to hundreds more.

Although it might seem modest, this was a form of exploration, and much danger attended their efforts in the early days. For Cooper the challenge was to combine the physical aspects of climbing, searching for new routes on tough, untouched rock, with the aesthetic; the *looking* at and exploration of those lines of ascent was true artistic adventure. He would always tuck his painting kit in his knapsack and the scores of sketchbooks that survive in the family archive witness his enthusiasm for the beauties found in rugged terrain. He once said 'I believe there is no place in the world that has as much variety of sculptured form in each square mile as there is in Lakeland.'

In 1938 he established his studio in Grasmere to show his paintings, his reproduction prints, and the sculptures of his talented new wife Ophelia Gordon Bell. His passion for landscape took him on painting expeditions many times to the Swiss Alps, the fjords of Norway, and once by cargo ship to Argentina. A meticulous draughtsman, he illustrated the Fell and Rock Climbing Club guides until the 1980s and designed the now iconic book jackets for John Hunt's *Ascent of Everest* and Hermann Buhl's *Nanga Parbat Pilgrimage*. And the five books on the Lake District that he himself created give ongoing pleasure to thousands of visitors.

A prolific and meticulous sketcher, Cooper's art was refined by his deeply rooted knowledge of the hills and a desire for simplicity, and his talents soon eclipsed the reputation of his famous father. His most spectacular paintings were often created in the evening or dawn, having walked miles to camp out and capture the play of light on the fell tops.

Cooper mainly used watercolour in subtle flat washes, simplifying forms and translating the indefinable quality of the light and atmosphere of the mountains into paint. His artistic explorations took him from the English Lakes to the far north of Norway.

Cooper's sketchbooks offer us a glimpse into his artistic explorations in the mountains and countryside of the Lake District. His watercolour boxes, palettes and other materials are also evidence of an intense artistic life and are very well used.

Life, I find, has much of climbing and painting in it – the contemplation, the challenge, the quick decisions and the sheer joy of arriving occasionally at the place where one longed to be.

REEVES' GREYHOUND PASTELS
MADE BY REEVES & SONS AT THEIR LONDON WORKS
Winsor & Newton, Ltd.
"DERWENT"
Colour Pencils
(SERIES Nº 19) OF SUPERFINE QUALITY
BRITISH MADE THROUGHOUT - FROM BRITISH - COLOURS.
DENSE, SMOOTH, LONG-WEARING.
BRASS PICTURE HANGERS
Raw Sienna
Cadmium Yellow
Lamp Black
Winsor Yellow

CHARLES DARWIN 1809-1882

My mind has been since leaving England in a perfect hurricane of delight & astonishment.

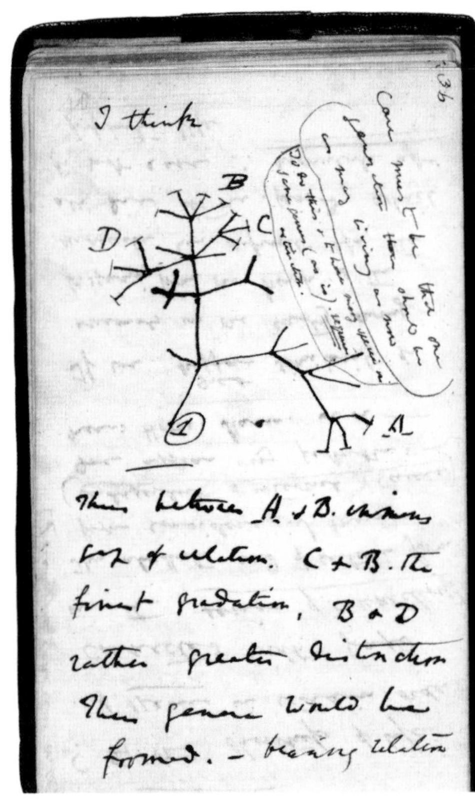

Darwin continued to use notebooks throughout his life to sketch out his ideas and observations. This page from 'notebook B' shows his sketch of the 'tree of life' drawn in 1837 - its branches as species.

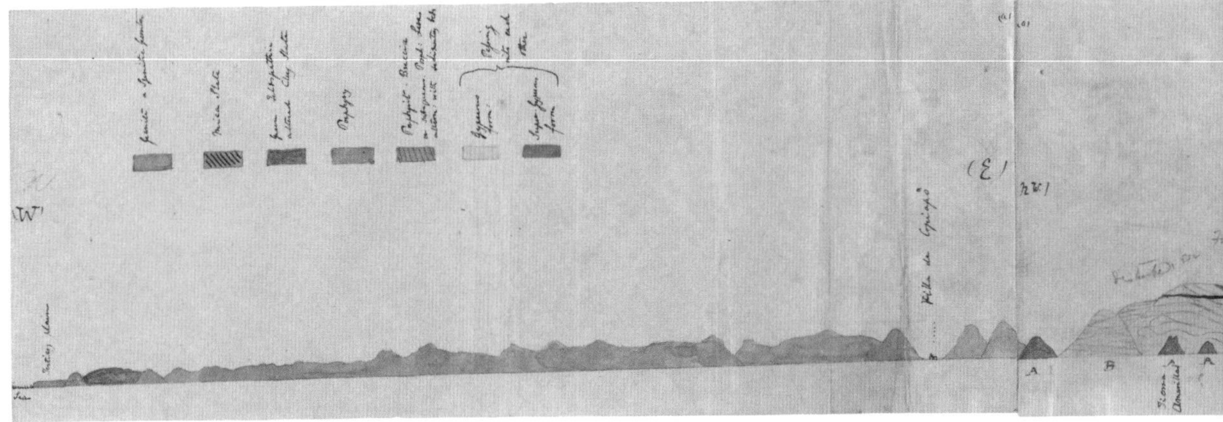

Two months into the voyage of HMS *Beagle*, 23-year-old naturalist Charles Darwin disembarked in Brazil, and experienced the wonders of a tropical forest for the first time. Bewildered by the density and variety of new species, he gazed at it all, took out his field notebook and began furiously to write. Recording even a fraction of this new world was a challenge: 'If the eye attempts to follow the flight of a gaudy butter-fly, it is arrested by some strange tree or fruit; if watching an insect one forgets it in the stranger flower it is crawling over ... The mind is a chaos of delight, out of which a world of future & more quiet pleasure will arise.' Darwin's observations from this journey would be the source of a theory that would forever change mankind's view of the world, and our place in it.

The early prospects for this great naturalist were not so illustrious, however. To his father's intense disappointment, he failed to become a doctor at Edinburgh University on account of his squeamishness during operations, and he squandered his time in Cambridge, preferring to go shooting and beetle-collecting rather than studying. But despite this, Darwin clearly had a brilliant and enquiring mind, and his college days were not entirely wasted. He learned taxidermy and attended extra-curricular lectures in botany, geology, zoology, hydrography, meteorology and mineralogy. Here he clearly impressed the Professor of Botany, the Reverend John Henslow, who put him forward as the naturalist on the *Beagle* in 1831.

Let the collector's motto be 'trust nothing to the memory'; for the memory becomes a fickle guardian when one interesting object is succeeded by another still more interesting.

For years Darwin had longed to follow in the footsteps of his hero, Alexander von Humboldt. His opportunity came with his appointment as naturalist aboard HMS *Beagle* in 1831. Independent of the ship's crew, Darwin embarked on countless overland journeys, observing, collecting and recording geology, geography, flora and fauna. This is a hand-drawn and coloured stratigraphical section eastwards from the coast at Tierra Amarilla, Copiapo, Chile.

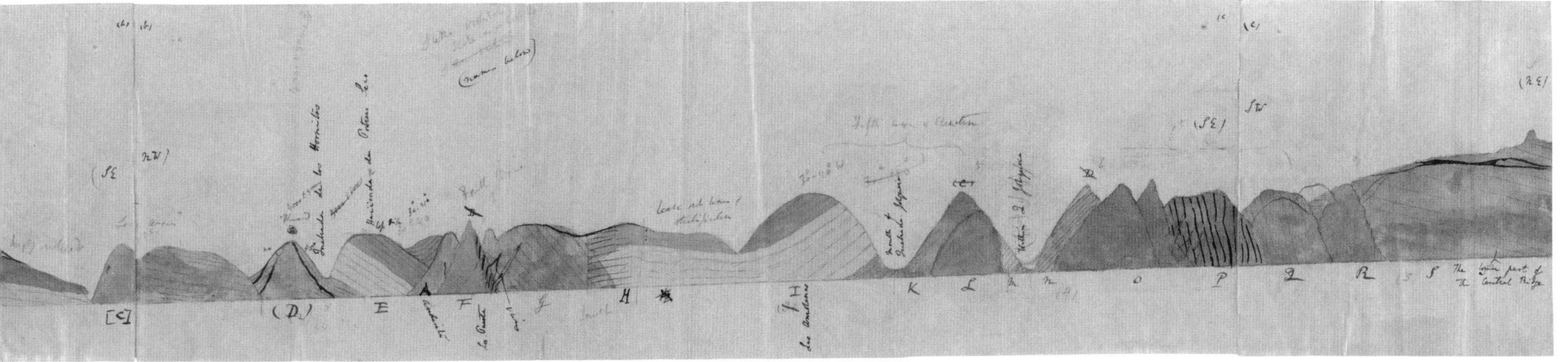

The five-year *Beagle* voyage would become one of the most important in maritime history and was the key formative event in Darwin's life, providing him with an unrivalled opportunity to make observations, collect animals and plants, and explore some of the most beautiful, intriguing and isolated places on Earth. Operating independently from the rest of the ship's company, Darwin entered into the spirit of adventure: he joined the carnival in Brazil, witnessed revolutions in Montevideo and Lima, and rode with gauchos on the pampas. He experienced an earthquake outside Valdivia and watched Mount Osorno erupt while visiting the island of Chiloé, all the while gaining more confidence as a naturalist and geographer.

At every opportunity Darwin travelled extensively overland. In Patagonia he made several expeditions on horseback, including a trek across the cordilleras from Valparaíso in Chile through the Portillo Pass to Mendoza in Argentina. Wherever possible he gathered specimens, building up an extensive collection of everything from insects and birds to invertebrates, plants and corallines, which filled the already cramped deck of the *Beagle* before being periodically shipped back to England. Throughout, Darwin methodically recorded his 'on the spot' observations in small field notebooks, and would then rewrite his notes every evening, forming a comprehensive 750-page journal.

On their last stage in Brazil before returning home, Darwin wrote: 'I stopped again and again to gaze on such beauties, & tried to fix for ever in my mind, an impression which at the time I knew must sooner or later fade away. The forms of the Orange tree, the Cocoa nut, the Palms, the Mango, the Banana, will remain clear & separate, but the thousand beauties which unite them all into one perfect scene, must perish; yet they will leave ... a picture full of indistinct, but beautiful figures.' Though the vibrancy of his experiences would fade, Darwin's *Beagle* notebooks would sustain a lifetime of thinking and be the source for his seminal work, *On the Origin of Species*.

AMELIA EDWARDS 1831-1892

It was wonderful to wake every morning close under the steep bank, and, without lifting one's head from the pillow, to see that row of giant faces so close against the sky.

Having reached the Second Cataract after weeks travelling up the Nile, Amelia Edwards opened her journal in February 1874 and wrote: 'In all this extraordinary panorama, so wild, so weird, so desolate, there is nothing really beautiful, except the colour. But the colour is transcendent ... I made no sketch. I felt that it would be ludicrous to attempt it. And I feel now that any endeavour to put the scene into words is a mere presumptuous effort to describe the indescribable.' Even so, she spent a lifetime both painting and writing.

Edwards showed a talent for writing at an early age. She had her first poem published at the age of seven and her first story at twelve. She would become a successful novelist and journalist, and, following the death of her parents, at 30 years old and unmarried, she embarked on a number of journeys. The proceeds of her writings allowed her the independence to live and voyage as she pleased. Together with a female companion, Edwards travelled through Belgium, the Dolomites and then, in 1873, through Egypt. Throughout, she constantly wrote detailed observations in her notebooks. These would later be published in her enormously popular travelogues, illustrated by engravings of her own drawings and watercolours.

Sketching and painting under the Egyptian sun, however, had its difficulties: dazzled by the light and wilting in the blistering heat, she commented it was like having a foretaste of cremation. And the sand was maddening: 'It fills your hair, your eyes, your water-bottles; silts up your colour-box; dries into your skies; and reduces your Chinese white to a gritty paste the colour of salad-dressing. As for the flies, they have a morbid appetite for water-colours.'

Edwards was particularly entranced by Abu Simbel. As she approached the temple by night, the colossi gradually appeared, ghost-like, in the moonlight: 'Even as we watched them, they seemed to grow, to dilate, to be moving towards us out of the silvery distance.' Observing that the northernmost Colossus was still disfigured from a plaster cast taken by Scottish Egyptologist Robert Hay some fifty years earlier, Edwards and her colleagues decided to make reparations. Makeshift scaffolding was improvised from spars and oars, and soon their boatmen were swarming over the great head, removing bits of plaster and tinting the white stains on the sandstone with thick black coffee.

The careless treatment of the Colossus by Hay and his team was symptomatic of a widespread ambivalence to the preservation of these valuable sites. Tourists carved graffiti on monuments; students of archaeology, taking wet paper 'squeezes' from wall paintings, were sponging away the last vestiges of original colour; and local tomb-raiders supplied the ever-constant demand for antiquities. Appalled by what she had seen, on her return to England Edwards became the motivating force behind the establishment of the Egypt Exploration Fund in 1882, with the aim of studying and conserving ancient sites. She also helped develop Egyptology as a discipline, endowing the Edwards Chair in Egyptian Archaeology at University College, London, and lectured widely in England and the United States. Called 'the most learned woman in the world' by the *Boston Globe*, Edwards is still referred to as the Godmother of Egyptology.

Edwards sketched herself drawing one of the giant statues of Abu Simbel, still partially buried in sand. Having discovered that the face of the northernmost Colossus still bore the traces of a plaster cast taken by Scottish Egyptologist Robert Hay, Edwards and her colleagues set out to clean it. Scaling improvised scaffolding, they tinted the white patches with coffee. 'Rameses' appetite for coffee was prodigious', she later wrote.

'The delights of sketching 1,000 miles up the Nile.' Edwards's caricatures, penned on letter paper while on her travels in 1888, provide a marvellous glimpse of her sense of humour. Possessing unusual stamina and a taste for adventure, she filled notebooks and sketchbooks with her observations.

CHARLES EVANS 1918-1995

Many men are happier, and find it less strain, to fight against wind and wet, cold and fatigue, than against telephones and timetables.

During his climbing expeditions, including to Everest in 1953, Evans would often be found writing letters, journals and postcards late into the night. They always included sketches of scenery and people for friends and family back at home.

On 26 May 1953 Charles Evans stood at the highest point on Earth then ever reached by man. With his partner Tom Bourdillon, he had climbed to within 90 m (300 ft) of the main summit of Everest. The final ridge lay before them, but with the oxygen in their cylinders running low and the day drawing on there was little choice but to head back down. Had they pushed for the summit as night fell they would probably never have returned alive.

Evans trained as a surgeon, and as a young man he joined the Royal Army Medical Corps, but he will always be remembered for his role as deputy leader on the 1953 expedition that climbed Everest. His first Himalayan expedition was to Annapurna II with Bill Tilman in 1950, and he also made an attempt on Cho Oyu with Eric Shipton, before being invited to join the Everest party. Just three days after he had himself stood so close to the ultimate prize, on 29 May 1953 his friends Ed Hillary and Tenzing Norgay finally took the first steps on the summit.

The Everest team returned to London to a heroes' welcome. Hillary and the leader John Hunt were knighted; Tenzing received the George Medal. The mountaineers were fêted wherever they went – except for Evans, who had quietly stayed in Nepal to do more climbing and make a map of the region. 'I wouldn't mind a party myself', he wrote to a friend, 'but I'd rather be in the mountains.' He always sent letters and postcards with drawings home, and in 1955 published a book of his sketches of the Everest expedition.

For many, Evans's efforts in 1953 were more than matched by his later role as leader of the first successful assault on Kangchenjunga, the third highest Himalayan peak, and considered a much harder climb than Everest. The summit is regarded by the people of Sikkim, on whose border it stands, as sacred and inhabited by gods, and in respect for this the climbers stopped just short of the top. It was a gesture that also said much about Evans's sensitivity to the mountain world and its people, and it is no surprise that he was greatly admired throughout his climbing life.

He later became Principal of the University College of North Wales. In time multiple sclerosis made climbing and expeditions impossible, and his career as one of the world's leading mountaineers drew to a close. Confined to a wheelchair, it was not long before he was unable to draw too, but he fought his illness with typical courage and good humour. He was knighted in 1969 and was President of the Alpine Club from 1967 to 1970. He died of pneumonia in a nursing home in 1995, within sight of the mountains of North Wales that he loved so much.

BY AIR MAIL
Rope Ladder below Camp III. Letter at back.
the Western Cwm goes - we call it "The Nutcracker".
With love Charles
BY AIR MAIL
AIR LETTER
IF ANYTHING IS ENCLOSED THIS LETTER WILL BE SENT BY ORDINARY MAIL.
4 Croxteth Drive
INDIA POSTAGE
CORWEN, N.W.
May 27th 1953
Thyangboche 6 6 53
Anne. Thank you for your
I've just written to
It has been a fine trip
model, I should say.
a big Expedition
with Each Step
Exactly according to plan,
very fine team spirit
I am off Eastwards
a fortnight, then
here + westwards
Katmandu with a
couple of old Sherpa friends -
One has just been having his hair plaited (once a month) by his Eldest daughter.
He is Da Tenzing + good fun.
There's a picture of him in the 1951 Everest Recce book, standing with Sen Tenzing outside the Embassy at Katmandu.
I hear the BBC has been after photos of me, Griff Pugh + Mike Ward — from the RGS —

RANULPH FIENNES 1944-

Alone in the wilderness, you come face to face with things that are impossible to imagine.

Ranulph Twisleton-Wykeham-Fiennes, known as 'Ran' to his friends – or 'the world's greatest living explorer' according to the *Guinness Book of Records* – inherited a baronetcy after the death of his father in action at Monte Cassino in 1943. Educated at Eton, he later joined his father's cavalry regiment – the Royal Scots Greys – before being seconded to the SAS. But, later becoming disillusioned with the army, he turned his attention to exploration and adventure.

After expeditions down the Nile by hovercraft, trekking over glaciers in Norway and navigating turbulent rivers in British Columbia, Fiennes was eager to mount a journey of true exploration. He needed to find a geographical goal that had not yet been achieved. Hillary and Tenzing had ascended Everest, and Francis Chichester had sailed solo around the world. They had been the first to do so, and those who followed in their footsteps were 'also-rans'. Priority was key.

'Why not', his wife Ginny suggested one day, 'circumnavigate the world, not the easy way, but along a line of longitude passing through both Poles?' No one had attempted such a journey before. They would need an icebreaker, a ski-plane for support and some £29 million of sponsorship to stand the remotest chance of success. At the time, the couple had £210 in the bank, owned a decrepit Mini van and a Jack Russell terrier. But this was a once-in-a-lifetime opportunity. In early 1973, the Transglobe expedition was sketched out on paper and planning began in earnest.

Leaving Greenwich in London in 1979, the team drove through Europe and sailed to Algiers, before driving by Land Rover through the Sahara and into the jungles of the Ivory Coast. At Abidjan they boarded the *Benjamin Bowring* and sailed to Antarctica. As Fiennes and his companion, Charlie Burton, set out over snow and ice, Fiennes finally felt like a true explorer. They crossed the continent in 67 days. Turning north, they then sailed to the Bering Strait and traversed the Northwest Passage using a Boston Whaler, before trekking towards the North Pole. Both men were at their absolute physical limits. But on 10 April 1982 Fiennes and Burton became the first men in history to have travelled over the Earth's surface to both Poles, and by August the Transglobe was successfully completed.

Fiennes later went on to mount a number of other extreme adventures: the first unsupported crossing of Antarctica; the discovery of the lost city of Ubar on the Yemeni border; the completion of seven marathons in seven consecutive days on all seven continents; and an ascent of Everest. Not all his expeditions have ended well. Frostbite, kidney stones and heart attacks brought some to a premature end. Fiennes, however, is still driven to ever more 'impossible' exploits as a means to raise funds for the charity Marie Curie Cancer Care.

He will perhaps never escape the pull of the polar regions. Of Antarctica he has said: 'Of one thing I am certain; this is a *marvellous* land, though you might not think so when you're lying rigid in your tent waiting for a blizzard to blow itself out, unable to hear anything but the roar of a cruel storm ... When you are finally able to crawl from your sleeping bag and feel the warm sun on your face, and know that you're alive, you come to feel the real joy of this place.'

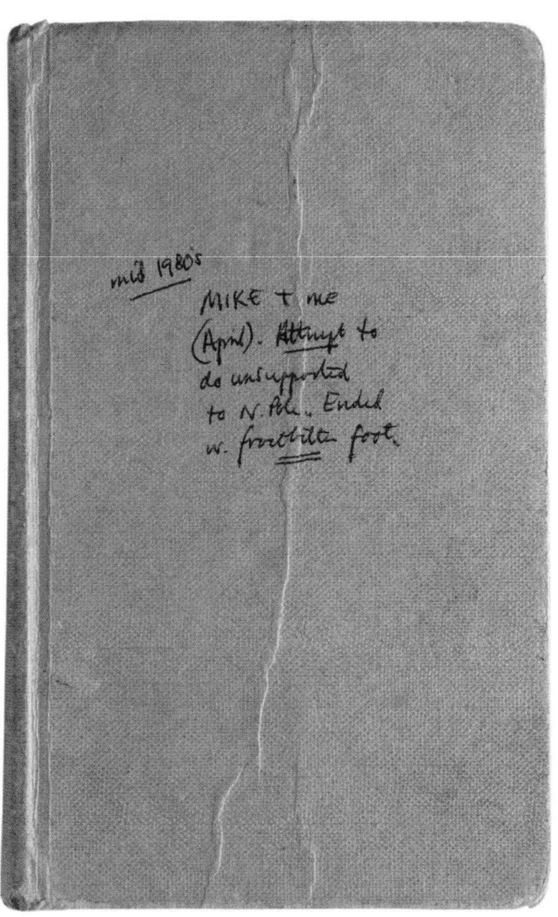

Scribbled on the cover of one of Fiennes's notebooks is a short note: 'Mid 1980s. Mike [Stroud] and me (April). Attempt to do unsupported to N. Pole. Ended w. frostbitten foot.' Inside are careful notes and calculations, plus a page of code for various situations, ice conditions and possible dangers.

Sit and listen awhile. You can hear your heart beat. But don't sit for too long. Keep moving or you may lose some of your fingers and toes.

MARGARET FOUNTAINE 1862-1940

I derive the greatest pleasure from travelling. I like the idea of knocking about the world and getting used to the ways and customs of men.

In 1978 a small group solemnly gathered in the archive vault of Norwich's Castle Museum to open an old chest that had remained sealed since 1940. Inside were twelve large volumes of diaries that had been maintained daily for six decades, along with mahogany cases containing some 22,000 butterfly specimens. Documented in the pages of the diaries were the extraordinary adventures of traveller and lepidopterist Margaret Fountaine, who had spent her life in relentless pursuit of both butterflies and wild-looking men.

Fountaine left England as a 29-year-old with no clear motivation save to mend her broken heart. A wealthy and generous uncle had provided her with the means to live an independent life, and she intended to spend her fortune on travelling the world. In Switzerland she discovered a love of collecting butterflies, and from that moment on her life as an intrepid butterfly-hunter truly began.

Inspired by an acute wanderlust and sense of romance, Fountaine tramped and rode through Europe, and then travelled to North Africa and beyond. Soon she was exploring the wildest, most remote areas of every continent, mostly with only a guide or translator as a companion. She regarded no destination as too harsh or dangerous. Unconventional in every respect, Fountaine favoured her own idiosyncratic butterfly-collecting outfit: a man's checked cotton shirt; a cotton skirt with extra pockets sewn on; cotton gloves, with the tips of the first finger and thumb cut off; a cork sun helmet and a compass strung round her neck on a heavy black chain. Although she had no formal training as a naturalist, she contributed articles to the *Entomologist* detailing her studies in Asia Minor, Algeria, Costa Rica, the Philippines and Greece.

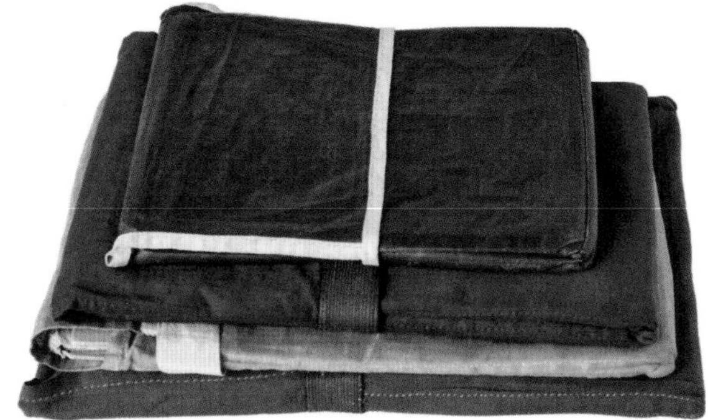

Fountaine's beautifully illustrated sketchbooks are enclosed in silk sleeves. Her fascination with butterflies began in Switzerland, but she travelled the world to study them - the page opposite is devoted to larvae and pupae found in South Africa, 1908-09.

Along with her diaries, her sketchbooks and her butterfly net, Fountaine always carried a flask of brandy – helpful for calming the nerves when the going got tough. But she was a fearless and enthusiastic traveller: she nimbly leapt off a train when it was about to derail, crossed a glacier in tennis shoes and several times nearly died of malaria; she was unfazed by earthquakes, tropical storms, and encounters with lions and poisonous snakes. One of her proudest moments was sharing a drink with notorious brigand Jacques Bellacoscia at his hideout on a Corsican mountainside. 'There is a direct and special protection over a pure and high-minded woman, which no man however base can break through', she later wrote.

Tall, attractive yet diffident, Fountaine throughout her life leapt from one disastrous love interest to another, until she eventually met Khalil Neimy, a married (as she subsequently discovered) Syrian, who for almost three decades would be her constant companion: her soul-mate. Together, she and Neimy would assemble one of the finest collections of butterflies in the world.

When Neimy died, Fountaine continued her travels, burying her grief in work. Even into her 70s she would think nothing of riding 65 km (40 miles) a day to secure a rare species for her collection. Eventually, though, her punishing travels would take their toll. She died aged 78 on a dusty road in Trinidad, her butterfly net still grasped tightly in her hand.

24.[b] Pupa of Papilio Policenes. Durban, (Natal.) Jan: 11: 1909.

6b. 28.[a]† Pupa of Precis Octavia, V. Sesamus. Dargle, Natal. Feb: 14: 1909.-

6a. 28.† Full grown Larva of Precis Octavia, var: Sesamus, on a leaf of its food-plant, Plectranthus Calycinus; Dargle, (Natal.) Feb: 9: 1909.

29: Larva and Pupa of Capys Disjunctus on a flower bud of Protea Hirta, inside which it feeds.- Discovered and presented to me by Mr G. F. Leigh, F.E.S.- Pinetown (Natal.) Feb: 11: 1909.-

17a. 30. Half grown Larva of Lepto-neura Dingana, hatched out, with two others, on Nov: 18: 1908, from ova laid by captive ♀. Feeding on grass. Barberton (Transvaal.) Feb: 27: 1909.

9a, 9b. 31. Larva (also pupa) of Pseudacraea Tarquinia, feeding on a leaf of Mimusops Obovata. Found by Mr G. F. Leigh, F.E.S. Pinetown, - (Natal) March, 1909.-

8a. 32. Full fed Larva of Precis Cloantha, on its food-plant Justicia Pulegioides: Bred from ovum laid, with many others, by captive ♀♀. Dargle (Natal.) March 23: 1909

VIVIAN FUCHS 1908-1999

There is a real difference between travellers and explorers: travellers go to places, whereas explorers go to acquire knowledge; they travel for a purpose.

After the Second World War, Antarctica was opened up by a wave of scientific research. During the International Geophysical Year, 1957-58, many nations established bases there for the first time, yet it was still a landscape that challenged the spirit of adventure. The blank map called out for completion. Though Amundsen and then Scott had reached the Pole in 1912, one major journey remained unachieved: the first crossing of the continent. Ernest Shackleton, who had attempted it – and failed – in 1914, had called it 'the last great polar journey'.

The man who would achieve this seemingly impossible dream was Vivian Fuchs, in 1958. He had actually begun sketching out the rough outlines of this audacious plan almost ten years before, when, as a geologist and leader of an expedition for the Falklands Islands Dependencies Survey in Antarctica, he had been confined to his sleeping bag for three days while the wind outside battered his tent. As the skies cleared, he continued on his sledging journeys, but the idea for his greatest adventure had been born.

Known to his friends by his childhood nickname 'Bunny', polar veteran Fuchs was a charismatic leader and diplomat, and later became a Director of the British Antarctic Survey and President of the Royal Geographical Society. He had read Natural Sciences at St John's College, Cambridge, where his tutor was James Wordie, the geologist and senior scientist on Shackleton's *Endurance* expedition that had attempted the Antarctic crossing. Wordie gave Fuchs his first taste of polar work, inviting him on an expedition to Greenland in 1929. Later, having met the eminent anthropologist Louis Leakey, Fuchs found himself in East Africa, where he was to spend a total of seven years working as a geologist, exploring the lakes and mountains of the Great Rift Valley. At the end of one expedition in 1934, accompanied by his new wife Joyce, Fuchs drove home overland, covering 12,370 km (nearly 8,000 miles) in 46 days.

Fuchs's great 3,220-km (2,000-mile) crossing of Antarctica from coast to coast – using a cavalcade of Sno-Cat vehicles supported by aircraft – would take some three years of effort and 99 days to complete. It was not just arduous, but dangerous too, as they had to drive across fields of concealed crevasses which opened up beneath them. Despite all the technological advances since Shackleton's day that had made their progress possible, it was still a formidable undertaking. During the entire journey, Fuchs kept detailed diaries; many notebooks, radio logs, telegrams and copious correspondence survive too. All were vital, considering the complex logistics of the expedition, but essential on his return home too, when he had to complete a book of the journey in just a few months.

Fuchs received news of a knighthood while in the bath at Scott Base on reaching safety. On his return to London he was awarded many more honours, including the special gold medal of the Royal Geographical Society, and would later use his profile to greatly improve the standing of polar science in Britain. He was a practical dreamer and, more important still, he had the fundamental grit and energy needed to get the tough job done. Yet he was also meticulous in his planning. As *The Times* reported: 'Nothing has replaced courage, endurance and accurate calculation as the indispensable equipment for a journey into these desolate regions in the face of the most savage weather in the world.'

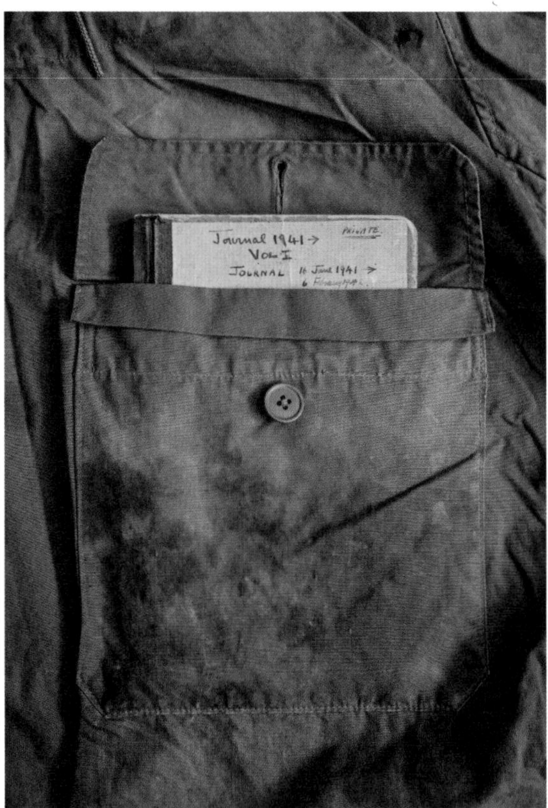

Fuchs's African journal from 1941 onwards, tucked in the pocket of a well-used expedition anorak. Opposite is a collection of notebooks and sketchbooks relating to his great Trans-Antarctic Expedition of 1955-58, which crossed the continent for the first time.

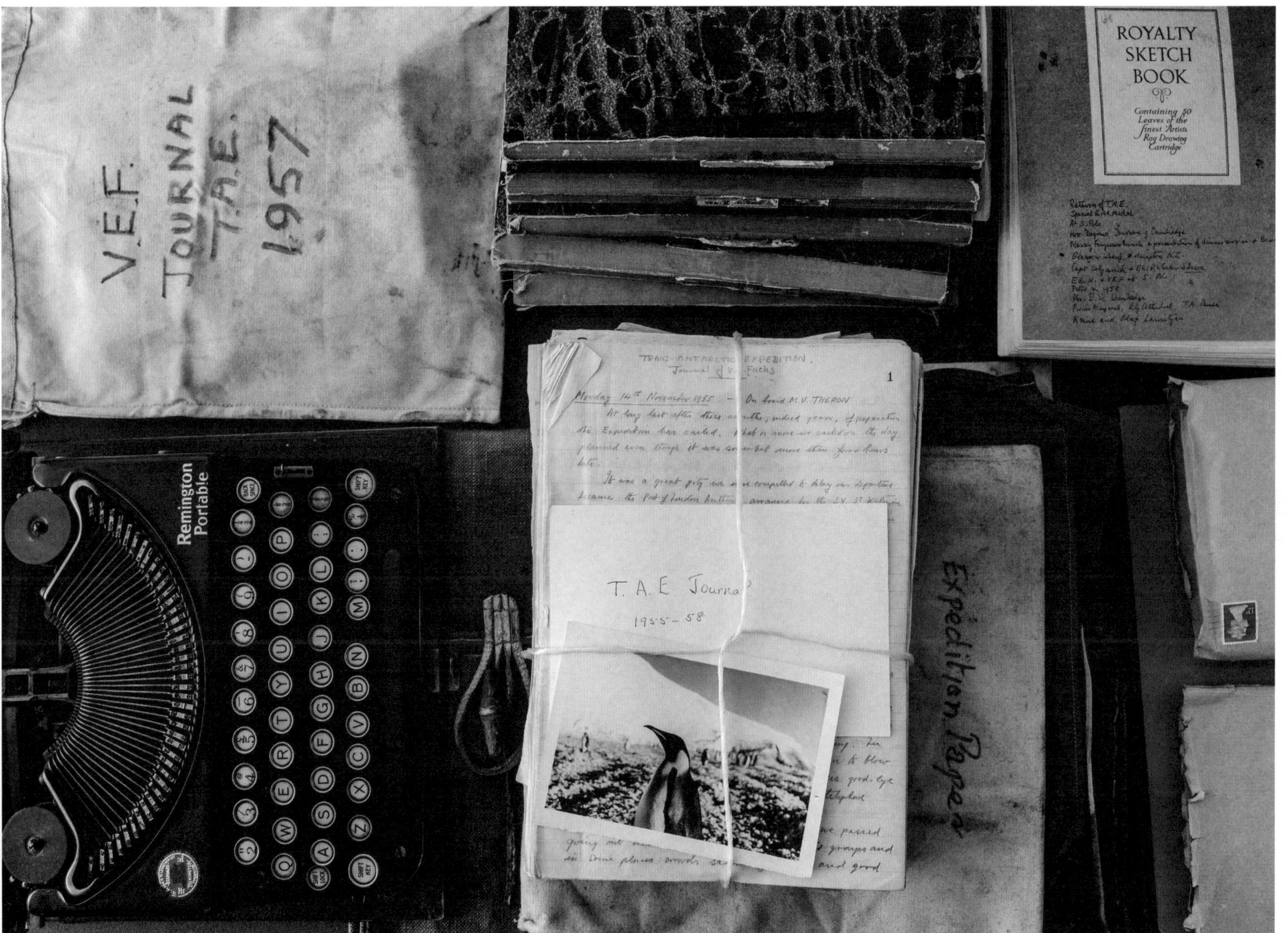

V.E.F. JOURNAL T.A.E. 1957
ROYALTY SKETCH BOOK
Containing 50 Leaves of the finest Artists Rag Drawing Cartridge
Remington Portable
TRANS-ANTARCTIC EXPEDITION
Monday 14th November 1955 — On board M.V. THERON
T. A. E. Journal
1955–58
Expedition Papers

EUGENE VON GUERARD 1811-1901

At every new place that shows any promise, swarms of diggers settle down like flies on a midden.

Encouraged by his father, a court painter to King Francis of Austria, Eugene von Guerard studied in Italy and Düsseldorf and was an accomplished artist. But on 18 August 1852, he boarded the *Windermere* at Gravesend, England, and sailed for Australia, hoping to make his fortune as a gold-digger. As the *Windermere* headed out to sea it passed close to a large three-masted ship carrying convicts and soldiers to Van Diemen's Land. The deck was thronged with human beings, most of them in chains. It was, Guerard wrote, 'a most depressing sight'. In contrast, he and his fellow passengers were brimming with expectation. For them, the Antipodean new world was a land of opportunity.

By the time Guerard finally arrived at the goldfields of Ballarat five months later, he had ridden on bullock carts through forests of immense gum-trees, camped by waterholes, been driven wild by biting flies and had made the 'unpleasant discovery' of a scorpion as a bedfellow. He had also encountered a man who had been attacked by bushrangers, robbed and tied to a tree. The prospect of making a fortune in Australia was alluring, but the reality was much tougher.

Armed with just a blanket, a pickaxe and a teapot, Guerard pegged out his claim and began to dig. It was a hard existence. By day, backs were strained and hands blistered as they worked the mines. Every evening, the weary diggers – Chinese, British, French and American – returned to their tents or makeshift shelters and roasted mutton over their fires. Prospectors rushed from one new site to another, slashing down forests and burrowing into the ground in their crazed thirst for gold. Behind them they left a trail of destruction and misfortune. There were highway robberies and violence between competing miners, leaving bodies scattered among the shafts. There were dust-storms and bush-fires. After a luckless sixteen months, Guerard admitted defeat. With little to show materially for his efforts, apart from his vivid, first-hand sketches of the life of a gold-digger, he travelled to Melbourne, where he hoped to have more success as a landscape painter.

But finding buyers for his paintings proved difficult. After holding an auction of his art, he began a series of sketching tours and joined the scientific expeditions of Alfred Howitt in 1860, then Georg von Neumayer in 1862. For the next sixteen years, Guerard travelled in the wilds of Victoria, Tasmania, New South Wales, South Australia and New Zealand, always with sketchbook in hand, recording in detail the forests of Gippsland and the Otways, the crater lakes of Victoria's volcanic Western District and the peaks of the Kosciuszko plateau. Later, these sketches would be the basis for large-scale canvases commissioned by wealthy patrons.

Guerard did go on to win the recognition he deserved. He was awarded the Cross of the Order of Franz Josef and held positions at the National School of Art, Melbourne, and the National Gallery of Victoria. Botanically accurate and geographically detailed, Guerard's majestic panoramas and sublime landscapes eventually secured his lasting reputation as one of the state of Victoria's most important colonial landscape painters.

Mining for gold in Chinaman's Gully, 1853. Guerard spent sixteen months in the Australian goldfields hoping to make his fortune, all the while sketching the activities and hardships of the miners. He would eventually have far more success in his career as a landscape artist.

In November 1862, as part of Professor von Neumayer's scientific expedition, Guerard reached the summit of Mount Kosciuszko, New South Wales. He would use his sketches from the expedition, including this panoramic view (top) to create one of his most famous paintings. As well as magnificent landscapes, Guerard's sketchbooks also provide intriguing and detailed glimpses into expedition life in the Australian wilds.

2nd May 1856.
no water.

N. XXII
1854—55—56 bis in 1857.
G. MERCER,
WHOLESALE AND RETAIL BOOKSELLER AND STATIONER,
AND
Account Book Manufacturer,
Letter Copying Books, Bankers' Passbooks, and Account Books of all descriptions, Ruled and Plain Papers, Sealing Wax, Pens, Ink, and every other Article in the Stationery Line, on the most reasonable terms.
N.B. Bookbinding of every description executed with neatness and despatch, and Paper Ruled to pattern.
102 Blätter

Guerard spent sixteen years travelling in the wilds of Victoria, Tasmania, New South Wales, South Australia and New Zealand. Often conditions were very tough: in the sketch opposite above he draws himself in a cave, with the words ‘no water’.

This sketchbook of 1854 to 1857, opposite below, marked a turning point in Guerard’s life. Leaving the goldfields behind he was now en route to Melbourne to begin his career as a landscape artist.

Above: In a sketchbook of 1857-59, Guerard drew this dramatic scene of a bush-fire tearing through the landscape.

[A bush-fire] is a grand, but terrifying spectacle, hundreds of trees with the flames rushing up their trunks, the foliage being consumed like fireworks, and the huge giants crashing to the ground on all sides, with a thundering noise, the sky red, with clouds of smoke flying upwards.

ROBIN HANBURY-TENISON 1936-

It has always been mankind's gift, and curse, to be inquisitive – this is what makes us unlike all other species. Without this curiosity we would all have stayed at home.

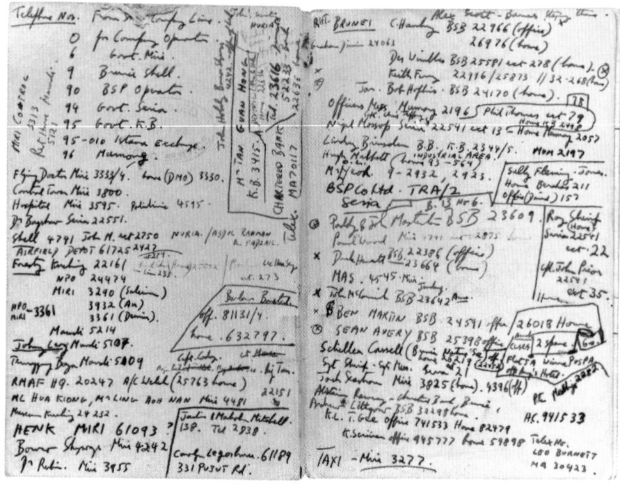

As scientists are beginning to explore the outer edges of our universe, there is still much that is unknown here on Earth. And that, says Robin Hanbury-Tenison, is what gets him out of bed in the morning. 'It's the ongoing challenge. Exploration continues in new forms. We're only now starting to realize how little we understand about nature. You can see this in the rainforest, in particular. I just hope it's not something we've realized too late.'

Though his days of adventuring are not quite over, the truly tough, long expeditions are beyond him. 'Not for me, that sort of life in the jungle. But I hope what I've achieved over the years might inspire others to try.' For his 80th birthday he has undertaken daunting challenges to raise money for the charity he founded, Survival International, which helps tribal peoples protect their lands and determine their own futures. This charity, in fact, is something he considers his most significant legacy.

As a child, the thought of foreign lands cast their spell. The maps he drew in coloured pencils still survive in his collections: ragged coastlines in purple, pink and blue, the *terra incognita* of a young imagination filled with ferocious beasts, wild jungles and marvellous mountain ranges. Escaping the confines of the nursery he would row out to a little island in a lake on his parent's estate, sleeping alone in a tree-house in the woods and imagining himself an explorer.

In 1957 he bought a decrepit Second World War Jeep and made the first overland trip from London to Sri Lanka; the following year it was the first land crossing of South America at its widest point. In 1962-66 he explored the mountains of the southern Sahara. He then crossed South America from north to south by river, and in 1968 was the first to navigate the Orinoco River by hovercraft. He has ridden the length of the Great Wall of China on horseback, explored the Outer Islands of Sulawesi in 1974, and Sabah and Brunei in 1976. In 1977-78 he was invited by the Royal Geographical Society to lead an expedition to an area now known as the Gunung Mulu National Park in Sarawak, one of the most remote and untouched regions of tropical rainforest then left in the world. His scientific team aimed to explore and study every aspect of this beautiful but hazardous terrain, from limestone pinnacles rising thousands of feet, to lush hidden valleys and vast unexplored cave networks, as well as the abundance of animals and plants. The expedition identified and photographed many new species.

A simple piece of advice that has fared him well, he says, is this: 'The most important thing to take on a journey is a notebook. It should be scribbled in every evening – at least two full pages describing what happened that day. If you don't do that you might as well not bother with a big expedition. Not only will you rapidly forget, but no one else will be able to share it. What's the point of going somewhere if you can't tell a great story about it ... a notebook is just what you need. It's the best investment you could ever make.'

Hanbury-Tenison has kept journals, notebooks and diaries throughout his life. Above left is one from childhood, showing a precocious interest in far-away lands. Above and opposite are a variety of records from his Mulu expedition of 1977-78, showing the range of ways that information can be captured and stored.

Limbang
R.H.T.
DAILY LOG
MULU 19
RHT.
DAILY LOG
MULU 1977-78
(2)
GENERAL
BOOK
+ACCOUNTS
(1)
ROYAL GEOGRAPHICAL SOCIETY
BASE CAMP
MULU EXPEDITION

CHARLES TURNBULL HARRISSON 1866-1914

It must be weary waiting for the poor wife, knowing not how we have fared thro the grim Antarctic winter – what dangers we may be meeting in this wild land.

While others collected geological specimens, Charles Harrisson sketched until his fingers were frostbitten. It was almost 30 degrees below. Later, as the winds gusted to 160 km per hour (100 mph), he was lifted into the air and carried 6 m (20 ft). As his team-mates huddled round the stove, forced to shelter for five anxious days until the storm blew itself out, he returned to his sketchbook and the nightly task of keeping his journal. In time he would improvise, cutting up an old pair of trousers to hang from his snow-goggles to protect his face, and fashioning a sketching box from an old wooden case to save his hands from the teeth of the wind. He drew in coloured chalks until the last of his supplies ran out. Harrisson was an artist in his element.

Born in Hobart, Charles Turnbull Harrisson, known to all as 'Chas T', was a 44-year-old field collector with a young family, and had already won admirers for his survey of Tasmania's rugged, trackless west coast. He was the only Tasmanian member of Douglas Mawson's legendary Australasian Antarctic Expedition of 1911-13. Just as other explorers were racing to the South Pole, here was an expedition devoted to science and sailing for an unknown shore. With little hesitation he joined up as its artist-biologist.

Harrisson's sketches and diaries graphically record the challenges faced by the eight-man Western Base party, which landed on the edge of a glacier in Queen Mary Land, over 2,000 km (1,240 miles) from Mawson's main hut in Commonwealth Bay. They were forced to build their own base on floating ice, well aware that if it were to break off they would float out into the Southern Ocean and likely never be seen again. Another hazard, the captain of their ship *Aurora* reminded them in his parting words, was that if he failed to reach port nobody would even know where they were.

Their achievements have largely been lost to history, overshadowed in the public memory by drama elsewhere; Amundsen won the Pole and Scott died in his tent. When anything is remembered of Mawson's expedition, it is mostly the unrelentingly severe winds that the main party endured – in the 'home of the blizzard', it blew hurricane force for almost a whole year – or people recall Mawson's heroic struggle for survival, sledging alone after his two companions died. But men like Harrisson, who also hauled their sledges tirelessly to chart new features or lay depots of provisions, who searched endlessly for team-mates gone astray, who went out each night in desperate temperatures to check on their scientific instruments, or dug through the ice to gather rocks that might give clues to the continent's history, these men also deserve credit as true explorers.

The Western Base party's leader, Frank Wild, was a polar veteran, having already served with Scott and Shackleton, and in his capable hands the party became a team of equals, achieving all their goals. Together they explored swathes of new land in bitter conditions and returned with useful records. And Harrisson's sketches allow us to see a little of the sufferings, and the satisfaction, of their pioneering experience.

Yet, within two years of his safe arrival home, Harrison was dead. He had made a brief visit to Macquarie Island as a fisheries officer, but on his way back to Australia his ship sank in a gale and vanished without a trace. All lives were lost.

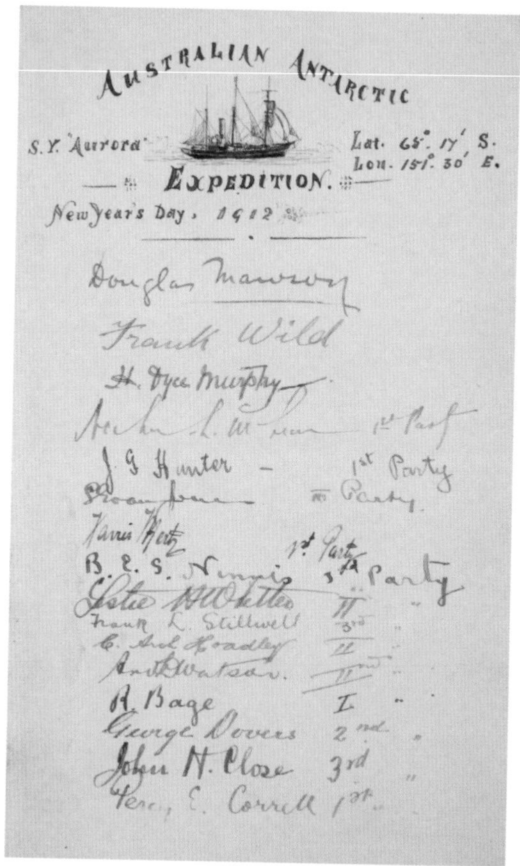
Australian Antarctic Expedition
S.Y. 'Aurora'
Lat. 65° 17' S.
Lon. 151° 30' E.
New Year's Day, 1912
Douglas Mawson
Frank Wild
J. G. Hunter – 1st Party
George Dovers 2nd
John H. Close 3rd

A page from Harrisson's diary for New Year's Day, 1912, signed by his companions as they sailed towards Antarctica.

7 September 1912. Sketching in this temp. even without 'blows' is bad – but add hard gusts! Twice before I got that rough sketch I had to run round to get some warmth!

Drawings from Harrisson's Winsor & Newton expedition sketchbook. Above left is of the SY *Aurora* anchored to an ice floe, 13 February 1912; and above right is labelled 'Our Antarctic home - The "Second Base".'

Harrisson's sketches of daily camp life provide an insight into the conditions that the men endured. Here they are shown sheltering and mending a tent in a cramped 'dugout' refuge. Opposite are 'Sketches from Memory' from his sledging journal of 1912, illustrating the difficulties of walking, let alone navigating, in a blizzard.

Overleaf: A selection of the many drawings from Harrisson's sketchbooks, including snow petrels, icebergs, cooking 'Hoosh', and enjoying Christmas dinner in the tent. He describes the sketch of a cave in glacier ice-cliffs as unfinished, since at 'minus 27°' he found it 'too cold for bare fingers'.

30 June 1912. We still have 7 or 8 months to wait for news of home. One blessing, time does not drag on our hands & but for the home ties, I should feel strongly the fascinations of the weirdness & beauty of these vast solitudes – the mystery of that lost dead land, hidden, we do not know even how deeply, beneath its eternal icy shroud.

Sketches from Memory
Eastern Depot Trip -
Ascending the ledge of the "Hippo." Rock.
How we came down the S. Eastern slope of the "Hippo"
A Sudden Squall - "Taken aback" "Here we are again!"
"Beware the awful avalanche!"
A collapsed tent. -
Navigation in a Blizzard -
Hanging on to your anchors!
The anchor drags! - &c - Capsize
Under reduced sail!

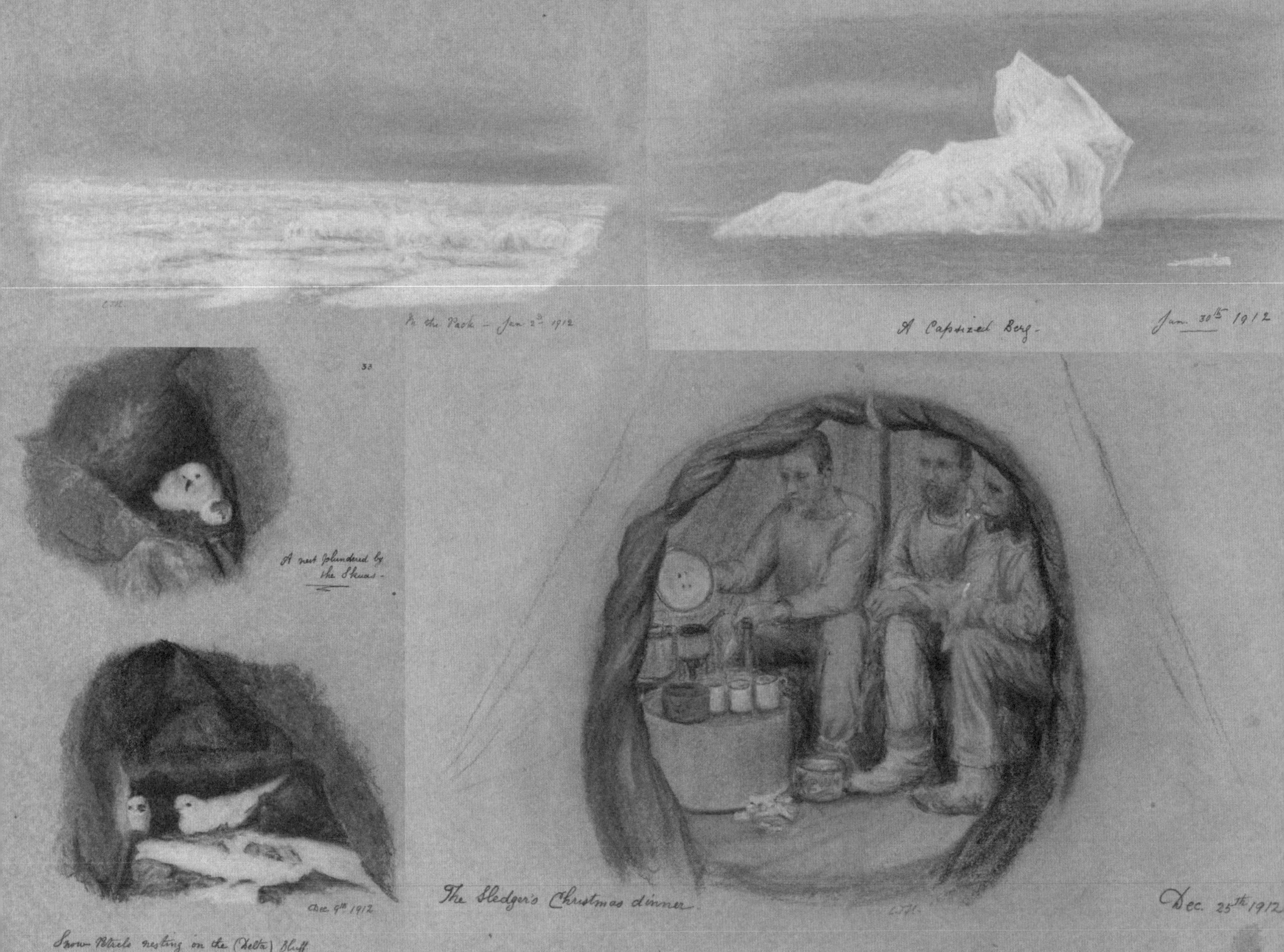
In the Pack – Jan 2nd 1912
A Capsized Berg –
Jan 30th 1912
33
A nest plundered by the Skuas –
Dec 9th 1912
Snow Petrels nesting on the (Delta) Bluff
The Sledger's Christmas dinner
Dec. 25th 1912

sketch of cave in Glacier cliffs
in Meteorological screen minus 27° —
it too cold for bare fingers!
May 17 1912
After the winter — The "Second Base," Sept. 21st 1912
Cooking "Hoosh"!
March 22nd 1912
1

SVEN HEDIN 1865-1952

I never walk in my own footprints. That is against my religion.

Swedish geographer Sven Hedin and his company of four men and their camels left the village of Merket on 10 April 1895 and headed into the desert. 'They will never come back,' a man said loudly as they passed. Hedin's aim was to cross the Taklamakan, the second-largest sand desert on Earth. Most people thought the journey suicidal. Its very name suggested the difficulties ahead: Taklamakan in Uyghur has been translated as 'place of no return', or 'desert of death'.

A few weeks later, they were in grave danger. One by one the camels died, and the men were crippled by thirst and exhaustion. Sandstorms buried their camp. The remaining camels refused to walk, instead lying down in the sand. The men lay beside them, pressing their faces against their flanks. On 30 April 1895, Hedin scratched in his notebook: 'mountains of sand in all directions, not a straw, no life ... God help us!' He abandoned his medicine chest, clothes, cameras and the thousand plates of already exposed photographs, and staggered on, carrying barely three days' provisions, and his precious diaries, maps, pencils and paper. Miraculously, just as life was ebbing away, he discovered a pool of fresh water.

By the time he had embarked on his 'death-march' in the Taklamakan, Hedin had already obtained a doctorate, was fluent in several languages and had undertaken two journeys through Persia. He went on to lead three further expeditions through the mountains and deserts of Central Asia, always with cameras and notebooks close at hand. He made climatological observations, collected rocks and plants, and recorded the topography in precise detail, in accurate maps as well as corresponding watercolour panoramas. His around 3,000 sketches and watercolours complemented his written observations, and eventually illustrated his numerous published travelogues.

Hedin discovered the Trans-Himalaya (for a time named the Hedin Range), Lake Lop Nur and the sources of the Brahmaputra, Indus and Sutlei rivers. In the Lop Nur Desert he discovered ruins indicating that the Great Wall of China had once extended to Xinjiang. He made the first precise maps of the Pamir Mountains, the Taklamakan, and sections of the Silk Road, Tibet and the Himalaya.

For the most part, Hedin was traversing areas closed to Europeans, dangerous territories overrun with bandits or whose rulers had an intense distrust of foreigners. Some who had ventured here before him had been tortured, thrown into vermin-pits, then beheaded. Despite employing disguises and hiding his sketchbooks in a bag of rice whenever officials rode up to his party, several times Hedin was arrested on suspicion of being a spy. Once he was nearly shot. No official could understand why a foreigner would make such detailed sketches and maps without some ulterior motive.

Hedin was a charismatic personality and a fantastic communicator. Prolific in his output, his scientific papers, lecture tours and gripping books for young people propelled him on to the international stage. He had mountain ranges, glaciers, plants, butterflies and even a lunar crater named for him. Later, however, his outspoken support for Kaiser Wilhelm II and then Hitler was met with ridicule and outrage. Nevertheless, his contribution to exploration is inarguable.

With yaks and camels, Hedin covered immense distances. Drawing and painting were both a means of recording his surroundings and for relaxation. Most evenings at camp he would sketch portraits of his companions or his Bactrian camels and their unusual 'hairstyles'.

Opposite: Hedin was both a skilled cartographer and artist. In addition to his highly accurate maps of previously uncharted regions, he produced meticulously drawn and coloured panoramas and scenes from his perilous journeys, including this one of a camp in Tibet in 1908, the tents weighted down against the icy blasts.

The adventure, the conquest of an unknown country, the struggle against the impossible, all have a fascination which draws me with irresistible force.

As a scientific explorer, Hedin conducted a great range of observations on his travels, seen here in 1894.

Opposite: In 1907, Hedin slipped unseen through the gates of Tibet's second city, Shigatse Dzong, late at night. The next morning there was uproar as the inhabitants discovered the foreigner in their midst; they believed he must have fallen from the sky. He later painted this image, based on one of his earlier sketches.

S. H-m. 1925

WALLY HERBERT 1934-2007

A pioneer has an unspoken responsibility to bring back something of value from his or her travels - a map, a unique discovery, or specialist knowledge that can contribute to the understanding of our planet.

Wally Herbert first went to Antarctica as a young man in 1956, spending two winters at Hope Bay and learning to navigate by the sun and stars. He mastered the art of sledging with dogs and was leader of the team that made the first crossing of the Antarctic Peninsula. On the Ross Sea side he would map vast swathes of previously unexplored country, and in 1962 his field party made the first ascent of Mount Nansen and covered huge areas of the Queen Maud Range. The team geologist secured the richest collection of plant-fossils yet found in Antarctica, and as surveyors they opened the gateway to the Pole, retracing Amundsen's route through the mountains down to the Ross Ice Shelf. All the while Herbert drew maps, filled journals, and whenever an opportunity arose made sketches and paintings.

He next headed to the Arctic, with a plan for an astonishing polar journey. After years of preparation, Herbert set out in February 1968 with three companions to attempt an impossible dream: the first surface crossing of the Arctic Ocean. The route would cover almost 6,000 km (some 3,720 miles) and would take sixteen months of effort and near continual danger on a surface as unstable and perilous as anywhere on Earth. There would not be a day when the ice floes on which they travelled and slept were not drifting in response to currents and winds. There was little hope of rescue, should they need it, and even turning back would have been difficult.

On 6 April 1969, Wally Herbert and his three companions stood at the North Pole. Trying to set foot on it, Herbert noted, had been 'like trying to step on the shadow of a bird that was hovering overhead, for the surface across which we were moving was itself moving on a planet that was spinning about an axis beneath our feet.' They had become the first undisputedly to reach the Pole by surface crossing. Too tired to celebrate, they set up the camera and posed for photographs But this was not the end of the journey – their aim was to cross the Arctic Ocean by its longest axis. They still had two months of daily fifteen-hour marches between the Pole and safety, before the ice on which they stood melted beneath them.

The expedition made landfall in Spitsbergen in May 1969. Their success was hailed by at the time as a 'feat of courage which ranks with any in polar history'. Yet within months the first footsteps were being made on the surface of the Moon; Herbert's expedition was instantly cast as something of another time, old-fashioned perhaps, as the wonders of space travel filled imaginations.

In the coming years, Herbert would become an award-winning writer and artist, documenting the fragile polar wilderness and the changing culture of the Inuit. Time and again he returned, even taking his wife and ten-month-old daughter to live among a small community of hunters in Northwest Greenland. Despite hardship and difficulties, Herbert simply loved the polar regions, particularly during the challenging winter months. 'The long polar night is a bewitching time of year to journey by sledge ... the experience of moving across a seeming infinity of sea-ice in the winter darkness has an almost mystical quality. There is no setting in the world more beautiful than a polar icescape illuminated by a full moon high in a cloudless sky.'

Herbert took his old school paint-box and three paintbrushes with him to Antarctica, in the hope of discreetly recording his impressions. In those days many of his companions saw painting as a waste of time. But his skills as an artist were useful in the field. Opposite are his surveying journals from Antarctica's Beardmore Glacier, where he sketched panoramic views of the prominent features from a survey point, noting down names and logging descriptions.

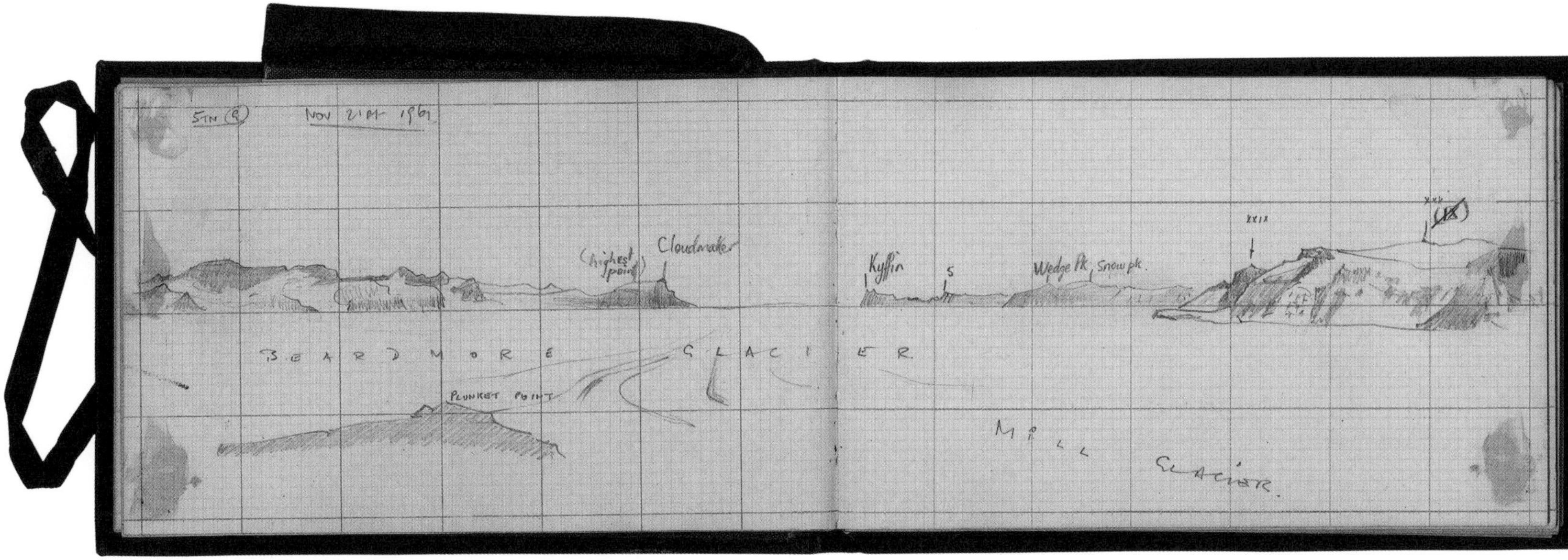
Stn (G) Nov 21st 1961
(highest point)
Cloudmaker
Kyffin
S
Wedge Pk
snow pk.
XXIX
B E A R D M O R E G L A C I E R
PLUNKET POINT
M I L L G L A C I E R

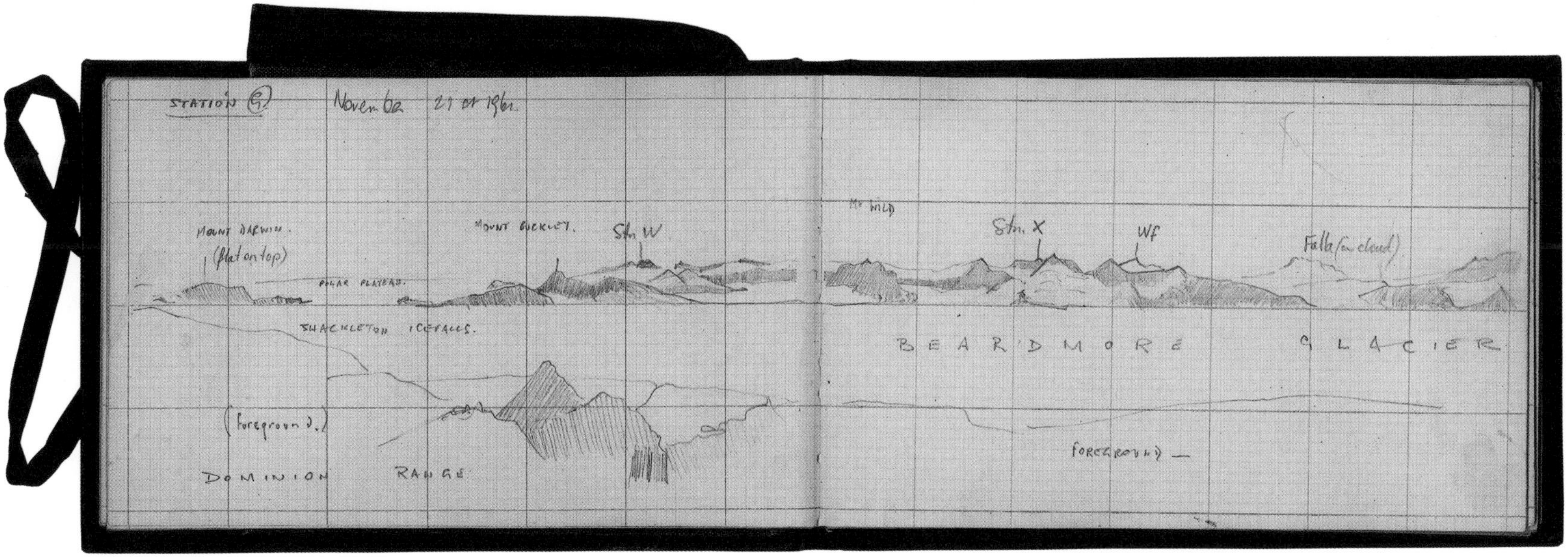
STATION (G) November 21st 1961
MOUNT DARWIN
(flat on top)
POLAR PLATEAU
MOUNT BUCKLEY
Stn W
Mt WILD
Stn X
Wf
Falla (in cloud)
SHACKLETON ICEFALLS
B E A R D M O R E G L A C I E R
(foreground.)
FOREGROUND
D O M I N I O N R A N G E

Wally Herbert's journals are full of insights and reflections, sketches, clippings from charts, even original photographs that he developed in a tiny darkroom in his polar hut. He employed an unusual technique for his hand-drawn maps: using plastic-covered paper, with a fine layer of printers' ink, shade was created with pencil and highlights by using a scalpel, scraping to the white paper beneath. It took enormous patience and precision. With the scraps left over, Herbert created some exceptionally beautiful artworks, including a portrait of his lead dog. Below is a triple portrait of an Inuit shaman turning his face towards the sun.

57

regime. If they bark during the night we must get up and check them in case they fight — if they fight we must get at them like lightning, not stopping to dress, and stop that fight. On one occasion this year a dog's eye was ripped out because a dog was too late in getting out of his tent.

But there are few greater satisfactions than to ride behind a dog team pulling like mad and in perfect formation. The dogs at Hope Bay are very big and strong and average 90 lbs apiece. A number weigh over the 110 lb mark. They eat 2 lbs of seal meat every day when on the move and the same amount every other day when at base.

A pack of healthy teams go mad when they are harnessed up and the noise is deafening until the moment they start, then apart from heavy panting silence reigns, and they pull like all hell let loose.

However the control of huskys that are a little excitable to say the least, is no mean task at times.

57a

"Five MPH all tails up" (one at back)

Notice in the photo that none of us are sinking into the snow — this type of surface is ideal for sledging, and very fast. There are so many things that can go wrong with a snow surface that when we do get a good one like this it is a pure joy to be alive. The dogs here are in remarkably good formation; not often as good as this!!

W.H.

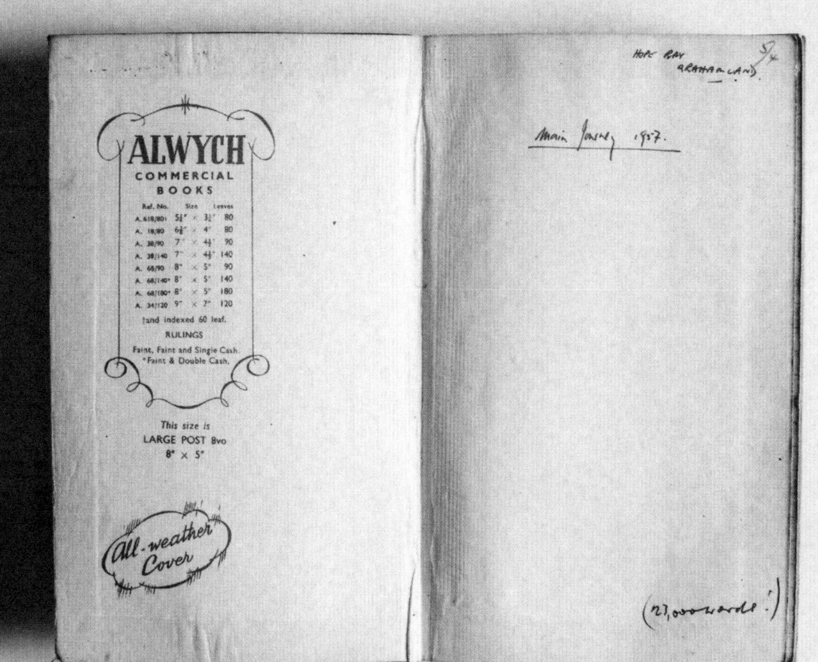
ALWYCH
COMMERCIAL
BOOKS
RULINGS
Feint, Feint and Single Cash.
*Feint & Double Cash.
This size is
LARGE POST 8vo
8" × 5"
All-weather Cover
Main Journey 1957.

Broadcast in New Zealand.
"A DOG'S LIFE"
by
W.W. Herbert
"CALLING THE ANTARCTIC" B.B.C - A special programme for the men down 'south'.
'On writing a book' - by WALLY HERBERT
Have you ever thought of writing a
Have you ever been wedged in a corner
sweat and perfume, while a few feet aw
"Calling the Antarctic".
First contribution by: Wally Herbert
broadcast April 23rd 1965

THOR HEYERDAHL 1914-2002

One learns more from listening than speaking. And both the wind and the people who continue to live close to nature still have much to tell us.

'Just occasionally you find yourself in an odd situation,' Thor Heyerdahl recalled: 'You get into it by degrees and in the most natural way, but when you are right in the midst of it you are suddenly astonished and ask yourself how in the world it all came about.'

This thought occurred to him during his voyage on the balsa-wood raft *Kon-Tiki*, along with five companions and a green parrot, as they drifted on the Pacific at the whim of the currents and the southeast trade wind. In all, they would spend 101 days on the fragile craft, sailing almost 4,500 nautical miles from Peru to Polynesia on a daring mission to prove his theory that prehistoric peoples from South America could have made the same journey.

Born in Larvik, Norway, Heyerdahl was encouraged in his love of nature by his mother, who taught him about Darwin and evolution. While still at school he ran a one-room zoological museum in his home, and roamed the local woods. In his teens he sledged into the mountains with his pet husky, 'braving storms and sleeping in the snow just to prove I could do things alone'. He studied zoology and geography at the University of Oslo, then, with his new bride Liv, sailed to the Marquesas Islands in Polynesia for a year-long study trip and honeymoon. Both believed that civilization was a destructive force, severing mankind's relationship with nature. They hoped to live as ancient peoples had done, surviving on the food they could gather and fish from the sea.

It was while they were in the Marquesas that Heyerdahl discovered what he believed compelling evidence that Polynesia had been discovered and settled by voyagers from South America, rather than Asia. His theory went against all current academic thought and was dismissed outright: such prehistoric transoceanic migration across the Pacific was regarded as impossible, given the craft and knowledge of navigation of early Peruvians. The common ethnological traits he had observed between the two cultures were said to be coincidental. In order to prove that such a voyage could have been undertaken and so vindicate his theory, Heyerdahl decided to build his raft based on illustrations by Spanish conquistadors and using traditional techniques.

On 7 August 1947 *Kon-Tiki* was grounded on a reef and Heyerdahl waded ashore on Tuamotu Island, in Polynesia, thus proving his theory at least possible. The narrative of his intrepid voyage eventually sold more than 30 million copies and was translated into 67 languages, and a film he made about it won him an Oscar.

Heyerdahl continued to mount expeditions well into his 80s. He led ground-breaking archaeological journeys to the Galapagos and Easter Island, then undertook a voyage in a replica of an ancient reed boat, *Ra*, from Morocco to Barbados to demonstrate that the ancient Egyptians could have sailed across the Atlantic to the Americas prior to Columbus – albeit succeeding only on the second attempt. It was the *Kon-Tiki* exploit, however, for which he earned lasting recognition. In later years, he came to despair of the celebrity that the expedition had brought him, believing that his image as a daredevil explorer meant he was not taken seriously academically. While he never quite received the scholarly acclaim he longed for, he was regarded as a leading figure in his native Norway, and continues to be an inspiration for a new generation.

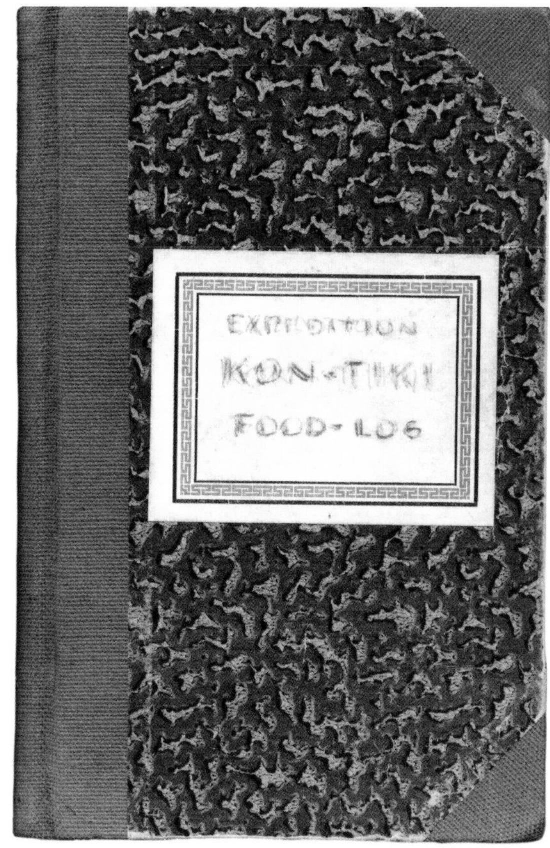

The food log of the *Kon-Tiki* expedition. Being so close to the water level, Heyerdahl and his companions discovered fish constantly leapt on to their raft, providing adequate sustenance during their journey: 'Our neighbourly intimacy with the sea was not fully realized by Torstein till he woke one morning and found a sardine on his pillow.'

Opposite left: Without engines to disturb marine life, the raft was constantly followed by dolphins and sharks. Fed with their leftovers, the sharks 'behaved like friendly dogs', Heyerdahl observed.

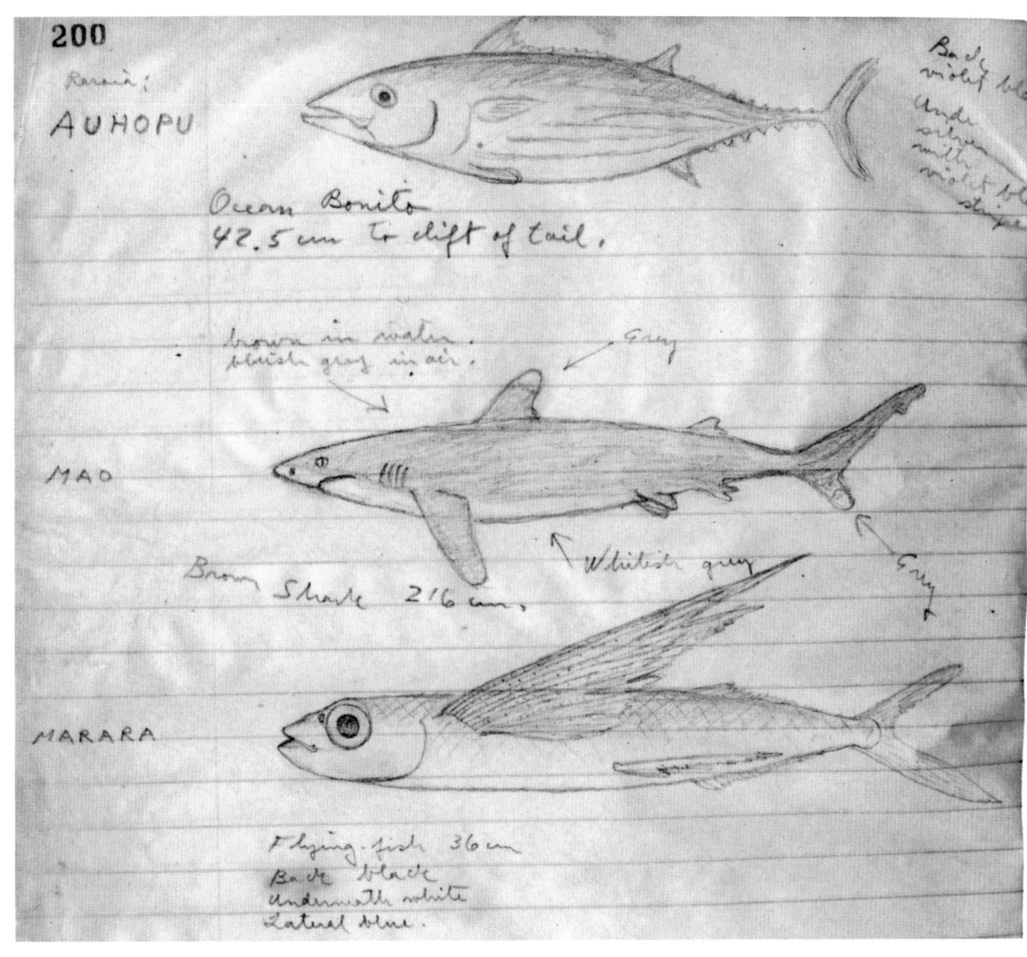

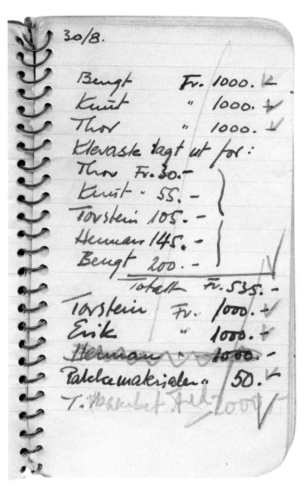

I have never been able to grasp the meaning of time. I don't believe it exists. I've felt this again and again, when alone and out in nature.

30/8.

Bengt Fr. 1000.
Knut " 1000.
Thor " 1000.
Klevaske tagt ut for:
Thor Fr. 30.-
Knut " 55.-
Torstein 105.-
Herman 145.-
Bengt 200.-
Totalt Fr. 535.-
Torstein Fr. 1000.-
Erik " 1000.-
~~Herman " 1000.-~~

A page from Heyerdahl's budgeting notebook. As with all explorers on any expedition, keeping track of expenditure was crucial. Here he details expenses for his team: Bengt Danielsson, Knut Haugland, Thor Heyerdahl, Erik Hesselberg, Torstein Raaby and Herman Watzinger.

ED HILLARY 1919-2008

When you go to the mountains, you see them and you admire them. In a sense, they give you a challenge, and you try to express that challenge by climbing them.

It was a long, freezing cold night, high on Everest on 28 May 1953. Tenzing Norgay boiled some soup, while Ed Hillary secured the guy ropes of their tent as best he could; clinging to a small ledge, it was the highest spot on Earth that anyone had ever camped. Both men struggled to sleep as the wind tore at the canvas. Yet the next morning the day dawned clear, and as Hillary opened the tent door he could see the outlines of 'icy peaks from horizon to horizon'. This was their chance. By 11.30 a.m. they would be standing on the summit of Mount Everest and the whole world would fall away beneath their feet.

Hillary was sixteen before he saw a mountain, but he immediately knew it was a world he wanted to explore and enjoy. He learned his craft of climbing on snow and ice in New Zealand's Southern Alps, and it was while on a shoestring expedition to the Indian Garhwal in 1951, with his friend George Lowe, that he managed to join a British Everest reconnaissance expedition, led by the enigmatic Eric Shipton. Hillary's sound mountain-craft and strength at altitude impressed Shipton, and he was invited to join the following year's training expedition to Cho Oyu, the formidable neighbour to Everest and the world's sixth highest peak. Lowe came too, and after they were turned back from the top by dangerous ice-cliffs, Shipton suggested that they might like to continue exploring. The young pair agreed without hesitation.

In June 1952 they crossed the Himalayan divide from Nepal down on to the immense glaciers of Tibet to explore secretly the great northern flanks of Everest. Standing on the Rongbuk Glacier, Hillary wrote: 'There was Everest, proud and aloof against a wind-streaked sky. The glacier was a shining pathway of ice sweeping up to the foot of the mountain.' And then came the 1953 Everest expedition led by John Hunt, and the morning in May that would shape the whole of his life. 'A few more whacks of the ice-axe, a few very weary steps, and we were on the summit of Everest', he wrote.

Although several climbs followed his Everest triumph, Hillary ironically suffered from ever more severe bouts of altitude sickness. But he channelled his considerable energies into other adventures. In 1957-58 he drove a converted farm tractor all the way to the South Pole, as part of the Vivian Fuchs expedition to Antarctica, pioneering a route up the Skelton Glacier and establishing depots on the polar plateau that were crucial to the expedition's overall success. Hillary was, in his own words, 'Hellbent on the Pole', and contrary to his orders made an audacious dash there, risking both fuel and supplies. He and his companions were the first men to reach the Pole overland since Scott, in 1912.

Hillary also immersed himself in river-rafting expeditions, before turning to the equally turbulent waters of political life. He devoted the rest of his life to the Sherpa of Nepal, through his foundation, the Himalayan Trust, building mountain airfields, bridges and schools, clinics and hospitals, and renewing remote Buddhist monasteries; he regarded this work as his finest achievement. Hillary summed up his incredible life with characteristic humility: 'Ever since I reached the summit of Mount Everest the media have classified me as a hero, but I have always recognized myself as being a person of modest abilities. My achievements have resulted from a goodly share of imagination and plenty of energy.'

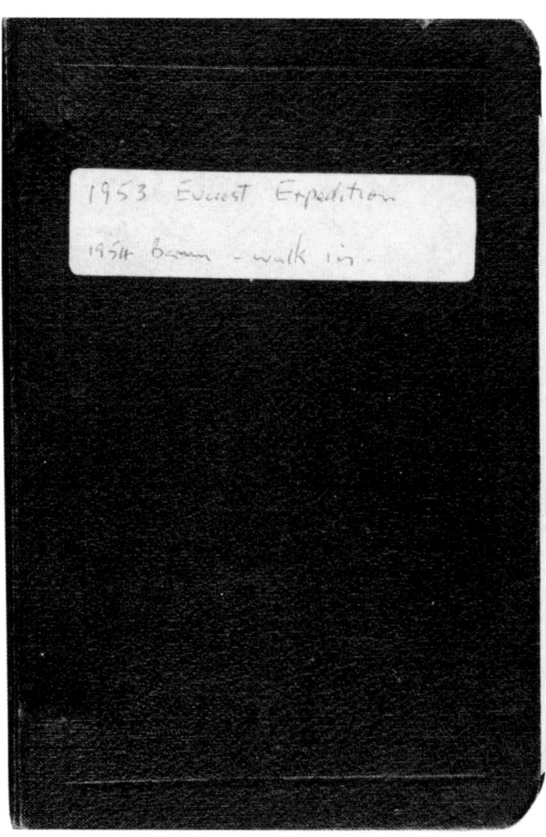

Hillary's journal from the 1953 Everest expedition. Opposite is his record of the morning that he and Tenzing Norgay reached the summit, 29 May. As he peeped out from their tent he 'indulged in the sensations of gazing over the world from our lofty perch'.

can be paid to Tenzing than to say that when one is leading a difficult pitch with him my support that the whole of one's attention can be devoted to the task ahead & only the gentle & insistent tug of the rope at one's waist is a constant reminder of the very capable sheet anchor at the other end

The summit

At 4 a.m. on the 29th May our second two hour spell of sleeping oxygen came to an end & we both stirred out of a not unpleasant dozing state. I untied the tent entrance next to me & peered outside. The whole world around was already lighting up with the early dawn & the rows after rows of icy peaks below were clearly outlined against the deep shadows of the sleeping valleys. It was very cold & the thermometer I had left outside read -27°C. The wind was completely still & everything was gripped in icy silence. For a moment in my still sleepy state I ~~savoured~~ indulged in the ~~strange~~ sensations of gazing over the world from our lofty perch & felt

WILLIAM HODGES 1744-1797

To give dignity to a landscape is my object. Whatever may be the value of my exertions, the design to amend the heart while the eye is gratified will yield me the purest pleasure by its success.

A portrait by Hodges of a Māori with facial tattoos.

Opposite: A map and profile view of Palmerston Island, a coral atoll in the Cook Islands.

Although much had been discovered on James Cook's first voyage, it had become clear that there were still large areas in the Southern Ocean where a great landmass might yet be found. Cook proposed a new search, circumnavigating the globe from west to east, taking advantage of the fierce westerlies that dominate these challenging southerly latitudes. It was to be another voyage into the cartographic unknown with a genuine scientific motivation, and yet an artistic impulse too. Through travellers' tales and wondrous artworks, the European world was beginning to fall under the spell of the south Pacific. Art and science combined in a seductive, and fashionable, landscape of imagining.

German-born Johann Reinhold Forster headed the scientific party, accompanied by his talented son Georg, with William Hodges hired as the expedition's official artist, or 'Landskip Painter'. Born the son of a London blacksmith, Hodges would become one of the outstanding landscape painters of his day, though in 1772 when the ships left England he was still young and little-known. He would prove an excellent choice: likeable and hard-working, attentive to detail yet alive to the subtleties of light, and intrepid enough to revel in the difficult environments into which he was thrown. He joined the ship at the last minute, bringing the total to 118 men aboard Cook's *Resolution*, with a further 83 aboard the *Adventure*.

Cook's course was set to the south. On 17 January 1773 his expedition became the first to cross the Antarctic Circle. On 9 February the two ships were separated in fog, but Cook continued his sweep to the south and reached Dusky Sound, in New Zealand's South Island, on 27 March 1773. After exploring islands in the Pacific, Cook again pushed south, crossing the Antarctic Circle for a third time in January 1774, achieving his farthest south. Following another winter in the Pacific and again navigating the ice edge, Cook finally headed north into the Atlantic. The ships dropped anchor at Spithead on the English coast on 30 July 1775 after an absence of three years and eighteen days.

Everywhere they had been Hodges had made sketches of landscapes and, crucially, the people they encountered, who often had not met Europeans before. On his return, Hodges would supervise engravings made from his sketches for Cook's official book, and the Admiralty employed him for two more years to create a number of grand oil canvases of scenes from the voyage. The vibrant immediacy of his shipboard sketches were replaced by idealized neo-classical set pieces to satisfy the tastes of the Academy.

Hodges then travelled to India with his painting kit, coping with the grief of losing his first wife through childbirth. He would spend over six years recording its landscapes and architecture. In later years his business interests failed, and following a run on the Bank of England his finances were in dire straits. His publications *Select Views in India* and *Travels in India* lost him considerable amounts of money and, disillusioned by bad reviews, he sold the contents of his studio and gave up painting altogether. He died in 1797 after an overdose of the laudanum he used to treat the gout he was suffering from; rumours would long persist that he had committed suicide. It would take many years for his artistic legacy to be fully appreciated. The explorer and great man of science Alexander von Humboldt later wrote that his desire to travel was first inspired by seeing artwork by Hodges.

Palmerston Island. Lat. 18. S. Lon. 163.5. W

N 28

The risk one runs in exploring a coast, in these unknown and icy seas, is so very great, that I can be bold enough to say that no man will ever venture farther than I have done ... thick fogs, snow storms, intense cold, and every other thing that can render navigation dangerous, must be encountered; and these difficulties are greatly heightened, by the inexpressibly horrid aspect of the country; a country doomed by nature never once to feel the warmth of the sun's rays, but to lie buried in everlasting snow and ice.

JAMES COOK, 1775

In the Antarctic, Hodges chose to use wash and ink to capture the special effects of light - here 'ice islands' with *Resolution* and *Adventure*. 'Truth', he would later write, 'is the base of every work of mine.' The challenge, even in difficult situations like this, was to attempt to depict nature faithfully. Cook appreciated Hodges's drawings so much that he kept many of them in his own portfolio.

Overleaf: On the left is Dusky Bay, New Zealand, March 1773; and on the right, the first depiction of the island of South Georgia, 1775.

N.32

N° 33

HECTOR HOREAU 1801-1872

I was left alone, with no companions except a manservant, more a master in my boat than a king in his kingdom.

Throughout the nineteenth century, a great number of European artists travelled to Egypt hoping to capture its exotic charm and document its antiquities. Among them was French architect Hector Horeau. Born in Versailles, Horeau studied at the École des Beaux-Arts in Paris. As an illustrator, he worked on the plates for Frédéric Cailliaud's *Voyage à Méroé*, an account of the French naturalist's expeditions in Egypt and Sudan. This experience would eventually inspire Horeau to make his own journeys to the region.

Horeau's first love, however, was architecture. Although little of his work still survives, or was ever built, he was well known as an enthusiastic proponent of modern urban planning and a pioneer of cast-iron architecture. Many of his progressive ideas were often technically impossible, such as his prescient proposal for the construction of a railway tunnel under the Channel between England and France. Although he won the competition to design the Covered Market in Versailles in 1839, and the palace for the Universal Exposition in London in 1851 (it was Jospeh Paxton's Crystal Palace that was actually built), neither of his designs were practicable until decades later.

As a young man, Horeau travelled extensively through Europe, then the Near East. He spent nearly two years exploring Egypt south from Alexandria. In 1838, dressed in Turkish garb in respect for local customs, he sailed up the Nile on a small barge from Cairo towards Abu Simbel. With an architect's eye he drew accurate plans, sections and elevations of the temples he visited, meticulously recording the depth and undulation of the infill of centuries of sand and debris within the temples before they were excavated. He sketched and painted Luxor, Karnak, the Valley of the Kings and the Colossi of Memnon.

Adding a sense of scale and human interest to his artworks, he populated the ruins with figures lazing in the shadows of the vast monuments of this ancient civilization. In one or two of his drawings, he shows graffiti from earlier tourists and visitors to the area: Greeks, Romans and Napoleonic soldiers. His watercolours would eventually illustrate his books: *Panorama d'Égypte et de Nubie* and *L'Avenir du Caire au Point de Vue de l'Édilité et de la Civilisation.*

Having lived in England for some years, Horeau returned to France in 1871 and took up the cause of the insurgents of the Paris Commune. Following its harsh suppression by the French army, Horeau was arrested and imprisoned. He was 70 years old. Released after several months, he never recovered from the ordeal and died in the city in 1872.

Horeau's draughtsmanship and great attention to archaeological and architectural detail in his sketches and watercolours of Egypt now provide a precious record of these ancient monuments. It would not be long before many were damaged by amateur archaeologists and treasure seekers.

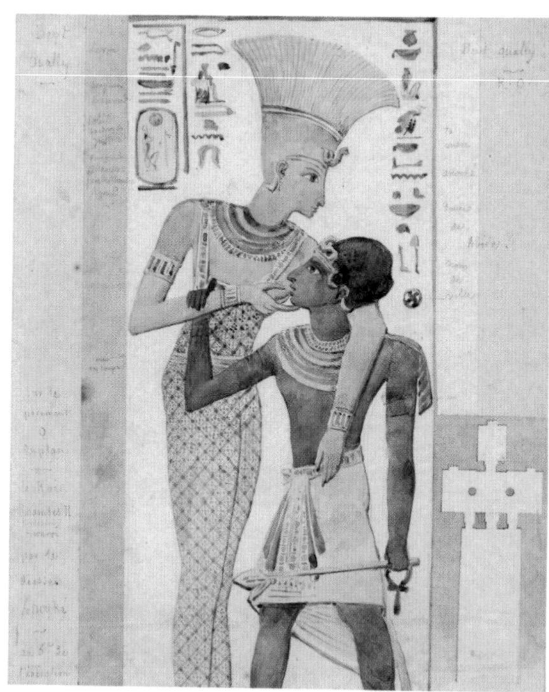

Horeau visited areas of Egypt and their monuments before they were excavated, and his watercolours provide a vivid colour record of murals that have since faded. Here the young king Ramesses II being suckled by the goddess Anukis at Beit el-Wali, and, opposite left, a *serekh* with the Horus-name of Ramesses II from Karnak. Opposite right: The rubble-filled entrance to the tomb of Ramesses III in the Valley of the Kings.

Horeau not only created detailed architectural drawings of temples, but also conveyed the joy of discovery and travel in his watercolours painted in situ, capturing the colour and the sense of heat. On the left overleaf is his painting of his arrival at the Second Cataract, in which he includes himself writing his name on a rock, 14 May 1838; and on the right he depicts his barge, which cost him 150 francs a month, moored at Abu Simbel.

de Karnac
salle hypostyle

Mr Horeau, arrivé à la 2e Cataracte, inscrit son nom sur un rocher

ALEXANDER VON HUMBOLDT 1769–1859

A man can't just sit down and cry – he's got to do something.

At a time when many areas of the world were still unexplored, Alexander von Humboldt ventured into remote areas, observing everything he could, and changed the way the world was understood. Undaunted, ambitious, implausibly talented, he was a true 'universal' man, a child of the Enlightenment who became the most widely respected scientific figure of his age. Among his many achievements, he can be regarded as the founder of the modern field of ecology and the first to call for global collaboration in the gathering of scientific data.

Born in Berlin, he was well connected and insatiably curious. He first travelled to England with his friend Georg Forster, who had sailed with Cook as a young naturalist, and together they visited Joseph Banks, revelling in the wonders of his herbarium. Humboldt inherited a fortune on his mother's death, which allowed him to resign from his work as a mine inspector and devote himself to planning a great scientific journey with another friend, the French botanist Aimé Bonpland. They had imagined overwintering in the Atlas Mountains in North Africa, and crossing the desert between Tripoli and Cairo, but soon their horizons broadened. They managed to persuade the King of Spain to give them permits to roam widely in Spain's South American colonies, and by 1799 they were crossing the Atlantic. Within a year they were paddling up the Orinoco and, with sketchbooks and instruments at the ready, plunged headlong into dense tracts of jungle where no Westerners had ever been.

The pair explored the coast of Venezuela, the Amazon, and much of modern-day Peru, Ecuador, Colombia and Mexico. Climbing mountains, making maps, catching electric eels, eating mud, pressing plants, revealing Inca ruins or the blueness of the sky, gathering bird droppings, observing the stars, bagging rocks – nothing was too large, or too small, to come under their scrutiny to be measured. They covered more than 9,650 km (6,000 miles) on foot, on horseback and in canoes. It was tough, often exhausting and frequently dangerous. The epic five-year journey cost Humboldt a third of his money, but resulted in over 60,000 specimens and a vast trove of daily data in his journals that would take a lifetime to analyse. In fact, he spent 30 years distilling and publishing the results, and it became in itself an ongoing and endless voyage of exploration in search of 'grand physical laws'. He always said his aim 'was to collect ideas rather than objects'.

At the age of 59 Humboldt made a trek across Russia, travelling in a carriage to the Chinese frontier and returning with a new concept of the Earth's magnetism. His first book, *A Personal Narrative*, was said to have inspired the young Charles Darwin to a life of science. His magnum opus, *Kosmos*, perhaps the most ambitious scientific work ever published, had as its goal the bringing together of everything he'd seen, read and imagined – no less than 'a complete physical description of the universe'. Making important contributions to nearly every branch of the natural sciences, it took him 25 years of endeavour, with the first volume published when he was 76 and the fifth and final volume nearing completion when he died, just short of his 90th birthday. The year of his death, 1859, saw the publication of *On the Origin of the Species* and Darwin would later write that Humboldt was 'the greatest scientific traveller who ever lived'.

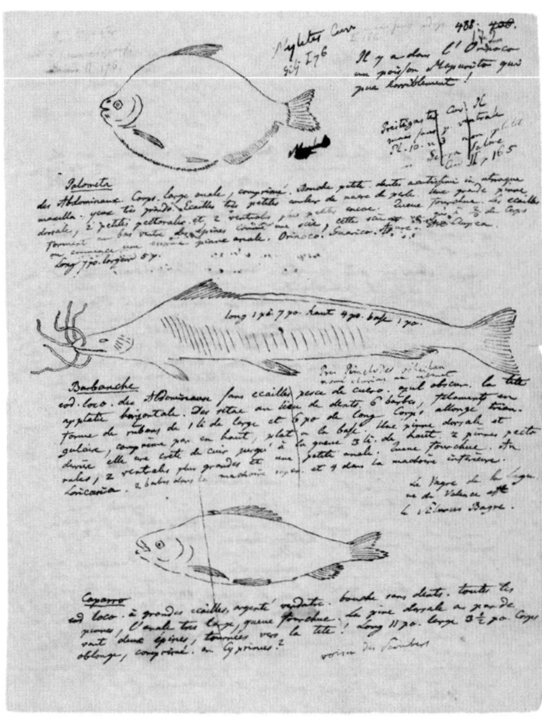

Humboldt's expedition diaries are densely written and immensely detailed, with small field sketches and tables of computation and observation. The journals held the raw material of his evolving scientific thinking. Opposite is his iconic cross-section profile of Chimborazo volcano in Ecuador. He sketched the beginning of this image on the spot, and it came to exemplify his vision for an ordered geographical ecology, in this case the zoned occurrence of different plants at different altitudes.

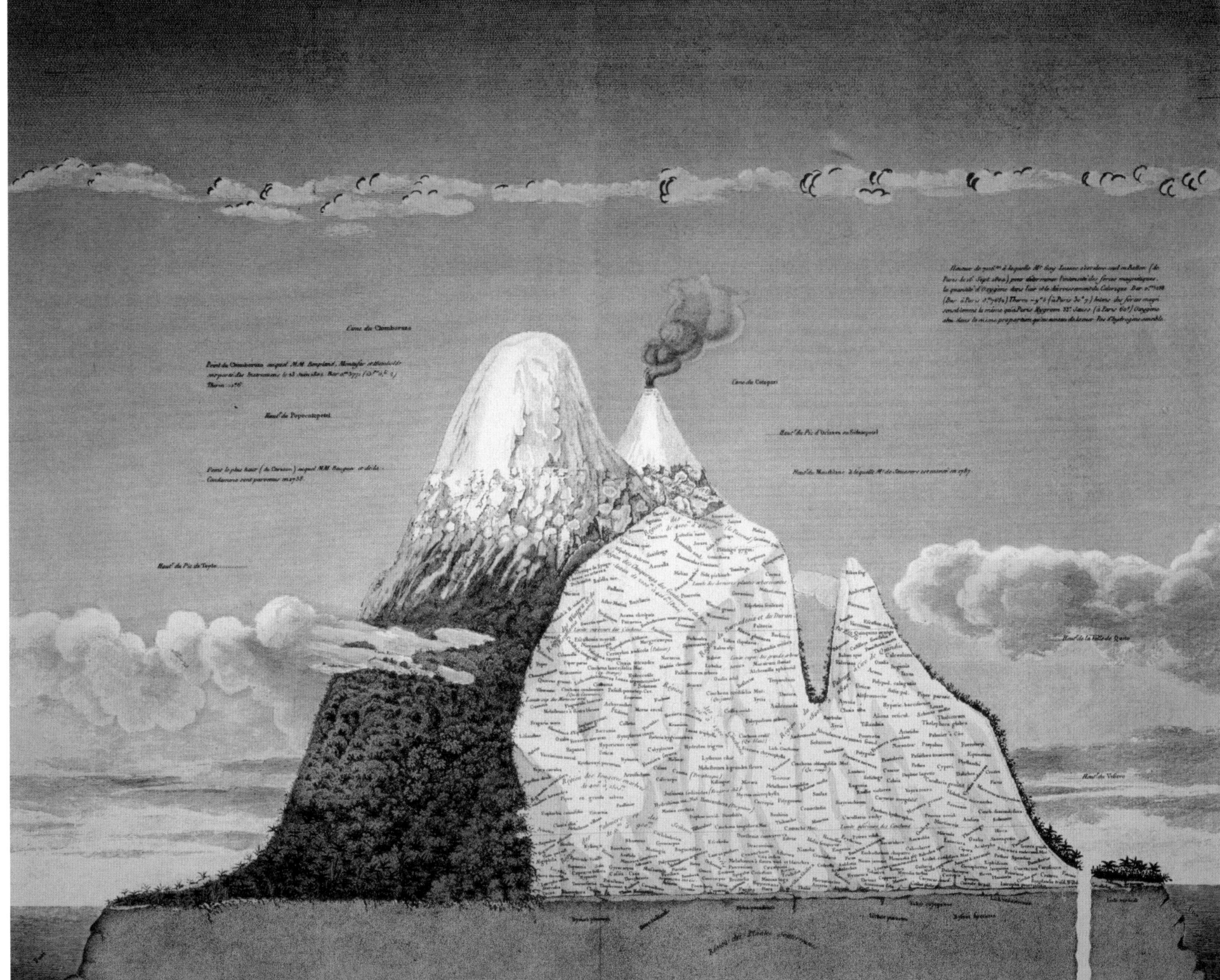

Cone du Chimborazo
Haut. du Popocatepetl
Cone du Cotopaxi
Haut. du Pic de Teyde
Haut. de la ville de Quito
Haut. du Volcan

ANOTHER WORLD

Alan Bean

My colleague on our moon walk, Peter Conrad, wanted to pick up a piece of rock, but the spacesuits made kneeling very difficult. So I grabbed a strap on his backpack, lowered him down and pulled him back up; it took just a few brief seconds. The moon rock in the painting contains a small piece of lunar meteorite found in Oman in 2001. *Rock'n'Roll on the Ocean of Storms*; textured acrylic on aircraft plywood, 2002.

Exploring is part of being human; people have always wanted to know what lies beyond the next mountain or across a faraway river. Partly it is just our natural curiosity: what is a place like? What would it be like to live there?

We landed at last in the Ocean of Storms; it was the Apollo 12 mission, November 1969. When I stepped out into this wilderness of ancient volcanic rock, one of the most important items of gear was the spiral-bound notebook clipped to the cuff of my glove. Within it were page after page of instructive reminders: checklists of essential procedures; the samples we needed to take; the kind of images that mission control wanted us to capture. Before we'd left, some friends in our backup crew had scribbled tiny cartoons and even sneaked a few pin-ups inside too. As we stood there on the surface of the Moon, you can imagine our smiles when we found them.

There were no blank pages in these special booklets, nor was there a spare moment to draw. We were on the lunar surface for just 31 hours and these notes were made to keep us perfectly on schedule. It was a ten-day voyage, for which I'd trained intensively for more than five years, and every precious minute spent exploring was filled with experiments and things to do and record. It all went according to plan, save for a few tiny slip-ups. We were the first to carry a colour television camera to the Moon, but lost transmission after I accidentally destroyed it by aiming at the sun. During splashdown in the Pacific, another camera dislodged from storage and struck me on the forehead, knocking me unconscious. I needed six stitches, but considering the dangers we'd just been through it was nothing.

I never tried to paint in zero gravity – it would be practically impossible – but looking back I wish I'd given it a try. We planted our flag, gathered rocks and took photographs. I could not take a sketchbook, but that first experience of leaving the planet in 1969 has provided me with sights that have lasted me a lifetime. As important as the images we obtained and the records we made was the simple act of being there, and looking. I began sketching in my mind. If you travel with open eyes your horizons can be limitless, and the things we beheld were almost unimaginable. Even now, almost five decades on, all I need to do is to close my eyes and remember. The visions of another world flood straight back.

Ever since my early days as a Navy test pilot, I knew I wanted to paint. I enrolled in night classes and continued my art training with private lessons in between the more dangerous missions. But it was only when I left NASA in 1981 that I devoted myself to making art full-time. Some of my colleagues thought I was having a midlife crisis, but I knew I just had to document the incredible things that I'd witnessed.

When I began painting, I realized that keepsake mission patches from my space suit were dirty with moon dust. I now add tiny pieces of the patches to the paintings, and with the hammer that we used to knock the flagpole into the lunar surface and the bottom of a bronzed moon boot, I sometimes add texture to the paint. I also use photographs to imagine the other Apollo missions that my fellow astronauts would undertake. My friend Neil Armstrong called my creations 'astro-artistry'. Through observation and memory, I try to conjure glimpses of our activities more than 320,000 km (200,000 miles) and many years away, to capture the spirit of our highest hopes. It was the fulfilment of a near-impossible exploration goal, and it captivated a generation. I want people to share the spirit of Apollo.

The next time I was shot into space was as Commander of the Skylab III mission in 1973. We lived for 59 days in America's first space station and flew some 24.5 million miles. During our daily operations, which included medical tests, solar observations and scientific experiments, I was also able to perform one of the first EVAs – an 'extravehicular activity' – a spacewalk. Floating so far above the Earth, I felt neither alone, nor afraid, just an overwhelming sense of privilege to be an explorer, being the first to do something, with the opportunity to discover the world anew.

Our Skylab station was abandoned the following year, having served its purpose as the most remote of all scientific bases – a pioneer outpost on the edge of an infinite ocean of nothingness. The station orbited Earth more than 2,470 times while it was occupied, logging thousands of hours worth of new data. The photographs of solar flares and coronal holes extended our knowledge of these extraordinary phenomena; and that's just one thing among a huge number of scientific achievements of Skylab. And yet, I feel the mission added so much more in terms of keeping alive the *spirit* of human potential. That's one true definition of exploration: realizing the dream of looking beyond the horizon.

If I were to sum up my life, I would say that I feel lucky. Of course, once I became a NASA astronaut my life was always going to be unusual, but what a journey it has been. I was the first artist in history to have visited another world and returned to paint my experiences. When I think about the artists who travelled on voyages to the unknown with the great navigators like James Cook, or who arrived on the shores of a new continent to settle and explore, I'm full of admiration for the hardships they endured and the challenges they faced. Imagine forests full of curious new creatures, encounters with new peoples, dramatic new landscapes never before beheld.

I know what it's like to gaze in wonder and to be humbled by what you see. The surface of the Moon might seem barren and sterile, but the richness and the colours are something I've always tried to convey. And, of all the things I've seen, nothing can compare with the thrill of looking back from the darkness of space and seeing the beautiful blue ball studded with fluffy white clouds, which is our home, the Earth.

Humanity's inner drive to explore the limits of our imagination and capability is something that is universal, and which expresses itself across the ages. As one of the twelve men to have walked on the Moon, I count myself blessed and I paint knowing what it was like to be there. What a privilege it was. It was a joy even just to look out of the window. I feel happy and – that word again – *lucky* to have been able to sail to the stars as the member of a great undertaking. As history unfolds, of course there will be many more. I'm certain that one day someone will be fortunate enough to stand on the surface of Mars. I just hope that they also take time to admire the view.

Looking up at the Earth, I moved into my spacecraft's shadow to get a better view without squinting; reaching up, I 'balanced' the Earth between my gloved thumb and forefinger. Our world, the whole Earth, was safely cradled in my fingertips. *Our World at My Fingertips*; textured acrylic with moon dust on aircraft plywood, 2005.

ALAN BEAN
©2005

MERIWETHER LEWIS 1774-1809

I was convinced they would attempt to rob us in which case ... I should resist to the last extremity preferring death to that of being deprived of my papers, instruments and gun.

When President Thomas Jefferson dispatched Captain Meriwether Lewis and William Clark to find a route across North America, there was little knowing what they might encounter. Some well-educated people of the time even believed that in the uncharted interior woolly mammoths and giant ground sloths roamed vast grasslands, where erupting volcanoes and a mountain of pure salt might be found, and that the explorers could discover a utopia populated by blue-eyed Welsh-speaking natives.

But the Corps of Discovery expedition was driven by real political and commercial interests. The Louisiana Territory, including the entire western portion of the Mississippi River drainage basin to the Rocky Mountains, had just been bought from the French, and it was vital to explore the geography, flora, fauna and resources of the land acquired. Expedition leader Lewis was urged to cultivate alliances among the Indians to check Spanish and British influence and determine which areas were ripe for colonization.

Raised on a plantation in Virginia, Lewis spent his childhood in the forests and wilderness of the Shenandoah Valley. Aged twenty he had joined the army and quickly rose through the ranks while serving on the frontier in Ohio and Tennessee. He became the personal secretary of President Jefferson, an old family friend, in 1801. Tall, athletic and with an adventurous spirit, Lewis was a champion for an emerging nation.

In May 1804, with William Clark, with whom he had served in the Northwest Territory, Lewis led 40 team members west on the Missouri River. After spending a winter with the Mandan Indians, they travelled by boat 4,145 km (2,575 miles) to the rapids below the Great Falls of the Missouri. Having portaged around the falls, they continued upriver until they reached the Continental Divide and the prospect of a long trek across the Bitterroots: 'tremendous mountains which for 60 miles are covered with eternal snow'. Abandoned by their Indian guides, the Corps became disoriented in blizzards and deep snow. With the last of their salt pork gone and game scarce, the men resorted to eating their horses. In desperation, Clark and several hunters went ahead and eventually returned with fish and dried roots obtained by the Nez Perce Indians, along with vital information on a route to the Columbia River.

On 7 November 1805, Lewis wrote jubilantly in his journal 'O! the joy'; they could see the sea at last. At the mouth of the Columbia River they built Fort Clatsop, then made the arduous return journey home, splitting the party in two to cover more territory before reuniting in North Dakota. They had discovered over 300 new species of plants and animals, forged relations with many Indian tribes and mapped much of the Missouri River and Pacific Northwest, confirming that the new nation of the United States extended from the Atlantic to the Pacific. Furthermore, they had established the potential for a vast commercial empire, transporting pelts from the interior to the Columbia River estuary for trade with Asia.

Lewis – 'the greatest pathfinder our country has ever had' – received a hero's welcome. But by October 1809, Jefferson's young protégé was dead, shot at a remote inn on the perilous Tennessee Trail. According to his friends, he had found the pressures of his new-found celebrity overwhelming. A heavy drinker, it is possible he took his own life. A broken column, the symbol of a life cut short, marks his grave.

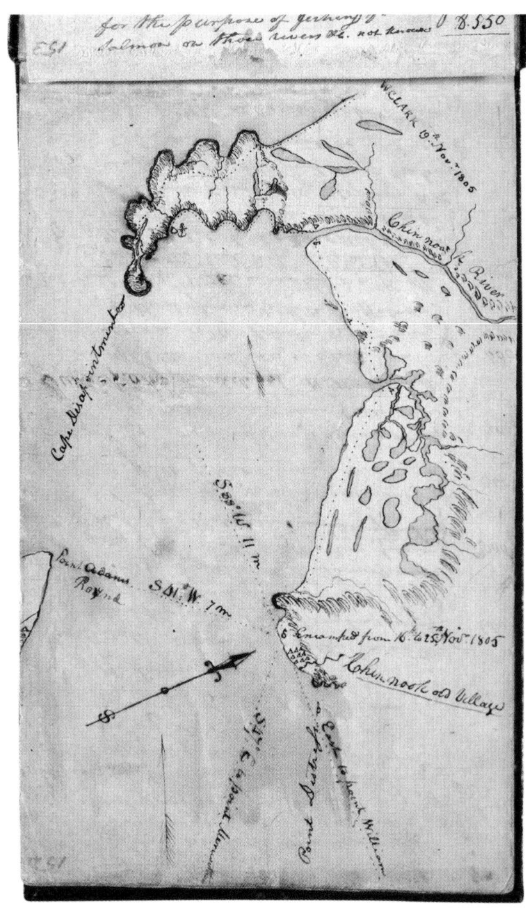

Sketch-map detailing Cape Disappointment, so named by English Captain John Meares in 1788 after he missed the passage to the Columbia River. For Lewis and Clark, it was a place of victory, where the Corps of Discovery achieved their principal mission of travelling across the continent to the Pacific Ocean.

Opposite: The Lewis and Clark journals consist of eighteen small notebooks of the type commonly used by surveyors in fieldwork. Thirteen of these are bound in red morocco leather, four in boards covered in marbled-paper and one in plain brown leather.

Lewis and Clark Codices.
Codex C. – Clark.
Journal
1804 – ... 1805.

Lewis and Clark Codices.
Codex A. – Clark.
Journal
May 13, 1804 – Aug. 14, 1804.
(complete.)
Clark's No. 1
Biddle's No. 1
Coues' A.
folios 92 – pages 184
Codex Aa
American Philosophical Society,
(FOUNDED 1743,)
104 SOUTH FIFTH STREET,
PHILADELPHIA.

Lewis and Clark Codices.
Codex D. – Lewis.
Journal
Apr. 7, 1805 – May 23, 1805.
Biddle's No. 4.
Coues' D.
American Philosophical Society
(FOUNDED 1743,)
104 SOUTH FIFTH STREET
PHILADELPHIA.

Lewis and Clark Codices.
Codex B. – Clark.
Journal
Aug. 15, 1804 – Oct. ...
(complete)
Clark's No. 2.
Biddle's No. 2.
Coues' B.
folios 90 pages 180
Codex Ba
American Philosophical Society,
(FOUNDED 1743,)
104 SOUTH FIFTH STREET,
PHILADELPHIA.

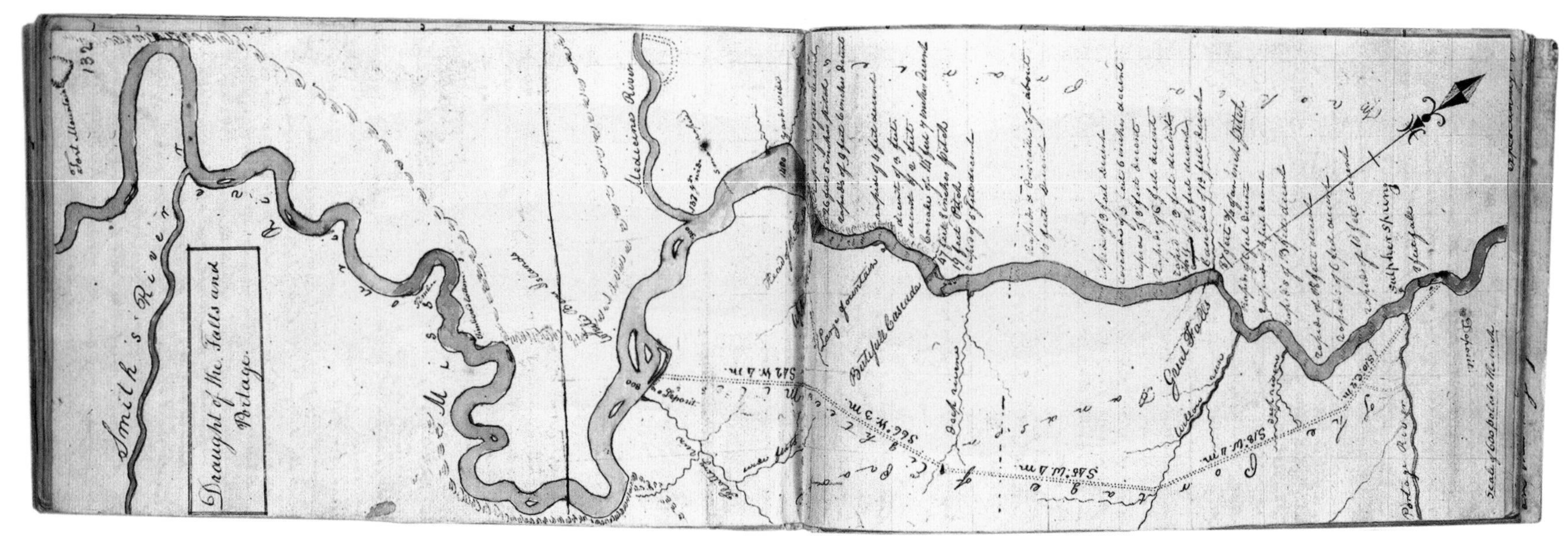

The journals of Lewis and Clark were filled with an enormous amount of data, from geographical and ethnographical notes to maps of each stage of their journey, observations on flora and fauna, and records of temperature and weather. This is a sketch of part of the Missouri River. They carried their notebooks sealed in tin boxes that were intended to protect them from the elements.

Pages from the expedition notebooks with drawings of a canoe and a salmon trout, along with copious notes. Time and again the Corps of Discovery realized the value of creating good relations with the Indians they met. Perhaps the most essential member on the team was Sacagawea, the Shoshone wife of their French Canadian interpreter. As Clark noted in his journal: ‘We find [that she] reconciles all Indians, as to our friendly intentions - a woman with a party of men is a token of peace.’ As a result, the Nez Perce Indians gave them food and shelter and advice on routes and canoe building, which ensured the eventual success of the expedition.

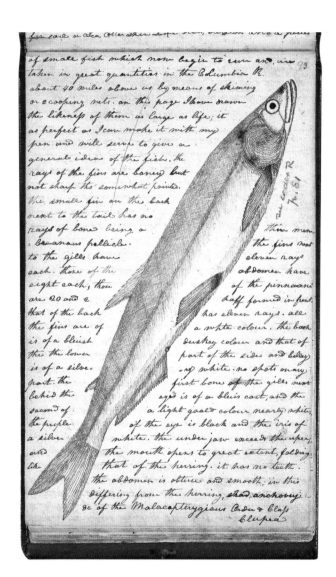

CARL LINNAEUS 1707-1778

In this dreary wilderness I began to feel very solitary, and to long earnestly for a companion.

On 12 May 1732, with the city of Uppsala behind him, 25-year-old botanist Carl Linnaeus strode out and headed north. Through the long Swedish winter he had spent many hours by the fire listening as his mentor, botanist and professor of medicine Olof Rudbeck, recounted stories of his expedition to Lapland 37 years earlier. Now, the old man enthused, it was Linnaeus's time to discover for himself the natural wonders of the wilderness.

Linnaeus first ambled up the Baltic coast. Over his shoulder was a leather bag in which he carried only the most essential equipment: a small dagger and spyglass, two maps, a letter of recommendation from the Royal Scientific Society of Uppsala, his journal and a parcel of paper stitched together in which he would dry plant specimens.

Having crossed miles of trackless country, Linnaeus finally arrived in Lapland and made his way to Jokkmokk. From there he crossed the Lapland Desert, then climbed the Lapland Alps. He explored valleys and lowlands, waded through wild rivers and marshes, and traversed mountains and glaciers with rain freezing into a crust of ice on his back. Some nights he shuddered violently with cold; on more fortunate occasions he ate reindeer tongue and sweet cheese with Sami nomads, and rested his head on pillows stuffed with reindeer fur.

During his five-month sojourn, Linnaeus covered some 7,700 km (4,785 miles) by boat and on horseback, and completed some 1,600 km (995 miles) on foot. He endured all manner of privations, had been shot at by a suspicious Lapp, was nearly swept over a precipice by violent winds and had narrowly missed being crushed by a rockslide. Despite all this, he had collected over a hundred specimens of plants new to science and filled his journal, *Iter Lapponicum*, with detailed notes and sketches, describing everything from the flora and fauna of Lapland to the beliefs and daily lives of the Sami. These formed the basis of his first book, *Flora Lapponica*.

Linnaeus's fascination with nature had started early. The son of a pastor, he was born in the countryside of Småland, in southern Sweden. When not exploring nearby marshlands and meadows, he spent his childhood tending the rectory garden with his father. This pastime, Linnaeus remembered, 'inflamed my mind from infancy onwards with an unquenchable love of plants'. It would also decisively influence the young botanist's life-work. One day his father, exasperated by his five-year-old son's forgetfulness, refused to tell him the name of another plant unless he promised to remember it. Linnaeus later said that from that moment on, he was determined 'heart and soul' to commit to memory every new plant name he was told. In years to come Linnaeus would lay the foundations for the modern biological naming scheme of binomial nomenclature used today, and would become known as the father of modern taxonomy.

Linnaeus continued to travel, and, in 1735, qualified as a doctor of medicine and was later appointed physician to the Swedish royal family. However, his plant studies and teaching remained the focus of his life. He was much loved by his students, and he actively encouraged them to travel the world in pursuit of science. Named by *Time* magazine as the fifth most influential scientist in history, he has been called the Prince of Botanists. As Swiss philosopher Jean-Jacques Rousseau declared, he knew of 'no greater man on earth'.

We reposed ourselves about six o'clock in the morning, wrung the water out of our clothes, and dried our weary limbs, while the cold north wind parched us as much on one side as the fire scorched us on the other, and the gnats kept inflicting their stings. I had now my fill of travelling.

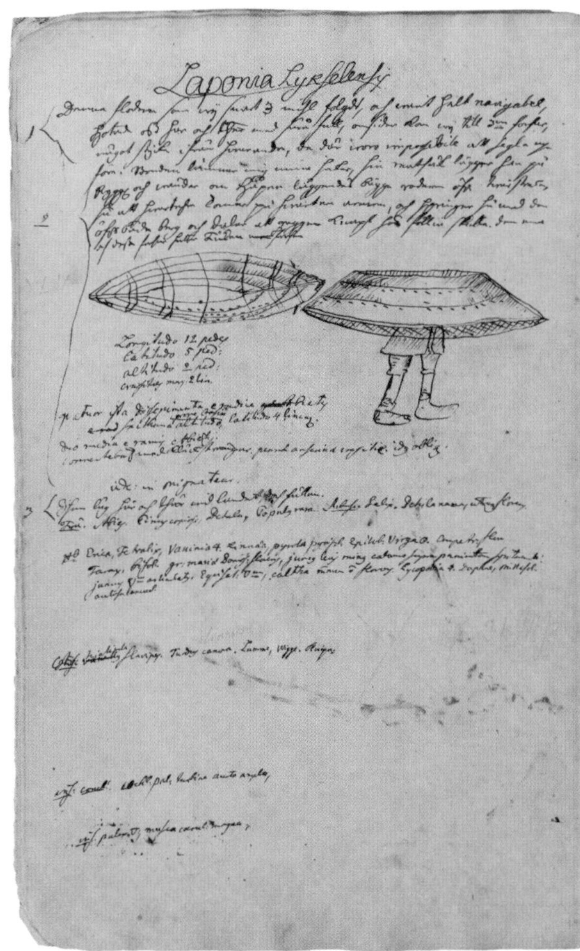

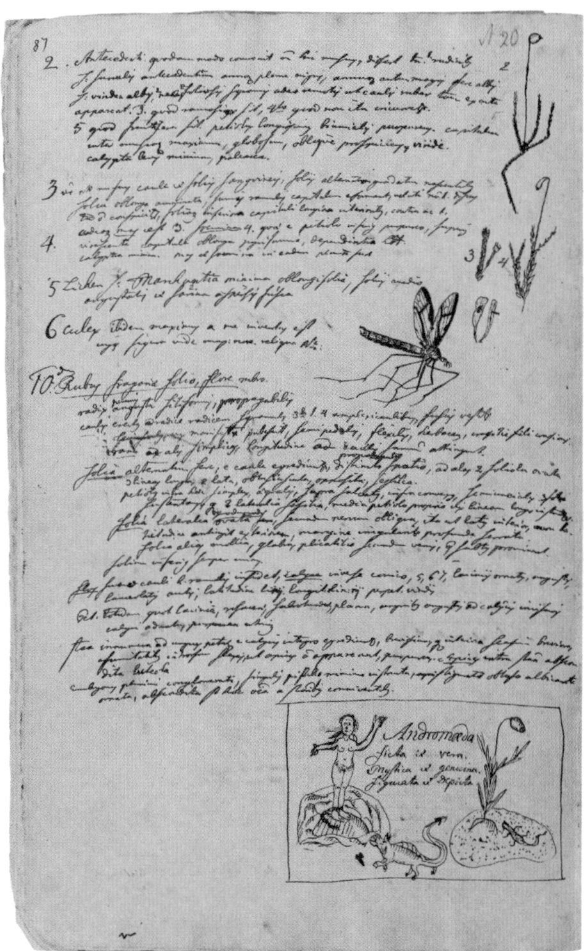

Linnaeus's Lapland journal, *Iter Lapponicum*, held in the Linnean Society of London's collections and illustrated with drawings of plants, animals and Lapps, formed the basis of his first book, *Flora Lapponica*, which was pivotal in establishing the reputation of the young botanist. This journal records every aspect of travel in the country, including a drawing of a Sami carrying his boat and details of its construction.

Far right: Linnaeus was particularly taken with a pink-flowered shrub he discovered in Lapland, which he named *Andromeda polifolia*, establishing a new genus based upon the allegory of Ovid's tale of Andromeda chained to the rocks as a sacrifice to the sea dragon, as illustrated by Linnaeus at the bottom of the page.

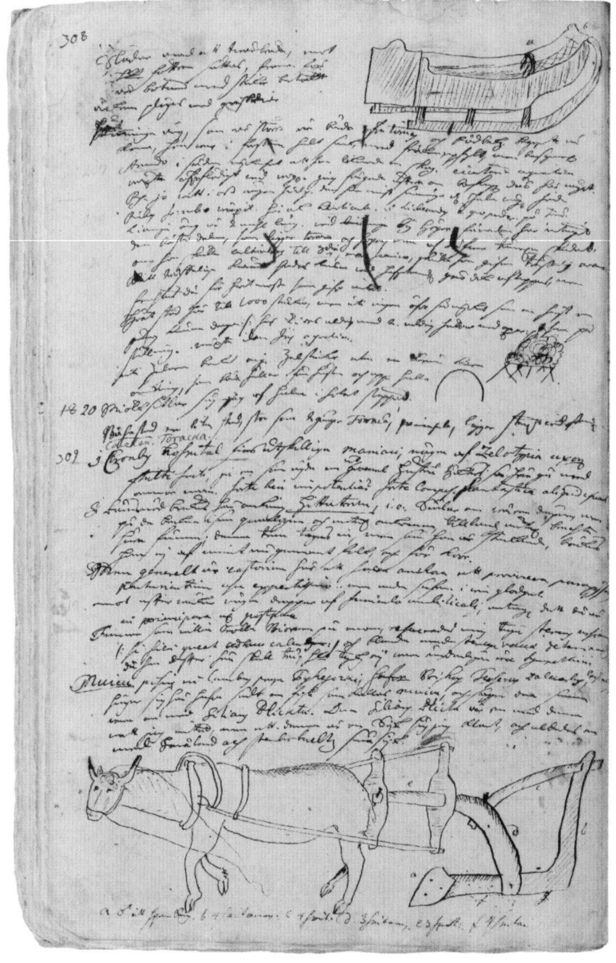

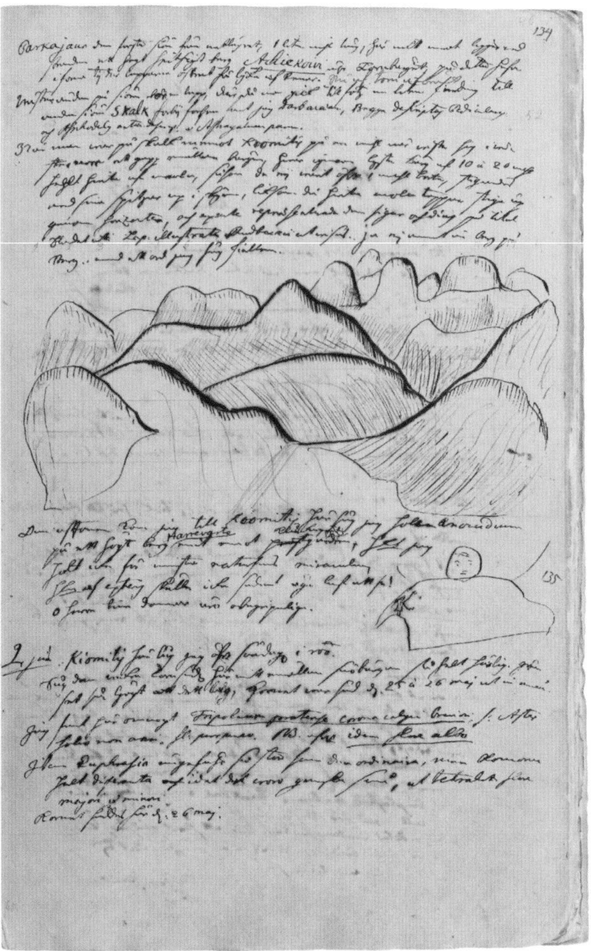

Pages from Linnaeus's Lapland journal, revealing his interest in everything he saw, including, opposite left, a drawing of a board game. He would go on to publish over 170 scientific works. After his death, his manuscripts and botanical, zoological and library collections, including his herbarium, were bought by the British botanist James Edward Smith and were subsequently acquired by the Linnean Society of London. Today, the Society continues to play a central role in the documentation of the world's flora and fauna - as Linnaeus himself did - recognizing the continuing importance of such work to biodiversity conservation.

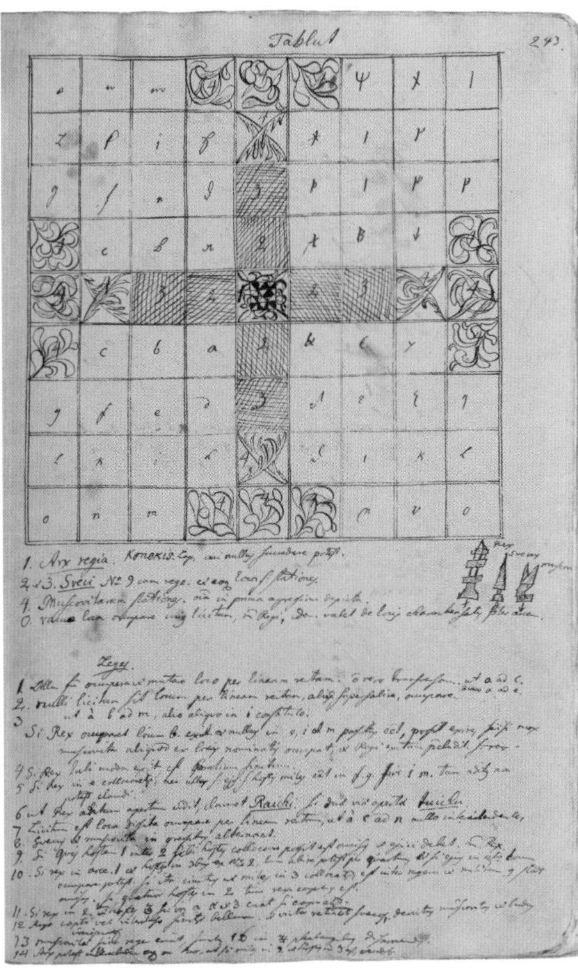

Overleaf: Linnaeus was a champion of the Swiss botanist Gaspard Bauhin's idea of giving all living things two names. Combining the theory of binomial nomenclature with his unique system of sexual identification, Linnaeus laid the foundations for a radically new form of classification. Although Linnaeus's proposal initially outraged his peers, his method would become standard. The page of a classification of insects is from Linnaeus's *Manuscripta Medica*. In *Spolia Botanica*, a short catalogue, Linnaeus classified plants from three different regions of Sweden (Småland, Scania and Roslagia) according to three different systems.

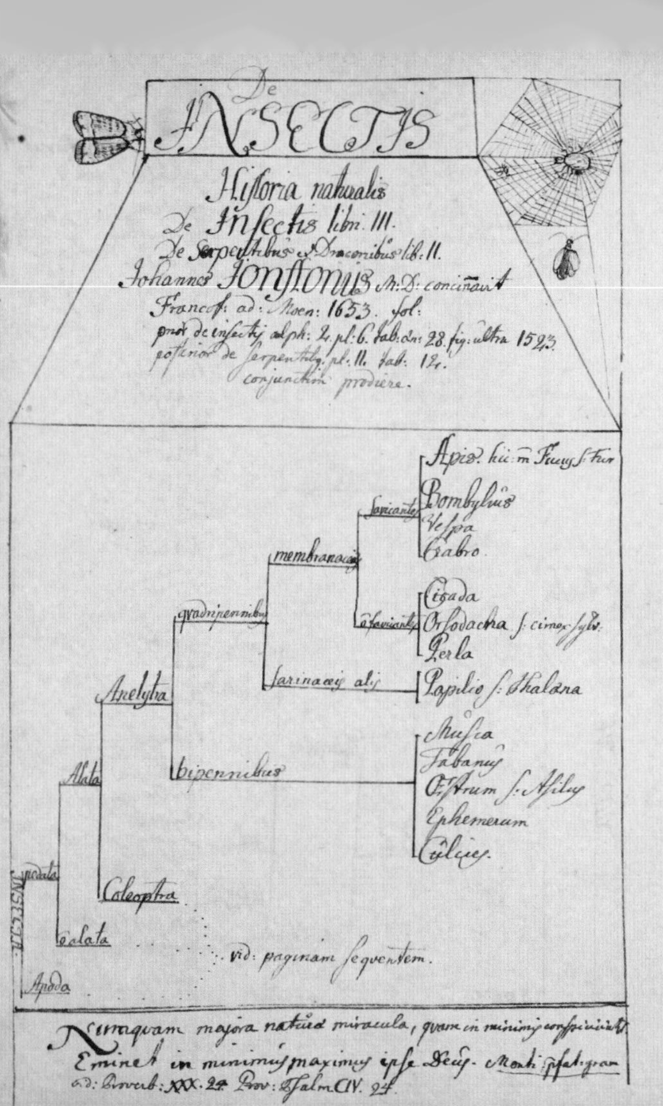

De Insectis

Historia naturalis
De Insectis libri III.
De Serpentibus & Draconibus lib: II.
Johannes Jonstonius M: D: concinnavit
Francof: ad: Moen: 1653. fol:
prior de insectis alph: 4. pl: 6. tab: aen: 28. fig: ultra 1523
posterior de serpentibus pl: II. tab: 12.
conjunctim prodiere.

INSECTA
pedata
Alata
Anelytra
quadripennibus
membranaceis
Saevientes
Apis. hic: m Fucus s. Fur
Bombylius
Vespa
Crabro
a saevientibus
Cicada
Orsodachna s. cimex sylv.
Perla
farinaceis alis
Papilio s. Phalaena
bipennibus
Musca
Tabanus
Oestrum s. Asilus
Ephemerum
Culices
Coleoptra
Exalata
Apoda

vid: paginam sequentem.

Nunquam majora naturae miracula, quam in minimis conspiciuntur.
Eminet in minimis maximus ipse Deus. Mont: praefat: gram
vid: Proverb: XXX. 24. Prov: Psalm CIV. 24.

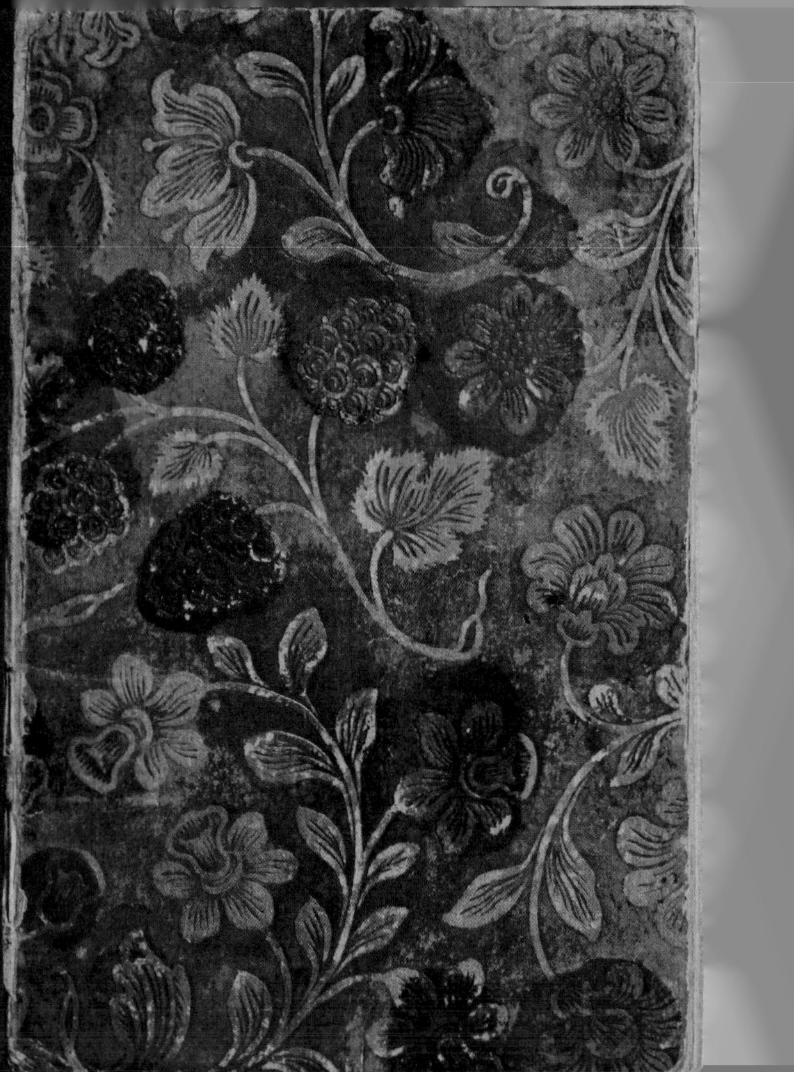

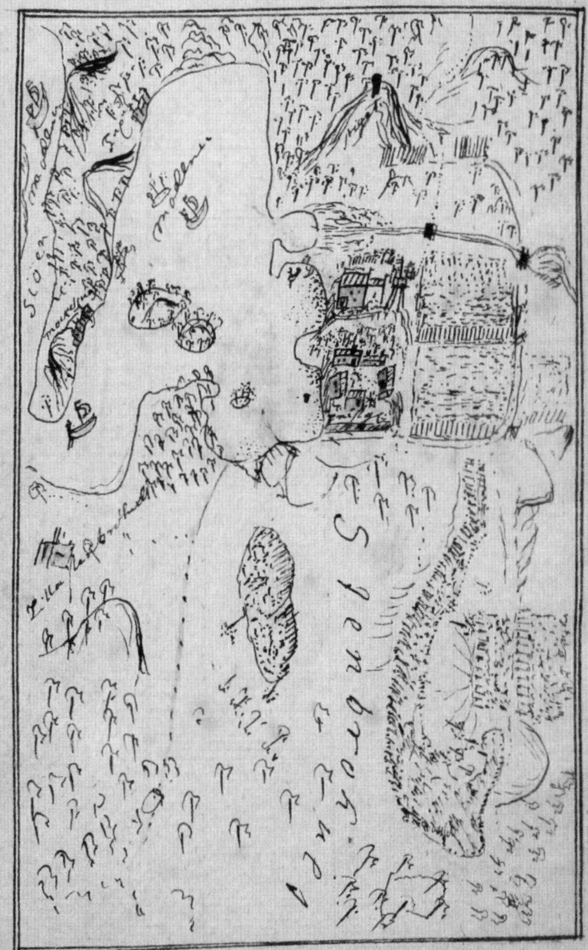

E Bibl. Linn. propriâ. 1784. J E Smith.

Spolia Botanica

sive

Plantæ Rariores

per

SMOLANDIAM

Scaniam

et

ROSLAGIAM

observata

et

enumerata

a

Carolo Linnæo Smoland.

Med: Bot: et Zool: Cult.

Stipend: Reg.

Upsal: 1729.

DAVID LIVINGSTONE 1813-1873

It had never been seen before by European eyes; but scenes so lovely must have been gazed upon by angels in their flight.

Scottish explorer-missionary David Livingstone endured heat, rains and mud, fever, dysentery and malaria, and hostile tribesmen and slave-traders ready to rob or kill him, but was sustained throughout by his faith and iron will. Born to a poor and pious family at Blantyre, Lanarkshire, Livingstone was working in a cotton mill by the age of ten. By 27 he had qualified as a doctor, been ordained and was exploring the interior of South Africa, searching for sites for new mission stations for the London Missionary Society.

Restless, driven and insatiably curious, Livingstone soon realized that opening up the continent was a means to further his missionary work. His journeys took him across the Kalahari, and in 1851 he reached the Zambezi. From Linyanti on the Chobe, he travelled across the Zambezi-Congo watershed to Loanda in west Africa and from there back to the east coast at Quilimane, discovering Victoria Falls en route. His 8,000-km (5,000-mile) journey encompassed the first authenticated crossing of the continent from coast to coast by a European.

Livingstone's vivid published accounts were a sensation in Britain and America. Through him the mysterious 'Dark Continent' came alive. Here was a man who had walked away from a lion attack, and had battled through thorny undergrowth, feverish, bleeding and exhausted, to discover great lakes, rivers, dense forests and verdant plains. There was one discovery yet to be made that drove him on, though he never succeeded: the discovery of the source of the Nile.

Nearing the age of 60, Livingstone reached the Congolese town of Nyangwe, one of the main slave-trading centres of the region. On 15 July 1871, a 'bright, sultry summer morning' turned into one of horror, as Arab slavers opened fire on the local inhabitants. Livingstone took cover and documented the barbaric scene: 'shot after shot falls on the fugitives ... who are wailing loudly over those they know are already slain – Oh let thy kingdom come.' Hundreds of villagers died in the massacre. It is remarkable that Livingstone's testimony survives: he had run out of paper and had to resort to using scraps of newspaper for his journal and the juice of berries for ink.

In Britain, Livingstone was presumed dead, or at the very least to have 'gone native'. While Livingstone was at Nyangwe, newspaper reporter Henry Morton Stanley set out in search of the 'lost' explorer. Eight months later, the young journalist was gazing in astonishment upon one of the most recognizable faces in exploration. Their famous meeting was immortalized by Stanley's words: 'Dr Livingstone, I presume?' – a phrase parodied to this day. The triumphant Stanley returned to Britain carrying Livingstone's prized Lett's Diary, letters and geographical reports. His account of his meeting with Livingstone was the first sensational news story to break simultaneously on both sides of the Atlantic.

Livingstone died in May 1873 near the headwaters of the Congo. He had lived and travelled among the African people for most of his life. His devoted companions buried his heart in a tin box under a tree where he had died, then carried his embalmed body to the coast, from where it was shipped back to Britain. In April 1874, Livingstone's body was interred with full honours in Westminster Abbey. His extraordinary rise from child factory-worker to national hero was complete.

Livingstone's eyewitness account of the Nyangwe massacre (above is a published illustration of it), written in berry juice on an old newspaper page torn from *The Standard*, led to the closure of the slave market in Zanzibar, a critical hub for East Africa's slave traffickers. The fragile paper and unusual ink made it indecipherable until recently, when spectral imaging technology was used to decode it.

XLVI Journal 15th July 1871

The reports of guns on the other side
of Lualaba tell of Dugumbe's men
murdering Kimburu and another for
slaves = Manilla is in it again = and
it is said that Tamwana gave him
3 slaves to sack the ten villages we
saw in flames = he is meeting his doom
in spite of mixing blood and giving
nine slaves for the operation = [illegible]
Nomenganga was his victim [illegible]
* [illegible] making one [illegible] to go
with Dugumbe's people to be [illegible]
in their blood quarrels

Chitoka about 1500 people came
though many villages were burning
before us = I saw three of Dugumbe's
people with guns in the market place
[illegible] wondered but thought it ignorance
and retired when 50 yards off two guns
were fired and a general flight took
place = [illegible] thrown away in terror
firing on the helpless canoes took
place = a long line of heads in the water
showed the numbers that would perish
for they could not swim two miles
shot after shot followed on the terrified
fugitives = great numbers died =
and a worthless Moslem asserted
that all was done by the people of the
English = this was spread through [illegible]
murderers are on the other side plundering
and shooting = It is awful = terrible
a dreadful world this = as I write
shot after shot falls on the fugitives
on the other side who are wailing loudly
over those they know are already
slain = Oh let thy kingdom come =

Went down to the confluence of the Misinjé and came to many of the eatable insect 'kungu' – they are caught by a quick motion of the hand holding a basket. We got a cake of these same insects further down; they make a buzz like a swarm of bees.

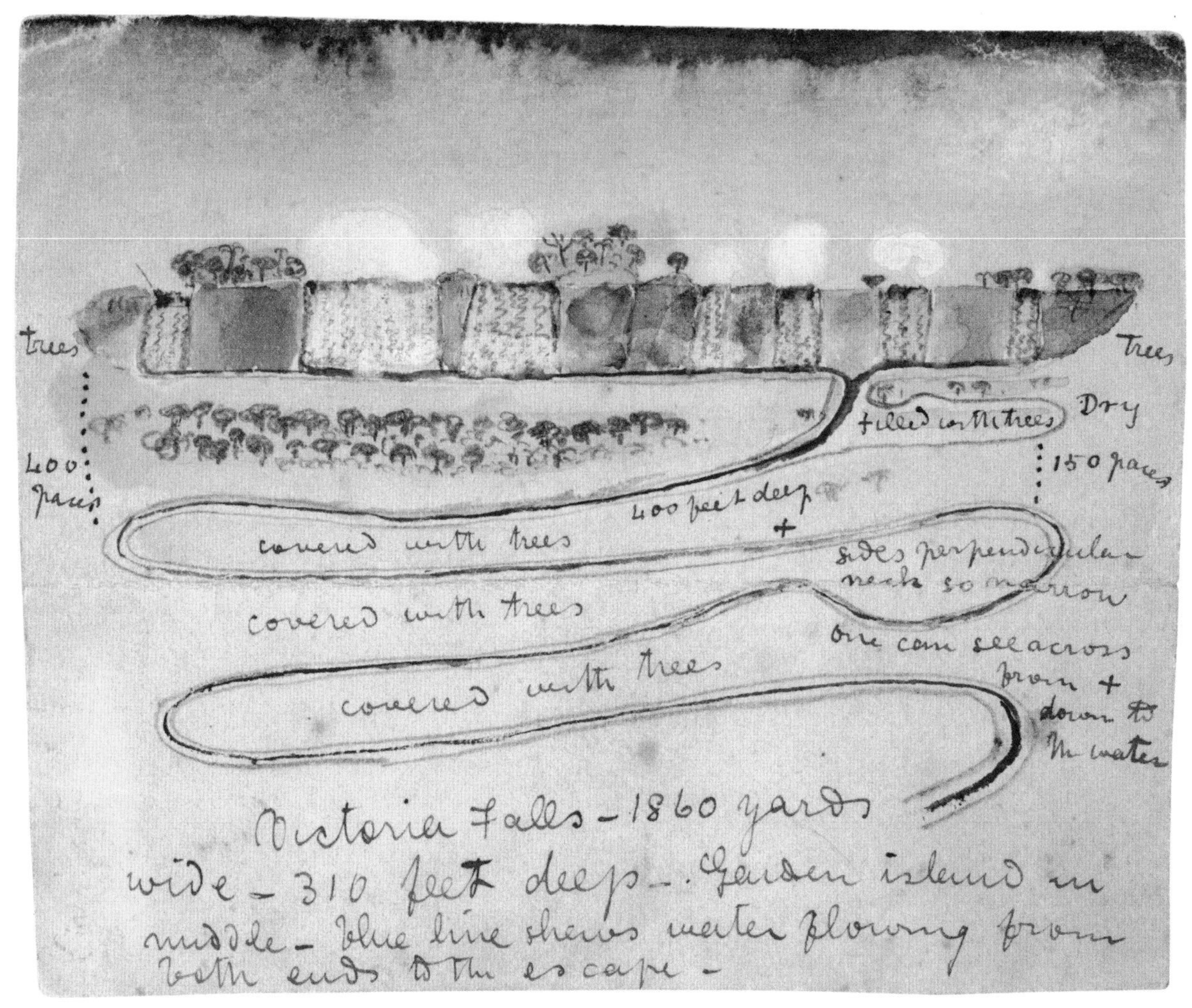

Livingstone's watercolour sketch of Victoria Falls is thought to date from his second visit in August 1860. The sketch is a means to document the width, height and configuration of the gorges cut by the Zambezi.

Opposite left: A committed diarist, Livingstone filled his journals with measurements of longitudes and latitudes, altitudes and rainfall, and maps. His map of Lake Shirwa and the River Shire, 1859, shows the route he took during his Zambezi expedition. Wherever possible, every creature, insect or plant was recorded.

Opposite right: Stanley continued Livingstone's geographical investigations and circumnavigated Lake Victoria, confirming it as the source of the White Nile. His hand-drawn pencil sketch of 1875 is the first time the lake's outline, in blue, was reasonably accurately mapped.

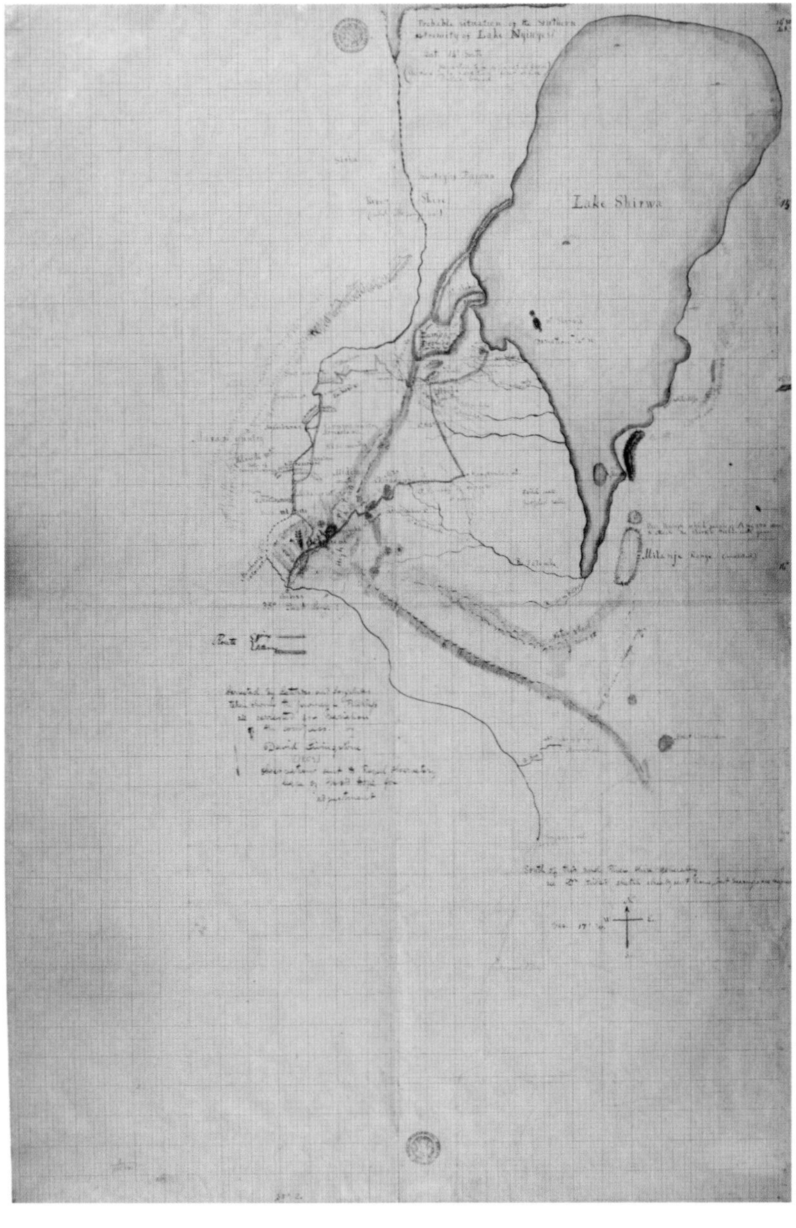

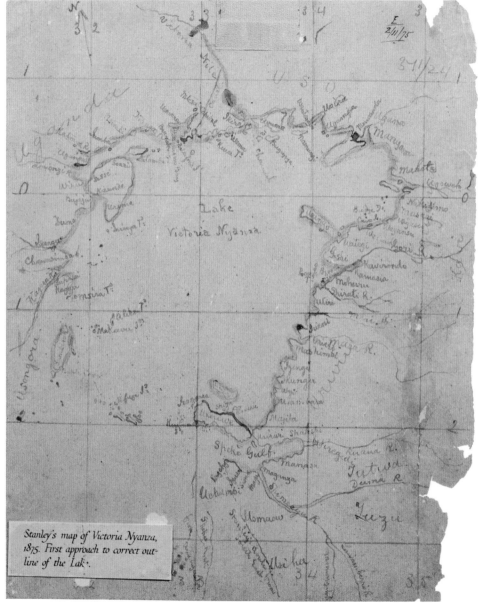

Stanley's map of Victoria Nyanza, 1875. First approach to correct outline of the Lak'.

GEORGE LOWE 1924–2013

Before we arrived Everest was still a dream. It was available for doubt and uncertainty. It still remained that way after we left. Within days the drifting snows had covered our footprints.

George Lowe, mountaineer and photographer, played a crucial role in the first ascent of Everest in 1953. His skills on steep ice – as much as his energy and sense of humour – were of huge benefit to the team, and his efforts greatly helped his best friend Ed Hillary reach the summit on 29 May. Lowe forged the route up Everest's Lhotse Face without oxygen and later cut steps for his partners up the summit ridge. It was Lowe who first embraced Hillary and Tenzing as they made their way down from the summit. He had been watching their progress from high on the South Col and climbed up to meet them. Hillary grinned, and after a short rest, looked up at his old friend, saying in his matter-of-fact way: 'Well, George, we knocked the bastard off!'

Lowe was born in New Zealand and grew up in Hastings, a small town on the North Island, the seventh child of a fruit farmer. He first met Hillary while working in the Southern Alps just after the Second World War and they soon struck up a friendship and tackled many peaks together. Once, trapped in a mountain hut waiting out a storm, they started planning and dreaming of greater climbs.

Throughout his travels, Lowe wrote letters home to his family. On his early expeditions the letters served as his journal, a sketchbook of memories, full of minor details and significant events. The majority of the letters Lowe wrote from Everest were to his sister Betty, who then made several hand-written copies to share with the family. In turn, they would then keep a wide circle of admirers updated with news, frequently before the local newspapers had full accounts of the climb. Yet these letters were more than just news – Lowe wrote in case he and Hillary never returned to tell the tale.

On the Everest expedition on the march out from Kathmandu Lowe wrote copiously, relaxing by streams in the morning sunshine or scribbling by hurricane lamp into the night, often too excited to sleep. As they climbed ever higher on the mountain, writing became increasingly difficult. From Camp III on 8 May: 'I've just had to have the ink bottle thawed over the primus to fill my pen – I had it in my boot thinking it may have escaped the cold – temperatures at night here are recorded at -30°F.' Halfway up the Lhotse Face and running out of ink, he radioed down to the lower camps and soon one of his companions lent him a much-coveted biro pen, in return for some extra tins of tomato juice.

After the success of Everest, Lowe and Hillary were invited on the Trans-Antarctic Expedition led by Vivian Fuchs, which traversed Antarctica. Lowe, ever versatile, was given the job of filming and photography, while also assisting in the sounding experiments that enabled a profile of the continent to be drawn beneath the ice, as well as daily tasks. He even found time to read *War and Peace* while driving standing up with his head out the roof of his snow-vehicle.

Lowe was a gentle soul, a fine climber and a wonderful man – funny, generous, positive in his approach to life and humble in his success. In 1958, after almost 100 days of driving over endless ice, dodging crevasses in whiteouts that frequently imperilled their lives, he was exhausted. Which journey was better, the journalists asked, Everest or Antarctica? 'Everest every time', Lowe replied with a smile. 'It's too dull here. One day's the same as another.'

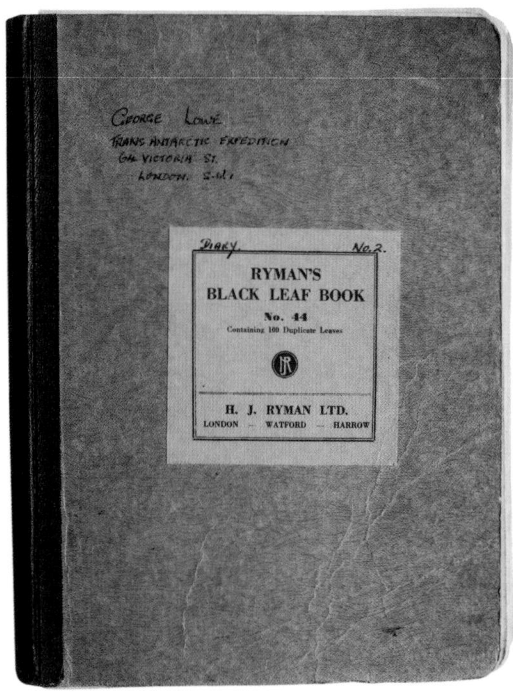

The cover and pages from Lowe's journal during the Trans-Antarctic Expedition. The drawing explains how they managed to recover a Sno-Cat wedged in a crevasse that had opened up unexpectedly beneath it. Overwintering in Antarctica, Lowe had a darkroom in the hut to process and develop film, and he carried many prints in his journal for safekeeping. From the South Pole he flew a batch of film back to London, and developed the remainder at Scott Base.

An attempt was made to fill in the hole. Within an hour of furious digging the change was unbelievable but true – Snow had been filled in to within five feet of the dangling under side.

Then a new & well worthwhile suggestion was made by Ralph. that of using the crevasse bridge to support the rear pontoons as Abel was pulled forwards & out. This was done in a couple of hours. – like this

WRACK + RUIN
RUMBLE
(Tension wire to hold)
Two cats in tandem ahead pulled Abel cleanly out
Crevasse bridge just spanned the distance & was anchored by ropes & (dead-men)
Snow filled in
Sledges pulled away

Abel emerged, to everybody delight & surprise quite undamaged. At 11 pm. we camped.

Monday. 19th December. 1957.

Probing & moving – all in these last days in cloudless blazing hot sunshine – We were sunburnt to a soreness most uncomfortable.

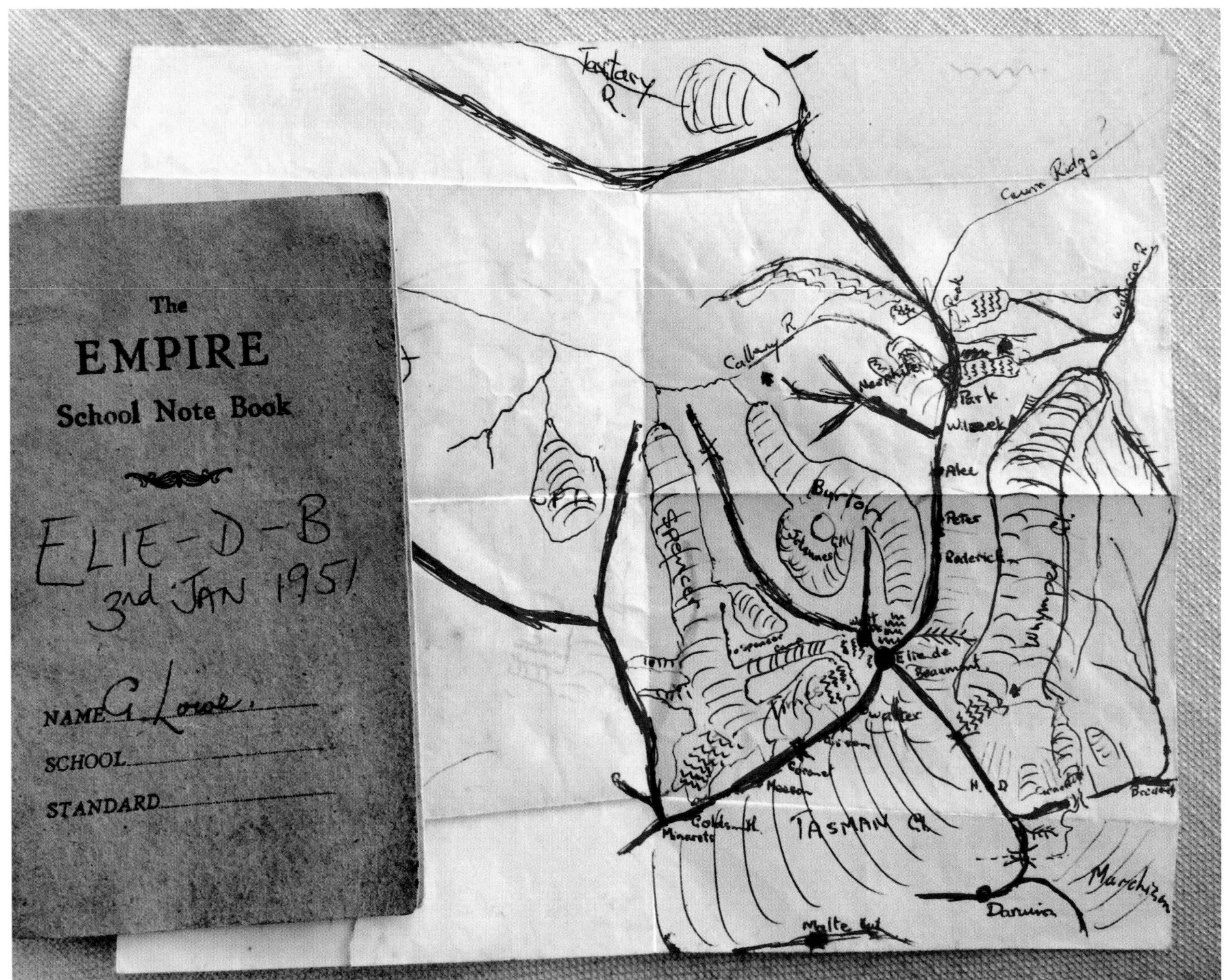
The
EMPIRE
School Note Book
ELIE-D-B
3rd JAN 1951
NAME G. Lowe.
SCHOOL
STANDARD
Callery R
Burton
Spencer
Elie de Beaumont
Walter
Coronet
TASMAN Gl.
Minarets
Darwin
Malte Brun
Park
Alec
Peters
Roderick
Whymper
Marchison

Base Camp.
2nd June

BRITISH MOUNT EVEREST EXPEDITION, 1953

(Himalayan Joint Committee of the Royal Geographical Society and the Alpine Club)

Dear Betty, Mum, Dad & all,

This will be short as the mail-runner is off to-morrow with all the important despatches & cables.

Probably at this hour or half day you will hear by radio of our success: Ed & Tenzing reached the summit at 11.30 last Friday 29th May. I was watching them from S. Col & went up to meet them on their descent to camp. It was quite a terrific moment. N.Z. was well to the front - as well as the Lhotse face work I got onto S. Col where I spent 4 nights & 5 days & carried a 50 lb load to Camp IX at 27900 ft.

I hope to tell you in detail of the last ten days as we march out to Katmandu.

We reached Base on 31st May & arrived absolutely played out & to-day - after two days of sleeping & eating we are just perking up.

To-day is a great day we are all around the wireless listening to the coronation service. The crown is just being placed & there is quite a hush amongst the boys.

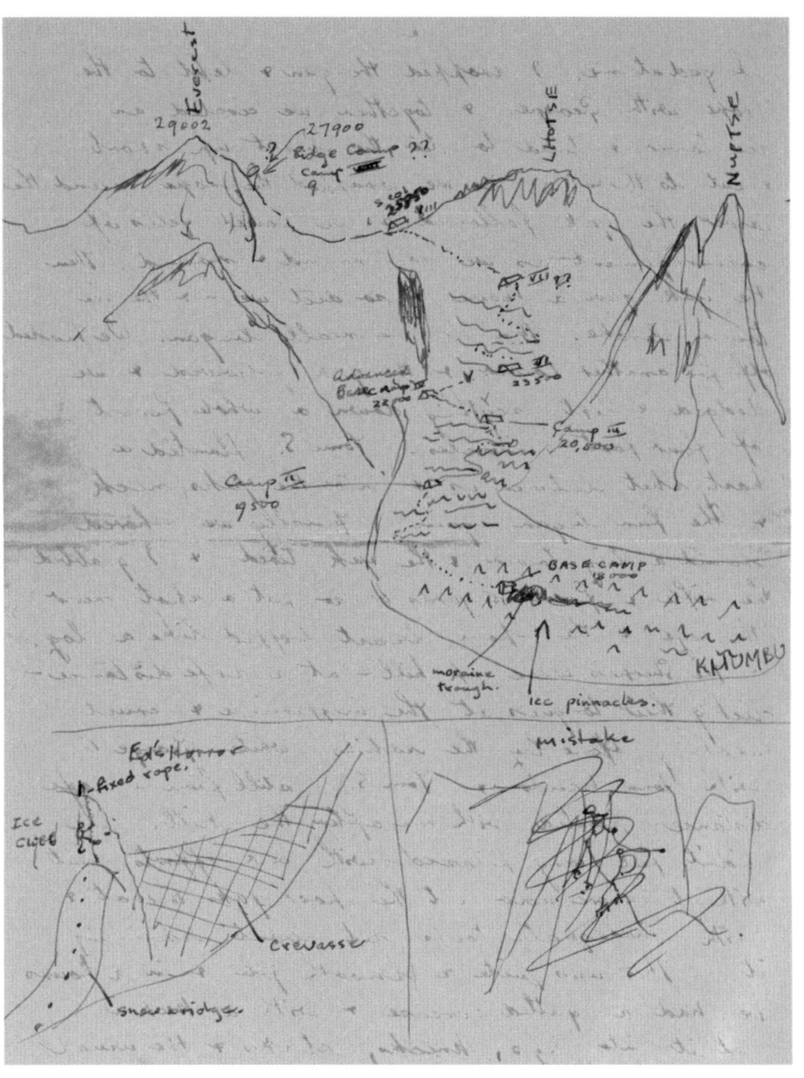

Opposite: Lowe's notebook and sketch-map from his 1951 climb of Mount Elie de Beaumont, where the objective was the striking Maximilian Ridge. Just to reach the foot of this ascent took several days of exploring, carrying heavy loads. It was one of many early New Zealand climbs that forged a lifetime friendship with Ed Hillary.

In 1953 on Everest, Lowe was able to fill in all the details of his experiences at length when back at Base Camp. These rare letters from the mountain provide a vivid, behind-the-scenes eyewitness account of a climb that would make history.

MAXIMILIAN DE WIED 1782-1867

This tent was large and painted red; at the top of the poles composing it some scalps fluttered in the wind.

Out of the dark thicket the warriors emerged. Aboard his river boat, Prince Alexander Philipp Maximilian de Wied waited anxiously for the strangers to make their intentions known. These 23 armed men dressed in white buffalo robes were Yanktonans, with a reputation as the most dangerous of all the Sioux. Indicating they came in peace, Chief Tatanka-Kta shared a pipe with Maximilian and his companions, and asked if they would negotiate a reconciliation with their warring neighbours. Two days later, the party were received by 600 'remarkably tall and handsome' Mandans, their painted warriors riding on panther skins and carrying whips of elk's horn. It was, Maximilian noted, 'a novel and highly interesting scene'.

By the time of this encounter in northwest America, 50-year-old German aristocrat Maximilian had experienced a great many adventures. He had participated in twelve battles as a major in the Prussian army, and had been a prisoner of war and awarded the Order of the Iron Cross for bravery. In 1814, at the end of the Napoleonic War, Maximilian had met Alexander von Humboldt in Paris, who had just returned from his five-year exploration of South America. The venerable explorer had a profound influence on the prince, becoming his friend and mentor. Passionately interested in ethnology and zoology, Maximilian resolved to leave the army and embark on his own expedition to South America.

Throughout 1815-17 Maximilian devoted himself to the exploration and scientific observation of the primeval forests of eastern Brazil. Despite battling constant rain and fever, he collected and catalogued thousands of specimens, and meticulously recorded every encounter with the indigenous people in his journals. On his return to Europe, Maximilian wrote up his findings, including *Reise nach Brasilien* – a monograph on the language and customs of the Botocudo people – now recognized as one of the great contributions to our knowledge of Brazil at the beginning of the nineteenth century.

Maximilian then set out for the 'desolate' prairies and mountain regions of northwest America in 1832, with the aim of providing a faithful record of the flora, fauna and indigenous peoples of the region before they were overtaken or extirpated by the tide of emigration from the Old World. From Boston he headed west with two men under his employ: artist Karl Bodmer and his brother's huntsman, David Dreidoppel. For the next two years they crossed the United States, navigating the Missouri River on steamships belonging to the American Fur Company. At Fort McKenzie they witnessed a bloody attack on an encampment of Blackfeet by Assiniboin and Cree Indians; in North Dakota, suffering from near starvation and scurvy, Maximilian spent five months studying the cultures of the Arikara, Hidatsa and Mandan Indians. At times, the temperatures plummeted so low that Bodmer's paints froze while he was trying to complete his portraits.

Although his huge collection of specimens was lost in a fire on his ship, Maximilian eventually returned home with more than 400 paintings by Bodmer, two live grizzly bear cubs, vocabularies of over twenty Indian languages and journals that ran into hundreds of thousands of words. His work provides one of the most complete and accurate records of the traditions and customs of many vibrant Indian nations before smallpox devastated the indigenous people of the Great Plains.

A shrunken head sketched during Maximilian's expedition to Brazil. He was a believer in recording absolutely everything that could be of interest. Each new species discovered, or indigenous tribe encountered, was captured in detail in his field journals and notebooks.

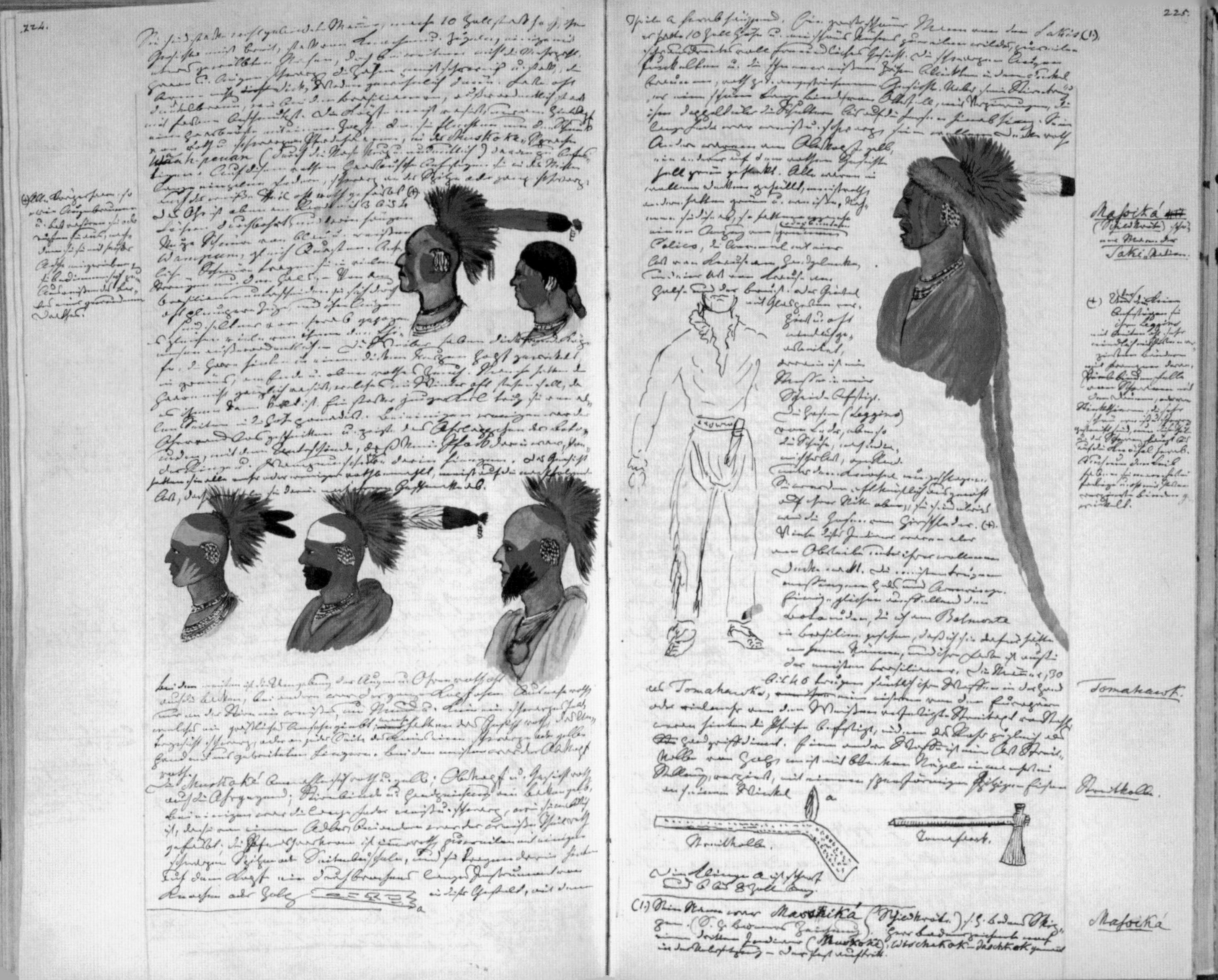
Tomahawk
Streitkolbe
Masoïka

Maximilian explored the southeastern regions of Brazil in 1815-17, returning with a wealth of information about the native flora and fauna and, most significantly, the Puri and Botocudo peoples. His treatise was later regarded as a pioneering ethnographic work. These sketches from October 1816 show 'shipping on the Rio Grande de Bellmonte' and, opposite, the Botocudos swimming in the river.

Badende Botocuden
im Rio Grande de Belmonte
October 1816.

Der Jäger beschleicht die Araras am
Rio Grande de Belmonte. Im October 1816.

A hunter stalks a flock of macaws on the banks of the Rio Grande in 1816, and, opposite, a dance of the Camacan in 1817.

Tanz der Camacans. Im Märtz. 1817.

MARGARET MEE 1909-1988

Go home, you can leave me. I have slept with jaguars.

Aged 47, British botanical artist Margaret Mee packed her artist's kit, journal, spare clothes and a revolver into a canvas rucksack, and headed into the Amazon Basin in search of rare plants and flowers. Over the coming months she travelled by dugout canoe with a local guide through the region of the Gurupi, a tributary of the Amazon River, pausing to record the flora in the canopies of trees they passed. She returned to her husband in São Paulo inspired: Amazonia, she declared, was now in her blood. She would spend almost four decades in Brazil, becoming a pioneering voice in conservation, and travelling more extensively in the Amazon than any other Western woman.

Mee's interest in art and travel was encouraged by her Aunt Nell, an illustrator of children's books, and her maternal grandfather, who had travelled the world for seven years waiting for his intended to accept his marriage proposal. Mee spent the war years as a draughtswoman in an aircraft factory, then, when peace was declared, studied art in London. She first travelled to Brazil with artist Greville Mee, later her husband. What was intended to be a two-year holiday became a lifetime's fascination. Short excursions to paint the luxuriant flora and hummingbirds in Brazil's southern coastal mountains only whetted Mee's appetite for longer journeys that would take her deep into the Amazon Basin.

Mee worked only from living plants, producing skilful renderings of the flora she discovered during her fifteen perilous plant-hunting expeditions. She returned each time with vibrant landscape paintings and meticulous botanical studies that allowed for precise identification of the species, several of which were new to science. These detailed and colour-accurate plant portraits established her reputation. Her work stands as one of the finest records of Amazonian plants and their habitats ever made. Sadly, it is now a record of a vanishing world. Mee's travels coincided with the beginning of commercial exploitation of the rainforests; she would become one of the first environmentalists to draw attention to the devastating impact of large-scale mining and deforestation in Amazonia. Many of the plants she drew are now extinct.

Petite and frail-looking, she was nevertheless a determined and fearless traveller. In her search for botanical treasures Mee journeyed thousands of miles, often alone, through remote and dangerous regions. She survived several shipwrecks; nearly died of hepatitis, malaria and starvation; held off drunken prospectors with her pistol and endured attacks by vampire bats and legions of stinging ants and biting flies. She continued her journeys well into her 70s, despite having an artificial hip and another that needed replacing.

Mee's long-held ambition was to paint the rare Amazonian Moonflower, which blooms and dies in a single night. It took 24 years of searching before she finally discovered the perfect specimen in 1988. Thrilled with her discovery, she waited patiently until the buds opened. Intoxicated by its strong perfume, the full moon and the sound of the night birds, she sketched by the light of a fluorescent torch. She was 78. Just five months later, she died in a car accident in England, shortly before the opening of a major exhibition of her paintings at Kew Gardens. She is remembered by colleagues for her courage and gentleness and her tireless struggle for the preservation of the flora, fauna and peoples of the Amazon rainforest. Her ashes were scattered beside the Moonflower.

I had to climb on top of the boat with all my sketching materials ... and sit down in front of the bud, waiting for it open. And it moved as it opened, you could see it opening. This was thrilling. And as it opened, a wonderful perfume came out, to attract the [hawk] moth ... which pollinates it. There was a full moon ... magnificent. And all the time the sound of the night birds.

Mee spent 24 years trying to discover an Amazonian Moonflower (*Selenicereus wittii*), which blooms at night, with its buds about to open. Aged 78, she finally found one ready to flower. She climbed on top of her boat with all her sketching materials and waited. Using a torch in the moonlight, she watched the flower move and open, and carefully drew it before it withered and died. It was, she recalled, a 'magnificent' moment.

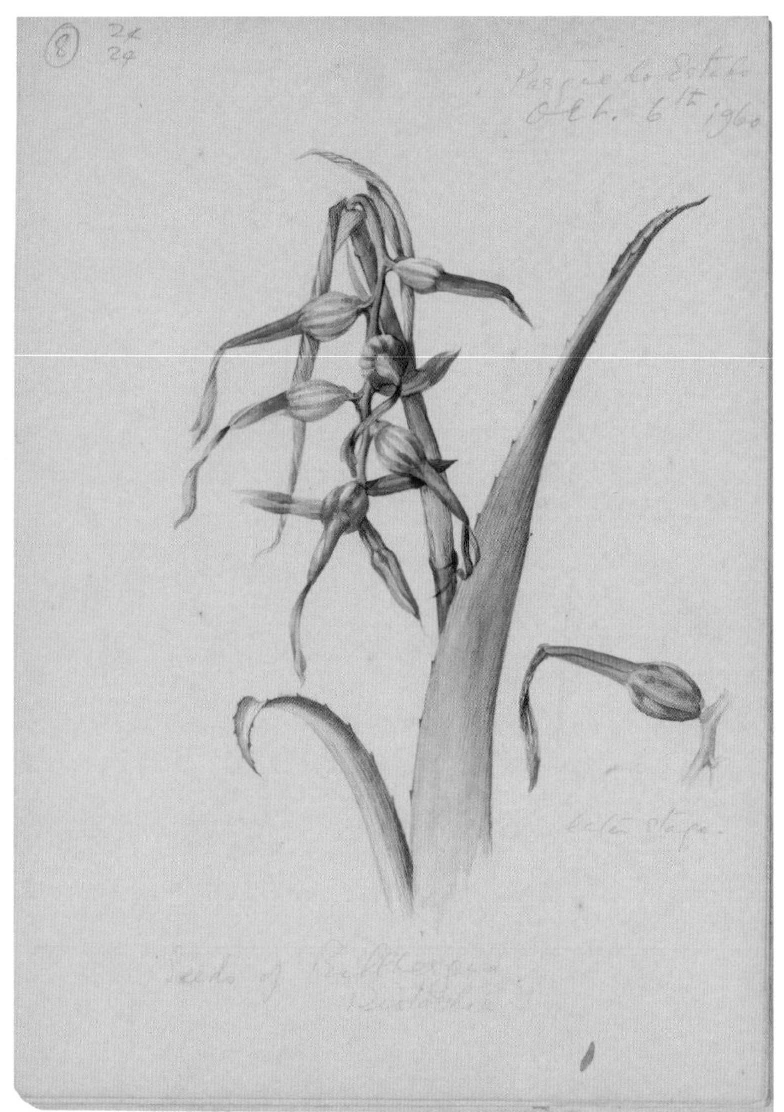

From her first expedition in 1956, Mee continued to create paintings, drawings and sketches of the flora growing along the maze of waterways of the Amazon Basin. It was not always possible to complete her paintings in situ - unpredictable weather or waterlogged canoes resulted in hurried sketches, but most were carefully annotated so they could be worked up into exquisite coloured sketches and paintings later.

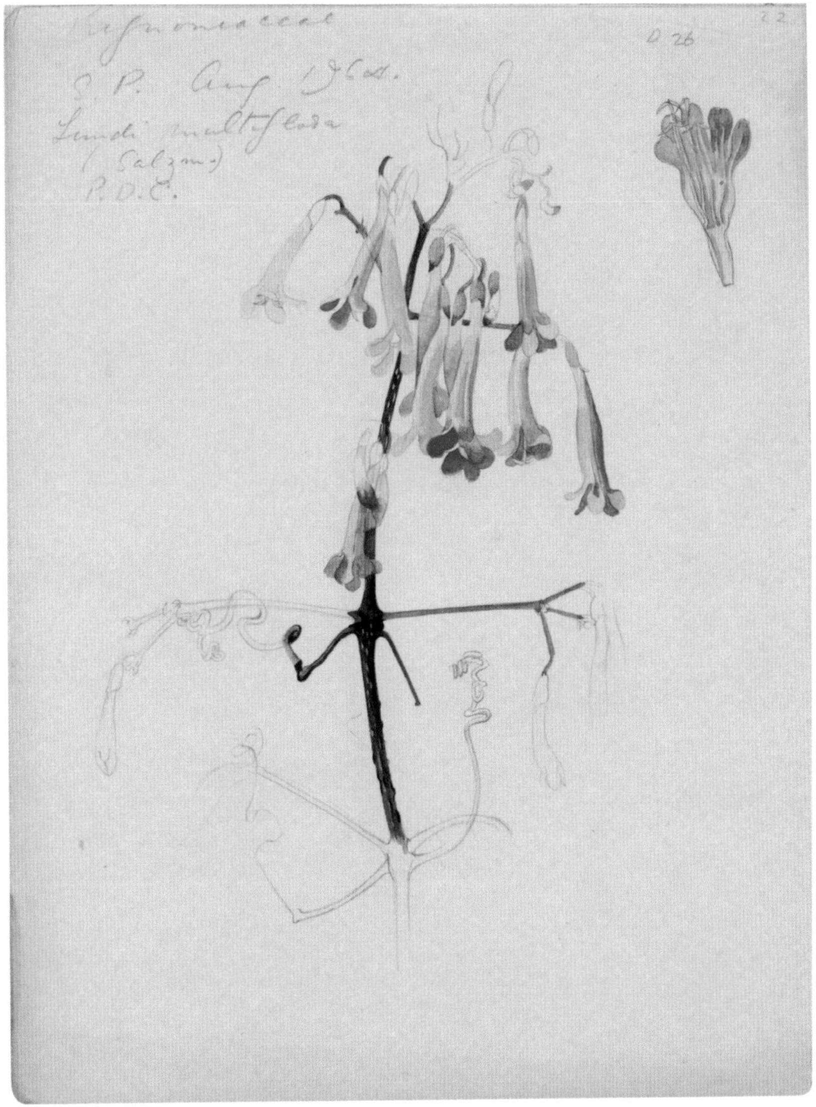

July, Aug 1962
Flowered March 63 in S.P.

MARIA SIBYLLA MERIAN 1647-1717

I would ask you to be so kind and not to send me any more dead creatures, for I have no use for them.

Maria Sibylla Merian was already collecting all the silk worms and caterpillars she could find in order to observe and draw the stages of their metamorphosis by the age of thirteen. A peculiar pastime for a young girl, one might think, but Merian was destined for an unconventional life.

Merian lived in an era of widespread superstition. While she was peering at caterpillars in Frankfurt, other cities were burning women for witchcraft. When she started her career, it was generally believed that insects were the spawn of the devil, generated by bad meat and rotting fruit – and few had the stomach or interest to look closely enough to prove otherwise. Merian was the exception. Her youthful interest soon developed into a lifelong fascination with insects, in particular caterpillars, moths and butterflies.

Although married at eighteen, Merian remained resolutely independent, keeping her own name and establishing her own business, which employed a cadre of confident female apprentices selling art supplies and silks hand-painted with flowers of Merian's design. After leaving her husband, she worked as a scientific illustrator in Amsterdam, examining the exotic flora, butterflies and insects from the Americas that had been collected by merchants and naturalists. The faded, ill-preserved specimens were a poor comparison to living subjects. Instead, she longed to observe their live behaviour and true colours.

It was time for her to do her own fieldwork. Aged 52, accompanied by her two daughters, Merian sailed to the Dutch colony of Suriname, to document the fauna and flora of that 'hot, wet land' in the northern jungles of South America. In her bags she carried her essential supplies: sketchbooks, notebooks, pigments and mixing materials and her favourite vellum – *carta non nata*, skin from unborn lambs – which held the colour of her paints like nothing else. For two years they gathered specimens, and fed and observed them as they underwent their mysterious transformations. The working conditions in the tropical rainforest were much more challenging than in temperate Europe, but with every image she wrote reams of notes, painstakingly documenting behaviours and locations of each species. Wherever possible she learned the native names for plants, fruits and insects, and their practical uses.

Malaria forced Merian to return to the Netherlands in 1701, where she immediately began to create her seminal book, *Metamorphosis Insectorum Surinamensium*. This depicted the life-cycles of plants and insects never before described or drawn, with the insects painted and printed life-size. The drama and the richness of her sketches and drawings were unparalleled. Some now argue that their consummate artistry diverted attention from her significant scientific contribution as an early modern naturalist and entomologist.

Merian changed pictorial conventions for depicting certain aspects of nature, challenging naturalists to look more closely at the relationships and behaviour between plants and animals. She has appeared on banknotes and stamps, and has had schools, ships and species named after her. But her greatest legacy was to remind us to keep our eyes open, to appreciate the smallest of beings, and, most of all, never to underestimate girls who collect caterpillars.

In her lifetime many dismissed Merian's extreme diligence of observation in sketching as fantastical, even as 'entomological caricatures'. Today her work is treasured in collections around the world. Above is a toad with hatchlings on its back, a pink-flowered plant and two shells, and opposite a caiman entwined with a false coral snake.

Merian became known for her unusual portrayals of wondrous natural subjects: she painted moths laying eggs, caterpillars feeding on their favoured plants, and butterflies and lizards extending their tongues towards potential food. She also depicted the entire life-cycles of individual species. Such close observation and artistic recording were pioneering, and would lay the groundwork for many natural philosophers who would follow.

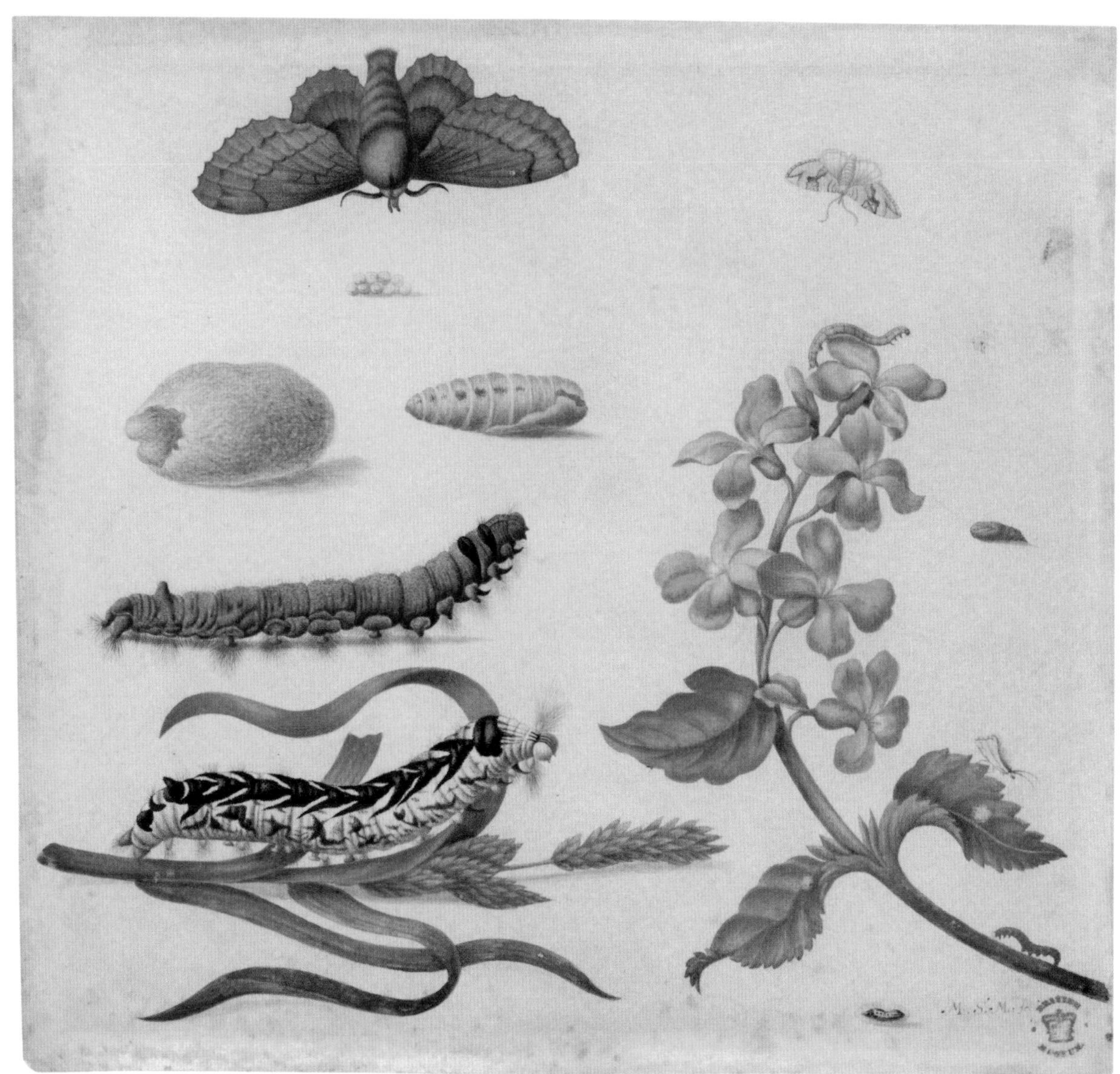

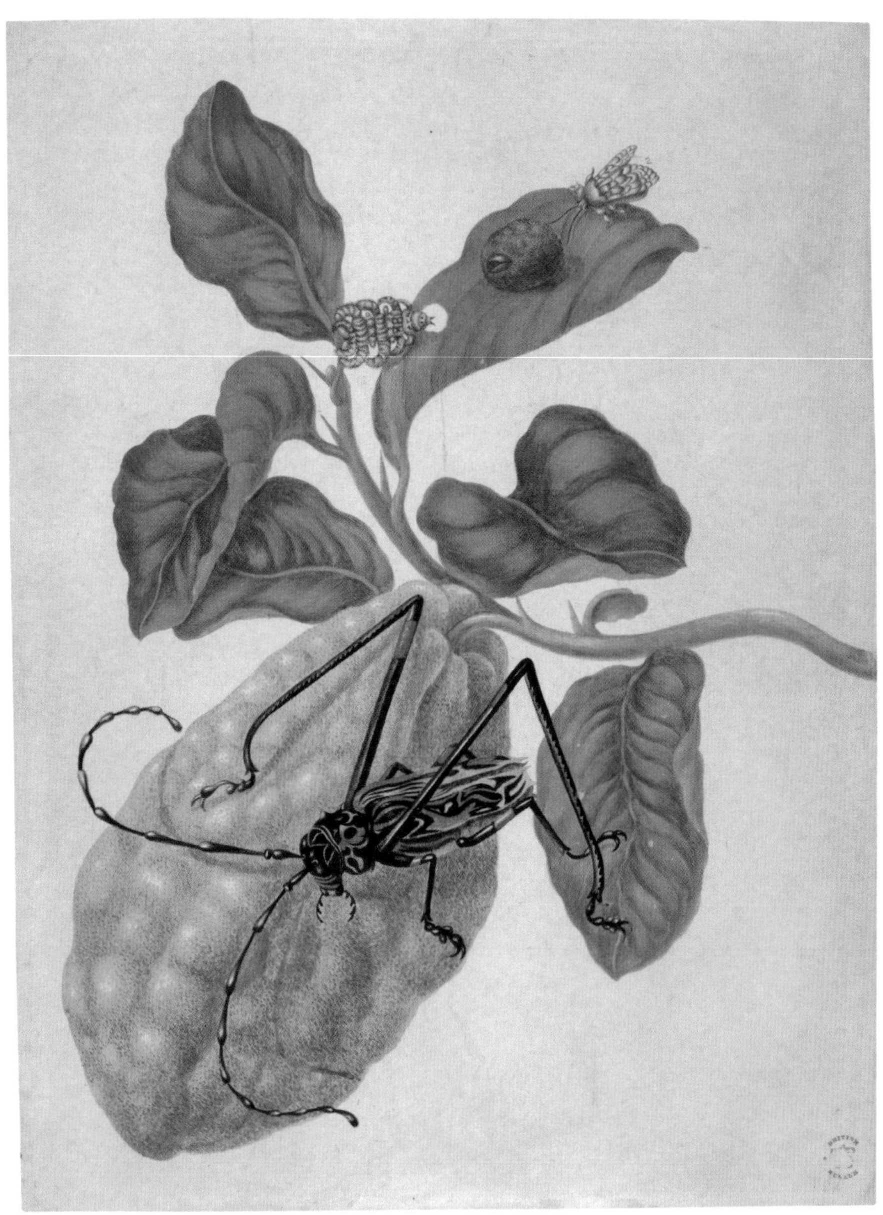

A harlequin beetle (*Acrocinus longimanus*) rests on the fruit of a citron tree, with a moth, caterpillar and larva on a leaf nearby. The citron was introduced to South America during the sixteenth century. Merian noted the fruits 'are candied; in Holland they are baked in gingerbread'. Of the beautiful long-horned beetle she wrote: 'Decorated with red and yellow flecks, shown resting on the fruit, it was added on account of its rarity to complete and decorate the engraving although I do not know its origin; I gladly leave it to others to investigate this creature further.'

A black monkey, possibly a kind of tamarin, sitting on the ground holding a Surinam cherry, which is indigenous to tropical Brazil. The small blue flower resembles the European Forget-me-not.

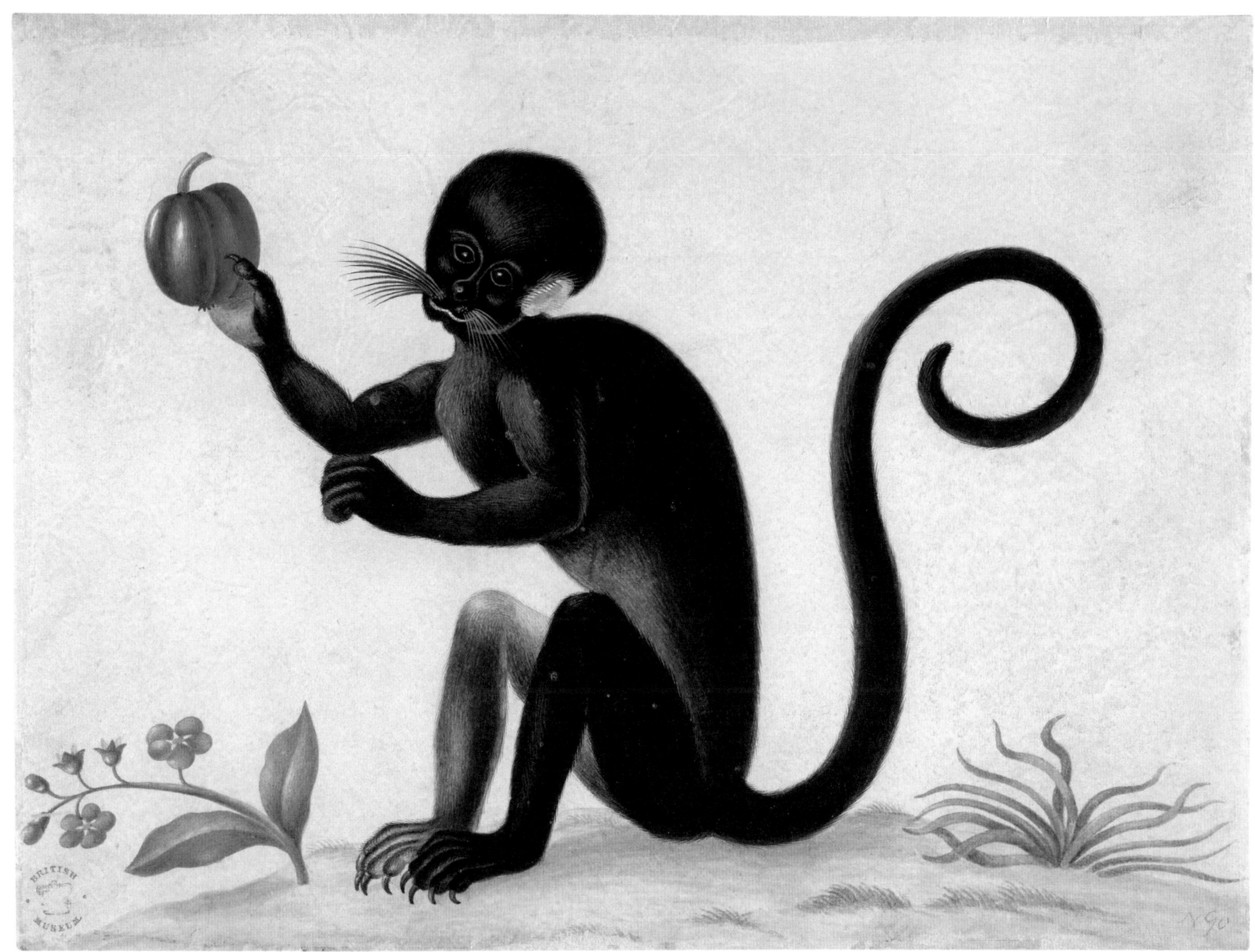
BRITISH MUSEUM

JAN MORRIS 1926-

There is just so much to write about without having to go very far.

A mad dash down through the Khumbu Icefall as night fell; a message wired in secret code to London. At last, news describing one of the great exploration achievements of the twentieth century: the first ascent of Everest, in May 1953. And it was Jan Morris who, by the flickering flame of a hurricane lamp, had typed out the story in her tent and achieved a worldwide scoop. 'I honestly didn't realize what a big deal it was at the time,' she remembers. 'I wasn't even that bothered by mountaineering. But it ended up being a rather big deal for me, a life-changing stroke of fortune. Doors opened, opportunities arose. I still find the world thrilling, but, I must admit, after sixty years or so, I'm tired of Everest. Sooner or later people will embark on a voyage to Mars. Now that really will change everything!'

Regarded as one of Britain's finest writers, Morris has directed her talents to the history and modern life of cities, cultures and peoples of many different countries. Her prose is lyrical, purposeful, revealing. Her evocation of Venice, for example, in this single sentence, perfectly captures her craft: 'It is a gnarled but gorgeous city: and as the boat approaches through the last church-crowned islands, and a jet fighter screams splendidly out of the sun, so the whole scene seems to shimmer – with pinkness, with age, with self-satisfaction, with sadness, with delight.'

Morris spent the first 46 years of her life living as a man. From school days she believed herself to have been born in the wrong body: she found herself, in her words, 'wrongly equipped'. She joined the army as an intelligence officer, serving in Italy, Palestine, and finally in Trieste, and her love of travel and adventure grew. After the war she pursued a career in journalism, taking a job as correspondent for *The Times*, and in 1953 was assigned to cover the British expedition to Everest. By serendipity and hard work her news of the first ascent arrived just in time for Queen Elizabeth's coronation, and her horizon became limitless. She made a 'dashing progress through unexplored desert' in a motorcar with the Sultan of Oman, and later sent back insightful dispatches during the 1956 Suez Crisis. Her first book, *Coast to Coast*, was also published that year, describing a road trip across America, and the later success of *Venice* allowed her to devote herself to her travels and books.

It was while working on a great trilogy charting the rise and fall of the British Empire – *Pax Britannica* – that Morris embarked on the most courageous adventure of her life: the transition from man to woman. Unable to have the operation in England, in 1972 she went to Casablanca to undergo sex reassignment surgery. The memoir she wrote of this experience a few years later, *Conundrum*, was the first published under her new name. She now lives with her partner Elizabeth in Wales, between the mountains and the sea, and there she has written more than 40 books of travel, history, memoir and the imagination.

'I don't think of myself as a travel writer,' she says. 'I've always written about my responses to the things that I see. Curiosity is at the heart of it, but I suppose much of it was just about me. How lucky I've been.' There is also one more book to come, *Allegorizings*, a final draft complete, though it will only be published posthumously. 'When I kick the bucket', she says with a smile, 'the presses will roll.'

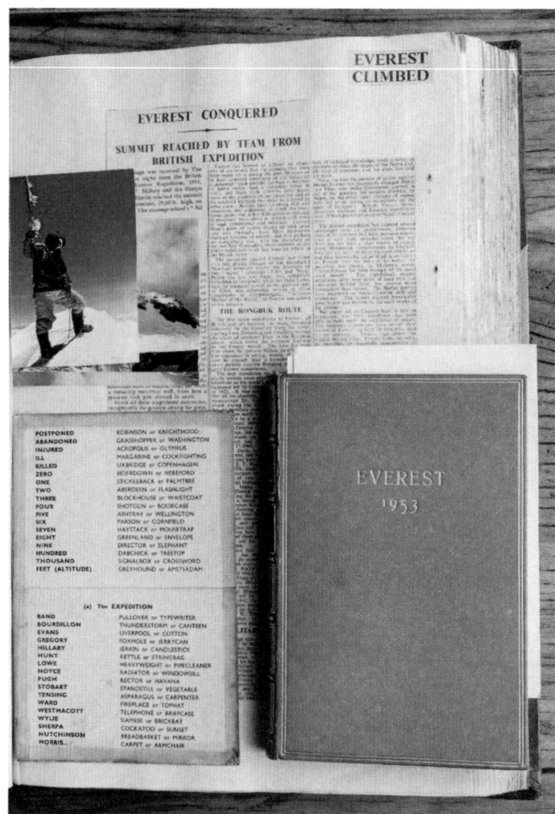

Morris kept scrapbooks throughout her years as a journalist. Her report of Hillary and Tenzing's ascent of Everest was sent to *The Times* in secret code; printed on waterproof cardboard, she kept it with her notebooks underneath her sleeping bag at night.

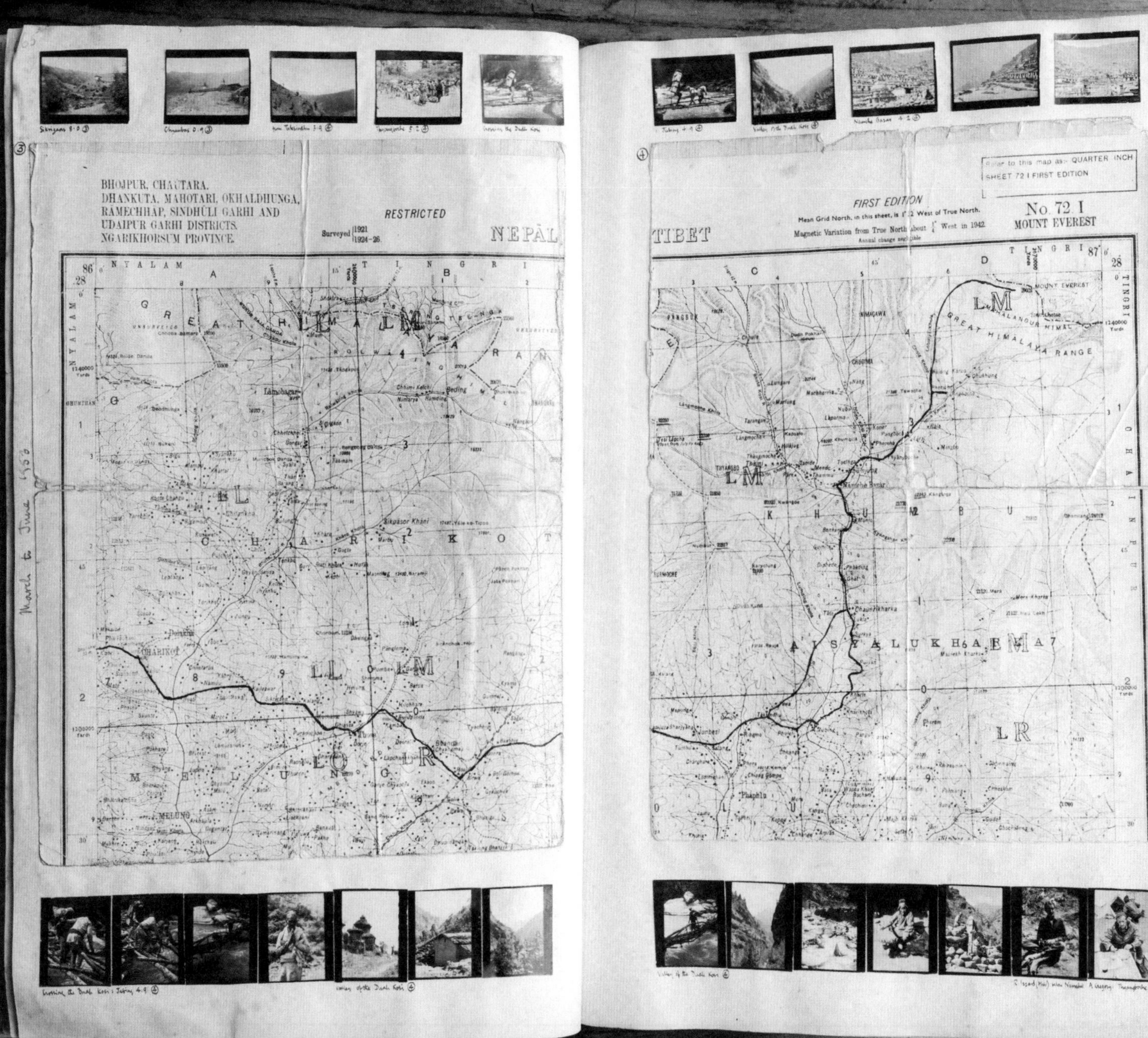

BHOJPUR, CHAUTARA.
DHANKUTA, MAHOTARI, OKHALDHUNGA,
RAMECHHAP, SINDHULI GARHI AND
UDAIPUR GARHI DISTRICTS.
NGARIKHORSUM PROVINCE.
RESTRICTED
Surveyed 1921 1924-26.
NEPĀL
TIBET
FIRST EDITION
Mean Grid North, in this sheet, is 1° 2' West of True North.
Magnetic Variation from True North about 1/4° West in 1942.
Annual change negligible
No. 72 I
MOUNT EVEREST
Refer to this map as:- QUARTER INCH SHEET 72 I FIRST EDITION
NYALAM
TINGRI
GREAT HIMALAYA RANGE
MOUNT EVEREST
CHARIKOT
KHUMBU
March to June 1953

EDWARD LAWTON MOSS 1843-1880

In this icy wilderness there is an overpowering sense of solitude, which adds greatly to the weird effect of moonlight on the floebergs.

A pioneering medical officer who saved many lives over his short career, Edward Lawton Moss was also highly skilled with brush and pen. He graduated from St Andrews in 1862, and in 1864 became a surgeon with the Royal Navy. Just a week later he was sailing on HMS *Bulldog* in the West Indies when they came under fire and the ship was lost. Having survived this he was posted in British Columbia, where he played a central role in founding one of the earliest medical institutions on Canada's west coast, the Royal Naval Hospital at Esquimalt on Vancouver Island.

Moss was appointed surgeon and artist to HMS *Alert* in 1875, under Captain George Strong Nares, on a voyage to the North Pole. Sledging teams charted new land and achieved a new farthest north hauling across the frozen Arctic Ocean, but despite regular rations of lime juice, and Moss's efforts to secure fresh meat, the ship's crew suffered from scurvy, and, blocked by impenetrable ice, they were forced to return early.

The Royal Navy was keen to paint a positive picture, and Moss's sketches and watercolours were widely reproduced as engravings in the press. They were also transformed into slides for popular magic-lantern lectures, long before film could circulate a polar expedition's heroics, or indeed, its tragedy. Moss was then posted to the battleship HMS *Research* in the Mediterranean, where he visited, and took part in, the excavations of what was believed to be ancient Troy. He next joined the training frigate HMS *Atalanta* on a voyage to Bermuda in 1880. The ship disappeared on the return journey and all hands were lost; no trace has ever been found. Moss was just 36.

Sledging parties haul their loaded sledges over the ridges of ice floes during the British Arctic Expedition to the North Pole in 1876. Moss made this sketch as the teams 'Bulldog' and 'Marco Polo' tried to make their weary way north.

Opposite: Godhavn harbour, on Disco Island, Greenland, with the expedition ships lying at anchor and Lyngemarken cliffs behind. Moss describes his sketch: 'A pair of Eskimo women, unmarried, as may be seen by their red top-knots, are busy with their laundry work at a pool amongst the glaciated rocks of the foreground.'

Arctic Ships & Valorous
Godhavn, Disco,
14 July -75
Lyngmarken Fjeld

If fortune did not favour us, the destruction of the ship was certain, and every preparation was made to meet such eventuality. Provisions and sledges were piled on deck ready to launch on the floes, and notes and sketches and carefully-selected specimens were packed into the smallest possible bundles, so that they could be pushed hastily into a pocket if it should be necessary to desert the ship.

Here Moss sketches the interior of what the expedition called the 'Unifiler House' - the unifiler was a piece of equipment with a suspended magnet for examining magnetic force. This was the third or fourth snow hut they had built for this purpose, approached by a long entrance passage, which the expedition dog, Nellie, is looking down. Moss noted that 'the dome and walls are covered with long feathery pendants of ice crystals'.

Moss wrote on the reverse of this sketch, opposite: 'Alert, Winter Quarters, 82.27 N, December 1875. Daily Routines. Digging out ice from top of hummock to melt for cooking and washing. About 10 inches of top of this hummock gives ice perfectly free from salt and the substitution of ice for snow has effected a great saving of fuel. The Marines had this duty.'

FRIDTJOF NANSEN 1861-1930

Suddenly I thought I heard a shout from a human voice, a strange voice, the first for three years. How my heart beat and the blood rushed to my brain.

Suspended between sea and sky, *Fram* drifted at the mercy of the currents and ice that held the ship captive on the Arctic Ocean. The men on board were in absolute isolation, with no certainty that they would return home and no means to communicate with the outside world. It was increasingly unlikely that *Fram* would drift to the North Pole as had been hoped, and even if she did, it could take five more years. Fridtjof Nansen, full of optimism at the outset of this grand enterprise, now felt as though he had led his men directly to purgatory. As the long polar night loomed, he took to his cabin and painted.

Nansen was already a national figure when he embarked on his 1893-96 expedition towards the North Pole. The 31-year-old Norwegian had by this time made the first traverse of Greenland on skis, spent a winter studying the West Greenland Inuit, gained a doctorate in zoology and conducted ground-breaking research into the central nervous system. His proposal had been to set a specially designed ship into the ice near the New Siberian Islands, with the intention of using the transpolar drift to carry him across the Pole. Although his ingenious design for *Fram* worked, Nansen and his men were carried helplessly off course.

In a final bid to reach the Pole, Nansen left Captain Otto Sverdrup in command of *Fram* and, with Hjalmar Johansen, skied north. They made a new farthest north record before they were forced to turn and head towards land, some 645 km (400 miles) distant. No matter how exhausted he was, Nansen kept to his daily task of writing in his leather-bound journal, into which was pasted a photograph of his wife Eva and daughter Liv.

They reached Franz Josef Land after 130 days of hard skiing, exposure and near-starvation – more by chance than by good navigation, for their chronometer watches had run down and consequently their longitude calculations were way off. They had reached land, but they still had to survive the winter and then kayak to Spitsbergen. Luck, however, was on their side. On 17 June 1896, fifteen months after they had left *Fram*, Nansen heard a stranger's voice. It was the English explorer Frederick Jackson, who had his base at Cape Flora. Six weeks later, Nansen and Johansen were on the *Windward*. They returned to Norway just days before *Fram* also entered home waters.

As a marine scientist and outdoorsman, Nansen believed the only way to travel well in the polar regions was to 'work *with* nature, rather than against her'. He designed his own equipment, pioneered the use of skis and sails on sledges, skilfully calculated adequate rations and mastered Inuit techniques of survival. Many still look to Nansen as the greatest polar explorer in history. He would also become a diplomat and humanitarian. In the 1920s he assisted the League of Nations to repatriate over 450,000 prisoners of war and stateless people with the help of the 'Nansen passport'. In 1922 he was awarded the Nobel Peace Prize. 'Perhaps what has most impressed all of us', the Chairman of the Nobel Committee declared, 'is his ability to stake his life time and time again on a single idea, on one thought, and to inspire others to follow him.' A tireless champion of people in times of distress, he was the true personification of a hero.

Pencil sketch of the Inuit Elias in 1888. Nansen overwintered with the Inuit of West Greenland after skiing over the inland ice - living, travelling and dressing as they did - and admired them greatly. He would use the techniques he learned in later expeditions.

In early January 1895, violent, prolonged tremors tossed the icebound *Fram* as if in an earthquake. Supplies were moved on to the ice in case the ship sank. An eerie calm then descended. Nansen sketched a parhelion in his journal and wrote 'the ice has [simply] discharged a cannonade for the high latitude ... Let it do its worst, as long as we move North.'

Overleaf: Two watercolours by Nansen of the evening and sunset on 22 September 1893. As the long polar night loomed, *Fram* made her way into the pack ice. In just a few days she would be beset. Nansen hoped that the transpolar drift would take them right across the North Pole.

M^c LAGAN & CUMMING, LITH^RS EDINBURGH
Kveld i Drivisen 22 september 1893.
Akvarelskisse

Ved solnedgang 22 september 1893.
Akvarelskisse

MARIANNE NORTH 1830-1890

I rested my painting-board on one of the great fan leaves, and drew the whole mass of fruit and buds in perfect security, though the slightest slip or cramp would have put an end both to the sketch and to me.

Taking her first lessons in oil painting in 1867, Marianne North was instantly hooked. It was, she described, 'a vice like dram-drinking, almost impossible to leave off once it gets possession of one'. She would go on to complete two circumnavigations of the globe, with wide detours north and south, in her mission to paint as many different species of plants as she could find.

North was the eldest daughter of Frederick North, an MP. When she was 25, her mother died, leaving her to fulfil the deathbed promise to take care of her father, and it would be decades before she discovered her freedom. She had sufficient wealth to be comfortably independent and felt no need or desire to find a husband. Sharing her father's passion for travel and botany, she decided to visit 'some tropical country to paint its peculiar vegetation in its natural abundant luxuriance'. In this she was supported by a host of influential family friends, including Charles Darwin, Francis Galton and botanist Joseph Hooker.

In 1871, armed with letters of introduction, North began a series of distant journeys. She spent time in Canada, the United States and Brazil. In Jamaica she rented a house in the old deserted Botanic Gardens and painted vivid oil paintings of the orchids and passion flowers outside her veranda. Between 1873 and 1877 she journeyed to California, Japan, Borneo, Java and Ceylon, then made an extensive tour of India. At Darwin's suggestion she sailed to Australia, Tasmania and New Zealand via Borneo, then travelled to South Africa and the Seychelles, to fill gaps in her collection.

North travelled alone and not for adventure, nor really to experience other cultures, but to capture in oils the extraordinary variety of plant-life across the world. Inhospitable terrain and hardship did nothing to dissuade her. She set up her easel and parasol and became completely absorbed in recording the details of a plant and its environment. She returned with vivid and accurate representations of ecosystems from all over the world rather than dried, faded blooms.

Encouraged by a successful exhibition in London, North proposed that a gallery for her paintings could be built, at her own expense, in the Royal Botanic Gardens at Kew, serving tea and biscuits to weary visitors. Her old friend Joseph Hooker agreed to the gallery, but not the refreshments. Irrepressible as ever, North decorated the door frames with pictures of tea and coffee plants. Recently renovated, the Marianne North Gallery remains a place where visitors can enjoy a visual tour of the world through over 800 exquisite paintings.

A distant view of Kyoto, Japan, drawn from outside North's paper window (above). In the foreground, on the right, is the top of a pine tree, clipped and trained to resemble a bank of turf.

Opposite: The bazaar at Mussoorie, May 1878. North visited India for two years and completed over 200 paintings. Mussoorie, she wrote was 'a long scattered place, covering an uneven ridge for about three miles, looking over the wide Dun valley on one side, and into the rolling sea of mountains on the other. The ever-changing lights and shadows over the great mountains were a continual wonder for me to watch.'

I painted all day, going out at daylight and not returning until noon, after which ... I used to walk up the hill and explore some new path, returning home in the dark.

In Ulwar in India in 1878 North encountered a 'whole street full of hunting cheetahs and lynxes' (opposite) and excitedly sketched the scene. 'All those wild beasts are chained to trestle-beds in front of the houses ... their keepers sitting or sleeping behind them.'

In Baroda, the elaborately decorated oxen pulling state gun carriages caught North's eye: 'At sunrise', she wrote, 'first came the gold and silver guns ... then came the Maharani's gold carriage, with silver wheels and gorgeous bullocks, quite hidden in silver draperies.'

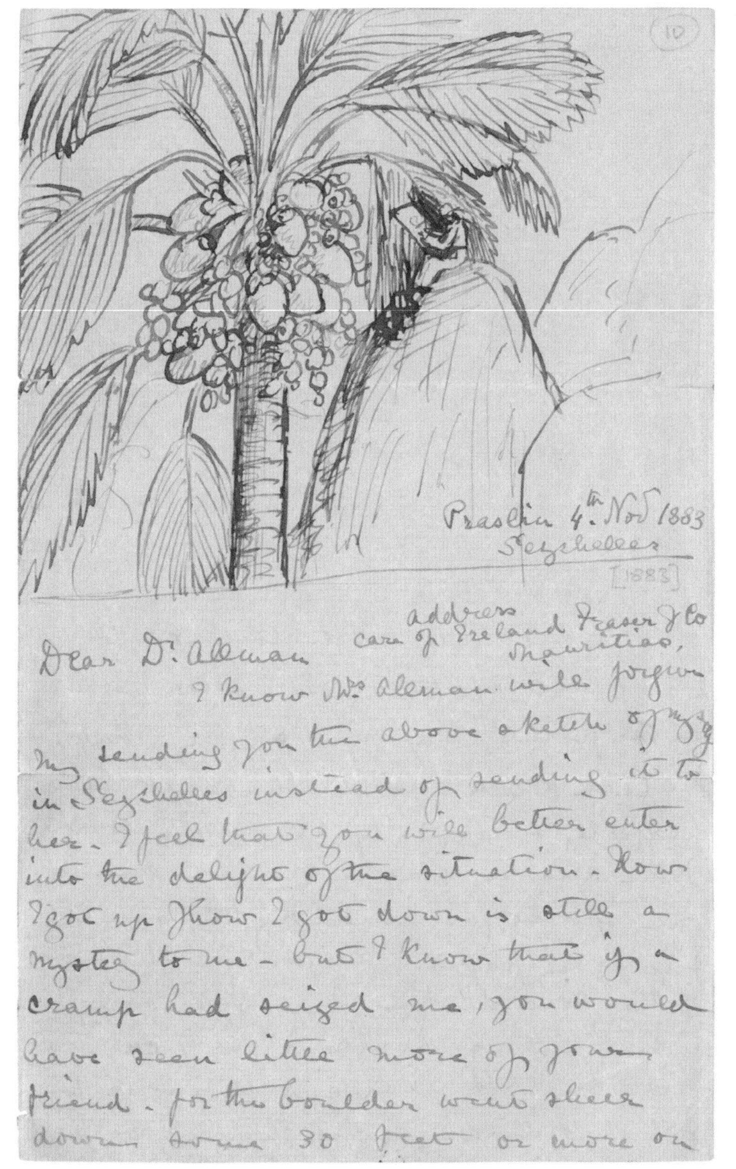
(10)

Praslin 4th Nov 1883
Seychelles

[1883]

address care of Ireland Fraser & Co
Mauritius,

Dear Dr. Allman

I know Mrs Allman will forgive my sending you the above sketch of my g[illegible] in Seychelles instead of sending it to her. I feel that you will better enter into the delight of the situation. How I got up & how I got down is still a mystery to me – but I know that if a cramp had seized me, you would have seen little more of your friend – for the boulder went sheer down some 30 feet or more on

My reflections in the middle of the suns image in the mist surrounded by iridescent halo just before sunset at Tongloo 12000 feet above the sea — India

In November 1883, North wrote to a friend from the Seychelles, illustrated with this little sketch of herself atop a large boulder (opposite left), so that he could 'better enter into the delight' of drawing the fruits of a tree up close. 'How I got up and how I got down is still a mystery to me - but I know that if a cramp had seized me you would have seen little more of your friend.'

In a fragile Indian sketchbook, only recently discovered and donated to the Royal Botanic Gardens at Kew (opposite right), is this sketch of North's own reflection in a lake, surrounded by mist and an 'iridescent halo just before sunset'.

An oil study of the impressive 'state elephant' of Baroda in 1879 (right). These elephants were, North recorded, 'painted all over, carrying about £5,000 worth of ornaments on their backs: all of them just had to be drawn'. Having sketched this extraordinary procession since sunrise, she admitted that she was 'nearly dead when dusk came'.

INFINITE BEAUTY

Tony Foster

Most of Foster's work is created outdoors, *en plein air*, in remote environments, camping and painting in the same spot until the work is broadly complete. Back in his studio, plan chests are filled with a lifetime's worth of careful observation: the essence of his adventures as an artist.

For almost thirty years I've drawn my inspiration from the sublime beauty of wilderness. My work is not just concerned with describing the landscape, but is about travelling slowly, living in wild places, and about the encounters with people, artifacts, flora and fauna. When I was first journeying it seemed like an adventure, and now it seems more like real life.

I'd like to think all artists are explorers. The more I see, the more I realize there's so much more to discover. And where better to go searching for inspiration than the wilderness. It's a privilege to be able to devote my life to trying to witness and record such things, and then bring back a glimpse of this beauty for others to enjoy. It does mean I'm away a lot though. From the Tropics to the Arctic, I reckon I've lived in my tent for more than seven years, all told.

From the moment I began exploring, my art has been about making journeys and creating marks on paper with paint. It's that simple. Each painting becomes part of an ongoing visual diary, a chronicle of my experience within the wilderness. When you make an artistic exploration the subjects are endless: from the first sight of a Himalayan mountain chain, or a hidden valley, to the shard of flint at the path-side, a feather or a shell turned over in the sand, a leaf burnished gold and blood red. Sometimes the fragment is indeed the whole. Like so many travellers today, and many explorers in the past, I see the journey as being as important as the destination.

My fascination is fed from these wild places. When my work is exhibited I get real pleasure from knowing not only that people are struck by the beauty of the scenes, but also that the resolve to protect these areas from depredation is strengthened. But that's a far greater aim than my basic wish: I explore to encourage others to do the same. And you don't have to travel to the ends of the earth to have a satisfying experience – some of my greatest pleasures are to take my paints to the small marsh beyond our village, or walk along the coast, a little further still. Whether in wilderness, or just a stone's throw from home, with practice it is possible to let the environment flow through you. Just wander and wonder. Sit still a while, breathe deeply and look.

I try to absorb everything around me. I rarely take a camera, but the one thing I'm certain to use is my journal. I find I must make notes every day, adding context to the ever-changing experience. All the small, mundane details are worth recording. Back at home, a few weeks or many years later, you never know when that kind of information might be useful to you – or indeed to someone else. Though it's raining, you're exhausted at day's end, it's getting dark, or nothing seems to have happened at all, pick up a pencil and make your mark on the page. Even the most terrible conditions are never boring; so scribble something down, anything at all.

Exploring is also about pushing yourself to attempt new things. It might mean going to ever more arduous and remote places, but for me creating difficult artworks is also the satisfying challenge. And devoting time to a place; I feel that is the key. By studying an area slowly I try to unlock more of its mysteries, and with greater insight, than if I were just to helicopter in, make a quick sketch or snapshot and retreat to the comfort of my studio. Time gives you experience and, eventually, authority. But most of all – if you forget being freezing cold or bitten to death by insects – taking your time brings real happiness. In the stillness as I paint, creatures emerge from the undergrowth, birds land nearby and as the sun moves across pools, flowers open. In Honduras, near the headwaters of the Rio Plátano, iguanas swim near my raft; an otter fights with a big fish; butterflies dance in shafts of light. A morning of silence is broken by the call of Howler monkeys.

By the time I finished a recent watercolour of the Grand Canyon, I'd spent a month painting on site, rolling up my paper at night into a protective metal tube, catching some sleep in the tent, slowly adding colour to the faint lines of my pencil sketches. Over the course of many journeys, and many other paintings, I'd walked over 650 km (400 miles), exploring the landscape from rim to river in search of the ideal vantage point to set up my camp. At 2 x 1.2 m (7 x 4 ft), it was my largest painting yet. Sketching underwater provides other challenges. Wearing an extra weight belt so I can sit firmly on the bottom, I scuba-dive to the sea floor and tuck in to paint fish at the coral's edge, but the longer I'm down the more the lead swells in my pencils and crayons split and crumble. My grip loosens for a second and my pencils are gone; just little flashes of colour torpedoing up to the surface.

Beauty is elusive, mercurial, and yet it's clearly all around us. Some of the most destructive forces in the world – water and fire – are at the heart of much that can be beautiful. Water is one of the hardest subjects for a painter, multiformed and yet formless too: boiling geysers, limpid pools, banks of dense mist, ancient ice, raging torrents. What colour is water, exactly? And how does it behave? So, I take time to explore it in all its moods and movements. I might get it wrong, but I must try. I think of artist John Ruskin, and the countless others who went before: 'Nature is painting for us, day after day, pictures of infinite beauty if only we have the eyes to see them.'

The notion of beauty is so hard to describe in words. But when I take up my brushes in the wilderness, immersed within the environment, I feel a little closer to a true definition of the word, and to what is best in our world. It is windless and quiet, an easy day on the tundra or in the endless desert. Or, perhaps we're deep in a forest gorge and now come the first drops of rain. I reach for my umbrella. I keep painting. Elsewhere, there's a storm brewing, or maybe the midday sun is baking my colours. High on a mountain's icy flank, the gathering sky grows thick and snow falls, or perhaps the sun is just starting its climb above a distant ridge. All around us, beauty is out there.

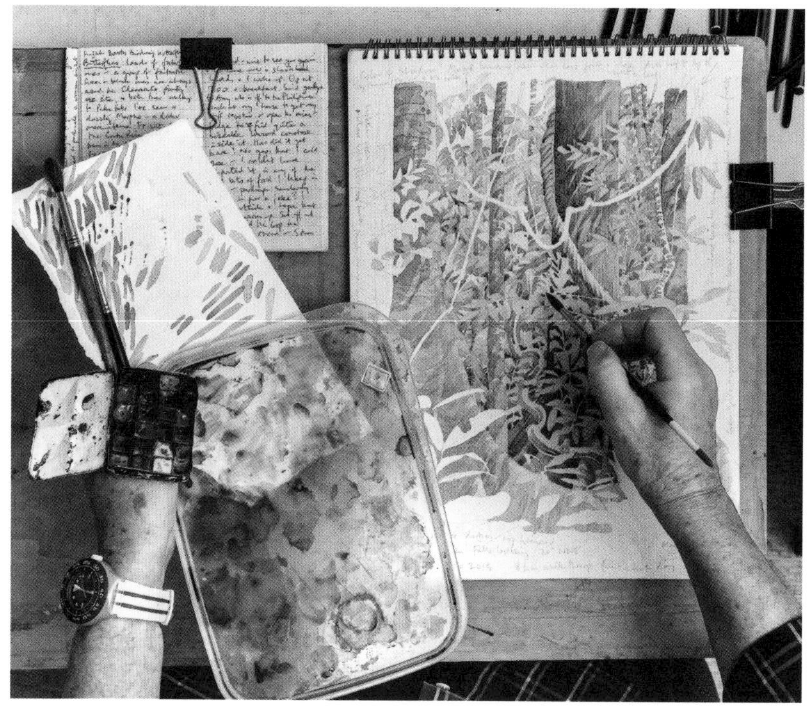

Foster's artworks are created with paints contained in a box the size of your hand. 'My exotic toolkit actually couldn't be more basic,' he explains. 'I take a few brushes and a mixing palette that's just the plastic lid of an ice-cream tub. At the heart of it are these two little tin paint-boxes. One is British, full of the earthy tones you might expect to find in the English countryside; and the other is an American colour set, packed tightly with sizzling bright paints like Winsor yellow, permanent rose, French ultramarine.'

Foster keeps a daily journal and makes copious colour notes to enable him to refine the work in his studio. He also collects small talismans from the field - twigs, feathers, pebbles, water samples, artifacts - which round out the record of a place.

MSR

EDWARD NORTON 1884-1954

I sketched feverishly, my water freezing as fast as I put it on the paper, as also my fingers.

A 'fine horseman, a keen shot, and enthusiastic fisherman, and a climber of prodigious courage and determination' – such were the talents of explorer Edward Felix 'Teddy' Norton. He was an able watercolourist too, filling a number of sketchbooks on his travels, while also collecting birds and flowers for the Natural History Museum in London. Yet, because he was so modest, few outside his family knew that he had a talent for painting, and it is only in recent years that his sketches have been brought to light.

Norton began climbing as a young boy, stalking chamois in the rocky hills of the Haute-Savoie above the chalet built by his grandfather, Sir Alfred Wills, himself a pioneering mountaineer and a founder of the Alpine Club in London. Later, he became a career army officer and a distinguished veteran of the First World War. He always climbed whenever he could, and in 1922 he was a member of the second British Mount Everest expedition.

With George Mallory and Howard Somervell he reached the then record height of 8,198 m (26,985 ft). Little was known about the effects of altitude and they were entering a new and dangerous world. They were the first men to climb without bottled oxygen beyond 8,000 m (26,247 ft) into what is now called by modern mountaineers 'the death zone', a place where for many mere survival is challenge enough.

On the next attempt in 1924, when the ebullient leader Charles Bruce fell ill, Norton took charge, and despite difficult weather and other problems, led an attempt on the summit. Again he climbed without oxygen, preferring to test himself against the mountain in pure style. His companion, Somervell, was unable to continue: his throat membrane had frozen and, choking on a lump of his own flesh, he sat down on the snow to die. Finally, the obstruction cleared in a flurry of blood. Norton went on alone to a height of 8,573 m (28,126 ft), reaching a great couloir on the north face and setting another altitude record that would stand for over fifty years before anyone would climb higher without oxygen. A few days later, Mallory and Andrew Irvine tried again for the summit, but neither man made it down alive.

Under considerable public scrutiny and press interest, Norton handled the tragedy with sensitivity. His first thought was to write touching private letters to the men's loved ones. His message to Mallory's widow included this sentence: 'You can't share a 16 lb high altitude tent for days and weeks with a man under conditions of some hardship without getting to know his innermost soul and I think I know almost as you do what his was made of – pure gold.'

In later years his love of nature continued, as did his strong dislike for publicity. He became an elder statesman of the climbing fraternity, valued for his integrity and knowledge of the Himalaya, though he modestly twice refused the presidency of the Alpine Club. He was happy, though, to offer guidance and advice to a new generation of climbers, including John Hunt in 1953, who would lead the team that finally made it to the top of Everest. He wrote to Norton, fresh from the mountain: 'To you goes a big share in the glory.'

For many years unknown outside the family, these sketches offer a vivid testimony of both the rigours and beauty of travel in Tibet at the dawn of the era of Himalayan climbing. While there was little chance to paint on Everest itself, Norton made good use of spare moments on the marches to and from the mountain, despite the biting cold of the endless plateau winds. In the sketch above, one of the climbers, Geoff Bruce, is 'addressing the porters in the blizzard on the East Rongbuk Glacier', 11 May 1924.

Rongshahr
Roses.
Our Camp covered with both sorts & the
iris on preceding page carpeted the ground
Primula
Sikkimensis
30/6/24
Rongshahr Valley
23/6/24
Everest
from Chogorong
15/6/24

Majestic Gaurishankar rises from the mist on 26 June 1924. Norton wrote some lines from Shakespeare's *Romeo and Juliet* opposite his sketch of the mountain in the Himalaya above the clouds: 'Night's candles are burnt out and jocund day Stands tiptoe on the misty mountain tops.' The night is over and the day comes.

The tent at the high mountain pass of Pang La, 27 April 1922, and Cho Oyu and Gyachung Kang seen the following day. Cho Oyu is the sixth highest mountain in the world, some 8,201 m (26,906 ft) high. The summit was not reached until 1954.

I must tell you, what Norton can't say in a dispatch, that we have a splendid leader in him. He knows the whole bandobast [arrangements] from A to Z, and his eyes are everywhere, is personally acceptable to everyone and makes us all feel happy, is always full of interest, easy and yet dignified, or rather never losing dignity, and is a tremendous adventurer.

GEORGE MALLORY, LETTER, APRIL 1924

Norton's affectionate sketches of members of the 1924 Everest expedition: John de Vars Hazard, John Noel, Geoff Bruce and George Mallory, who was later last glimpsed inching his way up the summit ridge before disappearing from sight.

Norton's view of Mount Everest from above Jikyop in April 1924. The fierce winds at altitude cause clouds to trail from its peak. 'The sky was cloudless blue, the country composed of every shade of pink, yellow and mauve,' he wrote earlier in his journal. 'Carbolic tooth powder, knife powder and wood ash mountains - the horizon encircled by row upon row of gleaming snow mountains.'

Mt Everest from
above Jikyop (60 miles away)
21/4/24

HENRY OLDFIELD 1822-1871

The hills on either side are richly covered with thick jungle ... all was wild, grand and very picturesque.

On 19 December 1851, British surgeon Henry Oldfield climbed on to the back of an elephant and headed into the jungle to hunt wild rhinoceros and leopard. Riding by his side was Jang Bahadur Rana, the powerful and controversial ruler of Nepal. Later that evening, they smoked, laughed, played chess and the flute, and cheered at the sound of musketry in the distance. Such experiences would cement Oldfield's friendship with the man later regarded as a dictator, allowing him unprecedented access to areas otherwise off-limits to foreigners.

Oldfield had joined the Indian Army Medical Service in 1846, and was appointed to the British Residency in Kathmandu during the early years of Jang's reign. He earned the ruler's trust, becoming his unofficial advisor and royal surgeon. With official blessing, he travelled hundreds of miles, meticulously recording the history, beliefs and society of the country in his journals. A keen artist, he created detailed watercolour sketches of villages, temples and shrines.

His impressive collection of drawings and writings would be published in two volumes, as *Sketches from Nipal*, in 1880, cementing his reputation as the principal British artist of nineteenth-century Nepal. At heart an antiquarian, Oldfield despaired at the neglect and ruin of the temples and buildings in the Kathmandu Valley. In years to come, the accuracy of his architectural observations would help to guide restoration projects on the very buildings he longed to preserve, though some have now been irreparably destroyed in the trauma of the country's recent earthquakes.

The Temple of Ganesha at Bhaktapur in Nepal. Oldfield was in despair when he came across sights that 'once profusely ornamented with elaborate carvings and grotesque sculptures in wood and stone ... now broken into ruins or overgrown with jungle'.

Oldfield often combined architectural details with scenes of daily life. The Dhunsar court of law in Kathmandu, opposite, lies deserted behind the fruit market; on the southern side are Fakir houses and other ruined temples.

Asoka's Temple - called Chillundeo - in the centre of Patun. Oldfield noted that the shrines here were elaborately finished, 'executed with an amount of care and accuracy which makes them very interesting and valuable'.

Thappatalli, the Residence of Maharaja Jang Bahadur, on the outskirts of Kathmandu (opposite). Oldfield forged a close friendship with the powerful and controversial ruler, and as a result was able to visit places and areas that other foreigners could not.

JOHN LINTON PALMER 1824-1903

La Pérouse says [the Easter Islanders] had an amazing fondness for the hats of their visitors; we found our trowsers equally coveted.

Were it not for his sketchbooks, Linton Palmer may well have disappeared entirely from history. His annotated drawings, compiled into six large albums and now treasured by the Royal Geographical Society in London, are a wonderful visual record of the places he visited during his career as a British naval surgeon in the mid-nineteenth century.

Palmer embarked on his first commission as acting assistant surgeon on HMS *Victory* aged 24. He would go on to serve on countless ships, exploring the Pacific, the East Indies and China, South America and the Arctic. In 1868 he was surgeon on HMS *Topaze* on its voyage to Rapa Nui (Easter Island), which resulted in the removal of the 'beautifully-perfect' stone statue, known as Hoa Hakananai'a, now displayed in the British Museum. Palmer produced many watercolours and sketches of the topography of the island, the statues and some of the resident chiefs. The people of Rapa Nui, he noted, were 'friendly, affable, and merry, excessively indolent, very fond of finery and adorning themselves ... Cannibalism was practised ... From some remains, and native testimony, we were led to infer that human sacrifice took place.'

Like many naval surgeons, Palmer developed a keen interest in natural history and ethnology. He spent his free time recording the lives, artifacts and environments of indigenous communities along the Pacific Northwest Coast of America, in Pitcairn Islands, Tahiti, China, Chile, Panama, Vancouver Island and the Bering Strait. He was an interested and educated observer, referencing his own experiences against the narratives of explorers past, creating a valuable record of remote, rapidly changing cultures.

Palmer's albums include many watercolours depicting places visited during his career as a naval surgeon. Copiously annotated, they are full of his observations of Pitcairn Islands, Rapa Nui, Tahiti, China, Chile, Panama, and right up to the edges of the Arctic Ocean. Opposite left are portraits and objects at Cape Classet and Vancouver Island, including paddles, fish rake and spears, and a bone club for killing fish. At far right are sketches of the indigenous people of Alaska, including an 'Esquimaux dandy' a 'Huskie woman' and 'Boy Boosey' - all regular visitors to HMS *Amphitrite* during its time in the region. He also includes a drawing of a small guillemot and 'Esquimaux costumes'.

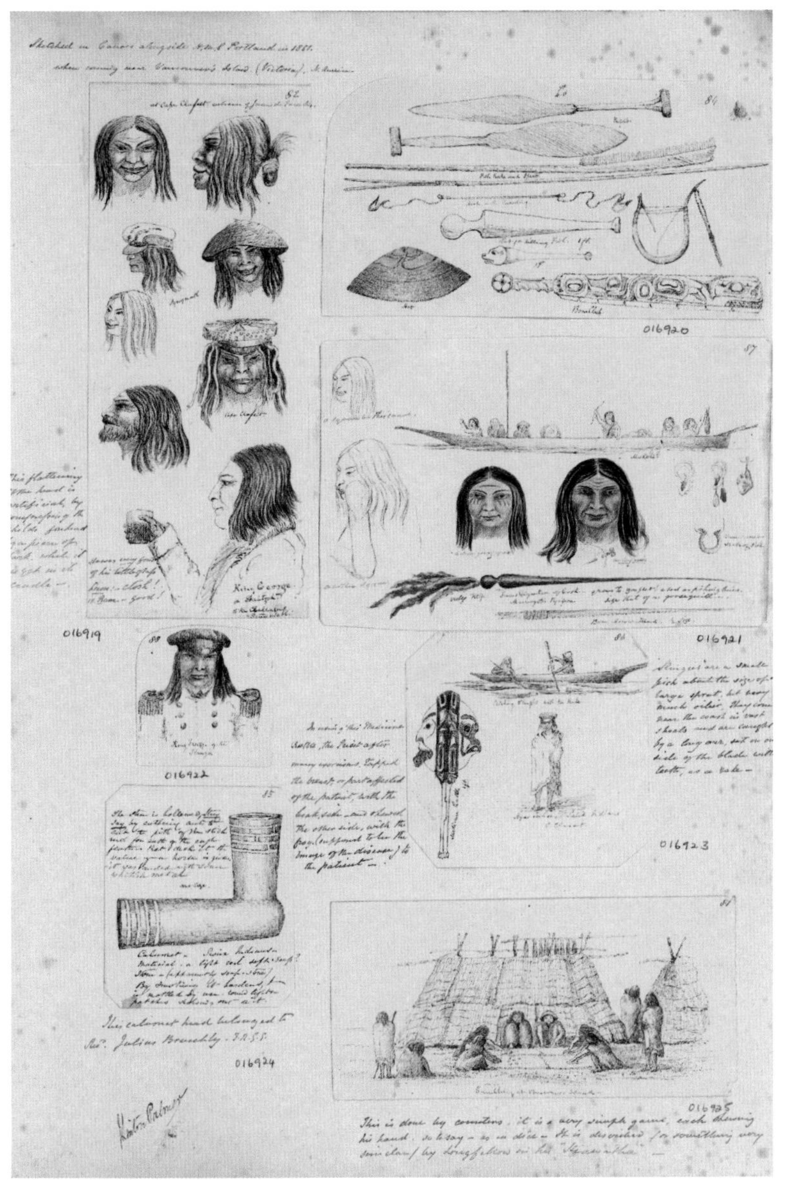

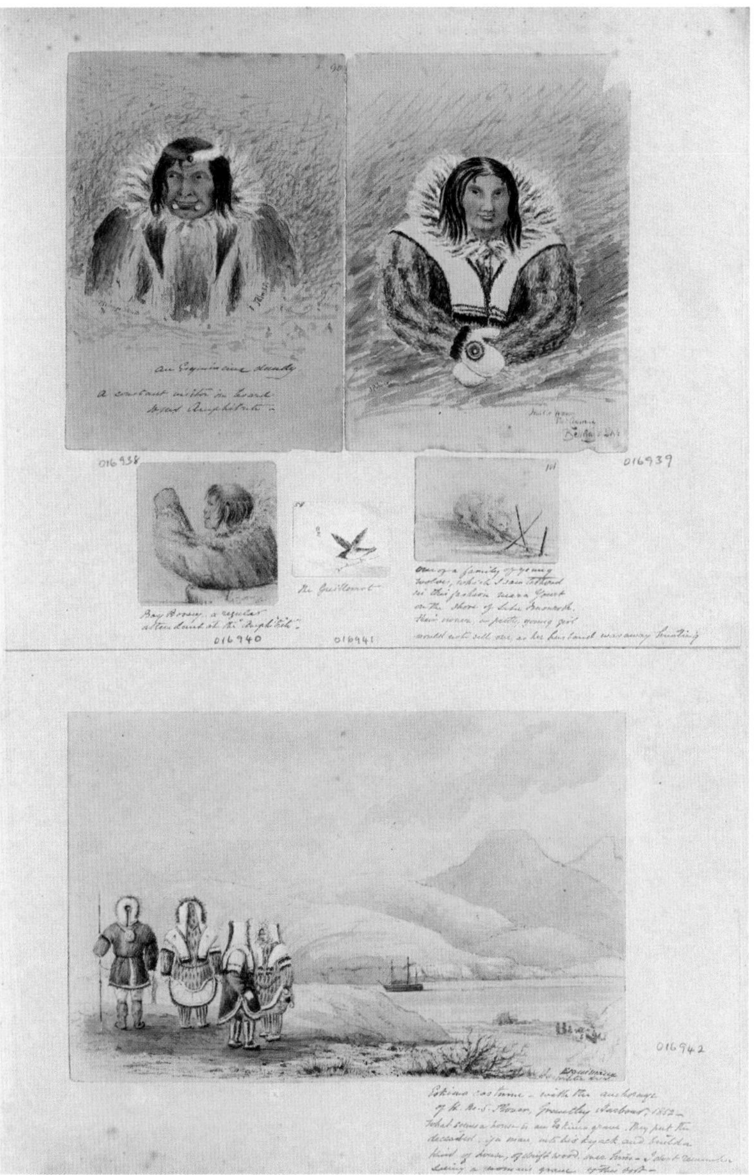

On the left are paintings and drawings of everyday life in Chile, completed during the voyage of HMS *Topaze* to the Pacific in 1865-69, and opposite left is the crater at Otu-iti, Rapa Nui (Easter Island), in 1868. Palmer made many first-hand observations of the statues: 'The head is very flat; the top of the forehead cut off level so as to allow a crown (hau) to be put on ... the face is square, massive, and sternly disdainful in expression; the aspect always upward ... the beautifully-perfect one Hoa-haka-nana-Ia (each image has its own name) ... is elaborately traced over the back and head with rapas and birds. It was coloured red and white when found, but the pigment was washed off in its transit to the Topaze.'

Palmer was particularly drawn by the body art of the 'Easter Islander' opposite right. 'Tattooing was practised by the women more elaborately than by the men, and completely ... both sexes wore ear-ornaments. The lobes were pierced, and distended very much. Large wooden ornaments, or the vertebrae of sharks, were inserted.'

Inside the Crater at Otu-iti –

01708

017084

One of the Images outside the Crater at Otuiti – These were generally in much better preservation than those elsewhere, the angles of the stone still sharp.

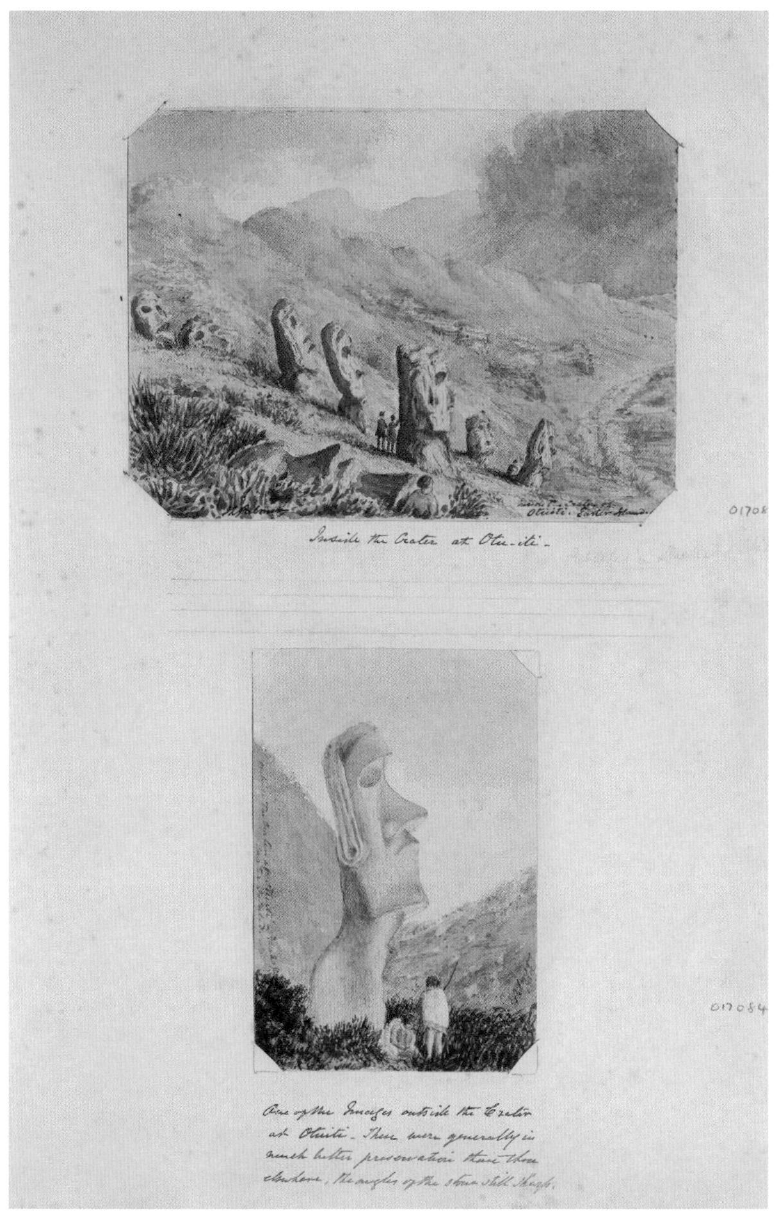

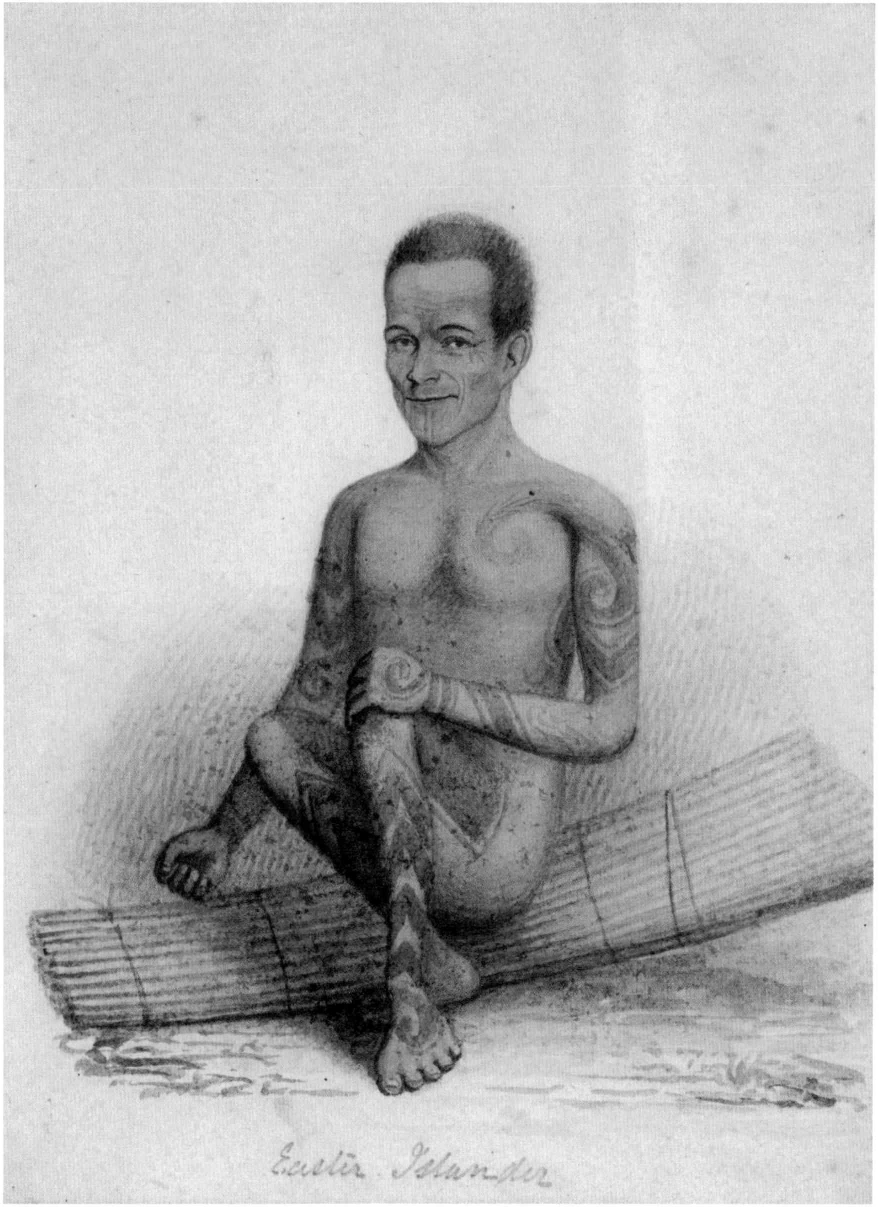

Easter Islander

SYDNEY PARKINSON 1745-1771

I made drawings of a great many curious trees, and other plants; fish, birds, and of such natural bodies as could not be conveniently preserved entire, to be brought home.

The Quaker son of a Scottish brewer, young Sydney Parkinson was happily drawing flowers in London when his skills caught the eye of the wealthy botanist Joseph Banks. The place was the 'Vineyard Nursery', essentially one of the first garden centres, importing exotic varieties for its well-heeled clients, and little could Parkinson have known that he would soon travel to the far side of the world. Banks first thought of taking him on a collecting jaunt to Lapland, before an altogether more serious opportunity arose. James Cook was about to embark on what would become the first of three great Pacific voyages, and Banks had bagged himself a berth.

Endeavour sailed from Plymouth on 25 August 1768 on essentially a collaborative venture between the Admiralty and the Royal Society. The principal aim was to observe the transit of Venus across the face of the sun, which would enable the distance between the Earth and the sun to be calculated. Added to this were secret instructions to search for the fabled southern continent – *Terra Australis Incognita* – whose location had aroused the speculation of cartographers for centuries.

Banks hired Parkinson as his personal draughtsman, with another artist, Alexander Buchan, given the task of creating the topographical views. But by the time the *Endeavour* reached Tahiti, the severely epileptic Buchan was dead. Parkinson would have to work tirelessly to fulfil Banks's demands, often sketching through the night in his cramped quarters. Rather like a modern-day expedition photographer, Parkinson was now expected to capture everything of interest: landscapes discovered and people encountered, and all the endless natural history specimens hauled on board.

For the rest of the ship's company, four idyllic months were spent in Tahiti, followed by an arduous running survey of New Zealand, which charted the entire coastline of the two islands, proving that it was not the northern tip of a great southern continent. Excursions ashore were limited, but every time a new creature was captured, Parkinson sketched furiously. For some he was able to complete detailed watercolours, but, overwhelmed by new material, for most a quick drawing had to suffice. Before the many plants wilted, notes on colour were quickly scribbled so that Parkinson might finish his images later on, perhaps during the long sea journey home or in quiet contemplation on their return to London. But, as fate would have it, this was not to be.

In April 1770 the expedition reached Botany Bay, and Parkinson would become the first European to observe and draw the Australian landscape, its aboriginal people and a kangaroo. Cook had decided to return home via the unknown eastern coast, but on 11 June *Endeavour* was trapped within the Great Barrier Reef and holed. Saving the ship, effecting repairs and then sailing her to safety may well stand as Cook's greatest feat of seamanship. The sad sequel is that while they were in dock at Batavia, fever and dysentery overran the ship; before they had reached the Cape of Good Hope, 30 men had died. The young artist was among them.

The ship finally reached England in July 1771 with over 30,000 plant specimens, many new to science, and laden with beautiful sketches, but without their diligent creator. Cook's journal entry for 27 January had been brief: 'Departed this Life Mr Parkinson, Natural History Painter to Mr Banks.' As with others, his diseased body was slung overboard.

Parkinson made this quick sketch of a kangaroo in June 1770 on the Endeavour River, near modern-day Cooktown in Queensland. It is the earliest known European depiction of the animal.

On the voyage out in 1768, local politics kept *Endeavour* at anchor off Rio in Brazil. It is likely Parkinson saw golden lion tamarins in the wild here (opposite left), though this image was possibly painted from a captive animal in London. It is now an endangered species. The Greater Bird of Paradise (opposite right) was also seen in the wild in New Guinea.

Silky Monkey Pennant quadr. 210

A page of Parkinson's pencil sketches likely made at Botany Bay, after 28 April 1770. It includes two Aborigines, one with markings on the chest and across the shoulders, resembling a crucifix, the other launching a spear from a spear-thrower with his right hand and holding a shield with his left.

Opposite: This wonderful album containing a collection of drawings made on Cook's first voyage survives in the British Library in London. On the left are four pen sketches of tattoos - 'Black stains on the Skin called Tattoo' - on the buttocks of some Māori who visited the *Endeavour* off Cape Brett, New Zealand, in November 1769. The ship's crew had first encountered tattooing in Tahiti, where some had even decided to get their arms marked, Parkinson included. The page on the right has two drawings, one of three highly decorated paddles, and the other with a musical instrument and a jadeite hand club, observed in New Zealand in October 1769.

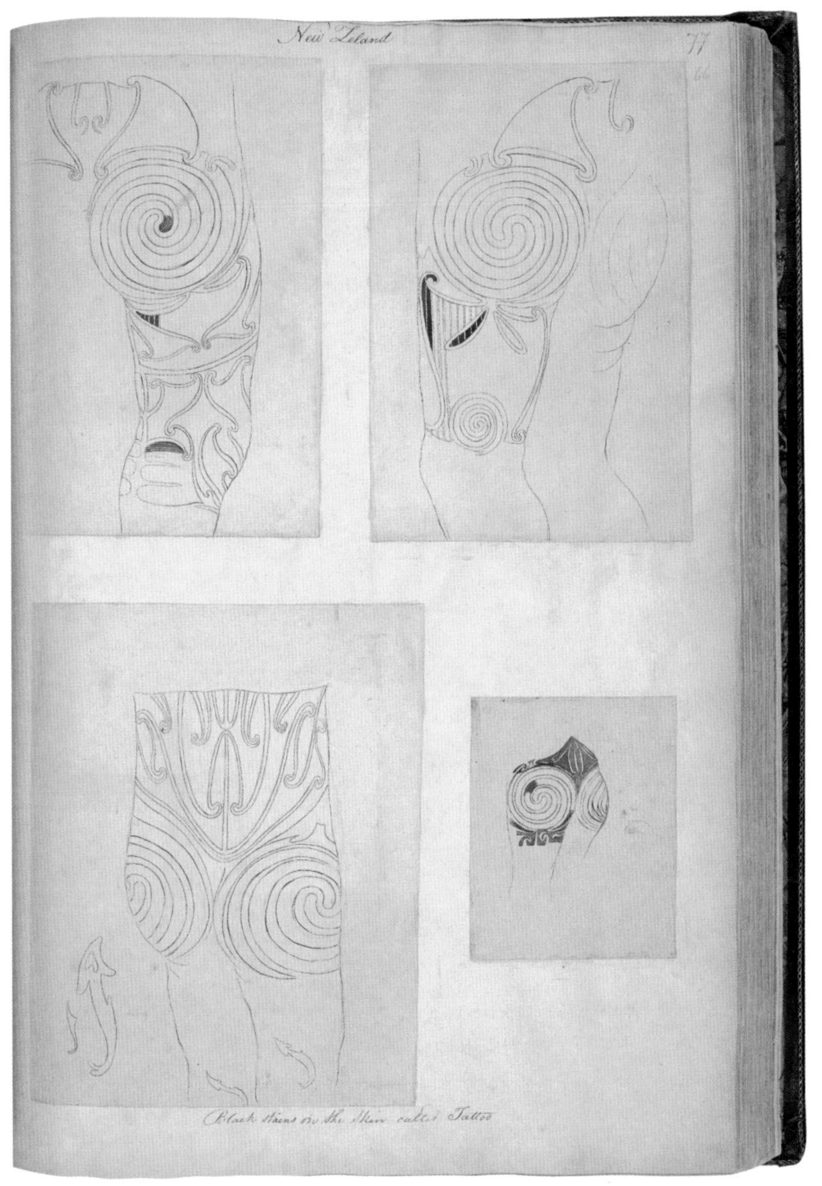
New Zeland
77
Black stains on the Skin called Tattoo

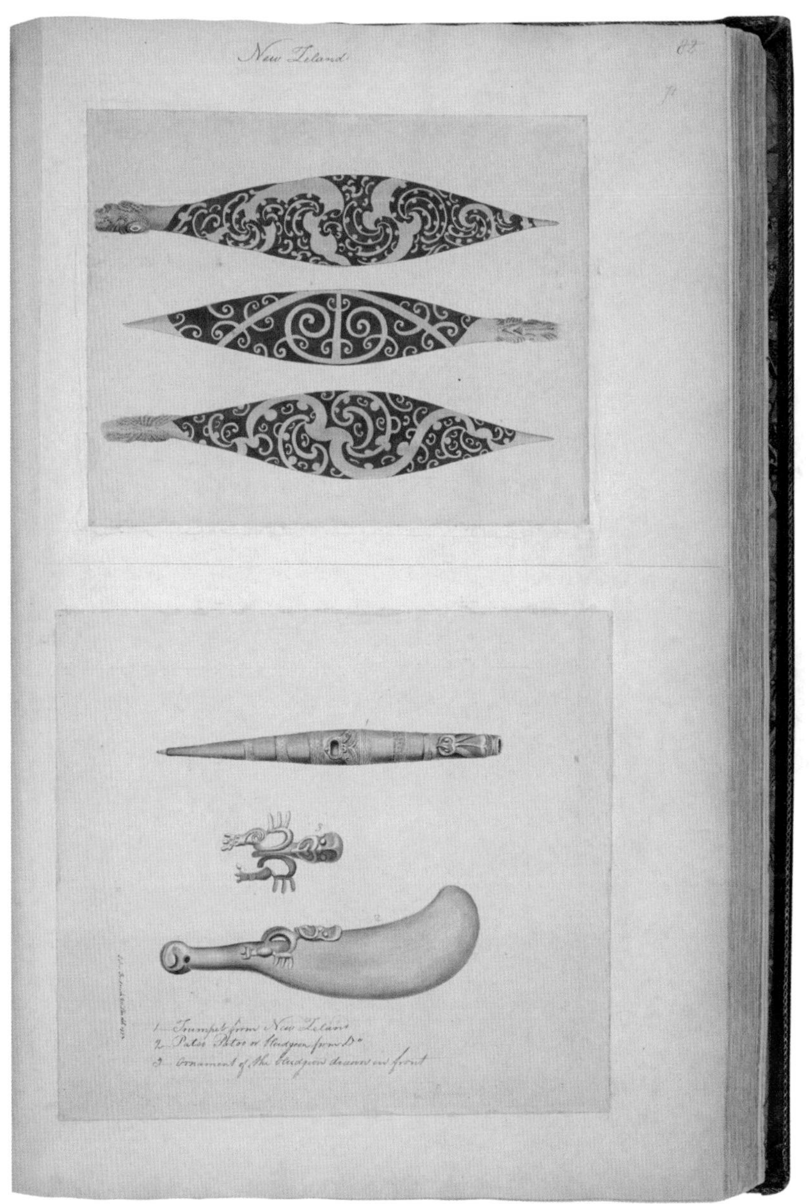
New Zeland
1. Trumpet from New Zeland
2. Patoo Patoo or Bludgeon from D°
3. Ornament of the Bludgeon drawn in front

TITIAN RAMSAY PEALE 1799-1885

The wolves were so bold last night that they entered our camp and carried off a fresh bear skin from the side of a fire.

On 21 June 1819 a steamboat left St Louis and started making its way up the wide Missouri River. On board was the nineteen-year-old naturalist and crack shot Titian Ramsay Peale, whose artistic skill had earned him his place on Major Stephen Long's expedition. Their aim was to explore and record the central and southern Great Plains and the Front Range of the Rockies – a vast, unspoiled wilderness inhabited only by Native Americans and the plants and game on which they subsisted.

Peale was the sixteenth child and youngest son of the American portraitist Charles Willson Peale, and shared his father's artistic and scientific inclinations. Aged seventeen he had his first illustrations published in Thomas Say's masterwork, *American Entomology*, was elected to the Academy of Natural Sciences and, with Say, embarked on his first expedition, to Georgia and Florida. Two years later, Peale was following in the footsteps of Lewis and Clark, whose specimens he had once helped to catalogue for his father's Philadelphia Museum.

Long's enterprise, however, would test his resources and resolve. With the steamboat encountering difficulties, Peale, Say, geologist Augustus Jessup and artist Samuel Seymour had to travel overland to gather what scientific material they could. But the prairies offered little shelter from the blistering heat and they suffered from shortage of food and water, heatstroke, sickness and exhaustion, and were tormented by biting flies.

Hardships aside, theirs was an experience awarded to few. Peale shared pipes with Kansa and Sioux chiefs and visited Omaha, Otoe, Missouri and Iowa villages, painting and sketching at every opportunity. A skilled hunter and taxidermist, he prepared skins and preserved specimens for shipment home. He filled his notebooks with drawings of insects, birds and butterflies, and sketched animals such as antelope and coyote, all unknown before their discovery by Lewis and Clark.

Although not as famous as some other artists of this genre, Peale was the first to capture on paper the landscapes, wildlife and inhabitants of western America. His painting of a Plains Indian on horseback with bow and arrow ready to shoot a charging bison was later lithographed and widely published in the 1830s. It became one of the standard images of the 'Wild West' and would influence countless artists.

More explorations followed before Peale sailed as naturalist on Charles Wilkes's United States Exploring Expedition (1838-42), the last fully sail-powered circumnavigation of the globe. One of the most ambitious American expeditions of the mid-century, the fleet of six ships explored parts of North America's Northwest Coast, Antarctica and a number of Pacific islands, from Fiji to Hawaii. Despite losing a large part of his collection when his ship was wrecked, Peale returned with a total of 2,150 bird-skins, 134 mammals and 588 species of fish.

Peale later became curator of the Philadelphia Museum, and would experiment with early forms of photography. He was, however, first and foremost a naturalist. As English explorer Charles Watson said: 'I met no one in the United States half so knowing or so keen after natural history as Titian Peale.'

Peale spent months with indigenous peoples of the Great Plains and Rockies, sketching and painting details of their daily lives, including a camp of the Otoe and a bark canoe being paddled by Maine returning from a moose-hunting trip in 1830; and, opposite, a spring camp beside the River Platte.

These four action-packed sketches, later adapted into book illustrations, document the bison-hunting skills of the Otoe people along the Missouri River, in what is now Nebraska.

The Wilkes expedition gave Peale the opportunity to witness and sketch places across the globe, from Antarctica and the Pacific to North America. Opposite, he depicts himself in Tahiti pursuing his favourite pastime: catching butterflies. An avid collector and expert taxidermist, he delighted in drawing and measuring everything, from bird-skins to animal skulls; overleaf, a selection of his sketches.

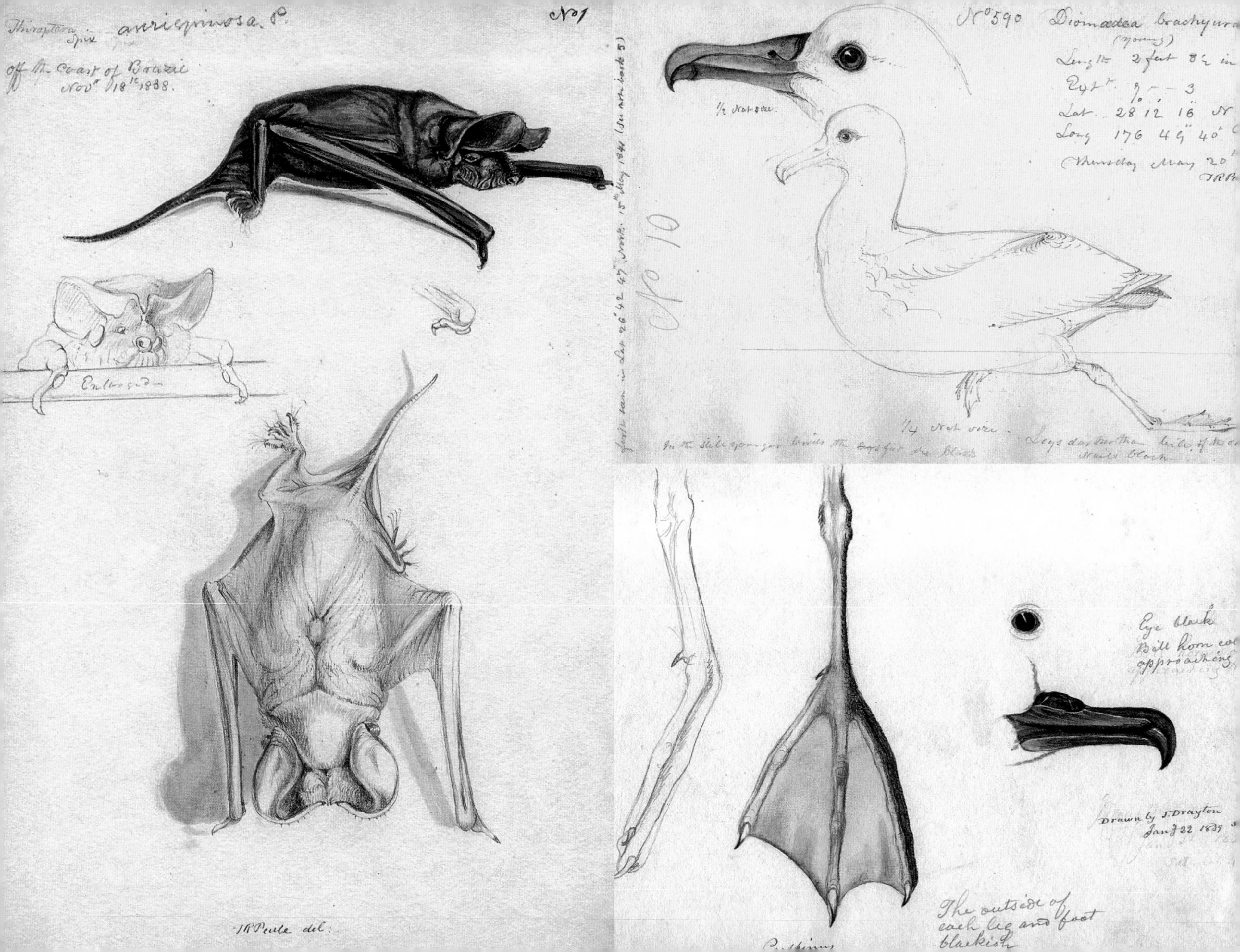
No 1
Off the Coast of Brazil
Novr 18th 1838.
Enlarged
J R Peale del:
No 590
Diomedea brachyura
(young)
Length 2 feet 8½ in
Lat 28 12 16 N
Long 176 44 40
Thursday May 20
½ Nat size
¼ Nat size
No 10
Eye black
Drawn by J. Drayton
Jany 22 1839
The outside of
each leg and foot
blackish

drawn on 22d of August and went into the ground the same day

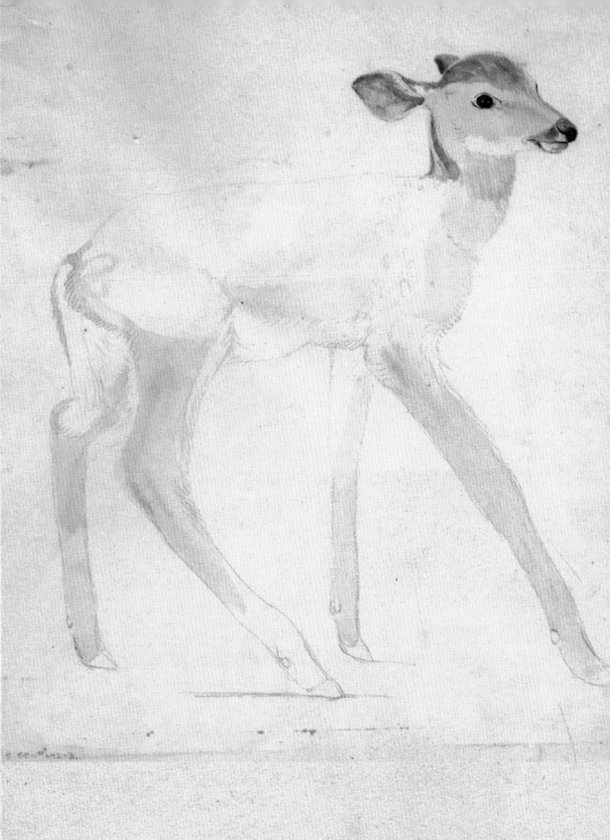

a. head (front) Nat: size
b Mandible double the Nat. size
c Labium double the Nat size
it is contractile and never drawn
except when the jaws are closed.

Carthagena April 4 183
Nat: size
Coloured from the living
Spec.m

TR Peale

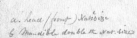

(No 1)

ROBERT PEARY 1856-1920

The Pole at last!!! The prize of 3 centuries, my dream & ambition for 23 years. *Mine* at last.

The above words are from one of the most controversial notebooks in the history of adventure and discovery. With these pencil marks, veteran polar explorer Robert Peary claimed the North Pole for the United States. The entry is dated 6 April 1909, a day that defined the culmination of his life's goal, something he had desired for many decades. The explorer and his team are standing triumphant at the top of the world. But perhaps they aren't.

Inconsistencies in Peary's records abound. The vital North Pole entry was not actually written in the field. Instead, this celebration of his achievement was written later on a loose-leaf page and inserted into the otherwise intact journal. Then there is the journal's strangely incomplete title – 'No. 1, Roosevelt to ---- and return' – as well as the almost super-human speeds at which he claimed to have travelled and his astonishing lack of observations for longitude. All contribute to the overall feeling now that Peary did not reach the Pole.

Today, the proof of the success or failure of any journey can be easily recorded. Satellites orbiting the Earth pick up GPS signals, and beam back coordinates, progress reports and even videos; a plane can fly overhead, confirming a location, or indeed bring home an explorer in distress. For those seeking out unknown frontiers before such technological advances, their observations, sketches, photographs and maps were all essential records – the proof that a discovery had been made. The word of a gentleman was simply not enough.

Given such an important geographical claim, Peary was asked to provide evidence to be examined and verified, both by his peers and those societies he had courted for their support. Yet, when requested to hand over his journal for closer inspection, Peary refused to comply: 'I do not care to leave it with anyone,' he replied flatly. 'I do not care to let it out of my possession; it never has been.' Peary was a formidable character with friends in high places. The committee charged with evaluating his claim accepted a cursory examination of his papers before they were safely sealed within a bank vault. They would remain unseen for over 70 years.

Peary was no stranger to the challenges of the exploring life. As a young man he had hacked through jungles and waded through swamps in Nicaragua, hoping to discover a potential route for a Trans-Isthmus Canal between the Atlantic and the Pacific. Unsuccessful, he had headed north, where his ambition was clear. 'Remember, mother, I *must* have fame,' he wrote home after his first Greenland expedition. He devoted the next two decades to exploring the Arctic, discovering and mapping hundreds of miles of coast and tundra, and losing almost all his toes to frostbite in the process. Aged 52 by the time he set out on this final polar expedition, Peary was certain that success would be his. But he was not the only American with his sights set on this most northerly point.

Just two days before Peary declared he had 'nailed the Stars & Stripes to the Pole', his former subordinate, Frederick Cook, telegraphed the press to say that he had reached the fabled spot almost a full year before. It was sensational news. But Cook had no proofs to back up his claim: his 'instruments, notebooks and flag' had been cached and subsequently lost. He was later jailed for fraud in connection with an oil promotion. Peary meanwhile was made a Rear-Admiral and awarded many gold medals from geographical societies that did not check his records. Eventually, the safety-deposit box containing his journal and observations was re-opened in 1984. Upon examination, several experts in navigation concluded that Peary, though his achievements were great, had not reached the Pole.

On every polar expedition Peary wrapped around himself this Stars and Stripes, sewn in silk by his wife Jo. At each successive 'farthest north', Peary would cut a square from the flag, and place it in a cache along with written notes describing his discoveries. The flag is as much an illustration of Peary's polar travels as his journals and observations.

This loose page with 'The Pole at Last' was inserted into Peary's Arctic notebook, detailing his proof of his achievement.

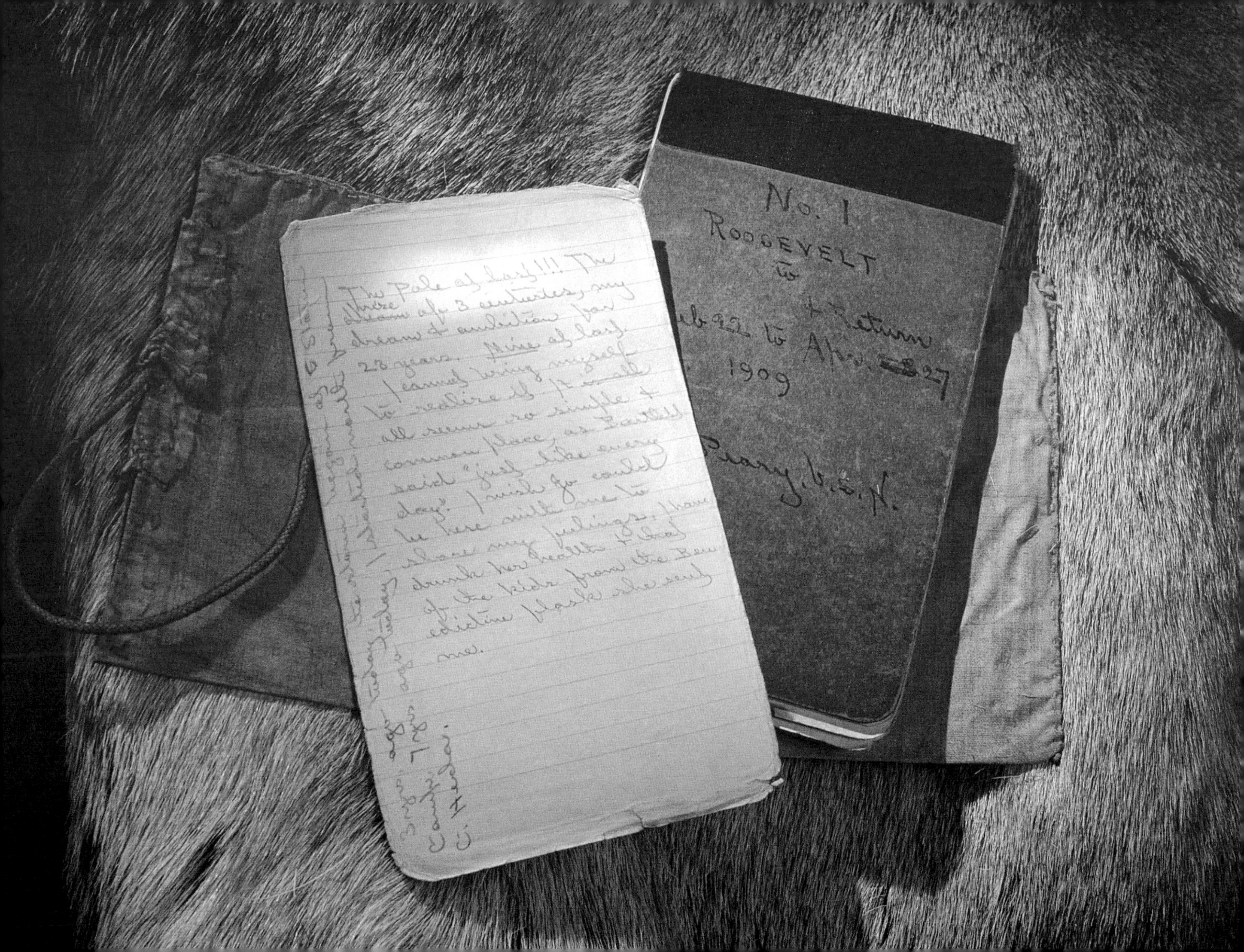
The Pole at last!!! The
prize of 3 centuries, my
dream & ambition for
23 years. Mine at last.
I cannot bring myself
to realize it. It all
all seems so simple &
common place, as Bartlett
said "just like every
day". I wish you could
be here with me to
share my feelings. I have
drunk her health & that
of the kids from the Ben
edistine flask she sent
me.
No. 1
ROOSEVELT
to
+ Return
1909

KNUD RASMUSSEN 1879-1933

From the earliest boyhood I played with and worked with the hunters, so that even the hardships of the most strenuous sledge-trips became pleasant routine for me.

Born on the west coast of Greenland, the son of a Danish missionary and his Inuit wife, Knud Rasmussen was an explorer whose life and discoveries went far beyond the conventional. From an early age he learned to speak the local dialect, *Kalaallisut*, drive sledges and hunt in the toughest conditions. At eight he had his first dog team, at ten his first rifle. Motivated by neither fame nor glory, Rasmussen's insatiable curiosity and genuine respect for the indigenous way of life allowed him to thrive in an environment where many Western men came and suffered.

After a brief career as an actor and opera singer in Copenhagen, he realized that his heart lay in the North. His first expedition in 1902-04 set out to examine Inuit language and culture, a theme that would shape all his future travels. Having finished his first book – a poetic travel journal interwoven with detailed accounts of Inuit folklore – he then ventured to establish a trading base at a site he named 'Thule', the most northerly post in the world. It became the base for a series of seven Arctic journeys, the 'Thule Expeditions'. As his main purpose was to investigate the spiritual life of the Inuit, even when following in the footsteps of previous travellers he was exploring uncharted territory. Rasmussen grappled with geographical theories, mapped little-known tracts of Greenland's northern coasts and amassed a vast trove of ethnographic data, all scribbled and stored in his numerous field notebooks.

Rasmussen's most significant exploratory journey was the huge 'Fifth Thule Expedition' of 1921-24. First taking a team to Arctic Canada to collect oral histories, excavate historic sites and recover artifacts, Rasmussen then travelled for sixteen months with two Inuit companions across North America to the Alaskan coast by dog-sled. Crossing the Bering Strait by schooner, his dream of exploring the remote tribes along the Siberian coast was cut short when his visa was refused. But he was the first European to complete the Northwest Passage by sled, and, more important still, the first to explore the origins of the Inuit people and appreciate the wondrous complexity of their shared culture.

Some of the groups of Inuit he met had never seen a white man. In his notebooks he wrote the stories they told him. At the time, most had no understanding of paper, which some thought the amazingly thin skin of a strange animal. When Rasmussen read their own words back to them, they were astonished that the *creature* – his notebook – had 'such an excellent memory!' Travelling and hunting among the Netsilik, he discovered much of their innate geographical knowledge. With the pencils he gave them they drew accurate maps of the land and sea for hundreds of miles around, which were invaluable to him as he continued on his travels. He filled 30 notebooks with hard-won data, later published in ten volumes, adding immeasurably to our understanding of Inuit ways before the influences of the modern world would change their lives forever.

Rasmussen died in 1933, after contracting pneumonia when weakened by a bout of food poisoning having eaten auks fermented inside a seal, a much-loved local delicacy not for the faint-hearted. Part of his philosophy of travel was always living with the people, not separate from them, yet his appreciation of Inuit food sadly proved his undoing.

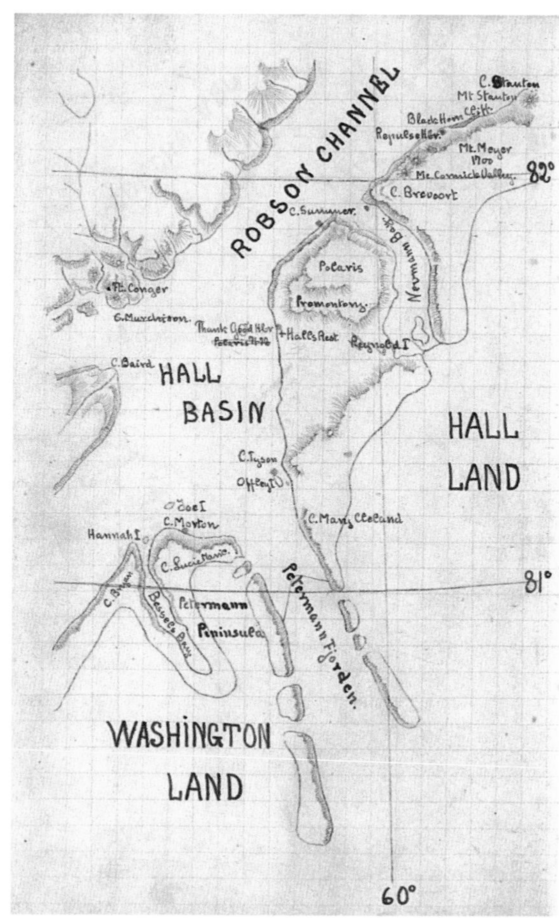

One of many small charts that can be found in Rasmussen's 1917 field journal, refining the known and unknown portions of the map of North Greenland. Opposite are three other notebooks from his wide-ranging explorations along Greenland's remote northern coasts. Filled with poetry, ethnography and cartography, they became essential sources for his later writings.

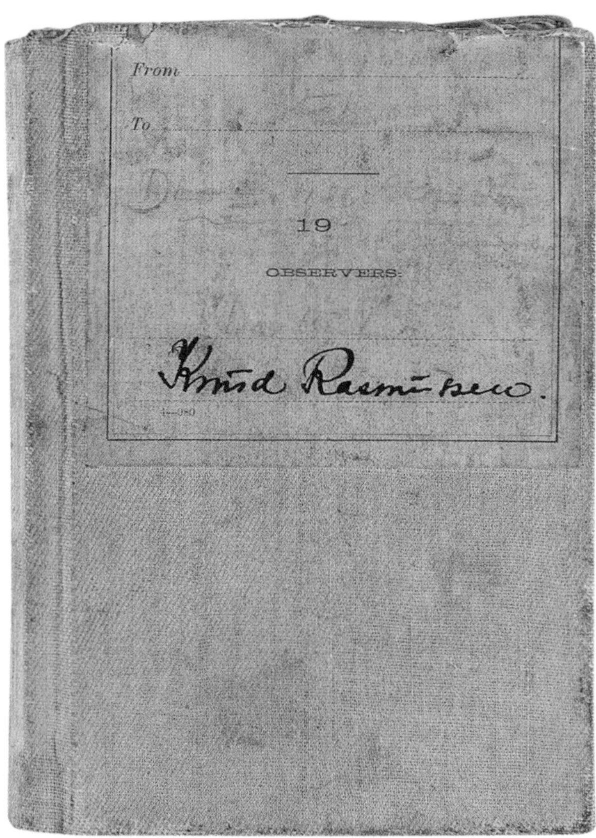

I am glad to have had the good fortune to visit these people while they were still unchanged; to have found … a people not only one in race and language, but also in their form of culture; a witness in itself to the strength and endurance and wild beauty of human life.

These sketches are from Rasmussen's first major expedition, when he journeyed north not in search of the Pole like so many others, but to examine Inuit culture. While other fame-seeking explorers travelled quickly over the land, Rasmussen took time to explore the spiritual life and customs of the Inuit he encountered. 'I have not sounded all the depths,' he wrote. 'One can never finish exploring a people.'

12

iparaŕâtigit' Gûte kisiat ugperilerat[illegible]go lamákua taimaimik [illegible] kiŭnĕrugput.)

uvanga Juva tamák isumavunga taimatussok taimanák orkarpunga nalugako

tarssumenga takussuse tamase saklakotamang; lase tainaselo inuvdluako, ivase asagase Jooa

PHILIP GEORG VON RECK 1711-1798

It thunder'd and lighten'd; and the wind being contrary and strong ... we lay under the Canopy of Heaven upon the bare ground, having made a good fire to warm our benumbed limbs.

In March 1734, just after the Georgia colony in southern British America had been founded by James Oglethorpe, a group of German Protestants arrived to create a new town, Ebenezer, as a refuge for Lutherans expelled from Catholic-controlled Salzburg. Among them was 25-year-old nobleman Philip Georg von Reck, whose intention was to bring back 'ocular proof' of this strange new world.

Enthusiastic and charming, but completely inexperienced, von Reck immediately took on the responsibility of finding a suitable site for the new settlement. Studying Oglethorpe's map of Georgia, he chose a place 'where there are rivers ... cool springs, a fertile soil and plenty of grass'. Within days, von Reck was riding through wild country to locate this new home, balancing on felled trees to cross rivers and sharing a fire and wild turkey with Native Americans. Soon, however, disagreements with the Salzburgers' religious leader saw him stripped of his responsibilities. Furthermore, the location for the new settlement had been poorly chosen. The town had to be relocated beside the Savannah River. Disappointed, von Reck returned to Europe and entered the Danish civil service.

Although von Reck's well-meaning efforts ended unhappily, his sketchbooks and journals provide a unique glimpse of the moment Europeans began settling in a new land. He observed the early markers of colonization – trees that had been barked to indicate where roads would be laid or bridges built. He made some of the earliest records of plants and animals in the area, and vividly documented Native American life. Above all, von Reck captured the hope of a new colony and the youthful wonder of discovery.

Von Reck was intrigued by the local people, and his field studies offer an important and early glimpse of North America in the 1730s. Here is 'the supreme commander of the Yuchi Indian nation, whose name is Kipahalgwa', while his sketch opposite shows the tribe embarking on a hunt in their lands, known today as Georgia.

(34).
Indianer welche auf die Jagd gehen. Fig.
Indians going a hunting

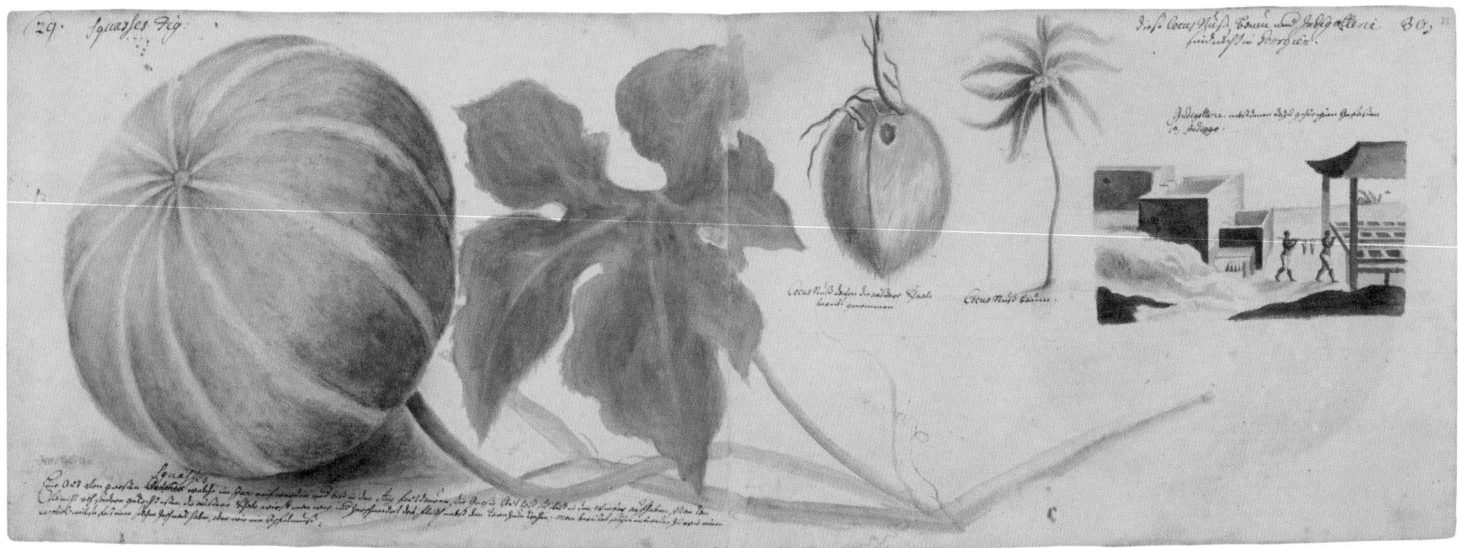

As a facilitator for the new colony, von Reck filled his sketchbooks with everything that might be of interest - from fruits and vegetables to scenes of indigenous daily life. Though not trained as a naturalist, he was fascinated by the plants and wildlife he encountered on his travels, including, as seen here, a water snake, chestnuts and an alligator - a 'sort of crocodile'. Many of his drawings were the first records of new species.

Roerich was as much a mystic as an artist. The most important thing in this world, he asserted, is the 'power of the spirit and culture', the basis for which is 'kind-heartedness, aspiration for knowledge and respect for beauty'. Above is the view to Kilas, Lahul, 1932; and opposite his drawing of Koan-In and Konya-Djonin, deep in the Himalaya in 1924.

NICHOLAS ROERICH 1874-1947

Deep ravines and grotesque hills rear up to the cloud-line, into which melts the smoke of villages and monasteries.

Nicholas Roerich gazed up at the Himalaya: 'Above the nebulous waves, above the twilight, glimmer the sparkling snows. Erect, infinitely beauteous, stand these dazzling, impassable peaks.' He had been fascinated by the geography and culture of this region since a child. Now, in 1923, along with his wife and son, he was embarking on a five-year journey that would take them through Sikkim, Kashmir, Ladakh, Sintzian (China), Siberia, Altai, Mongolia, Tibet and the Trans-Himalaya. As an archaeologist, he would search for a common source of Slavic and Indian cultures; as a philosopher he wished to understand eastern beliefs and discover traces of Jesus' fabled journey into the east; and as an artist he was inspired to vividly record some of the most spectacular desert and mountains areas in the world.

By the time Roerich arrived in northern India he was already an internationally recognized cultural figure. Born in St Petersburg, he had simultaneously studied law and art before travelling to Scandinavia, England and America, where he designed sets for Russian ballets and operas for Diaghilev and Stravinsky, established several cultural institutions and mounted large touring exhibitions of his unique paintings celebrating Russia's ancient past. It was the vibrant spirituality, culture and art of Central Asia, however, that would become his greatest inspiration.

Between 1923 and 1928, the Roerichs trekked hundreds of miles, enduring blizzards, sickness and fatigue. In Kashmir they had fights with thieves. In Ghund, hustlers fed their horses with poisonous grass, and wildcats crept under their son's bed. At Zoji their caravaneers threatened to leave for fear of avalanches. But they continued on, turning 'obstacles into possibilities', recovering their strength in remote monasteries and in villages fragrant with incense, wild mint, sage and apricots. By the end, Roerich had recorded new mountain peaks and passes, discovered archaeological monuments and rare manuscripts and had created over 500 artworks. The family settled in India and founded the Institute of Himalayan Studies. In 1934, they embarked on another expedition, to Inner Mongolia, Manchuria and China.

In his lifetime Roerich was celebrated for his creative genius, his extraordinary travels, his dedication to science and for his immense spiritual presence. His creative legacy speaks for itself, with numerous articles, books and essays and more than 7,000 paintings in collections all over the world. But perhaps more important were Roerich's guiding principles of human unity and friendship. His efforts to promote international peace through art and culture resulted in two nominations for the Nobel Peace Prize and the 'Roerich Pact': an agreement signed at the White House in Washington in 1935 obliging participating nations to respect museums, universities, cathedrals and libraries as they did hospitals during wars or civil conflict. In times of war, cultural institutions would fly Roerich's 'Banner of Peace' as protection. Roerich lived out his final years in the Kullu Valley in the western Himalaya. His body was cremated and his ashes buried on a slope facing the mountains he loved.

Nowhere, to one's recollection, is there such an open barricade of elevations. From this superb prospect one obtains an especially enthralling impression of the grandeur of the Himalayas — 'Dwelling of snows'.

Throughout his travels Roerich sketched and painted in situ. His vibrant sketches would often form the basis for other paintings once he returned home. Both works here are in tempera. The sketch of 1933 above was painted on canvas laid on cardboard, while that opposite was painted on a wooden panel.

INDISPENSABLE FRIENDS

David Ainley

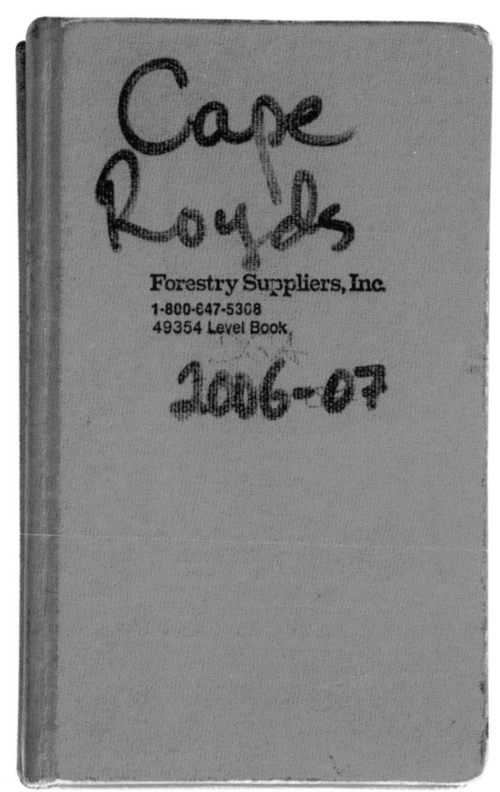

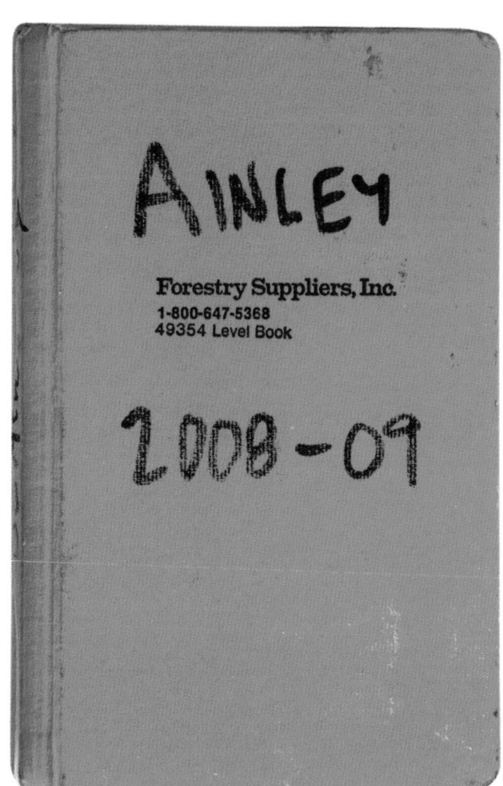

Brightly covered field notebooks are useful when working among the rocks and guano of an Antarctic penguin colony in summer. Mislay your brown journal and you'd have real trouble finding it again.

In an undergraduate course in ecology, taught by a herpetologist, I was schooled in the necessities of keeping a record of my observations. My field journal would become a sort of catalogue of nature, filled with endless notes that linked a specimen to the context in which it was found – date, time, place, habitat. Skinks, fence lizards, snakes, anything and everything that I collected or gazed upon. In graduate school, however, where I became immersed in the study of polar vertebrates, the conduct of science by collecting specimens had long since gone out of style, passing with the heroic era of Antarctic exploration. A catalogue like mine was thought of as quaint and old-fashioned, and what it represented politically incorrect – something of a bygone age when science was done only with a shotgun and specimen jar.

Nevertheless, I was inspired by books like *A Sand County Almanac* by ecologist Aldo Leopold and the experiences of the explorer Meriwether Lewis – a boyhood hero of mine. The lessons he had learned in the wilderness encouraged me to stick with my little notebooks. When embarking on his exploration of the American West, his mentor, Thomas Jefferson, had advised Lewis that 'knowledge unrecorded is knowledge lost'. This thought would ring in my ears and I knew that I must not miss a thing. On beginning my own research on Adélie Penguins on Ross Island, I was handed a leather-bound field book in which to record my observations and data, an advance beyond my scribblings in school notebooks. In an instant, my field book became an important element of the kit of the research team in which I worked. The data recorded within its tattered covers became invaluable.

Spending year after year among the ice of the Ross Sea, the field books that I accumulated were to become my most prized possessions. The habit had stuck. Quickly I had learned that in the high Antarctic where I worked, besides the books, a knife to sharpen my pencil was indispensable, any ink in a pen usually freezing. And any sort of electronic device just would not work, and would be unreliable. I also learned, from some anxious experiences, that a field book had to become 'un-losable'. Starting out, I once mislaid a book when trying to capture a skua with a net; it was often an athletic endeavour, with a bird diving one way, and my book flying out of my parka pocket in the other. Only after painstakingly retracing my steps was I able to recover it, its brown cover camouflaged among the endless boulders and frozen guano of the penguin colony. It was a huge relief – you can't imagine how happy I was. Thereafter I would plaster the journals with bright yellow tape in fat stripes. Eventually I found field books bound in vivid orange covers. In the polar snows, these were just perfect.

My field books were not works of literary merit, like those of Captain Scott and other early polar adventurers, but rather methodical recordings of data, by place, date and time of day – more like Amundsen's terse sledging journals perhaps, or the regular entries of a ship's sailing log. I kept weather records in a separate spreadsheet too. Early in a field season, my observations were written in sequence, but after a few weeks I would begin to compile detailed tables, which contained observations repeated on individual penguins, or of whale or seabird counts. At the same time, I made a log of each day's activities so I could keep a sense of how each season had progressed, day by day, storm by storm, and slowly my observational data were amassed. I sometimes drew little memory maps, too, for purposes of orientation, or if a thought occurred to me that I didn't want to forget, in it would go. A lurid little orange book was a treasury of my time and an essential part of my work when I got home.

In the shadow of Shackleton's hut at Cape Royds, my team now fixes satellite tags on penguins so we can monitor where they are hunting and how deep they are diving. Some carry computer chips and their weight and identities can be logged. Our camp is set up on the lava scree nearby, far enough away from the colony that we are not too often bothered by penguins plucking tent ropes in curiosity. Inside Shackleton's historic hut is an array of woolly jumpers, food cans and old wooden cases, tangible memories of those who went before. True, we now have Gore-Tex and solar power, but the conditions outside the hut are as challenging as they have ever been. The majority of my field research is still a case of spending time with penguins in person, watching silently for the slightest changes in behaviour, searching for patterns, and then trying to assemble the different pieces of the puzzle in my head.

Our research has identified the climate-related phenomena, as well as industrial fishing, that will define the future of these penguins. The Ross Sea is a fragile ecosystem, not long ago the last pristine ocean, and it requires understanding as much as protection. All knowledge that we can gain about this balanced biological system is essential if we are to approach conservation here with the urgency that it now needs.

Needless to say, after spending more than 35 seasons in the Antarctic, my shelves are now crammed with field books. Many of the entries have since been logged into endless computer spreadsheets and exist in digital pixels to be shared with colleagues instantly around the world. Nevertheless, the daily context in which the data really lived is only revealed by going back and slowly thumbing my way through the books, page after page. It's an enjoyable process returning to what have become, essentially, my indispensable 'friends'. Despite all the advances in technology that make regular fieldwork like mine at the edge of the world now possible, sometimes all you really need is clear weather, a notebook and a sharp pencil.

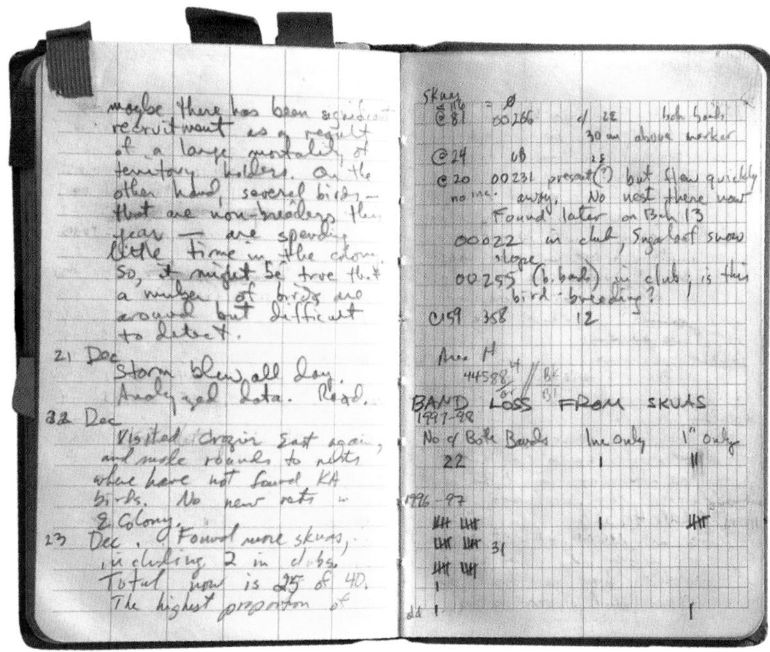

Inside these journals page after page of field notes, data and observations are recorded. Opposite, Ainley has divided a penguin colony up into manageable zones as he continues the painstaking task of logging and observing; it is data hard won, in often bitter conditions, and the summer season is short and light is fading fast. He must work quickly but also carefully.

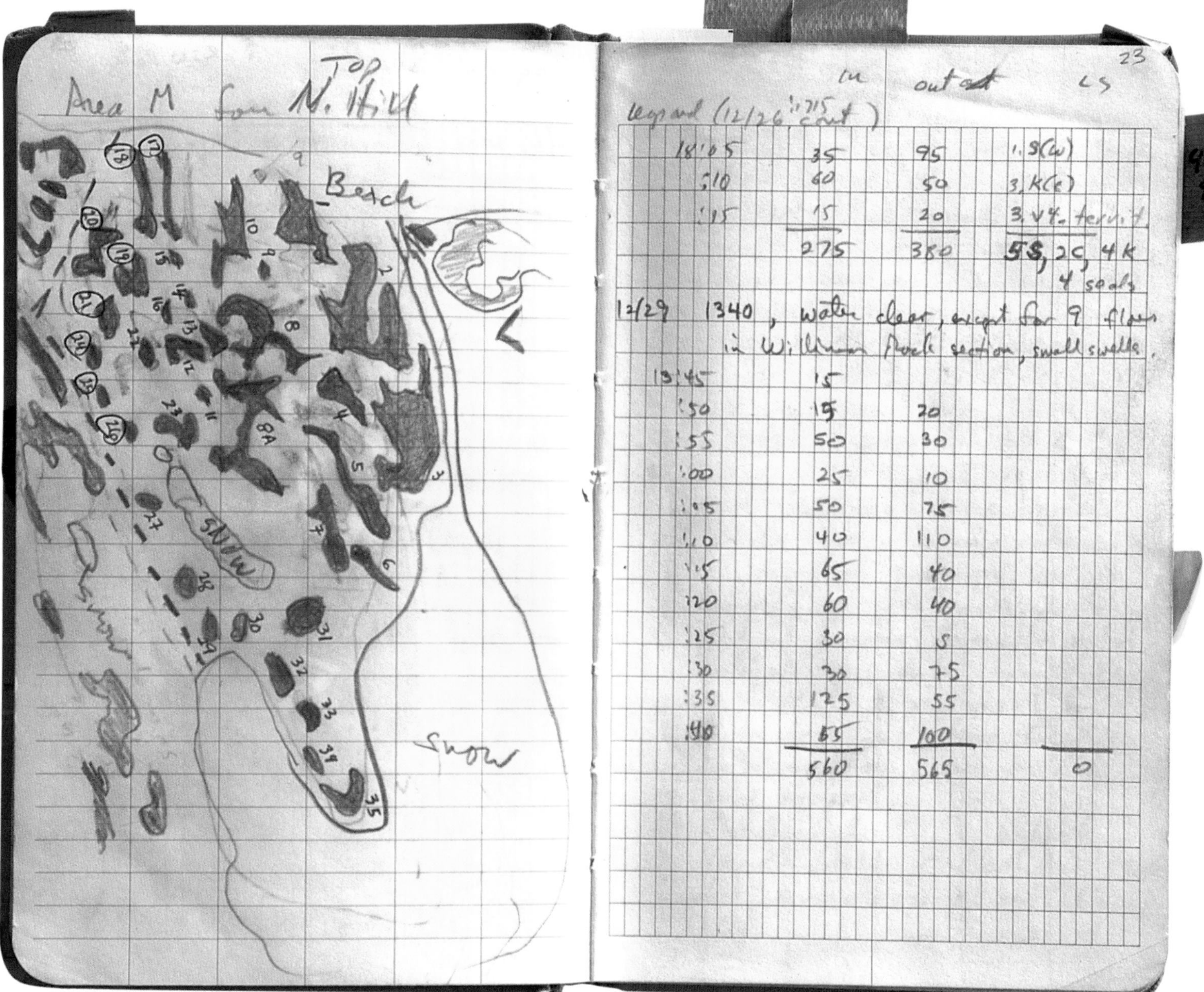
Top
Area M from N. Hill
Beach
SNOW
Snow
23
in
out
LS
leopard (12/26 1715 cont)
18:05 35 95 1, S(w)
:10 60 50 3, K(E)
:15 15 20 3, V4. terrvit
275 380 5S, 2C, 4K
4 seals
12/29 1340, water clear, except for 9 floes in Williams Rock section, small swells.
13:45 15
:50 15 20
:55 50 30
:00 25 10
:05 50 75
:10 40 110
:15 65 40
:20 60 40
:25 30 5
:30 30 75
:35 125 55
:40 55 100
560 565 0

ROBERT FALCON SCOTT 1868-1912

We shall stick it out to the end, but we are getting weaker, of course, and the end cannot be far. It seems a pity, but I do not think I can write more.

It could be argued perhaps that Robert Falcon Scott deserves to be remembered not for his exploring, but for his gift for writing under quite unimaginable circumstances. Though he has been maligned in recent years as incompetent, even reckless, such criticisms do injustice to a man whose achievements in Antarctica were considerable. It is true Scott made mistakes – as have so many others following after him – but it is hard to deny his courage, especially when you realize that small things in his favour might have turned tragedy into triumph. A storm of unprecedented severity ultimately denied Scott and his men survival. As the blizzard tore at his tent, he would write until his fingers could no longer hold a pencil. His companions died around him. Eventually he was alone. How had it come to this?

Scott had joined the naval training ship HMS *Britannia* at thirteen. Later, an unremarkable torpedo officer, he was plucked from obscurity in 1901 to lead the first British Antarctic expedition for over 50 years. Scott was not obsessed with the polar regions, unlike so many of those who travelled with him, and admitted that he only began reading polar books a few months before he left. Though unable to reach the South Pole, the *Discovery* expedition of 1901-04 was a huge success, making valuable contributions to the understanding of a continent still largely unknown, and successfully passing two winters in high latitudes. On his return, Scott was promoted to Captain in the Navy and later led the fateful second expedition, sailing south on the *Terra Nova* and reaching the shores of Antarctica again at Ross Island on 22 January 1911.

On 16 January 1912, after travelling for 77 days over almost 1,290 km (800 miles) of wild white desert, Scott and his companions – Edward Wilson, Henry Bowers, Edgar Evans and Lawrence Oates – were confronted with an awful discovery: a black flag. All around were sledge tracks and the imprint of dogs' feet. 'This told us the whole story,' Scott wrote that night: 'The Norwegians have forestalled us and are first at the Pole. It is a terrible disappointment, and I am very sorry for my loyal companions ... to-morrow we must march on to the Pole and then hasten home with all the speed we can compass. All the day dreams must go; it will be a wearisome return.'

They would never reach home. Their supplies dwindled and the weather grew worse. Time was running out. Evans fell during the march, and Oates gave his life for his companions; Scott, Wilson and Bowers lay trapped in their tent, as a fierce blizzard vented its fury outside. The three men summoned the strength to scribble letters to their families, in the hope that these last thoughts might be found. Scott managed to keep writing his diary to the very end. His final entry was dated 29 March, the day he is presumed to have died, and concludes with the line: 'For God's sake look after our people.'

Eight months later, in November 1912, a search party found the tent and the final wishes of these men were fulfilled. Their letters and journals were returned to those loved ones at home desperately waiting for news. Scott's words would resonate beyond the ice, and the public grieved at the loss; their failure was transformed into a noble sacrifice. Of the letters, the last that Scott penned to his wife is perhaps the most heart breaking of all: here was a man trying to brave death when all hope had gone. He added the words, 'To My Widow', at its head.

Captain Scott's final diary, perhaps one of the most famous journals of all, recovered when his body was found in 1912. A sacred object, within its fragile pages the tragedy is told.

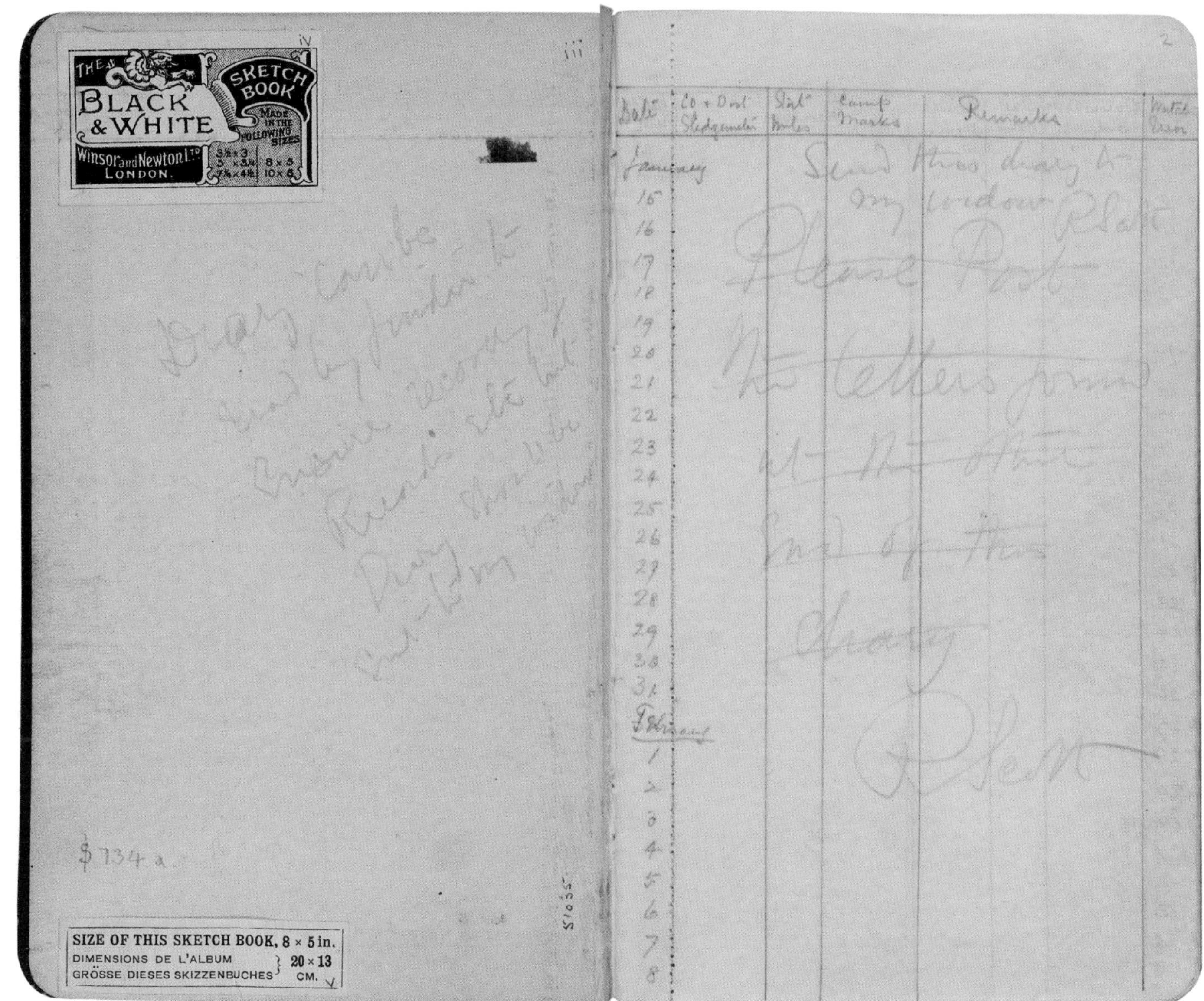

Aboard ship and in the base hut, Scott wrote a daily journal in large quarto books. On the sledge journeys he kept his diaries in smaller, 8 x 5 inch, 96-page artist's sketchbooks, writing in pencil on all the right-hand pages then sometimes turning the book to fill the rest of the volume. A green canvas wallet containing the three sledging diaries from the 'Southern Journey' was discovered beneath his sleeping bag by the search party that found the bodies of Scott and his companions, entombed in their tent in the snow.

Pages from Scott's journal for 17 and 18 January 1912. The entry for 17 January begins 'The POLE. Yes, but under very different circumstances from those expected. We have had a horrible day - add to our disappointment a head wind 4 to 5, with a temperature -22°, and companions labouring on with cold feet and hands. We started at 7.30, none of us having slept much after the shock of our discovery ... Great God! This is an awful place and terrible enough for us to have laboured to it without the reward of priority ... Now for the run home and a desperate struggle to get the news through first. I wonder if we can do it.'

Scott's final entry, 29 March 1912. 'Every day we have been ready to start for our depot 11 miles away, but outside the door of the tent it remains a scene of whirling drift. I do not think we can hope for any better things now. We shall stick it out to the end, but we are getting weaker, of course, and the end cannot be far. It seems a pity, but I do not think I can write more. R. SCOTT.' He then added: 'Last entry. For God's sake look after our people.'

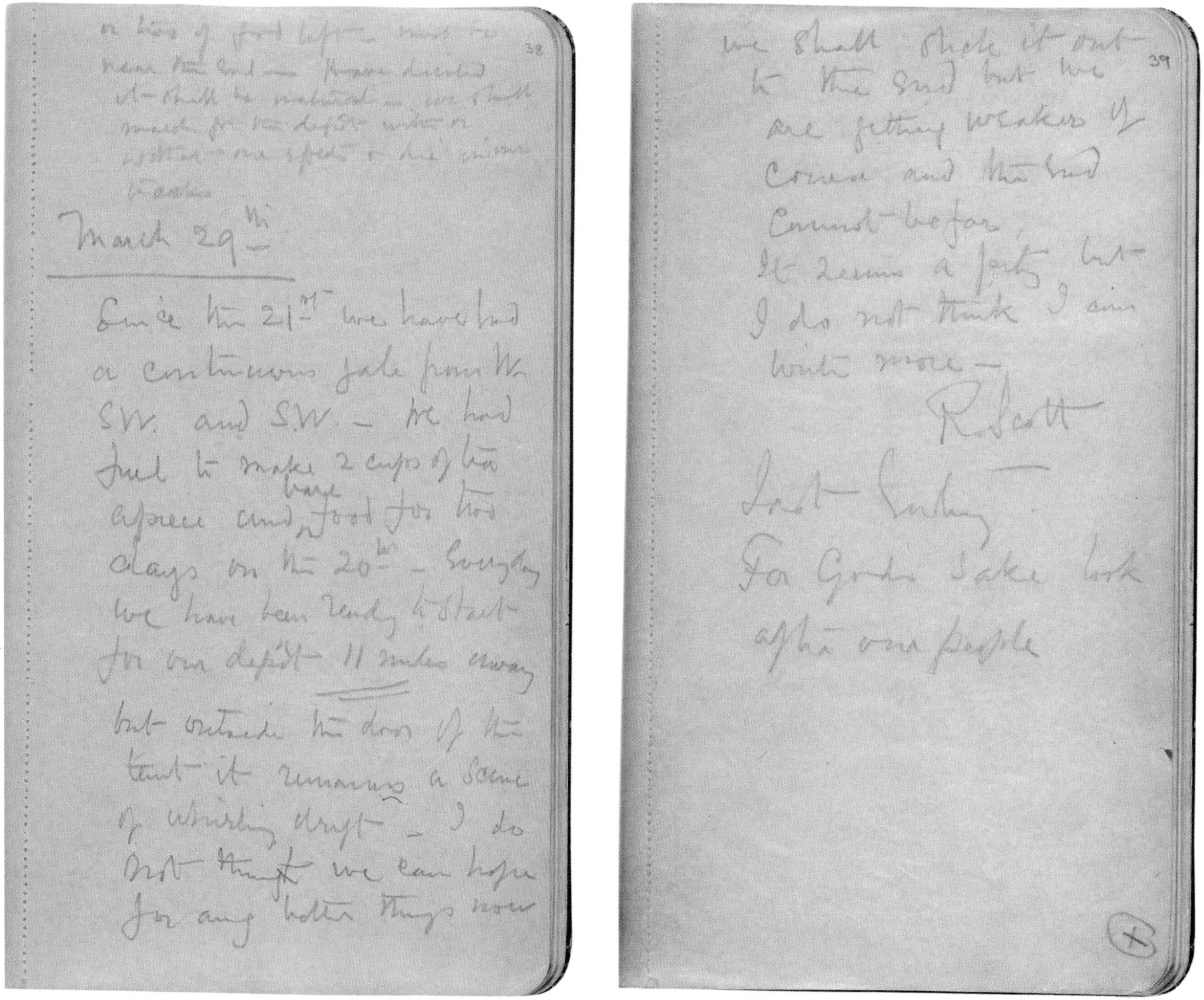

38

or two of food left — must be
near the end — Have decided
it shall be natural — we shall
march for the depôt with or
without our effects & die in our
tracks

March 29th —

Since the 21st we have had
a continuous gale from W.
S.W. and S.W. — We had
fuel to make 2 cups of tea
apiece and bare food for two
days on the 20th — Every day
we have been ready to start
for our depôt 11 miles away
but outside the door of the
tent it remains a scene
of whirling drift — I do
not think we can hope
for any better things now

39

We shall stick it out
to the end but we
are getting weaker of
course and the end
cannot be far,
It seems a pity but
I do not think I can
write more —

R Scott

Last Entry —
For God's sake look
after our people

ERNEST SHACKLETON 1874-1922

I feel I am no use to anyone unless I am outfacing the storm in wild lands.

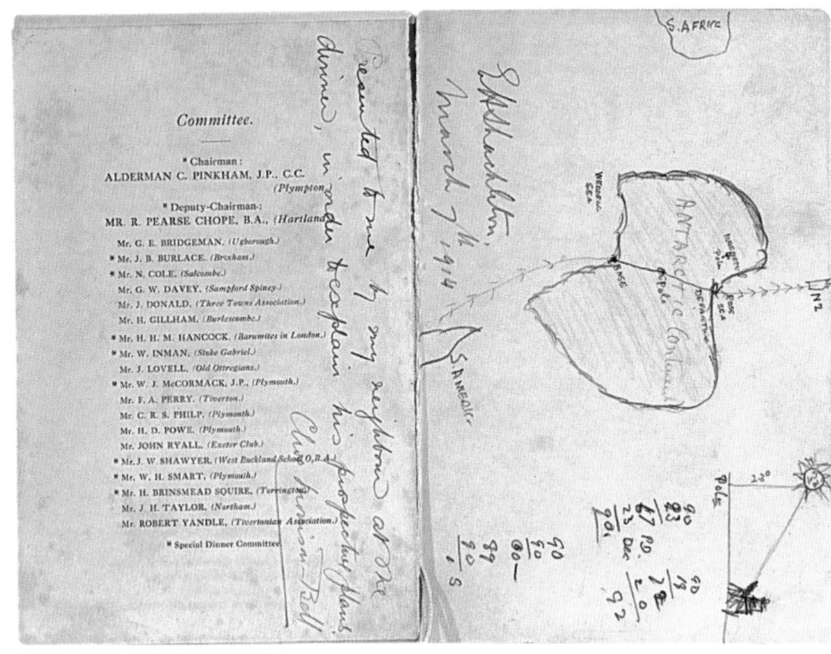

Committee.

* Chairman:
ALDERMAN C. PINKHAM, J.P., C.C. (Plympton.)

* Deputy-Chairman:
MR. R. PEARSE CHOPE, B.A., (Hartland.)

Mr. G. E. BRIDGEMAN. (Ugborough.)
* Mr. J. B. BURLACE. (Brixham.)
* Mr. N. COLE. (Salcombe.)
Mr. G. W. DAVEY. (Sampford Spiney.)
Mr. J. DONALD. (Three Towns Association.)
Mr. H. GILLHAM. (Burlescombe.)
* Mr. H. H. M. HANCOCK. (Barumites in London.)
* Mr. W. INMAN. (Stoke Gabriel.)
Mr. J. LOVELL. (Old Ottregians.)
* Mr. W. J. McCORMACK, J.P., (Plymouth.)
Mr. F. A. PERRY. (Tiverton.)
Mr. C. R. S. PHILP. (Plymouth.)
Mr. H. D. POWE. (Plymouth.)
Mr. JOHN RYALL. (Exeter Club.)
* Mr. J. W. SHAWYER. (West Buckland School O.B.A.)
* Mr. W. H. SMART. (Plymouth.)
* Mr. H. BRINSMEAD SQUIRE. (Torrington.)
Mr. J. H. TAYLOR. (Northam.)
Mr. ROBERT YANDLE. (Tivertonian Association.)

* Special Dinner Committee.

By the time Ernest Shackleton sailed towards Antarctica in January 1908, he had inspired the people of New Zealand to such an extent that 50,000 well-wishers crowded the streets of Lyttleton to catch a last glimpse of the explorers before they headed South. The enthusiasm for Shackleton's venture was so great that Raymond Priestley, one of the scientists on board, commented that several vessels of the accompanying flotilla were listing dangerously as passengers rushed across the decks to cheer as *Nimrod* passed.

One year later, Shackleton, with Frank Wild, Eric Marshall and Jameson Boyd Adams, was closer to the ends of the Earth than any human before. On 9 January Shackleton wrote: 'We have shot our bolt and the tale is 88.23 S. 162 E.' Exhausted, cold and hungry, the men unfurled their flag and planted it in the polar plateau. They were within 156 km (97 miles) of the South Pole but could go no further with any certainty that they would make the gruelling journey back to *Nimrod* alive. Shackleton took the wise decision to live to fight another day. 'Better a live donkey than a dead lion', he later said.

By the smallest of margins, Shackleton's team made it safely back. Although falling short of its main objective, the expedition had accomplished a new farthest south, discovered the location of the South Magnetic Pole and made the first ascent of Mount Erebus. Their reception on their return was as triumphant as if they had discovered the Pole itself. Knighted for his efforts, Shackleton was swept into a lecture tour that would draw in a cumulative audience of a quarter of a million.

Shackleton, 'the Boss', would come to be regarded as a visionary and a great leader of men, yet for others also a financial liability and a failure. Certain that he had struck a seam of good luck and wealth, Shackleton gave away his lecture fees to good causes and made a series of poor investments. By 1913, he was broke and restless. Both the North and South Poles had been claimed, and Captain Scott was the nation's tragic hero. It was clear that Shackleton needed a new, even more ambitious goal: the first crossing of Antarctica.

In August 1914 Shackleton's *Endurance* sailed south, but quickly became trapped in ice. As *Endurance* was crushed and sank, the men drifted on an ice floe for five months before taking to their three lifeboats and reaching the desolate Elephant Island. No sooner had they made landfall than Shackleton set out again by open boat with five companions on a journey of 1,290 km (800 miles) to South Georgia. Their perilous fifteen-day crossing of the storm-lashed Southern Ocean and subsequent traverse of the mountainous interior of the island to reach the whaling station at Stromness is one of the most astonishing feats in polar history.

Shackleton left England's shores for the last time on 18 September 1921. On 4 January 1922 Shackleton was in a pensive mood. The *Quest* had anchored at Grytviken, South Georgia, and together with his closest friends, Wild and Frank Worsley, he had relived the final episode of the *Endurance* expedition. That night he suffered a fatal heart attack. In the hours before his death he had written his final entry in his journal: 'In the darkening twilight I saw a lone star hover, gem-like above the bay.' Shackleton, the ever restless, charismatic Irishman had finally found peace.

The end came at last about 5pm – she was doomed, no ship built by human hands could have withstood the strain – I ordered all hands on to the floe.

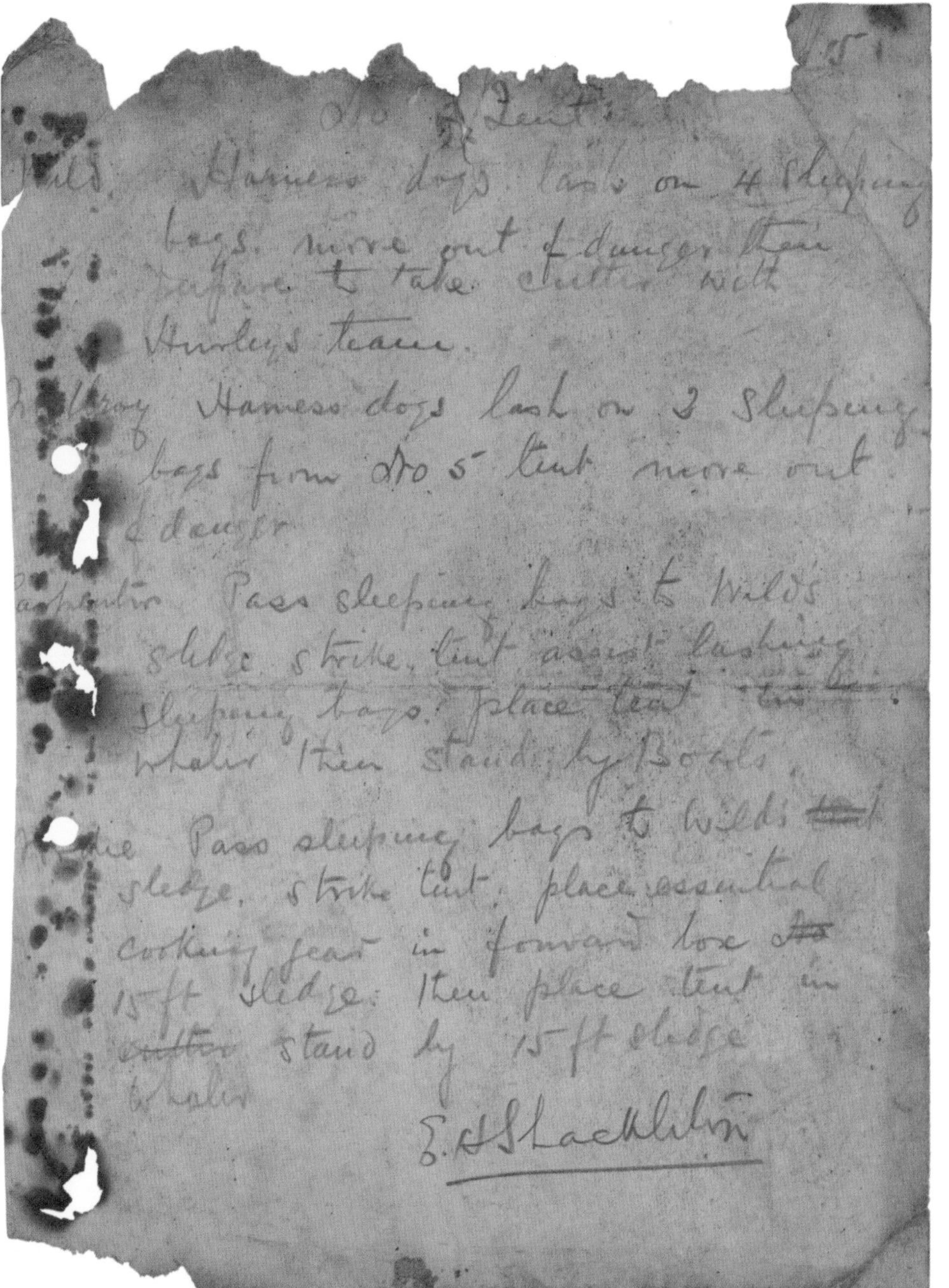

No 5 Tent

Wild Harness dogs lash on 4 sleeping bags. move out of danger then prepare to take cutter with Hurley's team.

McIlroy Harness dogs lash on 2 sleeping bags from No 5 tent move out of danger

Carpenter Pass sleeping bags to Wild's sledge strike tent assist lashing sleeping bags. place tent ~~in~~ whaler then stand by Boats.

Pass sleeping bags to Wild's sledge. strike tent. place essential cooking gear in forward box of 15 ft sledge: then place tent in ~~cutter~~ whaler stand by 15 ft sledge

E H Shackleton

Opposite: Preserved for posterity, a menu card bears a simple sketch by Shackleton, who was explaining to his neighbour at dinner in March 1914 his ambitious plan to cross Antarctica. As events would have it, Shackleton didn't even manage to set foot on the continent this time round. Yet, the *Endurance* voyage has gone down in the annals of polar history as one of the most remarkable stories of survival against all odds.

On 27 October 1915 Shackleton gave the order to abandon ship. *Endurance* had been crushed by the ice, leaving the men stranded on ice floes far from land. Shackleton worked out in detail what each man was to do if the ice broke under the camp, and pinned a copy of the instructions to each tent. The dark stains on the paper are smoke from the blubber stove.

Antarctic B.A.S. 86/87
N. POLE
2012
collins ideal...
SOUTH POLE 2012/3
Addresses
S.POLE → HER
KITE TRIP
summit
The International Trans-Antarctic Expedition
NOTE BOOK
Ruled Feint
NAME
SUBJECT
GEOFF SOMERS
Antarctic 86/87
A5 Feint
£2.79p
PILOT'S FLYING LOG
SAIL ATLANTIC
1989
Polar Expedition
Notes for Polar Season
03/04
CLUB
48 LEAVES
NOTE BOOK
IDEAL
ANTARCTIC
B.A.S. 86/87
1:5000 000
Collins
IDEAL
BOOKS
IDEAL
GREENLAND
GLACIO
TRAVERSE
2004
CHALLENGE

GEOFF SOMERS 1956-

Every journey changes you as a person. When you get safely home, the really miserable moments on a difficult expedition are always the ones you end up enjoying the most.

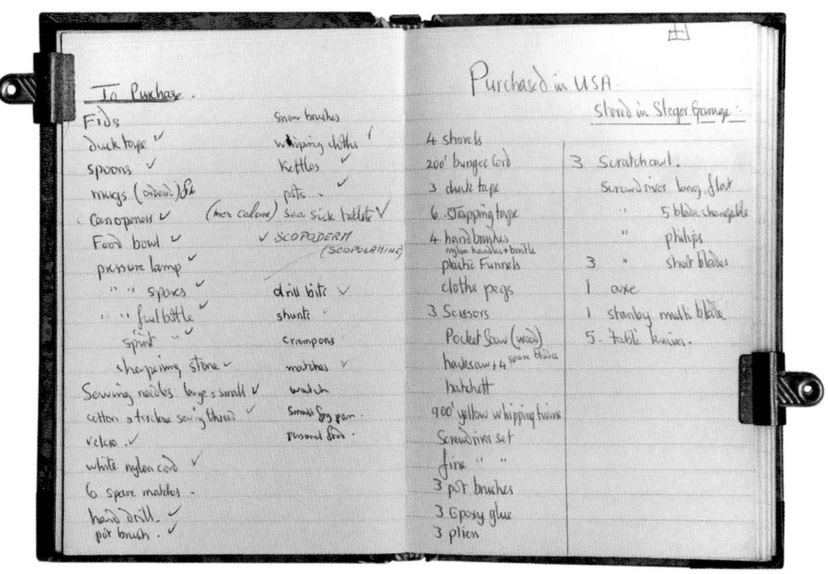

A formidable traveller, Somers has led expeditions over scorched deserts, through dense jungle and across icy wilderness. But he is most well known for his traverse of the entire Antarctic continent by its greatest axis – a seven-month, almost 6,200-km (3,850-mile) journey, using husky dogs to pull the sledges. To train for this, the team crossed the Greenland Ice Cap from south to north. During both of these adventures, Somers was responsible for the logistics, navigation and driving the lead dog team. Yet his achievements as a polar traveller go beyond borders or nationality; the crossing of Antarctica in 1990 was an achievement for all humankind, in that it brought together six men from different nations working towards a common cause: to focus the world's attention on this frozen continent.

Somers's five companions were Will Steger, an American environmental advocate, the designated leader of the team; Jean-Louis Étienne, a French doctor, who had skied solo to the North Pole, where by incredible chance he had met Steger; Qin Dahe, a Chinese glaciologist, who took daily measurements of ice and snow; Keizo Funatsu from Japan, also a dog trainer, who kept these crucial four-legged companions healthy; and Soviet scientist Victor Boyarsky, an Antarctica veteran who had spent a lifetime collecting data on ozone and weather in some of the world's most remote places. This was an impressive team of adventurers. The longest traverse of the continent was truly Antarctica the hard way.

The struggle to keep men and dogs alive and moving forwards was almost overwhelming. 'There were so many times when we were in danger', Somers admits, 'but we never really thought about it. We had to nurse two of the dogs for two months because they had frostbite in their legs; we wrapped them in jackets until a plane could take them off. Antarctica doesn't treat fools gladly, and life here can be very, very complicated. When the worst winds came, all we had were two layers of canvas between us and the outside. It would take less than two seconds for the tent to go and you would die.'

On foot, on ski and by kite power, Somers has now travelled some 22,500 km (14,000 miles) in the Arctic and Antarctic. He has led groups to the North Pole six times and has been to the South Pole a dozen times too, including a re-creation of Captain Scott's fateful journey using clothing and equipment as near as possible to those of the Heroic Age. Unlike Scott, of course, Somers was able to benefit from modern technologies, aircraft and radio, to ensure his survival.

Somers has also worked in Outward Bound schools throughout the world. As deputy director, he helped set up the Outward Bound school in Sabah, Malaysia, and, among other rainforest journeys, he crossed Borneo through remote jungle. In Australia, with three camels from the wild, he travelled from Perth across the deserts to Uluru, the 'Red Centre' of this remarkable continent. When not in remote corners of the world, he spends much of his time at home in England's Lake District, working through his copious journals and notebooks, writing his memoirs and planning new expeditions.

A lifetime of adventurous explorations produces a snowdrift of journals and notebooks. Each one is crammed full of details, both colourful and mundane: the real life of expeditions includes weather conditions and kit lists of essential supplies.

JOHN HANNING SPEKE 1827-1864

If I ever travel again, I shall trust to none but natives, as the climate of Africa is too trying to foreigners.

In the early hours of 19 April 1855, the silence of the camp was shattered by screams, gunshots and war cries. Running out of his tent, John Speke quickly despatched two of the Somali attackers before he was knocked to the ground by a tremendous club-stroke to the chest. By dawn, the camp was abandoned and looted. One of the expedition team was dead and Speke held prisoner, alternately being taunted and viciously stabbed with his captors' spears.

Remarkably, though bearing several deep wounds, two of them through his thighs, Speke managed to wrestle, run and punch his way through 40 armed men to safety. 'Lieut. Speke's escape was in every way wonderful,' his enigmatic expedition leader Richard Burton would later write. Yet in years to come, the two men would become bitter adversaries.

Speke had joined Burton in Africa after serving a ten-year commission with the Bengal infantry. The idea of an expedition in Africa appealed to his love of hunting as much as his sense of adventurous curiosity. But, naive of local customs, he would soon discover that the realities of African travel were immensely challenging: he became embroiled in clan disputes he could not understand and made few discoveries. With the attack on the camp by the Har Owel tribe, all hopes for the expedition were dashed. Speke was invalided back to England in June 1855, and it would be two years before he and Burton were reunited in Africa – with the aim to explore the interior further and determine the location of the long sought-after source of the Nile.

Eight months into their journey, Burton was battling with malaria and fever. With Burton incapacitated, Speke decided to lead his own party, and discovered the southern end of a lake, which he named Lake Victoria. Although unable to explore the area more fully due to local tensions, Speke concluded that he had discovered the source of the Nile.

In May 1858, with the support of the Royal Geographical Society, and to the consternation of Burton, Speke made his discovery public. Two years later he returned to Africa with James Grant to prove his claim. The geographical obstacles he encountered were trifles compared to the lengthy negotiations with rival clans, whose territories he needed to pass through. Speke spent months with the powerful chiefs Mutesa and Rumanika, gleaning knowledge of the region and winning their trust, recording details in his diaries and sketchbooks. Eventually he was given permission to proceed. On 28 July 1862, Speke pinpointed the place where the Nile issues from Lake Victoria. He named it Ripon Falls.

Speke returned to London, and at a special meeting held at the Royal Geographical Society in his honour he was welcomed by a riotous crowd. The adulation, however, would not last. Burton disputed his results, calling Speke a 'deluded nonentity' and highlighting that the discovery had not been verified by Grant, who had been too ill to join the final leg of the journey. On 15 September 1864, the day before an arranged debate between Burton and Speke, Speke lay dead: the accidental, some say suicidal, victim of a gunshot wound while hunting. Although Speke's shortcomings as a geographer and surveyor were many, his discovery of the source of the Nile was proved to be correct by the later explorations of Stanley and others.

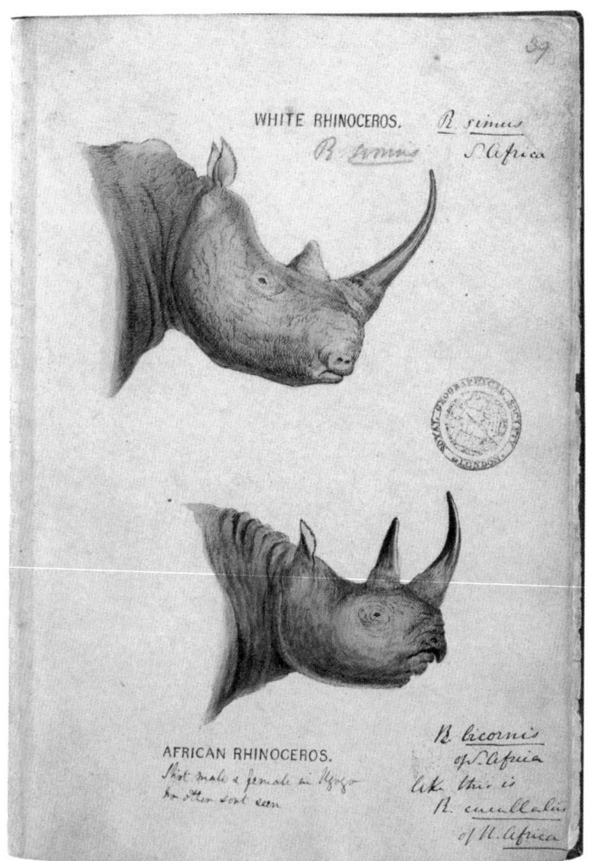

No 3
Mbwiga View of the Blue Mountain S. 60° W–

A big game hunter as much as an explorer, Speke wrote that he was 'always eager to shoot something either for science or the pot', hence perhaps his interest in the White and African rhinoceros. But he also sketched local life and landscapes, here 'Mbwiga, view of the Blue Mountain'.

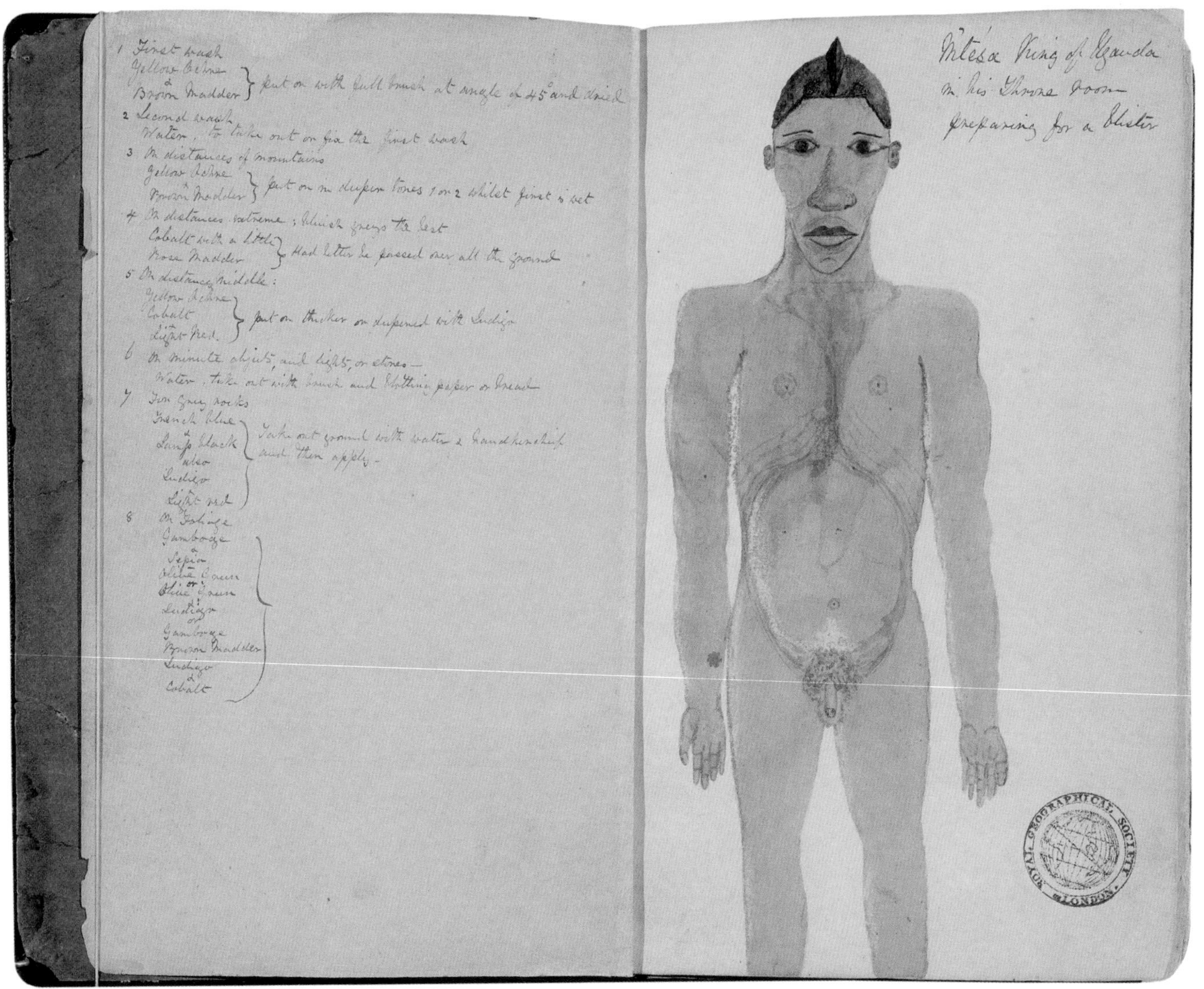

My first occupation was to map the country … The rest of my work, besides sketching and keeping a diary, which was the most troublesome of all, consisted in making geological and zoological collections.

Speke's diaries and sketchbooks provide the earliest eyewitness account of the Kingdom of Buganda, modern-day Uganda, and its people. He was fascinated by the rulers of the clans he met, seeing them as the true African aristocracy. Mutesa, left, was the ruler of Bunyoro, the most powerful kingdom Speke had to pass through. Speke included a sketch of his palace in his journal, opposite right, alongside the ubiquitous Ugandan cow.

260

Mtesa's Palace
1862
I.H.S

Uganda Cow

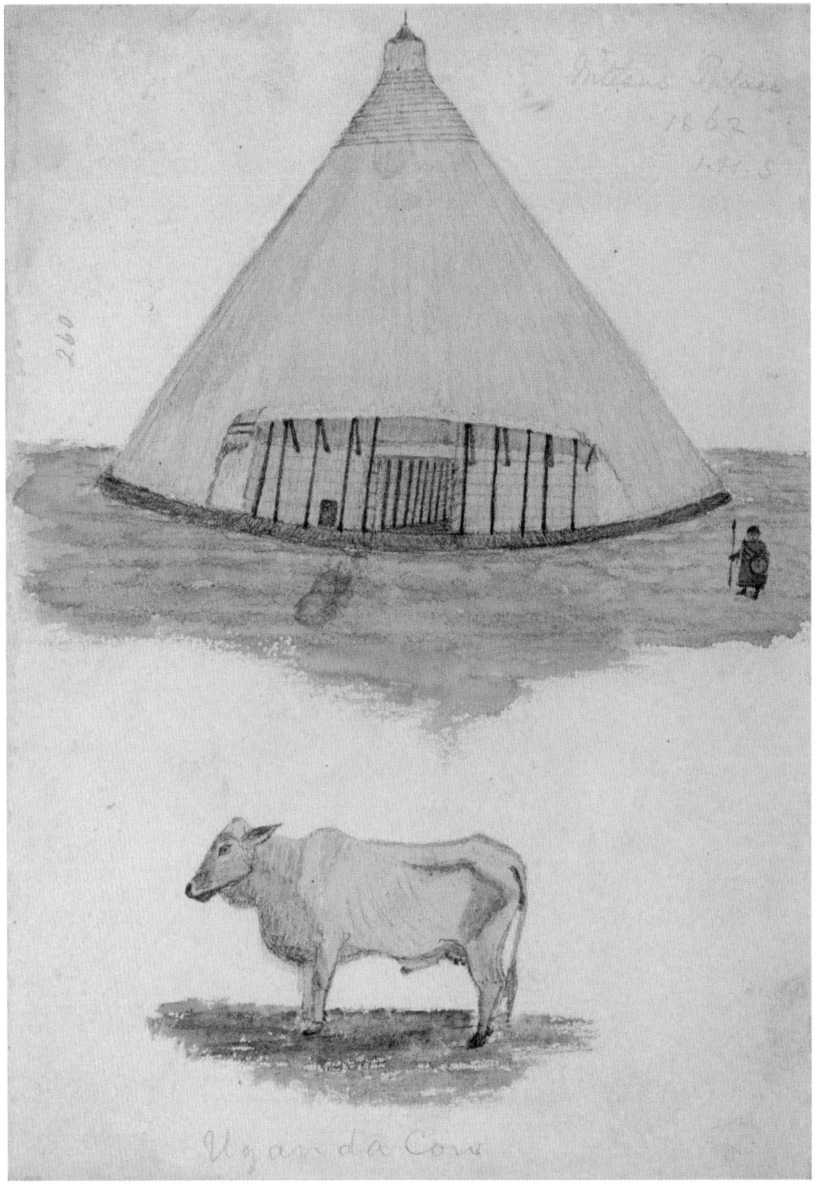

FREYA STARK 1893-1993

I have no reason to go, except that I have never been, and knowledge is better than ignorance.

'And then the wonder happened!', Freya Stark wrote as she entered the desert for the first time. Camels were appearing gradually, until she was surrounded by a herd of some 500 towering animals and their riders. 'I stood in a kind of ecstasy among them. It seemed as if they were not so much moving as flowing along, with something indescribably fresh and peaceful and free about it all ... I never imagined that my first sight of the desert would come with such a shock of beauty and enslave me right away.' Stark would become a highly respected Arabist and one of the most recognized travel writers of her time.

Born in Paris to liberal British parents, Stark had spent much of her childhood in northern Italy. A sickly child, reading the *Arabian Nights* was her escape. As the First World War broke out, she volunteered as a nurse at the Italian front, then became an art smuggler to make ends meet. All the while the East called. By the time she arrived in Beirut in 1927 for her first taste of desert travel, she was already conversational in Arabic and was learning Persian.

Stark had neither the aristocratic bearing nor the wealth of her predecessor, 'Queen of the Desert' Gertrude Bell, but she was just as intrepid and fearless. She slipped unseen into Luristan, an area under martial law, meeting the leaders of the Druze Rebellion. She was arrested by the French authorities on suspicion of being a spy, and charmed her way to freedom, before venturing into the hinterland of Lebanon and Syria where no Western travellers had been before. She crossed the Chala Pass and followed the Alamut River through Iran, correcting existing maps of the region as she went, while overcoming malaria, dengue fever, dysentery and measles, which she contracted from a child in a harem. In the wilds of Lamiasar she discovered the fortress of the famed cult of the Assassins, scaling the escarpment in stockinged feet as the approach was too slippery for her shoes. Her accurate maps and narrative of the journey won her medals from the Royal Geographical Society and the Royal Asiatic Society.

Throughout her decades of travel, Stark chose to write letters rather than journals. Composed in the field under the shade of a tree or ruin, these written sketches of her experiences were sent home to her mother and her publisher, and would later be worked up into over two dozen books – many now regarded as classics of travel literature. Eccentric, outspoken and self-assured, Stark was a larger-than-life figure, known as much for her gaiety and adventurousness as for wearing bold combinations of Arab garb and haute-couture dresses, with a large hat covering a scar from a horrific childhood accident. Like Bell, she was recruited by British Intelligence, becoming an enthusiastic propagandist during the Second World War.

After the war, Stark visited Central Asia, Afghanistan, China and the Himalaya. In her 60s she retraced the route of Alexander the Great through southern Turkey; in her 80s she voyaged down the Euphrates by raft. She continued to travel until she was 92. In 1972, she was named Dame Commander of the British Empire. She died aged 100 at her home in northeast Italy. In tribute, the Italian newspapers called her *la regina nomade*, 'the nomad queen'; in Britain, writer Lawrence Durrell declared her a 'poet of travel ... one of the most remarkable women of our age'. She thought of herself in more modest terms: 'I like to feel a pilgrim and mere sojourner in this world.'

Rather than keeping notebooks or journals, Stark chose to write letters. Composed in the field, these detailed sketches of her experiences were sent home to her mother and her publisher, John Murray, and would form the basis of her popular travel narratives. In these lively accounts, she captured a romantic world of nomads, caravans and harems at a turbulent time for the Middle East. A keen photographer, she also kept an extensive photographic record of her travels, here the Rock of the Assassins, Alamut, Iran, taken in 1930.

From Freya Stark,
c/o British Embassy,
Cairo.

17.11.41

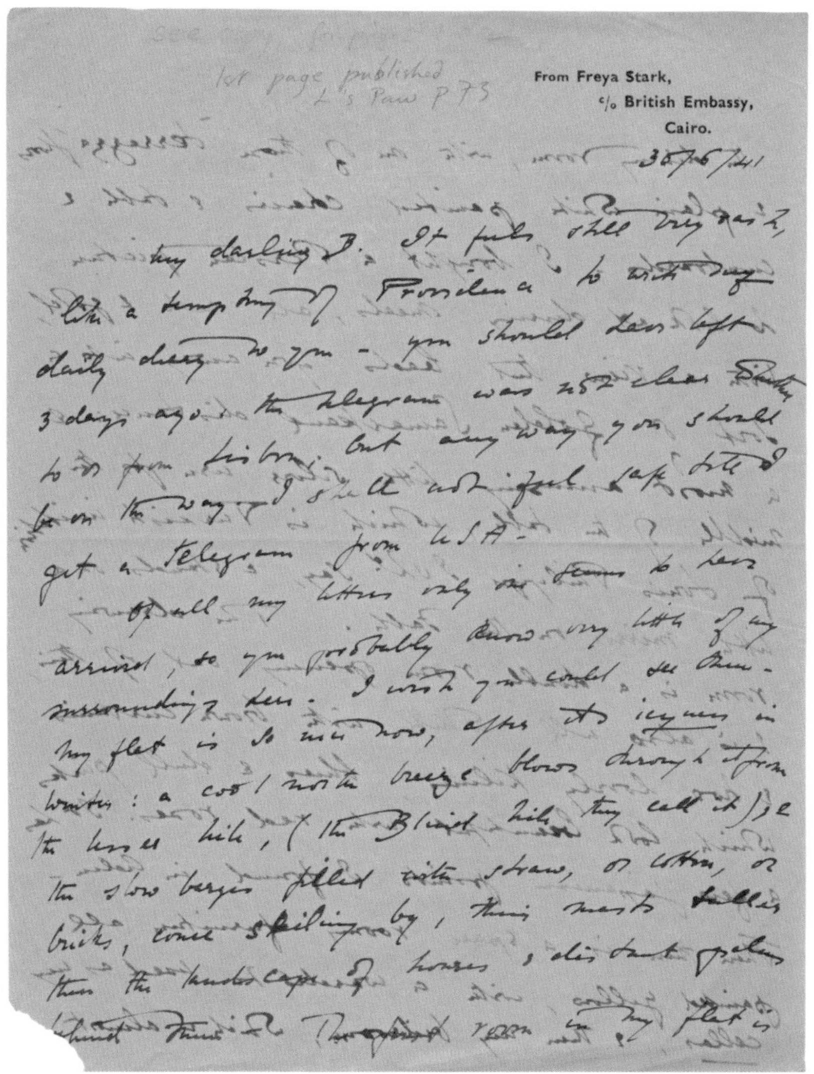
From Freya Stark,
c/o British Embassy,
Cairo.

To awaken quite alone in a strange town is one of the most pleasant sensations in the world. You are surrounded by adventure.

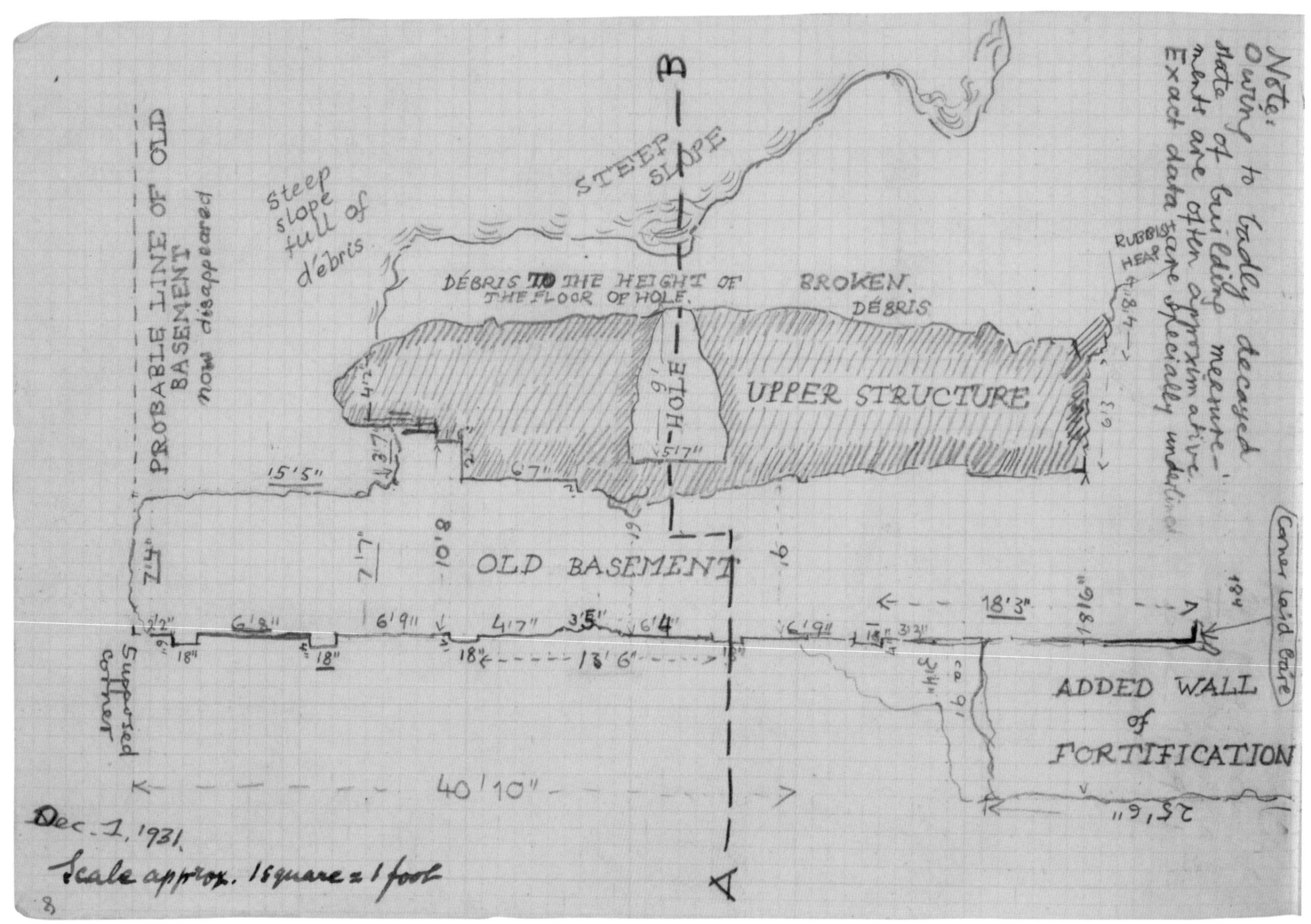

Note: Owing to badly decayed state of building measurements are often approximative. Exact data tape specially underlined
PROBABLE LINE OF OLD BASEMENT now disappeared
steep slope full of débris
STEEP SLOPE
B
DÉBRIS TO THE HEIGHT OF THE FLOOR OF HOLE.
BROKEN. DÉBRIS
RUBBISH HEAP
HOLE
UPPER STRUCTURE
OLD BASEMENT
15'5"
6'7"
18'3"
13'6"
40'10"
25'6"
Corner laid bare
Supposed corner
ADDED WALL of FORTIFICATION
A
Dec. 1, 1931.
Scale approx. 1 square = 1 foot

MARC AUREL STEIN 1862-1943

The sand-storms, which visited us daily, and the increasing heat and glare, had made the work very trying to the men as well as myself. It was manifestly time to withdraw from the desert.

In the decades before the First World War, many European explorers and archaeologists travelled in Central Asia. But one man stands out from the rest: Anglo-Hungarian geographer Marc Aurel Stein. Amid fierce rivalry to be the first to discover traces of long-lost Buddhist civilizations, Stein marched relentlessly some 40,250 km (25,000 miles), often in appalling conditions, conducting geographical and ethnological surveys and systematically uncovering shrines and tombs hidden for thousands of years beneath China's deserts. Tenacious and persistent, he was a force of intellect and curiosity whose name will forever be linked with the Silk Road. This fabled trade route linking China with the Mediterranean coast was also a meeting point of the civilizations of East and West, a conduit of culture, beliefs and technologies.

Having already put to use his surveying skills in India, Stein made three great Central Asian journeys between 1900 and 1916. His discoveries were exceptional: crossing the Hindu Kush, he was the first archaeologist to explore the Taklamakan Desert; the first to conduct a survey of prehistoric Iran; the first European to enter the Indus Kohistan, and the first to describe the mountain of Una as the site of Alexander the Great's siege of Aornos. In the Dunhuang oasis he found the Caves of the Thousand Buddhas (Mogao). Inside, was a hoard of early manuscripts hidden for some 800 years. Among the 40,000 scrolls Stein shipped back to England was a copy of the *Diamond Sutra*, the world's earliest known printed book, dated to AD 868.

Although physically slight, Stein could endure extreme privations and tackle the most difficult terrain in pursuit of his goal. So dry and lifeless were parts of the desert that he even discovered his own footprints from a journey he'd made seven years earlier. 'Time seems to have lost all power of destruction on this ever-dry ground,' he wrote in wonder. The relics he unearthed were immaculate, vividly preserved for centuries by the arid climate.

Stein became known for his heavily laden camel trains carrying away objects from the desert. The rightful place for these antiquities, he believed, were Western museums, where they could be preserved, studied and displayed. He was of the opinion that his removal of artifacts safeguarded them from damage or theft, having seen first-hand the desecration of similar sites in India, where 4,000-year-old bricks or stones from Buddhist temples had been carted off to build roads or used as railway ballast. He insisted that neither fame nor treasure-seeking was his motivation, but a greater understanding of ancient civilizations.

But, despite the scale and contribution of his journeys, China's later outrage at the 'theft' of their historic objects, coupled with his own publicity-shy personality, cast Stein into the shadows. However, described as 'The Greatest Explorer of Our Time' by a newspaper shortly before his death, Stein collected innumerable international honours, including a British knighthood.

Stein died in Afghanistan on 26 October 1943, just days before he was about to embark on another major expedition. He was 81. In Kabul's Christian cemetery, his gravestone reads: 'By his arduous journeys in India, Chinese Turkistan, Persia and Iraq he enlarged the bounds of knowledge ... A man greatly beloved.'

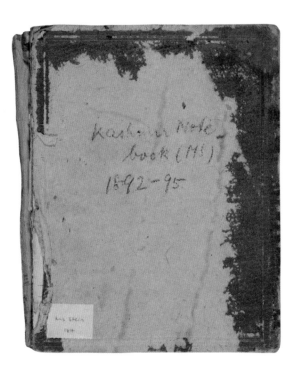

For Stein, the discovery and understanding of a lost civilization was worth any amount of privation. He chose the Chinese desert for his research deliberately for its obscurity. He relished being a pioneer; there was little competition in such a far-flung and hostile environment. His battered notebooks were as valuable to him as the treasures he shipped home. Opposite is his sketch of the ruined temple, known locally as 'Murti', in the Gamdhala Valley in a notebook from Kashmir. These early surveys would hone his skills for his extraordinary later journeys in Central Asia.

ABEL TASMAN 1603-1659

This land seems to be a very fine country and we trust that this is the mainland coast of the unknown South land.

Seafaring Abel Janszoon Tasman was a Dutch merchant skipper with a taste for far-flung voyages. The earliest known European explorer to reach the shores of Tasmania, Tonga and Fiji, he is most frequently heralded as the first to 'discover' New Zealand, though of course the Māori had been there for centuries. Tasman left little behind to mark his brief presence here – a couple of place names on the beginnings of a chart, a ragged line drawn in a vast ocean, a first brush stroke on the still incomplete map of the world.

His first voyage in 1634 was in the employ of the Dutch East India Company, and he honed his navigation skills patrolling the waters off Indonesia for rebels and smugglers. In 1639 he sailed in search of 'the islands of gold and silver' east of Japan. After a series of successful trading expeditions, he was given command of the most ambitious of all Dutch voyages, tasked with exploring the empty tracts of the chart in the Southern Hemisphere in order to solve the puzzle of the vast hypothetical landmass that might lie there. Was there a practicable sea passage across the Pacific to Chile, and would there be exploitable lands along the way?

He left the company's base in Batavia (Jakarta) in August 1642 with two small vessels: his flagship, the yacht *Heemskerck*, and *Zeehaen*, an armed transport ship. They reached Mauritius and then headed south before turning east and sighting land on 24 November at 42°20'S. Tasman skirted its southern shores, naming it Van Diemen's Land after the governor general of Batavia, but decided against further investigation and continued eastward. On 13 December he reached the coast of South Island, New Zealand, and explored the coast northward, entering the strait between North and South Island, assuming it to be a bay. It was here, on 19 December, that the Dutch had a violent encounter with the local Ngāti Tūmatakōkiri, in a place Tasman would later name 'Murderers Bay'.

Māori canoes came out to Tasman's ships as they were anchored in what is now Golden Bay. Tasman noted that the men had 'rough voices and strong bones'. The *Heemskerck*'s small boat was rammed and the sailors were attacked with paddles and clubs; three were killed and one mortally wounded. The canoes then raced back to shore out of range of the muskets and canon which opened fire from both ships. As Tasman weighed anchor and set sail, eleven canoes approached again but were fired on, with one Māori in the leading boat struck down by canister shot.

Tasman left New Zealand waters in January believing he had discovered the western shore of a great southern continent, naming it 'Staten Landt' in honour of the Dutch state legislature. He reached Batavia on 14 June, completing a ten-month voyage, effectively circumnavigating Australia without seeing it. Tasman ventured south again the following year to define Australia's northern coastline, but this resulted in failure as he did not discover lands of potential wealth for his backers. In 1647 he resumed command of trading fleets, this time on a mission to the islands of Siam, and was also pressed into service fighting the Spaniards in the Philippines. The following year, when drunk, he attempted to hang two sailors who had disobeyed orders, and his reputation never recovered. He retired to captain his own small cargo ship, the sea still calling him, but his days as an explorer were over.

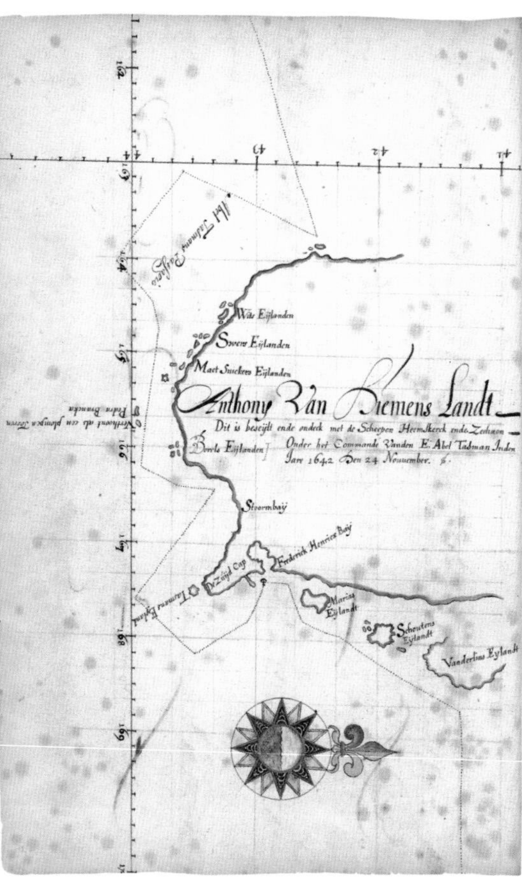

The earliest chart of the surveyed coast of 'Anthony van Diemens Landt', the southern tip of Tasmania; Tasman was the first to sail along it in 1642.

Coastal profiles (opposite) were an essential part of a seaman's journal. It is likely that many people sketched in this way on the voyage, though the most talented artist was Isaac Gilsemans. The sketches were collected and several 'definitive' journals were later compiled. Tasman dictated the text to his draughtsmen and signed the finished result.

Aldus vertoont hem t Landt op 4 desember 1642 op de Zuyder Breete van 42 grad. 38 Minuyten als het 2 Mylen
N.W. ten W.
N. ten W.
Aldus vertoont hem t lant op 4 Xber 1642 op de Zuyder Breete van 42 graden 40 Minuyten als het vaste
Maria Eylant
Z.W. ten Z.
W.Z.W.
Landt 4 a 4½ Mylen ende d' Eylanden 2½ a 3 Mylen
W.N.W.
N W ten W
N. W. ten N. d' E. Hr. schoutens Eylant
N. en N ten Westen
Vertooningh op 5 Xber 1642 Als het 8 Mylen van
N ten W en N N W
Z.W. ten Z.
Z.W. en Z.W. ten Z.
Z.W.
Z.W. ten W.
W. d' E. Hr. vanderlyns Eylant
W. ten N. ende W.N.W.

All the lands, islands, points, turnings, inlets, bays, rivers, shoals, banks, sands, cliffs, rocks etc., which you may meet with and pass, you will duly map out and describe, and also have proper drawings made of their appearance and shape.

New Zealand was first seen by European eyes when Tasman came upon the west coast of South Island. Onboard, Isaac Gilsemans sketched the coast from just north of Punakaiki up to Rocky Point, today's Cape Foulwind. Different events of that fateful encounter are imagined here. These and other sketches are the first European representations of this land and of the Māori, and had a significant influence on European perceptions. Any drawings that were made at the time, or during the voyage, have been lost and these may be the earliest that survive. The full truth is impossible to determine.

On 5 January 1643 a group of islands northwest of North Island was sighted, which they named 'The Three Kings', coming to anchor there on Twelfth Night. Wanting fresh water they tried making a landing, but were discouraged by the rocky shore and heavy surf, and by 30 or so inhabitants who shouted 'with rough loud voice' and threw stones from the clifftops (opposite).

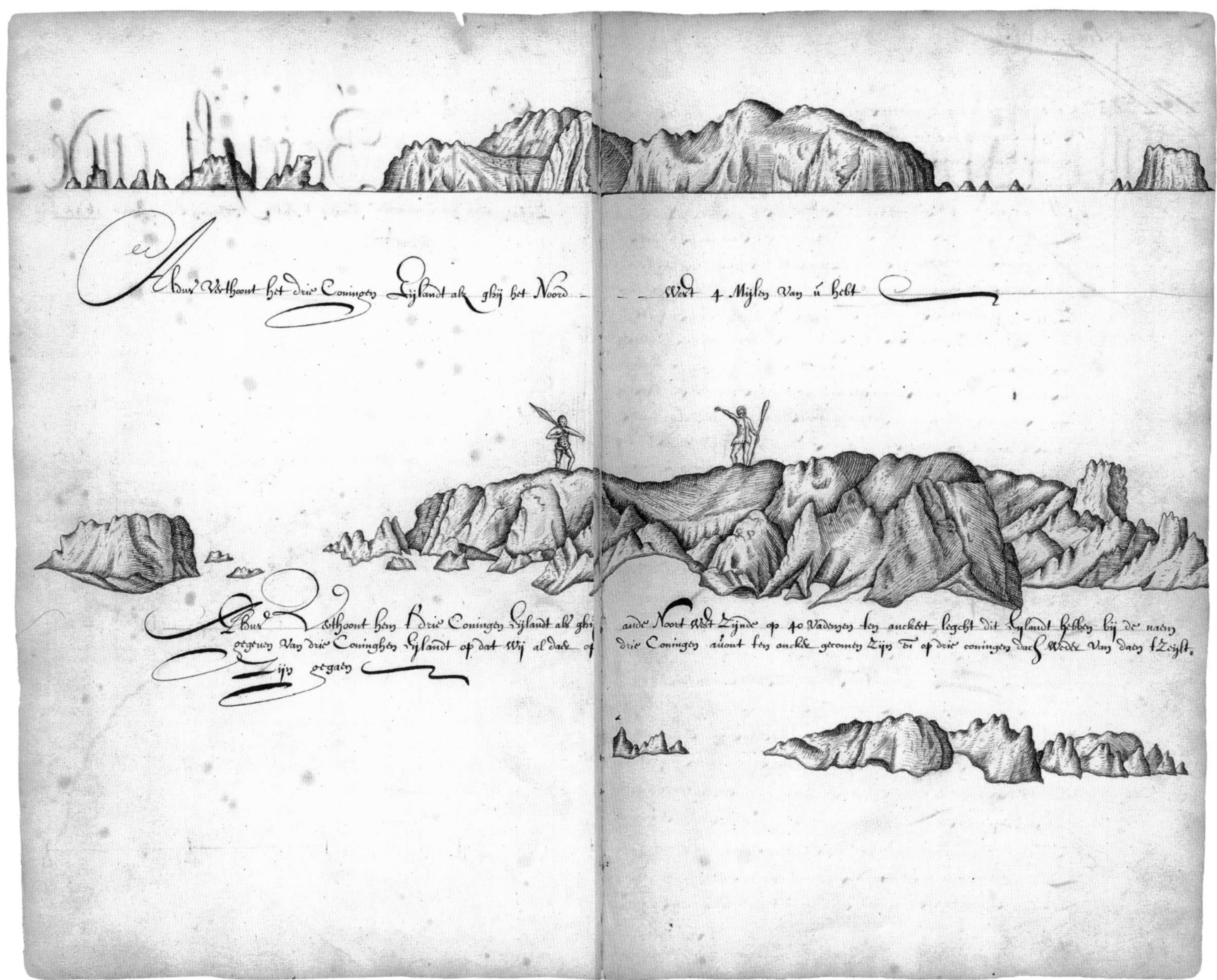

Aldus vertoont het drie Coningen Eylandt als ghij het Noord — — West 4 Mijlen van u hebt
Aldus vertoont hem t drie Coningen Eylandt als ghij ande Noort West Zijnde op 40 vademen ten ancker legcht dit Eylandt hebben bij de naem gegeven van drie Coninghen Eylandt op dat wij al dade op drie Coningen avont ten ancker gecomen Zijn en op drie coningen dach weder van daen t Zeylt Zijn gegaen

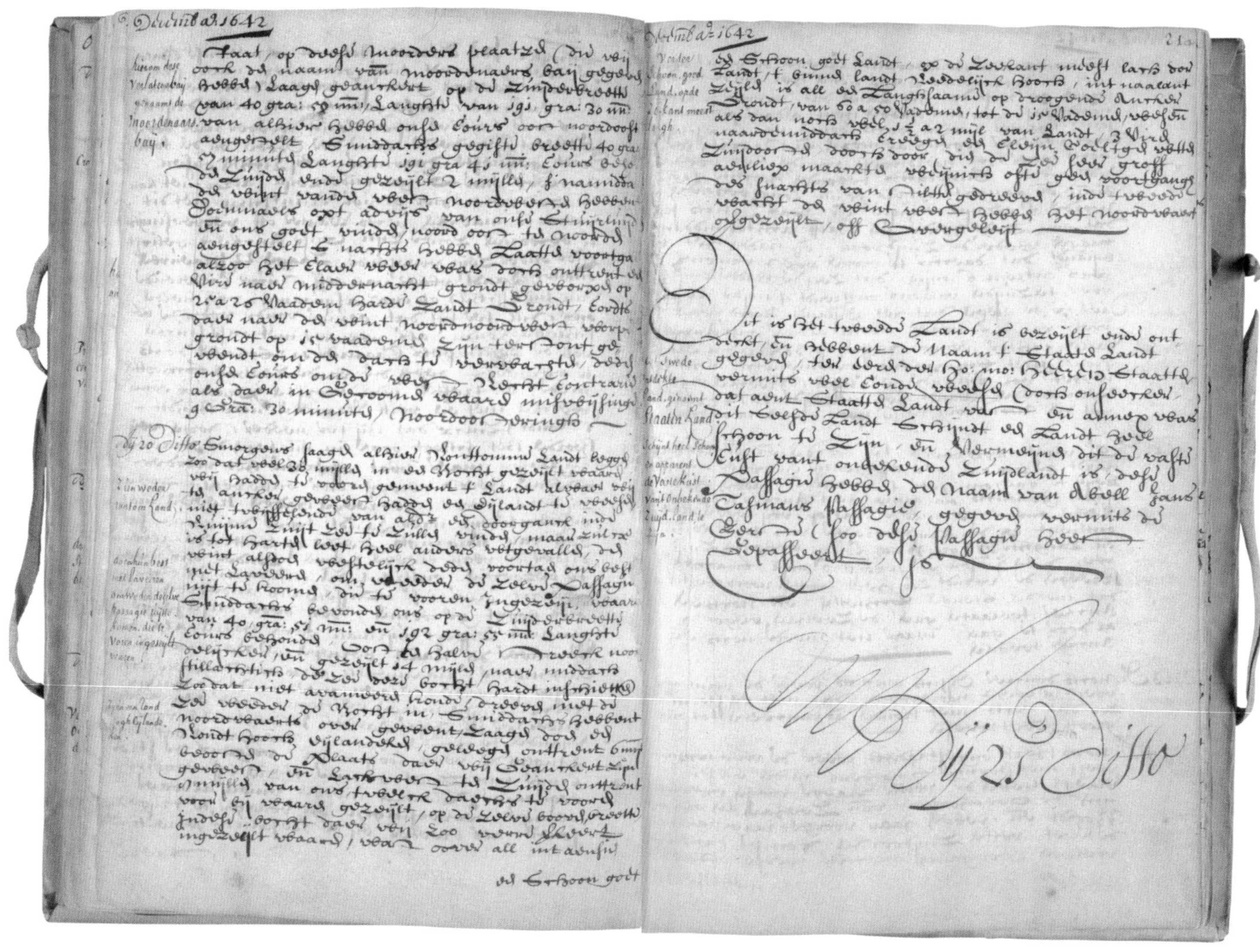

Tasman's original journal of the first voyage was lost, but two other later versions survive. The 'Huijdecoper' manuscript, housed at the State Library of New South Wales, is one of these versions; the other is held in the collection of the State Archive in The Hague in the Netherlands.

Although the translated title of the map opposite suggests otherwise - 'This work was put together from different writings as well as from personal observation by Abel Jansen Tasman, A.D. 1644' - it is now thought to be neither by Tasman nor from 1644. But it is still hugely important for being one of the few first-hand records of Tasman's route.

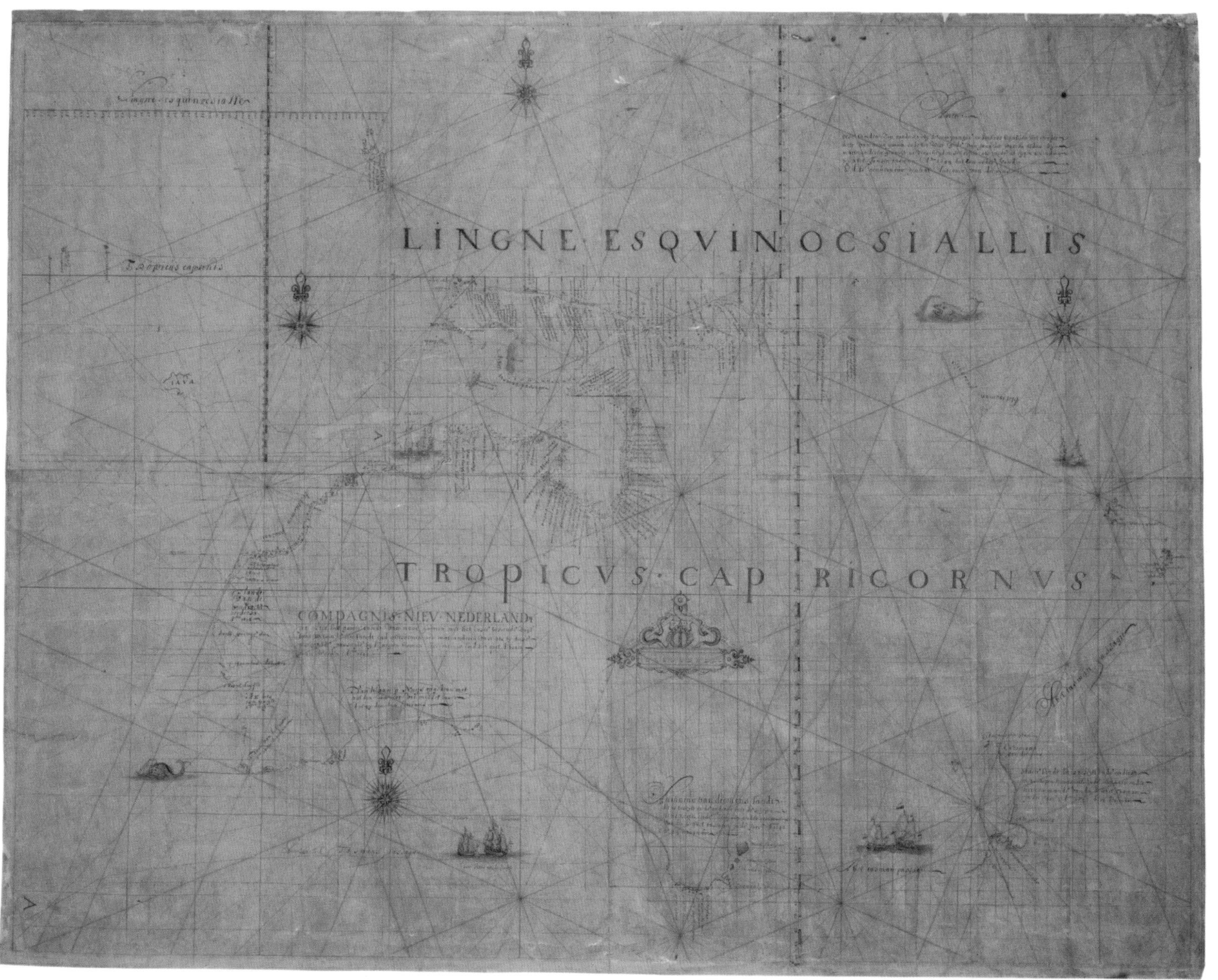
LINGNE ESQVIN OCSIALLIS
TROPICVS CAP RICORNVS
COMPAGNIE NIEV NEDERLAND

JOHN TURNBULL THOMSON 1821-1884

There is something exhilarating in daily coming on new country, and in descrying new objects of interest. We are now beyond the range of the white man, and the country is utterly desolate of inhabitants.

The story of this engineer turned explorer-surveyor is also the story of the exploration of southern New Zealand. Though navigators such as James Cook were the first to draw in ink the coastlines of this new country on the chart, men like John Turnbull Thomson ventured inland to fill in the blanks. Tough and resourceful, travelling with packhorses and enduring all weathers, for thousands of miles they sketched and mapped their way up the rivers and through the mountain systems of a rugged wilderness.

Born in England, Thomson emigrated to Malaya at the age of sixteen in the employ of the East India Survey, and led a rough, lonely life surveying in the jungles of Penang. His talents drew him to Singapore in 1841, and for the next twelve years he distinguished himself in surveying the colony and helping to construct roads, hospitals and bridges. His greatest engineering feat undoubtedly was the Horsburgh Lighthouse, which still stands on a rocky outcrop in the Straits of Singapore, but the effort took its toll on his health and he returned to England to recover. In search of a more temperate climate, he eventually arrived in New Zealand in 1856 and was soon offered the post of Chief Surveyor of Otago.

His first task was to select a site and establish a layout for the new town of Invercargill, which he gave a wide main street and ample reserves. More adventurous challenges lay ahead as he embarked on two long reconnaissance surveys of the little-travelled interior. Thomson met the Māori chief Reko at Mataura, who it is said drew a map of the southern region on the dirt floor of his home. That knowledge would help to guide Thomson on his journey. He mapped large tracts of Southland, explored the headwaters of the Tasman River, measuring the majestic Mount Cook and the 'lofty, snowclad' Mount Aspiring, which he sighted and named in 1857. It was known to the Māori as *Tititea*, the 'peak of glistening white'; it would be over fifty years before it was first climbed.

Back in Dunedin, Thomson built yet more bridges and wrote his first book, *Some Glimpses into Life in the Far East*, but even more significantly he created the first accurate map of Otago, published in 1860. This was *real* exploration; those small fieldbooks crammed with hard-won data and observations brought definition and opportunity to this new country, eventually opening some seven million acres for sheep-farming and settlement. The discovery of gold in Tuapeka in 1861 accelerated this change, with new roads and land claims soon spreading across the map.

Having taught himself to paint, Thomson was also a prolific amateur artist, working up all manner of paintings from the sketches in his fieldbooks, which were a resource that inspired him for many years. After an international transit of Venus collaboration brought a new impulse to science in New Zealand, the government formed a national Survey Department, with headquarters in Wellington, and Thomson was appointed the country's first Surveyor General in 1876. He later retired to Invercargill, the town he had helped found, to enjoy time with his large family – nine daughters in all – living together in the house he designed. His final happy years were spent painting, philosophizing and penning books.

Thomson frequently painted himself into his sketches. On the far left opposite he is sitting sketching the view of 'Tulloh Blangah Hill' - now Mount Faber - in the new colony of Singapore, where a signal station, flagstaff and observatory had been set up in 1845. Above, he can be seen happily surveying on 'Dome Mountain' in Southern Otago on 17 February 1857. His poor companion had left his coat down at their camp. It was later reported that on this expedition he had 'travelled on foot over 1,500 miles of difficult country, carrying his theodolite and swag of clothes on his back, and driving pack horses laded with flour.'

Thomson painted these vignettes of his exploring life in 1877, depicting those pioneering first surveys of Otago and Southland. The first watercolour is 'Snowed up. Hawkdun Mts, 2 January 1858', then 'Ascending Longslip Mountain, 17 December 1857', and lastly 'Crossing the Horse Range, 10 November 1857'.

J.T.T.
1877

COLIN THUBRON 1939-

Sometimes a journey arises out of hope and instinct, the heady conviction, as your finger travels along the map: Yes, here and here ... and here. These are the nerve-ends of the world.

Exploration is continuous. Though it might appear to some that there is little left to discover in the world, such a narrow view of exploration is an impoverished one. Countries, cities, individuals are constantly changing, and at every step there are new things to experience and observe. Maps fall out of date even as they are printed. The challenge has always been to wrestle something of value from the difficulties of the field. Today it can just as usefully be a scientific discovery as something as simple as pen marks on a page. Each has the power to change the way we think.

Colin Thubron is a traveller whose writings and insights have made a significant contribution to our understanding of the world, its people and cultures. In their capacity to delight and inspire, his books have reached as wide an audience as any explorer before him. Though many years separate him from writers that he most admires – Robert Byron, Freya Stark, Patrick Leigh Fermor – he shares their spirit of individualism and adventurous curiosity, and the gift of rich, elegant prose.

He has been drawn to worlds that his generation found threatening: China, Russia, Islam. 'My desire has always been to humanize the map. To know these cultures more fully and share them with others for whom they are inaccessible. This is my basic impulse. Others might be overwhelmed by the prospect of tough journeys in these sorts of places, but for me the opposite is true: the more remote, or misunderstood, the better. It's seductive. I have grappled with Russian and Mandarin half my life. Trying to learn the language has been essential. If I can bring back a little of the strangeness and richness of my experiences then I feel that the effort of the journey has its reward.'

Thubron worked as a publisher and a freelance film-maker before having 'the courage to take the plunge' and try life as a writer. 'It was a risk, but the need to write was beginning to consume me. So I went to live with an Arab family in Damascus. I was twenty-five. I took a chance and it opened a future.' *Mirror to Damascus* was published in 1967 and more books on the Middle East followed, but it was his journey by car through western Russia during the Brezhnev era that really established his reputation as a writer willing to roam widely beyond the conventional. Fascination and the element of danger are ever present, particularly so in his 11,265-km (7,000-mile) journey detailed in *Shadow of the Silk Road*. His expedition to sacred Mount Kailas in Tibet offered the chance to communicate more personal concerns. 'With the death of my mother, I became the last of my family. I felt compelled to mark this passage, to walk through bereavement.'

The practicalities of his work have changed little since Damascus. He writes longhand in notebooks every day. 'Which means a rising level of panic about losing them as a journey goes on,' he admits. 'They are invaluable. I write down everything I know I will forget after a few months. It might be whole passages, or just impressions: an encounter, a conversation, the shape of someone's eyebrows, the smell in the back of a train, the texture of a rock. These are just as important as the bigger sense of the landscape around you. The details stored in your notebooks are what gives the description life.'

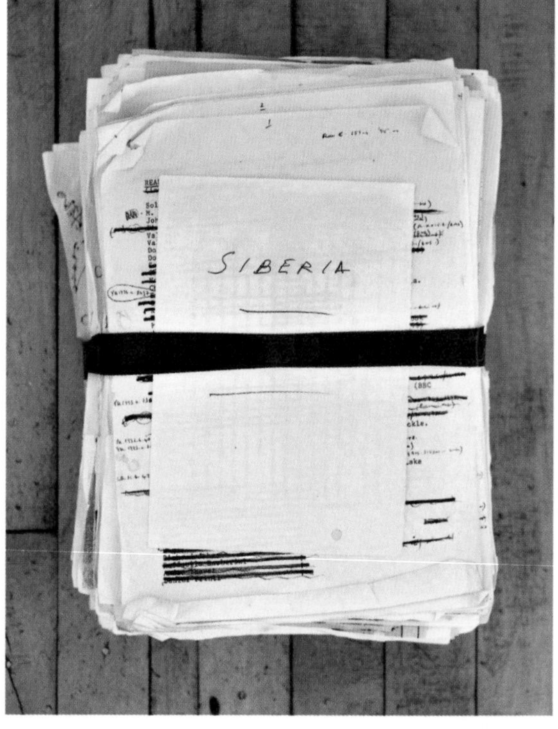

With much effort, a long journey is gradually reduced to a pile of paper bound with a rubber band. From field to manuscript, a book is born. 'It's a fantasy to think writing just flows. I have to struggle like hell. It's a mass of corrections. But it all begins with my notebooks. History, landscape, chance conversations with people; all of these things find a home in them and when I return they are essential to my memory ... these pages mark the continuation of my travels.'

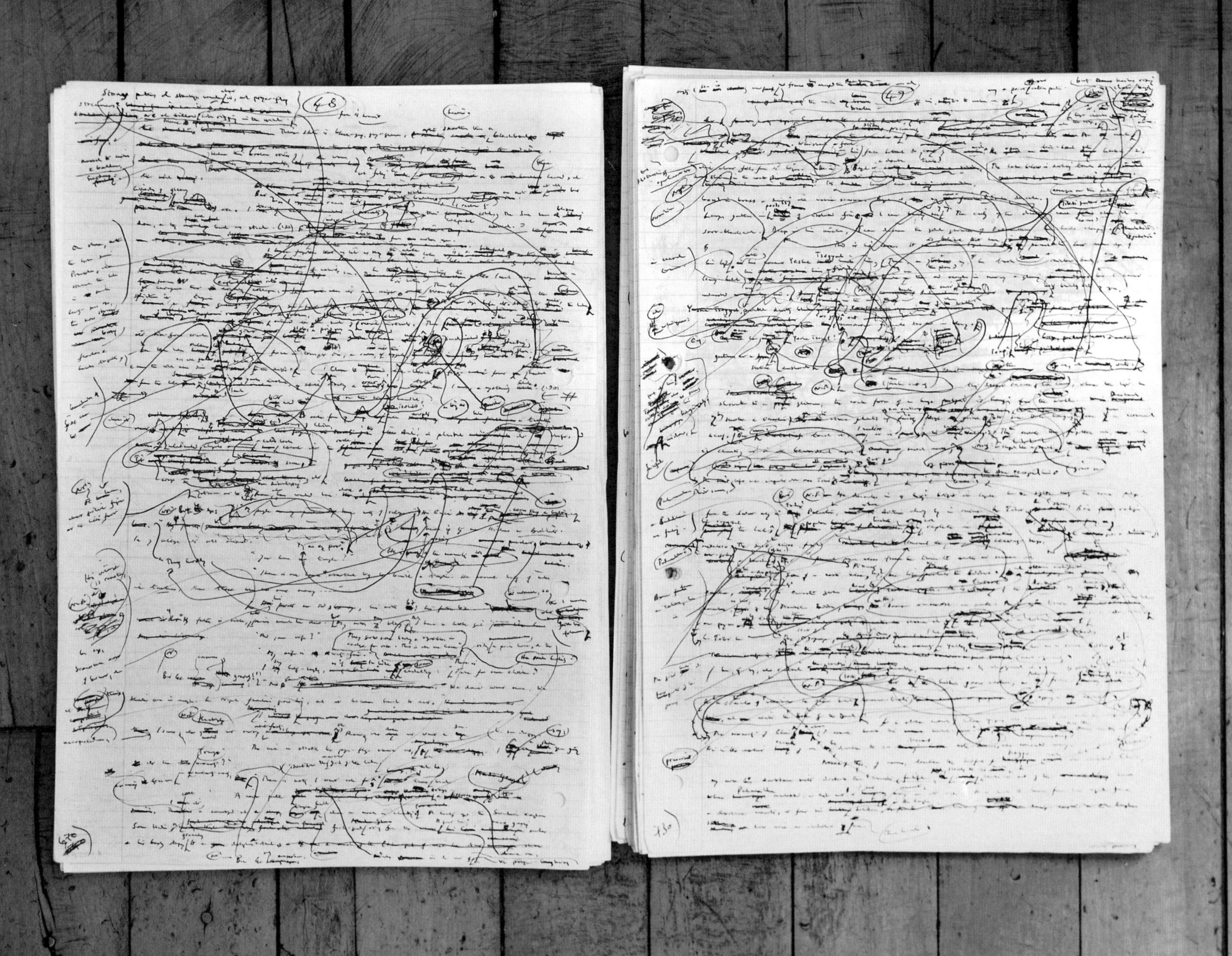

ALEXANDRINE TINNE 1835-1869

If anything were to happen to me, during my travels, if I would be killed, which is a reasonable possibility ... you will not lament me. I have never understood the happiness of growing old.

In the late 1850s Africa was the focus of intense geographical activity, with some of the greatest names in African exploration – Speke, Burton and Livingstone – vying for the prize of being the first to discover the source of the Nile. Less well known was Dutch noblewoman-explorer Alexandrine Tinne. Ambitious, formidably well connected, spirited and optimistic, she had no reason to doubt her own success in pursuit of the same aim. Although barely remembered today, she had as much determination and mettle as any of her male counterparts.

Born in The Hague into one of Holland's most affluent families, with close links to royalty, by nineteen Tinne had already visited much of Europe, and was about to embark on a journey through Egypt. With her mother she trekked by camel and donkey to the Red Sea, visited Damascus and toured the Holy Land, Syria and Lebanon. Three years later, Tinne led another major expedition into Sudan, with the intent of finding the source of the Nile. 'They must be demented!' wrote explorer Samuel Baker White as Tinne's party left Khartoum. 'A young lady alone with the Dinka tribe ... All the natives are naked as the day they were born.' White, it seems, was more concerned about Tinne's modesty than her safety. Tinne, with her mother and aunt, would sail by steamer farther up the White Nile than any European women before them.

But with the source of the Nile clearly unobtainable, Tinne decided they would instead navigate the marshlands of the Bahr el-Ghazal, a tributary of the Nile, then explore the interior overland towards Lake Chad. They would never reach their goal. Stalled by months of heavy rains, Tinne's mother and servants fell ill. One after another they died. This was followed also by the death of her aunt. Blaming herself and grief-stricken, she moved to Cairo, then sailed around the Mediterranean. In 1869 she set out again, with the aim of being the first Western woman to cross the Sahara.

Tinne had never seen the need to travel lightly. On the Nile, three boats had been required to carry her luggage, which included – beyond the usual expeditionary equipment – a Chinese porcelain tea service, silver cutlery, an easel and painting supplies, a camera and developing apparatus, and a library of books. Now travelling overland, her caravan of over 100 heavily laden camels was a sight to behold. Two months into her journey, a Tuareg chieftain, Bu Bekker, heard rumours that the great water tanks of the 'Blonde Sultaness' were filled with gold, and sent men to investigate. In the oasis of a wadi a quarrel broke out between Bu Bekker's warriors and Tinne's servants. Tinne intervened, raising her hand in peace. Believing she was reaching for a gun, a Tuareg warrior slashed off her hand. The caravan was looted, several others killed, and Tinne was left to bleed slowly to death, alone in the sands.

A surviving Sudanese servant reported the murder to the authorities. Tinne's body was never recovered. Young, privileged and female, with no published narratives or diaries, Tinne's legacy faded into obscurity. Nevertheless, she had gained the respect of her peers. In a memorial, David Livingstone said: 'None rises higher in my estimation than the Dutch lady, Miss Tinne, who ... nobly persevered in the teeth of every difficulty.'

On her travels through Egypt, North Africa and the Near East, Tinne gathered botanical and ethnological specimens and made skilful drawings of people, places and archaeological monuments, observing everything in watercolours and prose. Opposite is her sketch of one of her encampments in the desert. She spent much of her life away from home - overleaf is her 'Bedroom in Beirut', where she stayed for many months in 1856, before attempting to discover the source of the Nile.

Encampent in desert.

MATUSHKA
Beyrouth ?

Overall, I have been content with my life – I have lived well … I have had fun. I am in no hurry to die – but if it happens, fine – a short life, but a happy one! I have now been to that unknown region and I shall return to it again, perhaps out of instinct, like a fly drawn to a flame.

Tinne's heavily laden caravans were conspicuously lavish, and would lead to her brutal death, aged 33, at the hands of Tuareg. Many camels were used solely to carry her blotting paper and immense plant collection.

Known to some as the 'Blonde Sultaness', Tinne managed to journey far beyond the conventions and expectations of other aristocratic women of her time. In these sketches, side-by-side, she draws herself at a ball in 1855 and then in a Bedouin tent a year later.

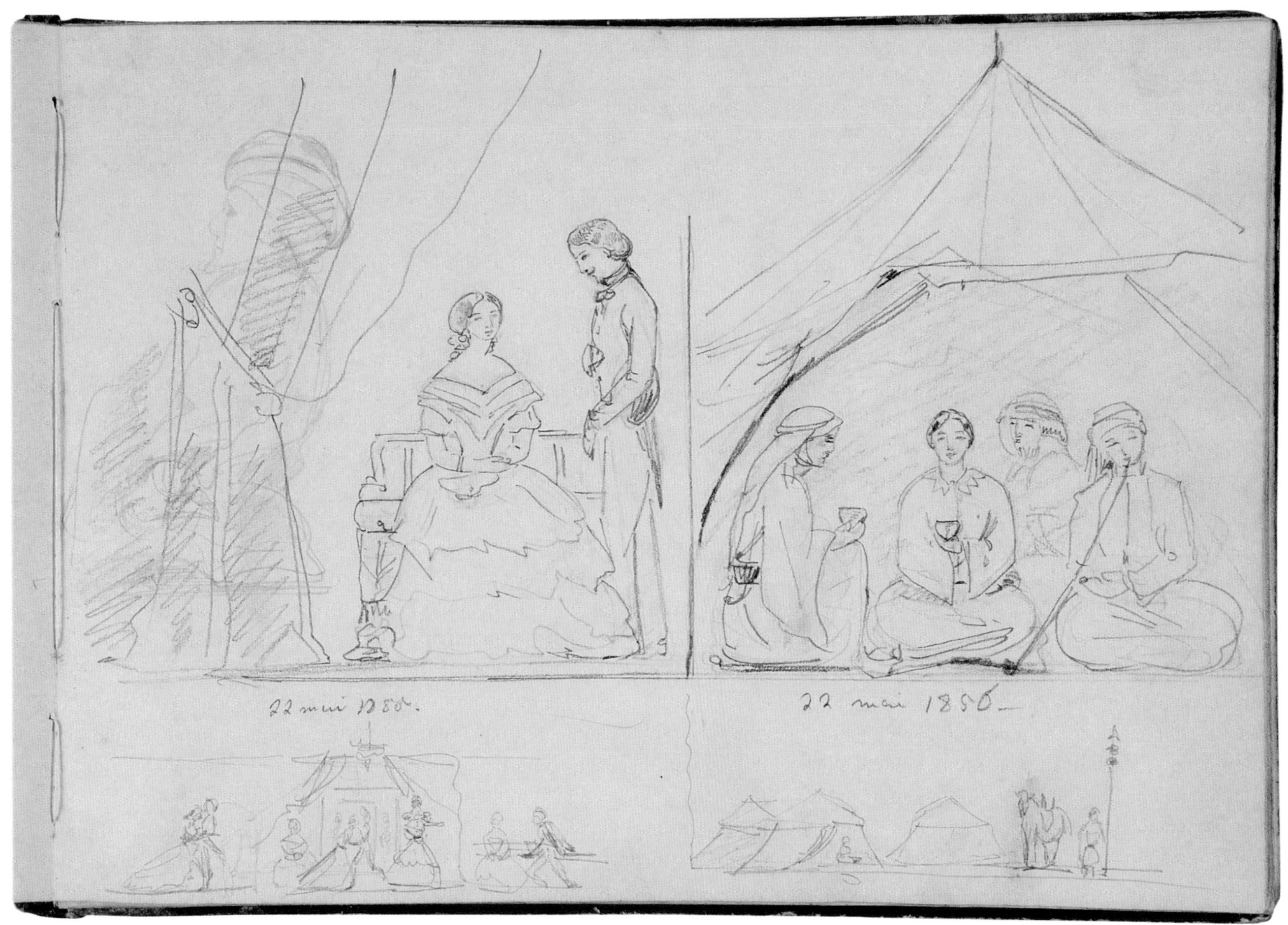
22 mai 1850.
22 mai 1850_

MAKING YOUR MARK

Wade Davis

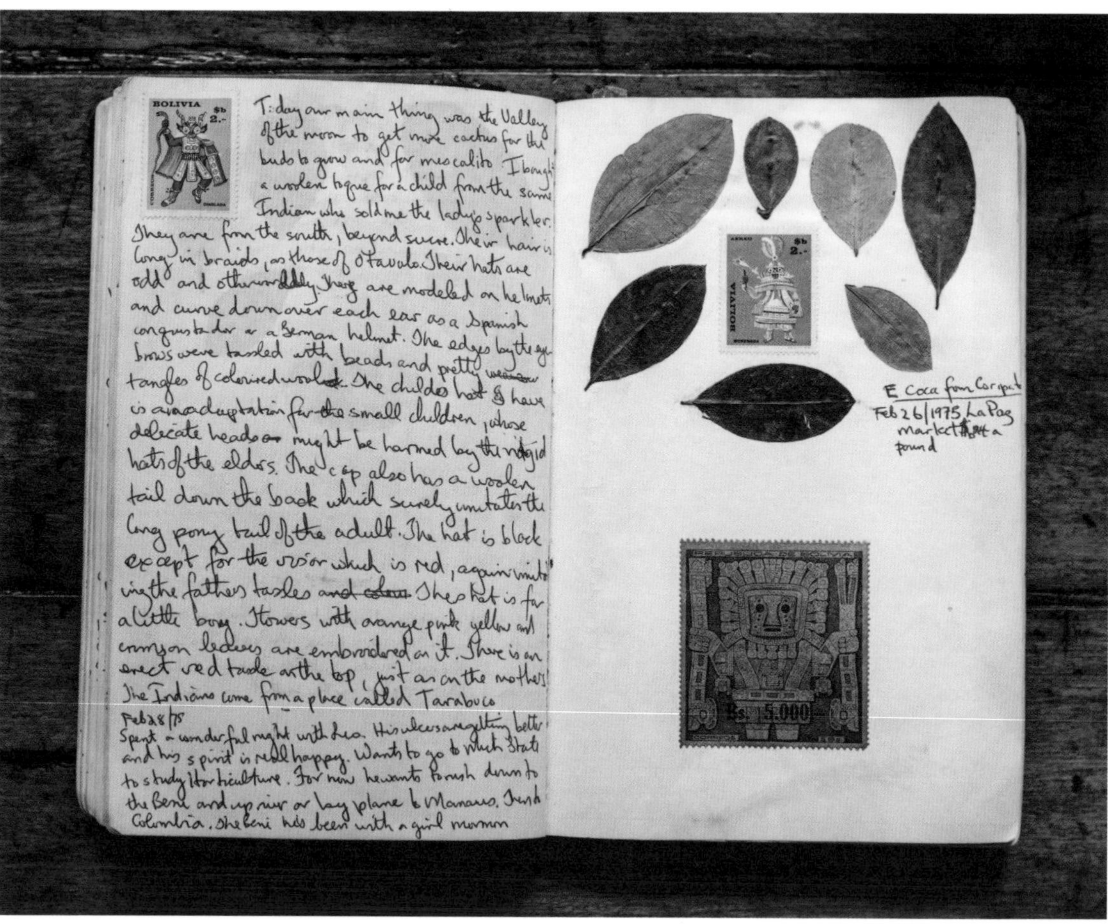

Inside every journal is the story of a finished journey - a completed route perhaps - yet every journey changes over the years and its revelations can be made anew. As Davis reminds us: 'As an explorer I've always wanted to find those great stories of wonder found within various cultures that teach us something about human experience. In this sense, if we travel with open eyes and minds exploration will never end.'

Exploration has a power beyond the material. It may be defined not just in new discoveries but in new ways of thinking. The true purpose of space voyages, for example, or at least their most profound and lasting consequence, lay not in wealth secured but in a vision realized, a shift in perspective that would change our lives forever.

One morning in the winter of 1974 I was sitting in a café in Harvard Square with my college roommate. By chance, a *National Geographic* map of the world was on the wall, a foot away, right in front of our eyes. David looked at the map and then at me, then lifted his arm to touch the Arctic. He looked back to me and I watched as my arm rose and landed on the Amazon. Had it hit Italy I might have become a Renaissance scholar. Within days my friend would leave for the Arctic. As for me, having decided to go to the Amazon, there was only one man to see, Richard Evans Schultes, the legendary plant explorer who had sparked the psychedelic era with his discoveries of the so-called magic mushrooms in Oaxaca in 1938. Three years later he had disappeared into the northwest Amazon of Colombia where he remained for twelve years, travelling down uncharted rivers, living among unknown cultures, all the time enchanted by the wonders of the rainforest.

I found him in his fourth-floor eyrie at the Harvard Botanical Museum. I explained that I wanted to go to the Amazon and collect plants, just as he had done so many years before. Barely twenty, I knew little of South America and less about plants. Asking nothing of my credentials, he peered across a stack of dried herbarium specimens and asked, 'Well, when would you like to go?'

A fortnight later I left for South America, where I remained for fifteen months. Just before leaving Cambridge, I stopped by his office, hoping to pick up a few tips. He had three vital pieces of advice. First, I was to avoid high leather boots, as all the snakes strike at the neck. Second, he recommended that I take a pith helmet, because in twelve years he had never lost his bifocals. Third, he insisted that I not come back from the forest without having tried *ayahuasca*, the most powerful hallucinogenic preparation of the shaman's repertoire. Then he handed me two letters of introduction, which, as it turned out, might as well have come from God, such was his reputation throughout Colombia and beyond.

I left for South America with a one-way ticket, and no plans. I had just a small backpack of clothes, and two books, George H. Lawrence's *Taxonomy of Vascular Plants*, and Walt Whitman's *Leaves of Grass*. In the frontispiece of my journal I wrote: 'risk discomfort for understanding'. At the time I believed that bliss was an objective state that could be achieved simply by opening oneself unabashedly and completely to the world. Both figuratively and literally I drank from every stream, even from tyre tracks in the road. Naturally I was constantly sick, but even that seemed part of the process – malaria and dysentery fevers that grew through the night before breaking with the dawn. Every adventure led to another. At one point on a single day's notice I set out to traverse the Darien Gap. After nearly a month in the swamps and rainforest I became lost for a fortnight without food or shelter. When finally I found my way to safety I stumbled off a small plane in Panama City, drenched in vomit from my fellow passengers, with only the ragged clothes on my back and $3 to my name. I had never felt so alive.

That traverse of the Darien inspired me to seek a life that had previously been beyond my imaginings, one of exploration and discovery, free and content to move undaunted through realms of the spirit that had no boundaries. Travel not just as adventure – though excitement there would be – but as transformation, as a movement through sacred space. I learned that if you place yourself in the way of opportunities, in situations where there is no choice but to go forward, no option but success, you create a momentum that in the end propels you to new levels of experience and engagement that would have seemed beyond reach only months before. You hurl yourself into the abyss only to discover that it's a feather bed.

Through all these months my anchor was my pen, my solace a diary. In many ways the journal was the only thing that kept me grounded. In later years my scientific notebooks would become quite disciplined, as one might expect, with detailed accounts of botanical observations, ethnographic experiences, geographic descriptions. But those first two volumes of journals, decorated as collage, with a scattering of insights, outbursts of confusion, raw expressions of awe, were very much the emotional ramblings of a young man on a personal quest.

I would later come to understand travel not as scientific inquiry, but rather as pilgrimage, with each step taking one closer to the goal, which was not a place but a state of mind, not a destination but a path of illumination and liberation that is the ultimate quest of the pilgrim. Hemingway once said that the most important preparation for a writer is to have led an interesting life, to have something to say that the world needs to hear. At the time I had no aspirations to be a writer, but I desperately wanted to live an interesting life.

Along the way I learned a number of lessons. Life is neither linear nor predictable. A career is not something that you put on like a coat. It is something that grows organically around you, step-by-step, choice-by-choice, and experience-by-experience. Everything adds up. No work is beneath you. Nothing is a waste of time unless you make it so. An elderly cab driver in Bogota may well have as much to teach you as a wandering sadhu in India or a mystic saint in the Sahara. There were tens of thousands of teachers out there that I did not even know that I had.

The work you do is just a lens through which to view and experience the world, and only for a time. The goal is to make living itself, the act of being alive, one's vocation, knowing full well that nothing ultimately can be planned or anticipated, no blueprint found to predict the outcome of something as complex as a human life. If one can remain open to the potential of the new, the promise of the unimagined, then magic happens and a life takes form.

On that first long journey, while living in the mountains of Colombia, I met a Kamsa shaman who told me something I have never forgotten. 'In the first years of your life', Pedro said, 'you live beneath the shadow of the past, too young to know what to do. In your last years you find that you are too old to understand the world coming at you from behind. In between there is a small and narrow beam of light that illuminates your life.'

If you can look back over a long life and see that you have owned your choices, then there is little ground for resentment. Bitterness comes to those who look back with regret on the choices imposed upon them. The greatest creative challenge is the struggle to be the architect of your own life. It was through travel that I became a writer, and it was through the wonder of being a writer that I learned to be patient, not to compromise and to give my destiny time to find me. And it all began with those first journals, and that promise to 'risk discomfort for understanding'.

At home in British Columbia, Davis is surrounded by the memories and materials of his extraordinary exploring life. His journals are sacred objects: they are talisman and keepsake, old friends and trusted companions. They are full of insights, describing the joy and challenge of difficult expeditions, of finding routes through dense jungles, but also being rewarded with encounters with remarkable people and their cultures.

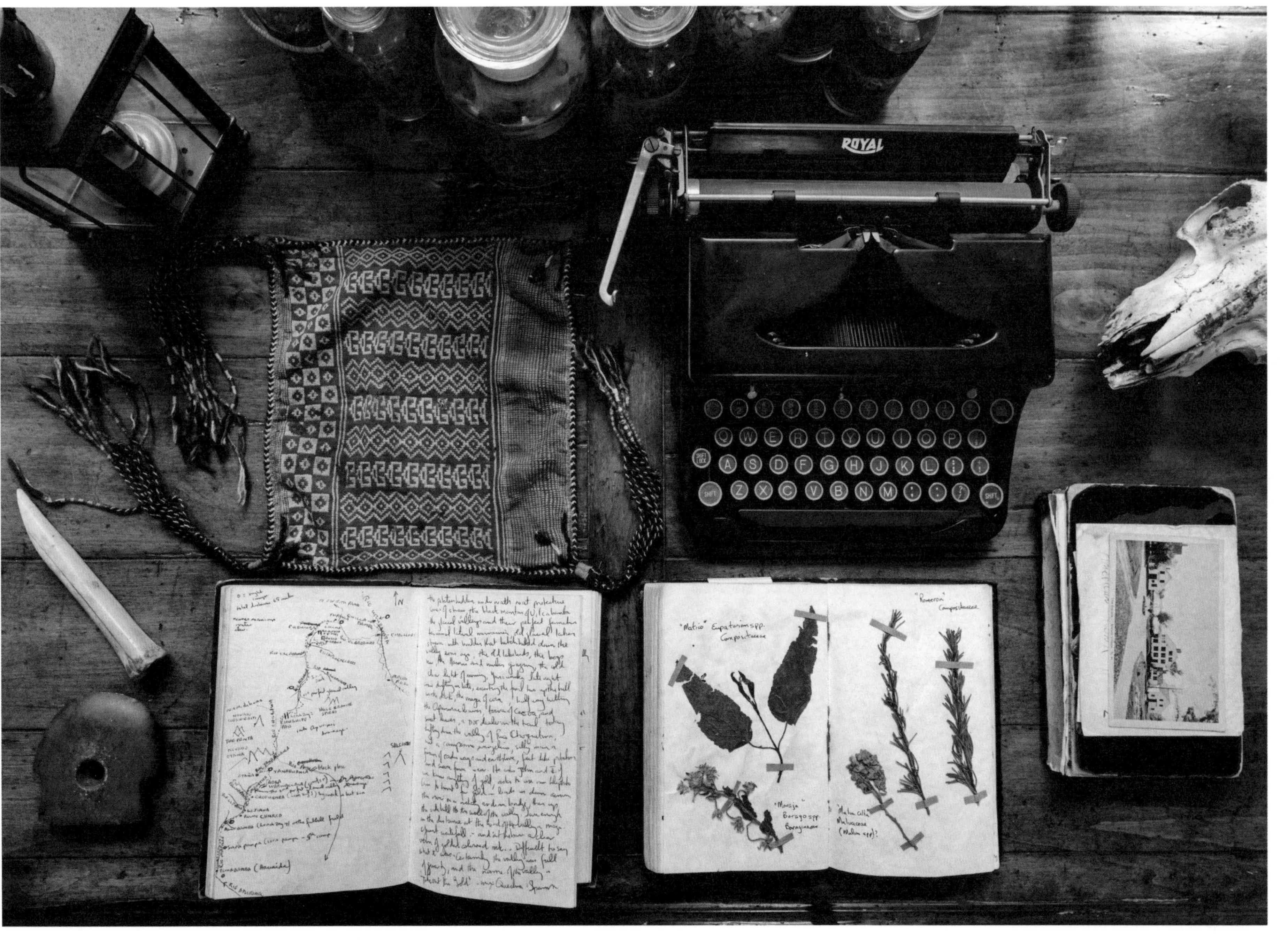
ROYAL

OLIVIA TONGE 1858-1949

The fresh water crab has been known to crawl stealthily up a Lady's petticoats and suddenly nip her thigh.

In 1908, Olivia Francis Tonge picked up her Winsor & Newton sketchbook and wrote a 'Curious Fragment': 'And it came to pass that a certain Grandmother, when that she had come to nigh on two score years and ten; and had gotten long in the tooth, spake to herself thus – Lo, will I now paint ... and verily no man mote stop her'. She was about to leave her familiar life behind and journey to India on her first great adventure.

Born in Glamorganshire, Tonge (née Fitzmaurice) had grown up with her father's stories of his explorations of Australia as assistant surveyor on HMS *Beagle*. He was a keen naturalist and landscape painter, and had encouraged these skills in his daughter. Acutely short-sighted, she was unable to share her father's love of landscapes, but instead quickly became adept at painting flowers, birds and reptiles. At 50, widowed, and with her children grown, Tonge embarked on a new phase of her life. She travelled to the region of India and modern Pakistan twice, and over three years toured Sindh, Calcutta, Darjeeling, Mussoorie, Lucknow, Karsiyang and Karachi.

Within the pages of sixteen sketchbooks Tonge created an exquisite and eclectic visual record of her travels. Elements of Indian culture, artifacts, flora and fauna jostle together with personal annotations: toads squat next to delicately wrought jewellery; a bird sits on a battle belt. Although not among the most well-travelled artists of her time, nor the most prolific, nevertheless Tonge beautifully captured the vibrancy of the lands she travelled through.

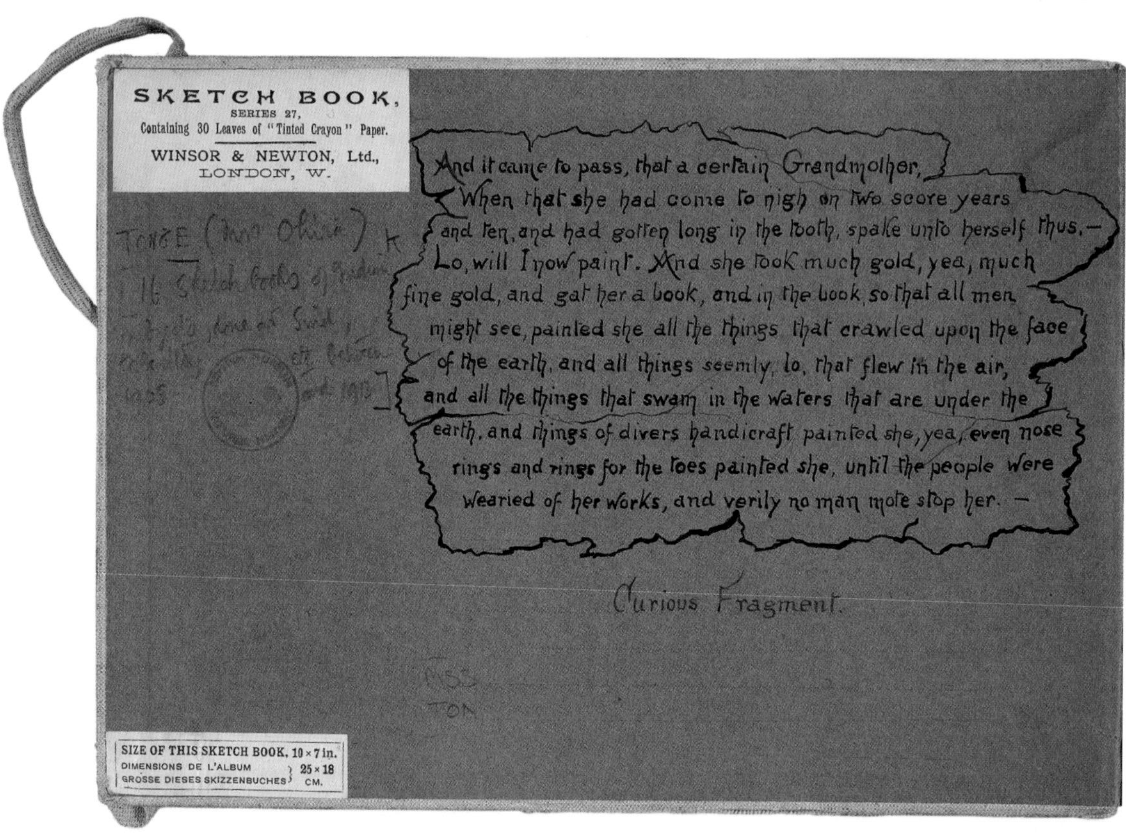

Tonge wrote this note on the inside cover of one of her sketchbooks. Not so much journals as a visual record of her travels, they vividly capture anything that caught her attention, such an oceanic crab that 'swims with the grace of a Swallow's Flight' and 'feeds upon living Prey, and chases it with the Speed of a Shark'. Her sketches excel in combining unusual elements with personal annotations, overleaf jewellery and a frog and toad, and 'The Indian Mugger, or Man eating Crocodile', which she says 'are quite tame and live for Centuries'.

This
Crab is
among Crus-
taceans what the
Albatross is among Birds,
sustaining itself for Days
together without
needing
rest.
It
feeds upon living
Prey, and chaces it
with the Speed of a Shark.
The
Oceanic Swimming Crab,
Neptúnus pelágicus.
A Crab that swims with the
grace of a Swallow's Flight.

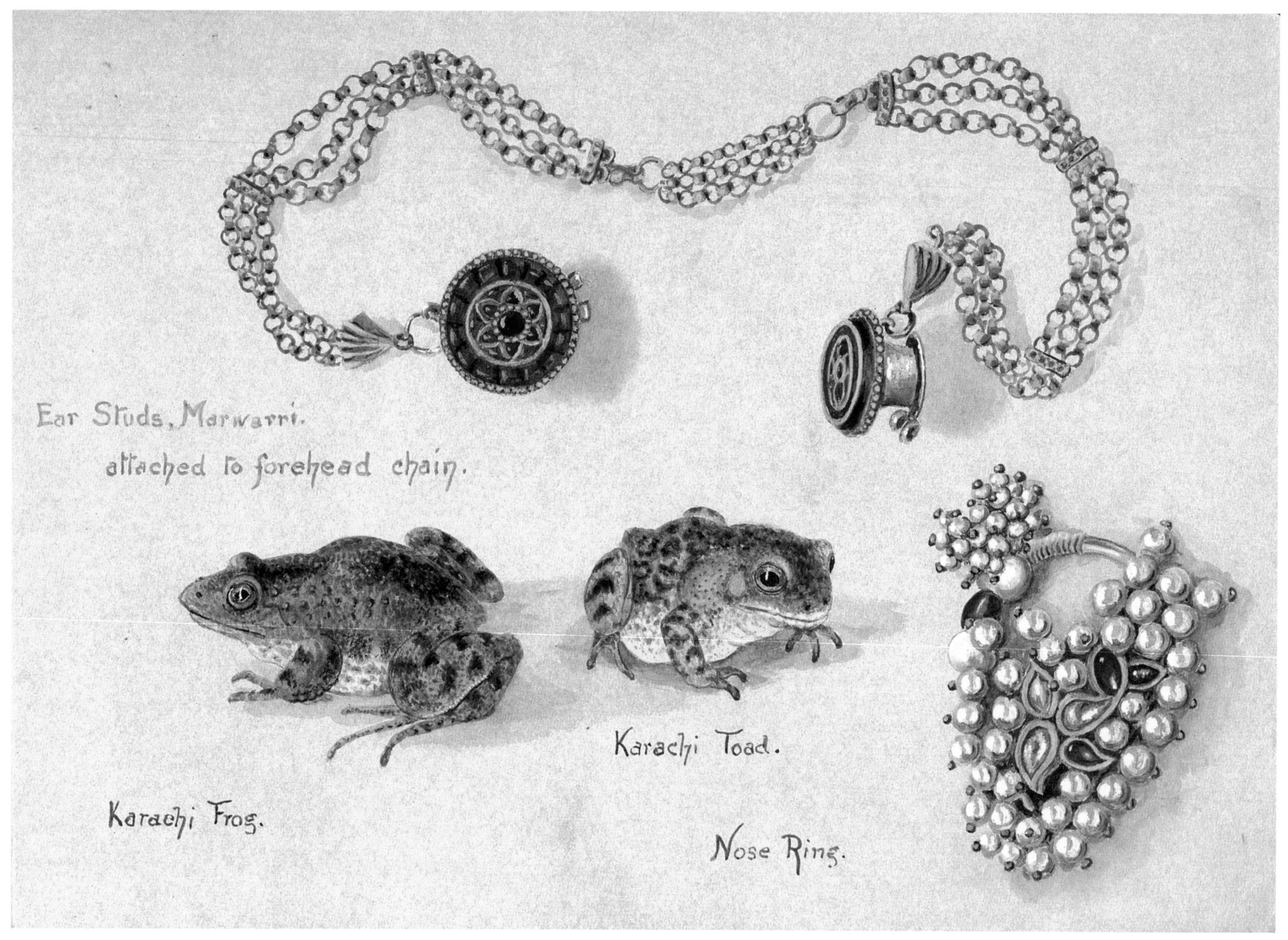
Ear Studs, Marwarri.
attached to forehead chain.
Karachi Toad.
Karachi Frog.
Nose Ring.

These Muggers are usually from 10 to 15 feet
in length, but sometimes attain 30 feet.
They are Sacred to the Hindoos, and
when attended and fed at a Shrine
or Temple, they are quite tame,
and live for Centuries.
The Indian Mugger,
or Man eating Crocodile. Mugger Pir. Karachi.
Elephant Grass.

NAOMI UEMURA 1941-1984

In all the splendour of solitude ... it is a test of myself, and one thing I loathe is to have to test myself in front of other people.

On 26 February 1984, two climbers found a diary in a snow cave high on the slopes of Mount McKinley in Alaska, North America's highest mountain. It belonged to Naomi Uemura, who had disappeared two weeks earlier after planting the Japanese flag on the summit. Along with his diary, Uemura's 'self-rescue' device was discovered – bamboo poles tied over his shoulders that would span any crevasse he fell into, allowing him to pull himself out. In some ways he was a victim of his own success, a rescue mission had not been organized earlier for fear of offending him. It seemed inconceivable that Uemura, the consummate mountaineer and polar traveller, could be in trouble.

Born in Hidaka, Japan, the sixth and youngest son of a rice farmer, Uemura took up mountain climbing as a student at Meiji University, in the hope, he later joked, of 'improving my skinny appearance'. Naturally shy, mountaineering appealed to his love of solitude. He soon became well-known for achieving feats alone that had only ever been attempted before by teams. He made solo ascents of Kilimanjaro, Aconcagua, Mont Blanc and the Matterhorn. In addition, he walked the length of Japan, floated 6,000 km (3,728 miles) down the Amazon solo on a raft, made the summit during the first Japanese Everest Expedition in 1970 and also achieved the first solo ascent of Mount McKinley.

In 1978 Uemura set out across the sea ice with nineteen huskies from northern Ellesmere Island to make the first solo journey to the North Pole. By the time he reached the Pole 57 days later, he had negotiated hundreds of pressure ridges, had almost lost his dogs through thin ice, and survived a raid from a polar bear which ate all the dog food, destroyed his tent and tore apart his sleeping bag, with Uemura still in it. When the bear returned the following night, Uemura shot it and fed the meat to his hungry dogs.

Increasingly, he travelled light and fast, paring his equipment down to the bare minimum: instead of a tent he slept in snow caves and he carried very little fuel, planning to eat cold food. It was this, perhaps, that was his undoing. In 1984 Uemura returned to McKinley. Although he had already climbed the mountain solo in 1970, his aim now was to climb in winter. Making good progress, he quickly achieved his aim, reaching the summit on his 43rd birthday. He later spoke by radio to Japanese photographers. Delighted, he was making his way back to camp. He was last spotted the following day by a small plane, before thick storm clouds swallowed the mountain.

The diary left behind described the harsh conditions he had suffered before making his final summit bid – crevasse falls, temperatures of minus 40°C and inadequate fuel to melt his frozen food supplies – but it also showed his humour and inner strength, documenting the songs he sang to stay focused on his goal. Uemura's body still lies somewhere on the mountain, and it appears his spirit resides there too. In 1988 Alaskan climber Vernon Tejas became the first person to summit McKinley and return safely in winter. While sheltering in a snow cave from a storm, Tejas confessed he had said hello in Japanese to his predecessor, and had 'felt his spirit up there'. Uemura had completed all he had set out to do, so perhaps this great mountain is a fitting final resting place for this exceptional traveller and gentle, unassuming human being. As he once said: 'Out there on the rocks, I feel exceedingly happy.'

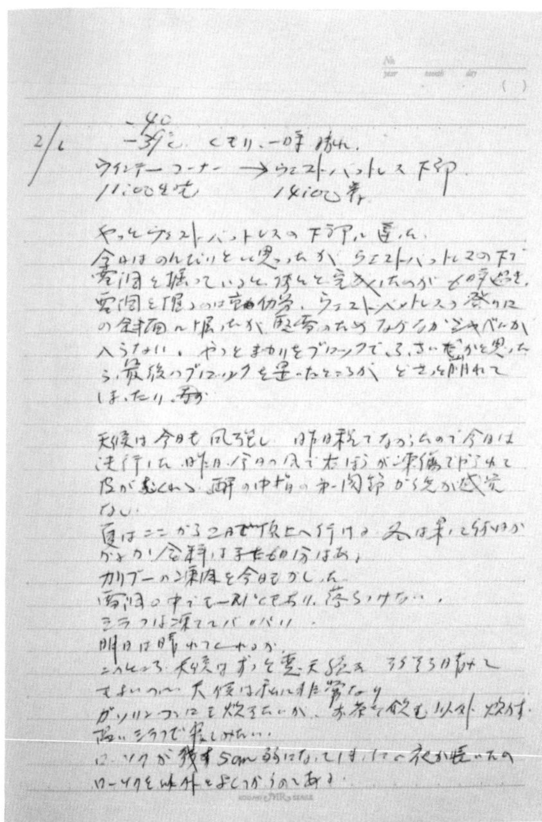

A page from the 'cave diary' discovered after Uemura disappeared on Mount McKinley, having successfully reached the summit in February 1984. His body was never recovered.

These sketches are from Uemura's journal from his solo crossing of the Greenland icecap from north to south. In May 1978, Uemura climbed the Academy Glacier from Independence Fjord. The dotted line details the crevasse zone and short black lines mark where two of his dogs were lost to crevasses. The second sketch shows the layout of Uemura's expedition tent, with his sleeping bag in the centre and a rifle ready to hand behind his head.

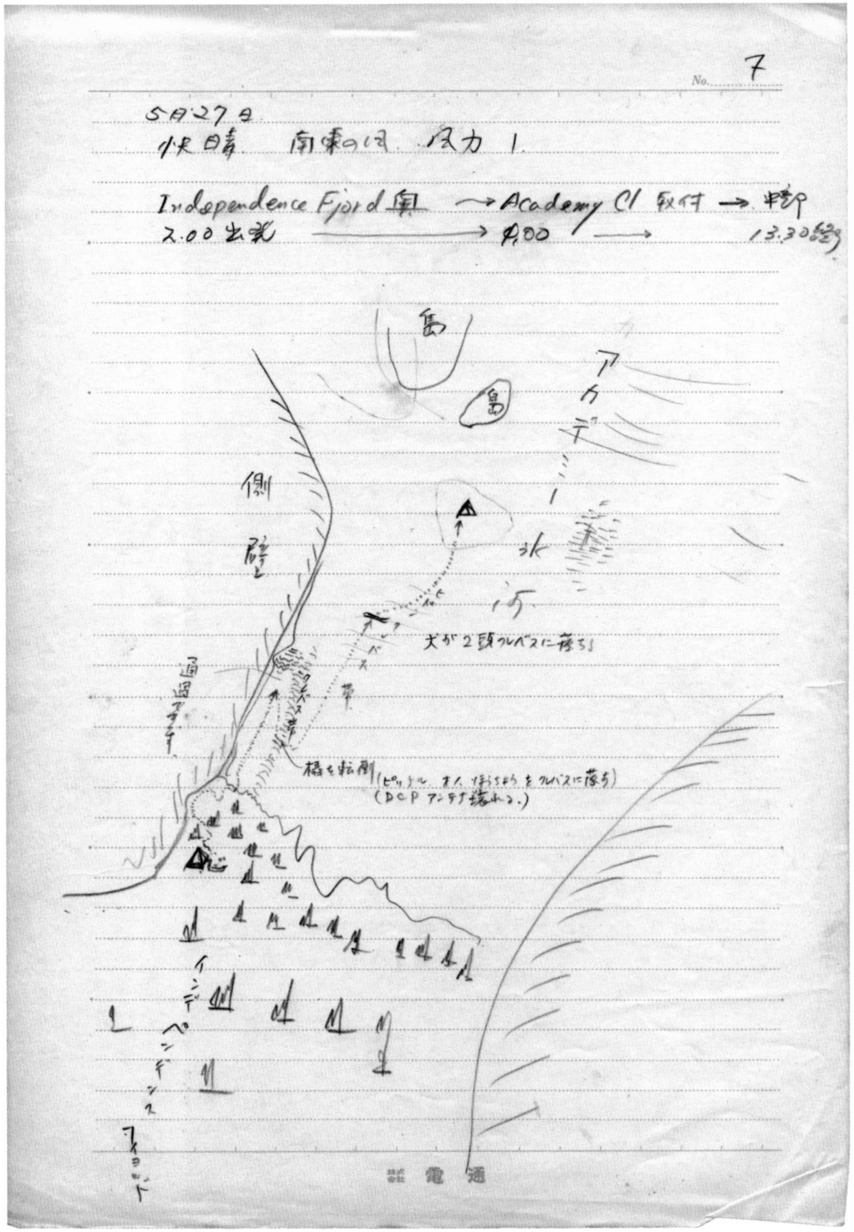

No. 7

5月27日
快晴 南東の風 風力 1.

Independence Fjord奥 → Academy Gl 取付 → 中部
2.00出発 → 4.00 → 13.30到着

島

島

アカデミー氷河

側壁

犬が2頭クレバスに落ちる

クレバス

橇を転倒 (ピッケル、オノ、ほうちょう をクレバスに落ち)
(DCPアンテナ壊れる。)

インデペンデンスフィヨルド

電通

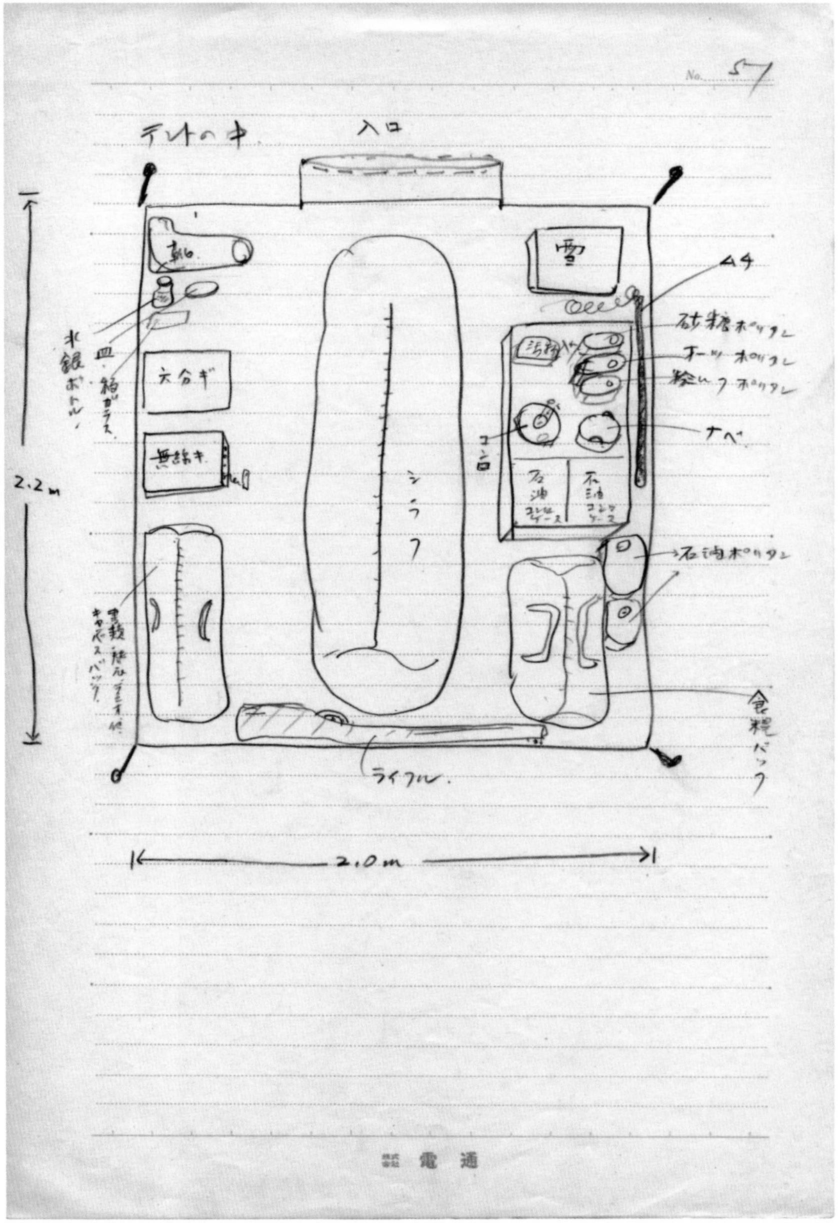

No. 57

テントの中

入口

2.2 m

靴

水銀ボトル

皿

箱ガラス

六分ギ

無線キ

雪

ムチ

砂糖ポリタン

オーツポリタン

粉ミルクポリタン

コンロ

ナベ

石油コンロケース

石油コンロケース

石油ポリタン

シュラフ

食糧バッグ

ライフル

2.0 m

電通

GODFREY VIGNE 1801-1863

A shooting-jacket I have always found, on account of the numerous pockets, to be the best travelling dress, and in one corner of these I always carried a pair of warm socks and slippers.

Little is known about the intrepid Godfrey Thomas Vigne, a wealthy lawyer who went exploring, often in disguise, to indulge his passion for art. He first attracted public attention jaunting across America and Canada in 1831, publishing an account of his whistle-stop six-month journey, but it was his next adventure that earns him recognition here.

Leaving England on a ship bound for India in 1832, he passed through Persia and spent the next seven years travelling in the western Himalaya. He rode into Kashmir and Ladakh and made forays into Tibet and Afghanistan. Like the dashing Scottish explorer Alexander Burnes, who had reached Kabul in the spring of 1832, Vigne can be considered a pioneer, travelling through a dangerous country that had rarely been seen by Western eyes.

Vigne got himself out of tight spots by drawing pictures, usually for alarmed villagers or angry chieftains, who would swing from 'fury to a chuckle' on seeing their faces rendered in watercolour. 'I put them in good humour by scratching off two or three caricature portraits, and distributing a little medicine.' As war brewed, Vigne escaped unnoticed; the flamboyant Burnes was later cut to pieces by an angry mob.

On returning safely home, Vigne described his extensive journeys in two books – *A Visit to Kabul and Afghanistan* in 1840 and *Travels in Kashmir* in 1842 – which gave a valuable view of this part of the world, just as other nations, Britain and Russia in particular, were beginning to compete for supremacy there. A few years later, with the public eager to see the peripheries of empire for themselves, Vigne's account and drawings even inspired a huge circular panorama of Kashmir in the heart of London's Leicester Square.

His wanderlust unsatisfied, Vigne had already set off on more adventures. He was as happy on remote islands in the West Indies as he was in the jungles of Nicaragua and Mexico, though he died in 1863 before he was able to see his next book come off the press. His greatest luxury on the trail was a portable chair – 'the indispensable accompaniment of dignity' – in the seat of which was fastened his sketching gear, a thermometer and sextant, and the apparatus for brewing a pot of tea. He described himself as neither 'a professional author nor a commissioned tourist', wandering for his own amusement into areas that were politically sensitive and frequently risky. He seems to have had few motives beyond his simple wish to go 'roving in new and fabled lands' and apply his paintbrush and pen to the people he encountered along the way.

On his overland trek into Persia, Vigne joined a caravan of laden mules to climb the Kosapinar Pass in March 1833. In the sketch opposite we glimpse the valley of Hezar Cham in the northern mountains of modern Iran. The Chalus River runs through a dramatic gorge and Vigne 'wandered with delight among the forest-clad mountains'.

Vigne's portraits of the people he met on his travels provide us with intimate glimpses of characters and local customs - and often proved useful to him at the time to ease tensions when in a tight spot.

From left: Ameer Khan, a Lohani chieftain, joined the expedition and Vigne painted him in Kabul in September 1836; Murtaza Khan, the head of a family of the Shia Qizilbash, met Vigne near Ghazni and also accompanied him to Kabul; and the bride of the Qizilbash leader Murtaza Khan.

Vigne encountered the Persian general Abdul Samut in 1836 at the court of Dost Mohammad, then ruler of Kabul. He took an instant dislike to him, but was persuaded for his own safety to draw his portrait and give him the bottle of brandy he was demanding. Abdul Samut later moved from Kabul to Bukhara, where he became the right-hand man of the notorious emir, and was allegedly responsible for numerous cruelties.

ALFRED RUSSEL WALLACE 1823-1913

Everything was gone, and I had not one specimen to illustrate the unknown lands I had trod, or to call back the recollection of the wild scenes I had beheld!

As the ship burned, Alfred Russel Wallace scrambled into the lifeboat and looked on in dismay as his collection of thousands of insects, plants, bird-skins and journals was engulfed by flames, then sank without trace. In his hands was a small tin box containing a map, a few notebooks and drawings – the only surviving records of his four years of discovery and research along the Rio Negro in Brazil.

Surveyor and self-trained naturalist, Wallace had arrived at the mouth of the Amazon with entomologist Henry Walter Bates in 1848. Both in their mid-twenties, the friends intended to fund their expedition to South America by selling specimens to collectors in England. The men then split up, with Wallace travelling up the Rio Negro to areas previously unexplored by European naturalists. He delighted in collecting: 'With what pleasure had I looked upon every rare and curious insect I had added to my collection! How many times, when almost overcome by the ague, had I crawled into the forest and been rewarded by some unknown and beautiful species!'

Yet by 1852 the physical toll of tropical exploration forced Wallace to leave the region. He had nearly died from malaria several times, had accidentally blown off part of his hand with a loaded gun, and had returned to the city of Pará to discover that his younger brother, who had sailed to Brazil to join him, had succumbed to yellow fever. Deeply saddened, Wallace boarded the brig *Helen* and sailed for home. Twenty-six days later, *Helen* was engulfed in flames and his precious specimens were irretrievably lost.

Undeterred, a year and a half later, Wallace left England for the Malay Archipelago. He would spend nearly eight years, visiting every important island in the group. This time, Wallace would bring home an astonishing 126,500 natural history specimens, including over 200 new species of birds and more than 1,000 new insects.

The Malay Archipelago was the ideal geographic setting for studying species distribution. After crossing a deep channel between the islands of Lombok and Bali, Wallace noticed strikingly different animals and birds. He realized he had crossed a divide between two zoological realms: on one side the animals were typical of Asia, on the other of Australasia. The invisible boundary is now known as Wallace's Line. The Archipelago was also the setting for what Wallace would later describe as 'the central and controlling incident of my life'.

In February 1858, feverish from malaria, Wallace had an epiphany. Opening his notebook, he jotted down his first thoughts on the origin of species. During his recovery, he enlarged on his idea and sent the complete essay to Charles Darwin. Darwin was taken aback by Wallace's hypothesis – he had conceived the same notion twenty years earlier, but had only shared it with his closest friends. Later that year, the two naturalists were presented as co-realizers of the theory of evolution by natural selection.

Wallace would spend a further fifty years applying himself to a formidable array of scientific subjects. From his start as an impoverished surveyor, he had become a leading evolutionary theorist, a pioneering scientific geographer and prolific author. Although always in Darwin's shadow, the modest, gentle and honourable Wallace was affectionately known as 'the Grand Old Man of Science'.

For almost eight years, Wallace travelled around the islands of the Malay Archipelago, covering some 22,530 km (14,000 miles) in native crafts; these are his bird and insect notebooks from 1858. His time here was fundamental to his later inspiration as a man of science.

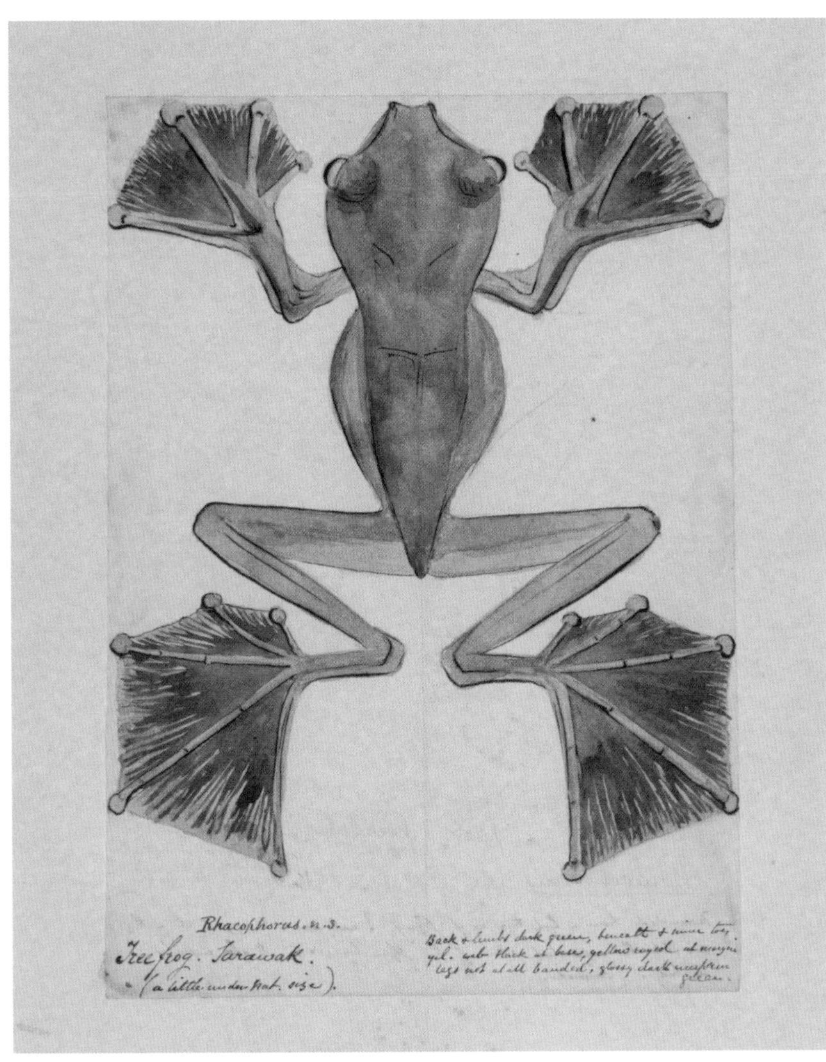

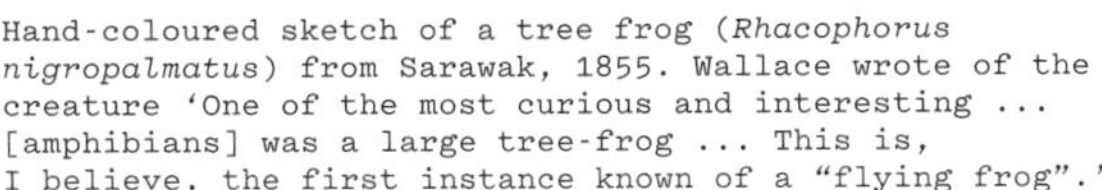
Hand-coloured sketch of a tree frog (*Rhacophorus nigropalmatus*) from Sarawak, 1855. Wallace wrote of the creature 'One of the most curious and interesting ... [amphibians] was a large tree-frog ... This is, I believe, the first instance known of a "flying frog".'

A rainforest tree in a clearing at Simunjon coalworks, Sarawak. This was one of Wallace's most productive localities for observation and gathering: 'On one day I collected 76 different [species], of which 34 were new to me. By the end of April I had obtained more than a thousand.'

Birds which are Migratory in Malacca
appearing in Nov. with the N.E. Monsoon & leaving
in March at the change to the S.W. monsoon

Muscipeta paradisi. (Lin. sp.) & two other species
one all rufous, the other all black, all with
middle tail feathers equally long.. "Gen. Rappa"
also a small gray flycatcher.

Buceros cassidix. Macassar
bill of ♂ 1/3 size..

♀ bill shorter – all orange
ridges at base deeper & more in
number? older.. iris or. red.

Called by the Dutch at Macassar "Year-bird" from
the ridges on the bill which are said to show the
age of the specimen; Eats fruit, but also insects which
it picks off the bark of the branches when it alights
such as Lamia 5-maculata, large elaters &c. These it
kills by crushing in its mouth. It also crushes the fruit
before swallowing.

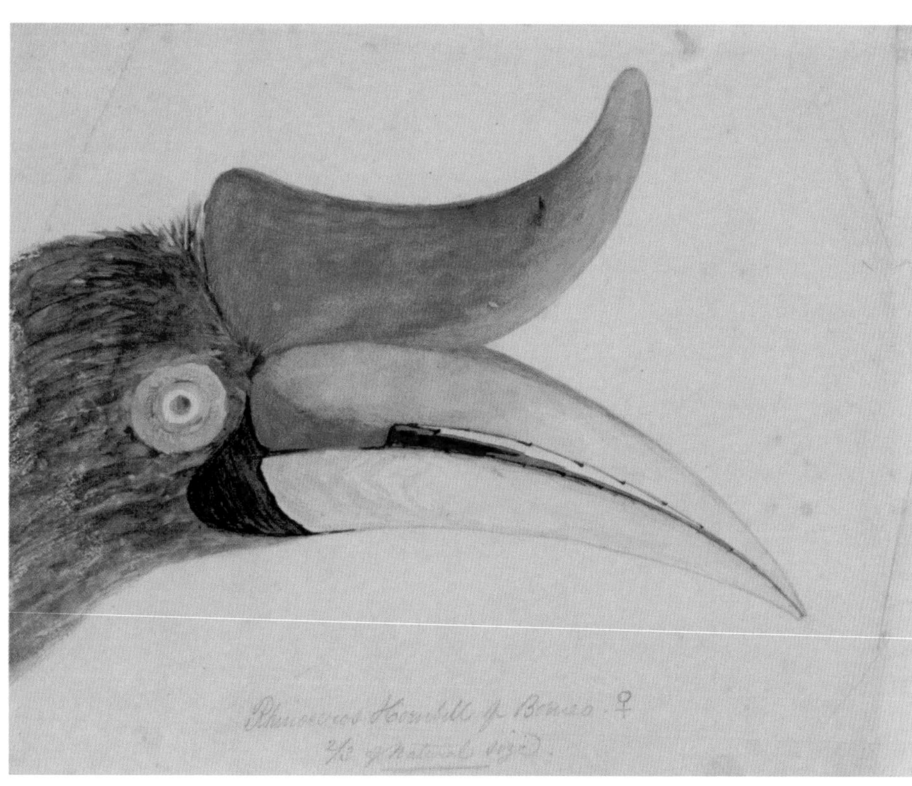

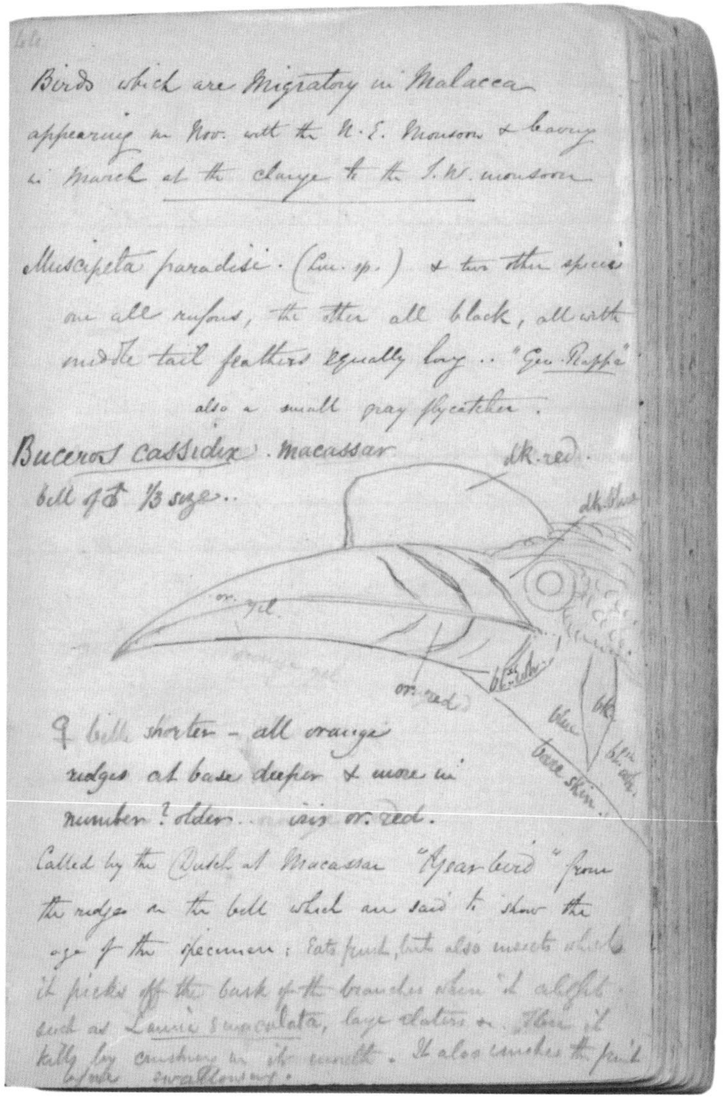

The head of a female Rhinoceros Hornbill (*Buceros rhinoceros*) painted by Wallace in Sarawak in 1855. His notebook in Makassar the following year contains more detailed notes on the birds he observed, including another wonderful hornbill.

Even now, while writing by the last glimmer of twilight, the vampire bat is fluttering about the room, hovering among the timbers of the roof … and now and then whizzing past my ears with a most spectral noise.

Now bound safely in albums, these sketches were among the handful of precious items that Wallace was able to salvage from his 1848-52 expedition to Brazil, when his vessel *Helen* caught fire and then sank on his return voyage home. His huge collection of drawings and specimens was engulfed in the flames.

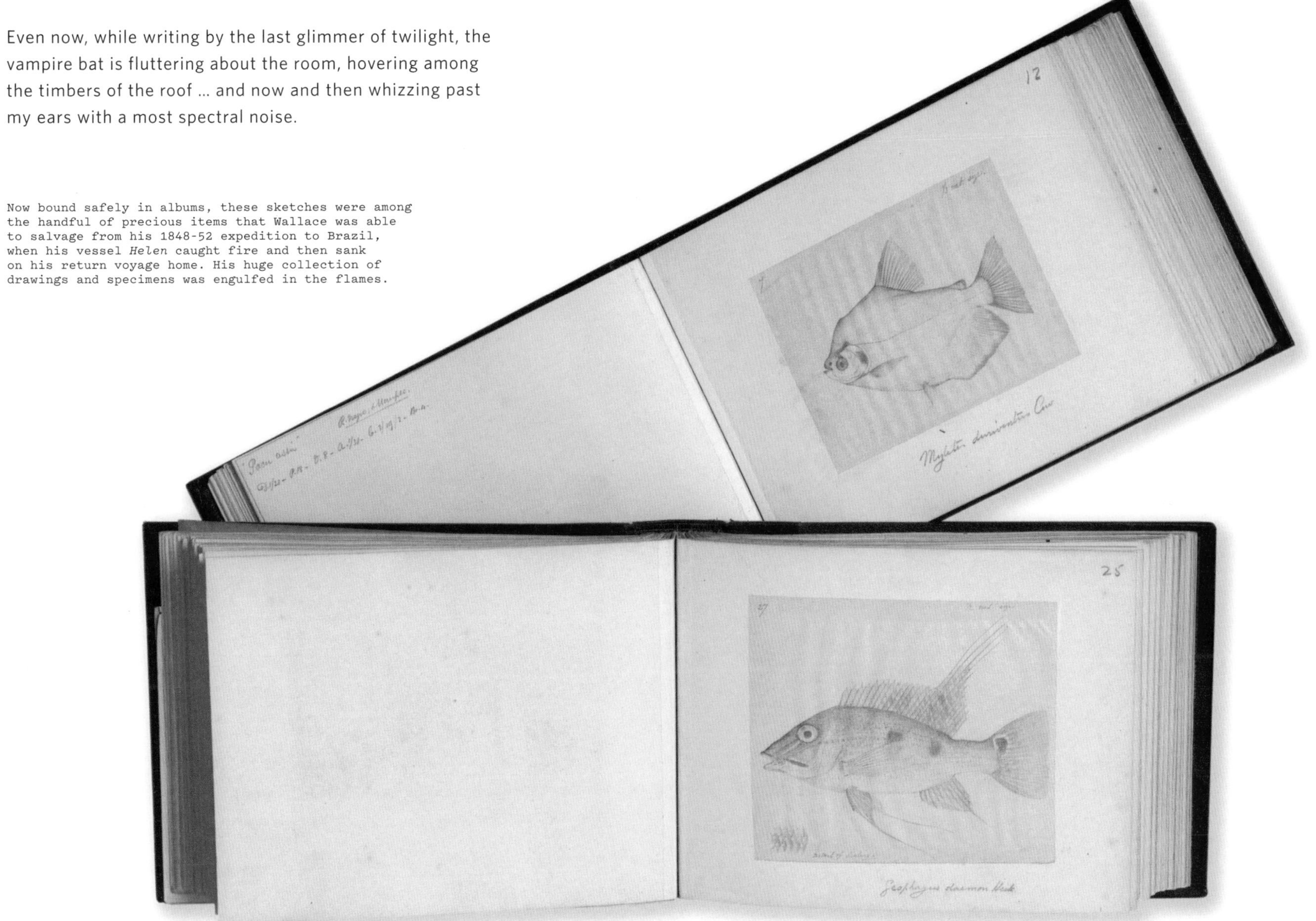

JAMES WALLIS 1785-1858

I now remember poor Jack ... guiding me thro' trackless forests with more kindly feelings than I do many of my own colour, kindred and nation.

Newcastle, Australia in 1816 was a grim, infant town: a penal settlement that was home to some 250 dangerous convicts who slept three to a crib in soulless barracks. The summers were oppressively hot; there were sandflies and mosquitoes, and outbreaks of dysentery, fever and cholera. The one preöccupation among the prisoners was escape. For Irish-born career soldier James Wallis, however, Newcastle was a place of opportunity.

As Commandant of the penal settlement from June 1816 to December 1818, Captain Wallis immediately began an ambitious expansion plan for the settlement, building new stone barracks for convicts and his men, as well as a hospital, a workshop, a school and a church. With no clergyman available, he read services himself. An amenable character, Wallis soon made close relationships with the local indigenous people, becoming particularly friendly with the chief of the Awabakal, a man named Burigon or 'Jack', with whom he would go on hunting and exploring expeditions.

When off-duty, Wallis spent his time sketching. Two hundred years after he arrived in Australia, his album of drawings and paintings was discovered in the bottom of a cupboard in Ontario, Canada. Illustrating the local indigenous people, flora, fauna and landscapes, this forgotten album, created as a gift for his new wife, has become a significant pictorial record of a fledgling colonial settlement. Finally, Wallis's historical contribution is gaining recognition as the earliest depictions of the now flourishing city of Newcastle and, in a broader sense, the representation of an emerging nation and its indigenous peoples.

'The Fish of New South Wales'. As a gift for his new wife, Captain Wallis compiled an album filled with exquisite renderings of the local flora, fauna and indigenous people.

Wallis became close with local indigenous peoples of New South Wales, particularly with 'Burigon', known as Jack, seen here on the left; the figure in the centre is in full warrior dress. Wallis's paintings show a familiarity with his subjects that was extremely rare for the time.

BURIGON
NERANG DOLL
TRIMMER
in Warriors full Dress
WALKER
NERANG WOGEE
These figures of the Natives are all drawn by Major Wallis 46 Regt
These Natives all sat for their Pictures

JOHN WHITE d. 1593

A skilful painter is also to be carried ... to bring the descriptions of all beasts, birds, fishes, trees, townes etc.

Little is known about the curious life of John White, but a few things are clear, including that he was a very talented artist and a courageous one too. The exceptional watercolours he created gave the Elizabethan world its first glimpse of America, shaping perspectives of the New World for more than 200 years.

Born sometime in the 1540s, in May 1577 White had his first taste of adventure, sailing with buccaneer Martin Frobisher on a prospecting expedition in search of a northwest passage to the riches of Asia. They explored the shores of Greenland and Baffin Island, though returned with little more than fool's gold and wild tales of people seen for the first time. White recorded a skirmish with the Inuit, which sadly would be the first of many lethal encounters between European and indigenous peoples as different worlds collided in the years ahead.

'America' had first been named in 1507, inked on a map that credited its discovery not to Columbus but to the Florentine sailor Amerigo Vespucci, who had realized that beyond the Caribbean lay a 'Novus Orbis' or New World. When White was appointed as artist to the 1585 expedition to Virginia promoted by Walter Ralegh, his task was to capture it all with paper and paint. White's art offers an insight into the raw experience of risking everything to establish a new community on hostile shores, of enduring the hardships of a voyage as it approaches a new land, of witnessing new forms of life at every turn. He sketched in graphite pencil, coloured with vermilion, indigo, red ochre, powdered gold and silver leaf. In the flying fish and turtle, jellyfish and firefly, sturgeon and land crab he drew, here was a peculiar and bountiful new Eden.

White was joined ashore by Thomas Harriot, a linguist and surveyor, and together they explored the coasts and nearby settlements, recording the wildlife and creating detailed maps of the coastline of what is now North Carolina. White's art was to be used to encourage further investment and colonists for a new plantation here. They were images crafted for Ralegh, made to inform and impress Elizabeth I, the Virgin Queen. It was art as propaganda as much as it was a pioneering observation of nature.

Whereas many who followed him painted merely crude and barbarous savages, White's rendering of the Algonquian-speaking Indians who lived in the forests is sensitive and free of later stereotype. They cultivate the land and fish using effective technologies – weirs, nets and spears – and live in organized settlements. White returned to England, and the good relations with the Indians that his watercolours record broke down, as the first settlers struggled to feed themselves and turned to force. In 1586 the colony was abandoned and Francis Drake evacuated the survivors.

In 1587, White sailed again to Virginia, with more than 100 colonists, as governor of a second settlement on the Chesapeake island of Roanoke, where they built a small fort. His granddaughter, Virginia Dare, was born there, but White had to leave her and her mother, along with the others, in a desperate voyage to bring back supplies. He had hoped to return in months, but the approaching war with Spain meant he didn't reach Roanoke until 1590, by which time not a single person could be found. The mystery of the 'lost colony' of Roanoke has never been solved.

White's sketch of a skirmish at 'Bloody Point', Frobisher Bay, in 1577, depicts one of the first of many lethal encounters between Europeans and indigenous peoples as explorers discovered and claimed new lands. Here the Englishmen fire their guns at the Inuit who wield their bows from the cliff above.

One of the earliest charts of the New World, showing the east coast of North America from Chesapeake Bay to the Florida Keys. Drawn by John White in 1585, it located all the major coastal features and includes the arms of Walter Ralegh, as well as dolphins, whales and other sea beasts.

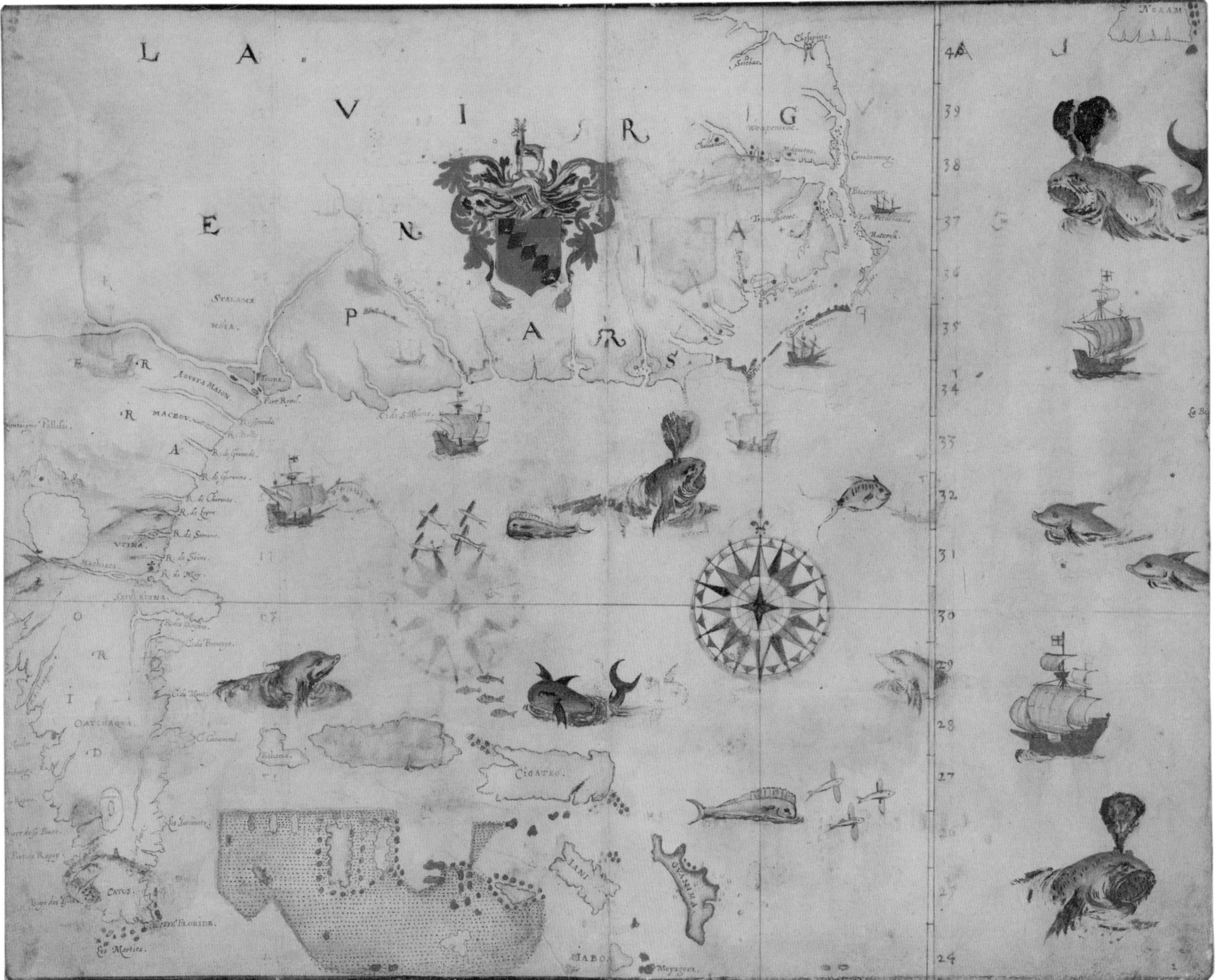

L A V I R G
E N I A
P A R S
Chesepiooc
Weapemeoc
Croatamung
STALAME
NOIA
ADVSTA MAION
Port Royal
MACEOV
VTINA
OATCHAQVA
C. Canaueral
Bahama
CIGATEO
IANI
GVANIMA
CATOS
DE FLORIDE
Moyaguez
40
39
38
37
36
35
34
33
32
31
30
29
28
27
26
25
24

White recorded the North Carolina Algonquian Indians, their language and way of life, creating the earliest views of human settlement in America. This drawing of the village of the Secotan Indians in North Carolina, 1585, features not only their daily life and crop rotation but also, in the lower right, a precious glimpse of a religious ceremony, possibly a 'green corn festival'.

'A cheife Herowans wife of Pomeoc and her daughter of the age of 8 or 10 years.' The child is holding a doll wearing Elizabethan dress. Harriot remarked that the children he met 'greatly delighted with puppets and babes which are broughte oute of England'.

Opposite is a remarkable drawing of a ritual dance, perhaps the 'green corn festival' also seen in the drawing far left. White's task was to 'drawe to life' the New World's natural bounty and the character of its inhabitants.

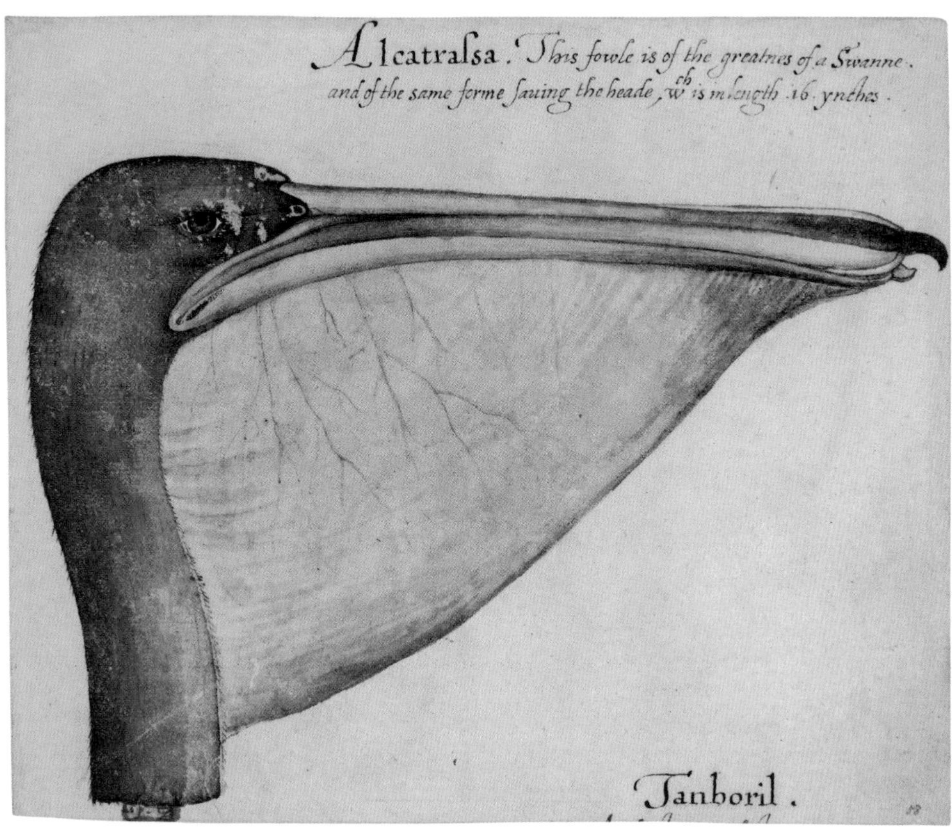

Alcatrassa. This fowle is of the greatnes of a Swanne. and of the same forme sauing the heade, wch is in length 16. ynches.
Tanboril.

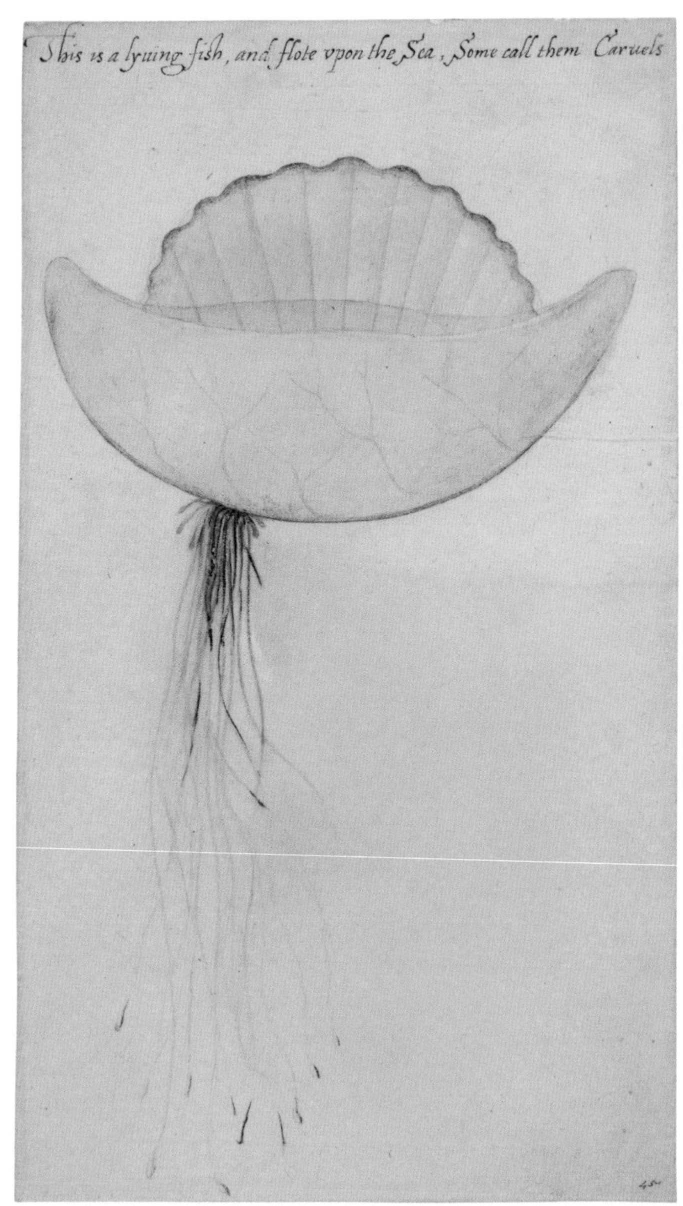

This is a lyuing fish, and flote vpon the Sea, Some call them Caruels

From thence we returned by the water side, round about the North point of the Iland, untill we came to the place where I left our Colony in the yeere 1586 ... and as we entred up the sandy banke upon a tree, in the very browe thereof were curiously carved these faire Romane letters C R O: which letters presently we knew to signifie the place, where I should find the planters seated, according to a secret token agreed upon betweene them and me at my last departure from them.

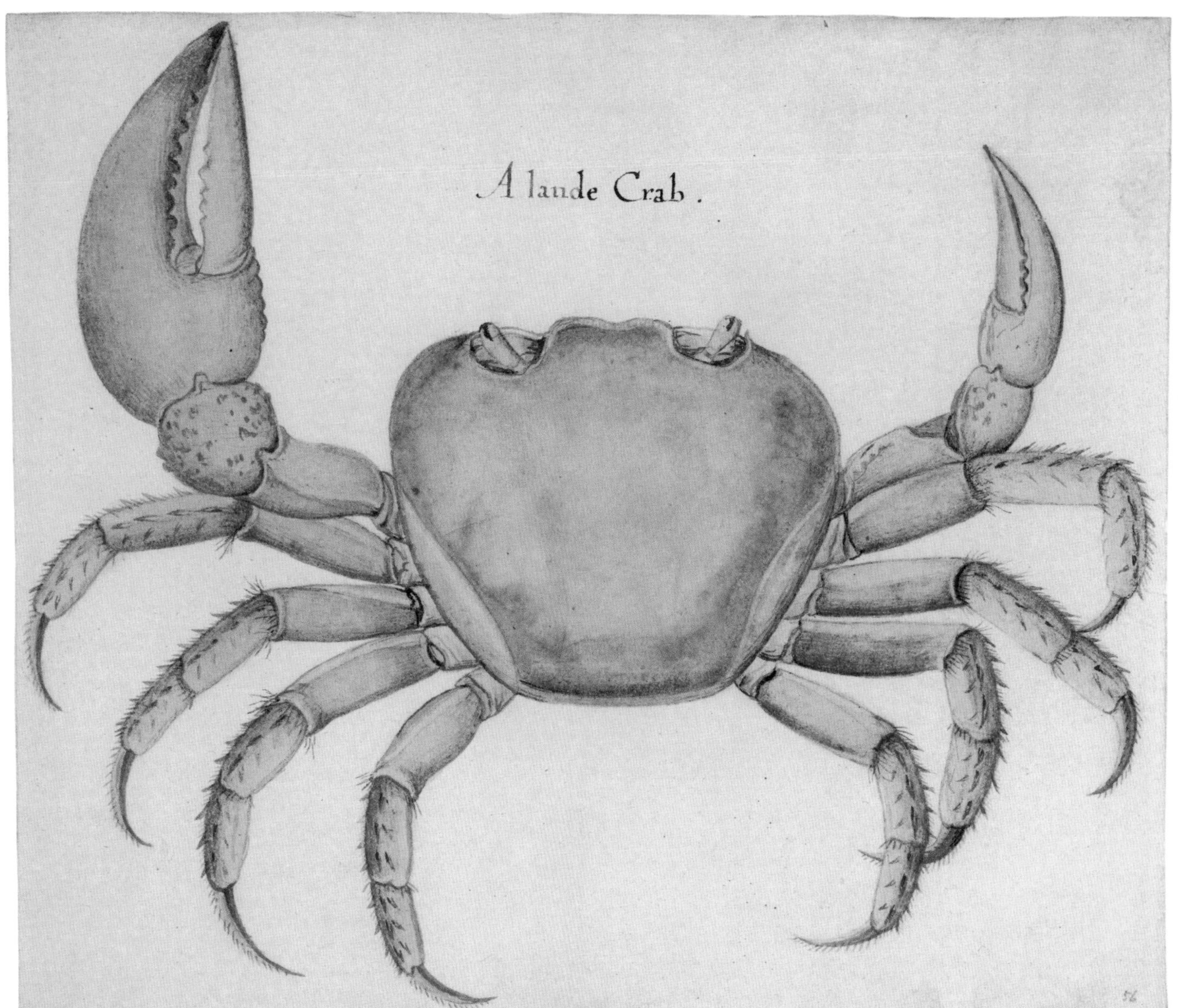

White's watercolours survive in the British Museum, London. It is incredible to think that they were made at a time when America, and its inhabitants and unknown creatures, was seen for the first time by Europeans, merely a line of trees on the far horizon. Shown here are an Eastern Brown Pelican, a 'lande crabe', and a huge Portuguese man o'war jellyfish - the name given it by sailors because its translucent body was shaped so like their caravels. The blue tentacles deliver the potentially fatal sting.

52 1910—MAY 24. ○ Full Moon 5.39 a.m.

	NAME AND ADDRESS	23 M	24 T	25 W	26 TH	27 F	28 S	29 $	£	s.	d.

Jan 4 Evans — We turned out as usual at 5.45 am and there was some delay in getting off as Teddie Evans & his party of Crean & Lashley came along with us for a mile before turning back to go home. I was very sorry for Teddie Evans as he has spent 2½ years in working for a place on this polar journey. We are now 5 & as we have only 4 pairs of ski Bowers has to go on foot just behind Scott & myself

12½m

87°45

Oates
Scott
Bowers
Evans
Wilson

Our sledge is a pretty high pack

tank
5 sl. bags
Cooker
instrument box
biscuit boxes
tank

We had a perfect day without wind - calm & hot sun - but temp -16.8° though so warm & took a bit of a sun bath in the evening. The surface was bad, heavy sandy drifts and

EDWARD WILSON 1872-1912

The snow is soft and one sinks in at every step, making the walking very fatiguing. Supper, sleeping bag and breakfast are joys worth living for under these conditions.

Within a small leather satchel, tucked carefully into an instrument box, they found a sledging diary, two sketchbooks and a final letter to his wife – here were Edward Wilson's last thoughts, written as a blizzard raged outside the tent. Eight months on, three bodies now lay frozen in time. Could anything in exploration be worth such a miserable death?

Born in Cheltenham, the second son of a local physician, Wilson went to Cambridge as an undergraduate to read Natural Sciences. His college rooms were said to be littered with drawings and the bones and skulls of numerous birds. Self-taught, his sketching developed well, aligned with his passion for ornithology. Wilson was assistant surgeon, artist and vertebrate zoologist on Scott's *Discovery* expedition, sailing south in August 1901, just three weeks after he was married. He had also learned taxidermy at the British Museum and began sketching seal skins and skeletons there, training his eyes.

A deeply religious man, Wilson's sympathetic character and genuine care for his shipmates made him one of the most admired on the voyage; he was known fondly as 'Uncle Bill'. Scott relied heavily on him for guidance and moral support. During the long winter night he worked up many paintings from his sketchbook in the relative warmth of hut and ship by candle and gas light. In the summer he would sketch outdoors, and, nearly snow blind at the end of a long day's sledging, admitted that 'sketching in the Antarctic is not all joy, for ... your fingers are all thumbs, and are soon so cold that you don't know what or where they are.'

After the return of *Discovery*, an exhibition of Wilson's pictures was held at the Bruton Gallery in London. Wilson was one of the first men to 'convey an accurate idea of the beauty and subtlety of Antarctic colours. Often these records were as precise as photography and much more pleasing.' Among the throng of viewers was Joseph Hooker, then aged 88, who as a young naturalist had accompanied James Clark Ross to Antarctica over six decades before. 'I made an effort to see the Antarctic sketches,' he remarked, 'they are marvellous in number, interest and execution ... the heads and bodies of the birds by Dr Wilson are the perfection of ornithological drawing and colouring. They are absolutely alive.'

Appointed Field Observer to the Grouse Disease Inquiry, Wilson spent several years on the moors of Scotland, painstakingly dissecting and then illustrating over a thousand birds. In 1910 he returned again to the Antarctic with his friend Captain Scott, joining *Terra Nova* as expeditionary artist, zoologist and Chief of the Scientific Staff. He led a party to the Emperor Penguin rookery at Cape Crozier in June 1911, in the middle of winter and for much of the time in total darkness; a formidable effort later described as 'the worst journey in the world'. They returned to the safety of their hut more dead than alive, and all for the sake of three eggs.

Wilson was an automatic choice as a member of the final party to push for the Pole. On the return journey, in March 1912, he died alongside Scott, sheltering in their tent on the Great Ice Barrier. In the final days, Scott had written to Wilson's wife: 'If this letter reaches you Bill and I will have gone out together ... he died, as he lived, a brave, true man – the best of comrades and staunchest of friends.'

Wilson's diary and sledging sketchbooks transport us to his fateful journey. On 14 November 1911 there was a wonderful parhelion, but with no time to paint he carefully jotted down colour annotations. 'In full swing', above, shows the daily effort of manhauling heavy sledges.

In the morning, you put on frozen socks, frozen mitts and frozen boots, stuffed with frozen damp grass and rime, and you suffer a good deal from painfully cold feet, until everything is packed up again and strapped on the sledges, and you are off to warm up to the work of a beast of burden. There's a fascination about it all, but it can't be considered comfort.

An ardent ornithologist, Wilson sketched Emperor Penguins with delight on both of his expeditions to Antarctica. On 8 April 1902 about fifteen were seen across the ice and the men raced out to drive them closer to the ship, where they were killed in the name of science. 'It was not a pleasant job, in any way,' Wilson wrote in his diary, 'but an opportunity not to be missed, for no one has ever seen this bird in any numbers before and it is our duty to bring back as good a collection as we can.'

The original sketch-map by Wilson showing the track of his remarkable journey from Cape Evans to Cape Crozier and return, 27 June to 1 August 1911. It was a feat later made famous in the classic book *The Worst Journey in the World*. With two companions, Wilson had gone in search of fresh Emperor Penguin eggs laid in the depths of an Antarctic winter, enduring a desperately hazardous journey in darkness, the loss of their tent and temperatures plummeting to minus 70 below. Cherry-Garrard later wrote: 'Antarctic exploration is seldom as bad as you imagine, seldom as bad as it sounds. But this journey beggared our language; no words could express its horror.'

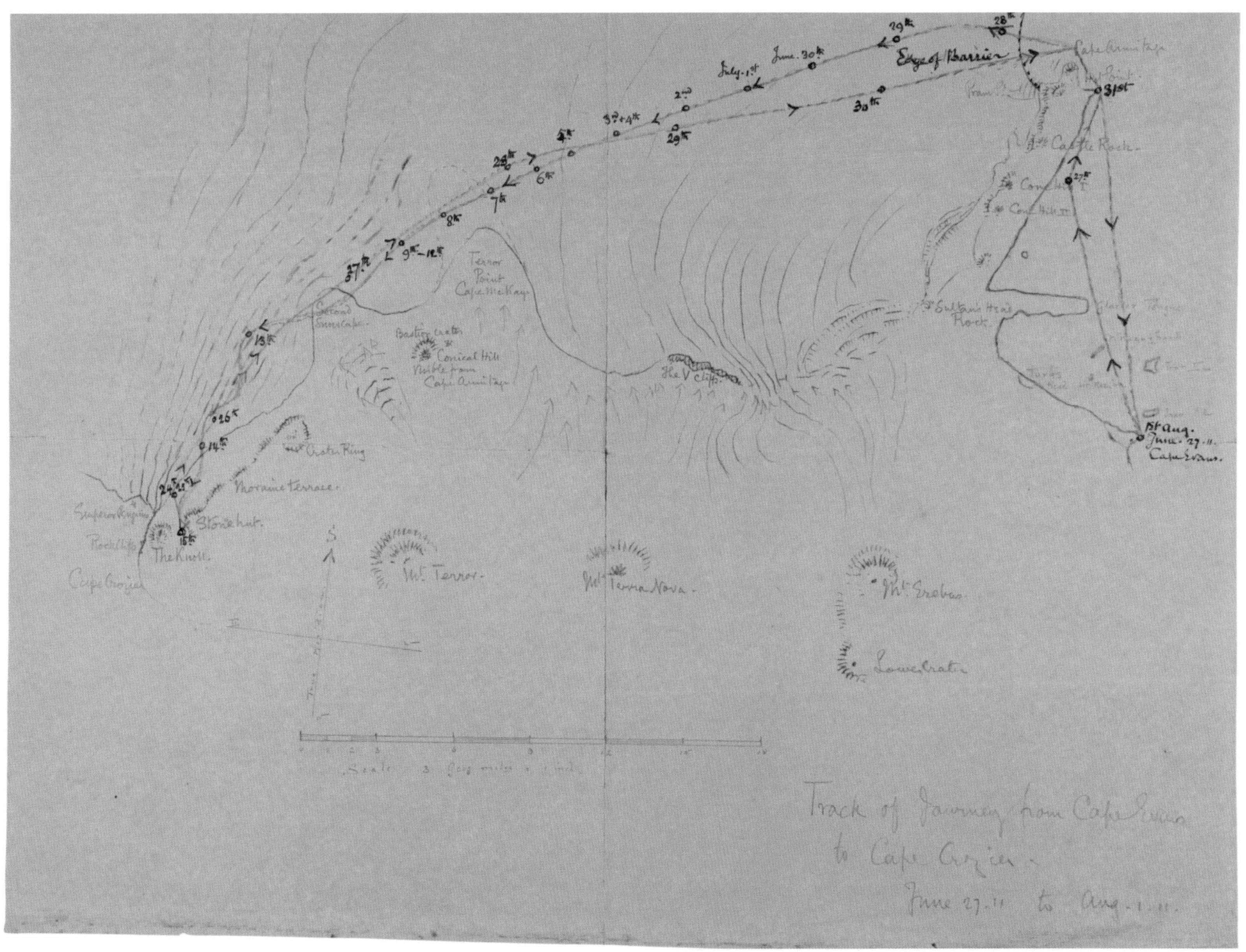
Edge of Barrier
Cape Armitage
June 30th
July 1st
Castle Rock
Terror Point
Cape McKay
Conical Hill
visible from
Cape Armitage
Sultan's Head
Rock
Crater Ring
Moraine terrace
Stone hut
The Knoll
Cape Crozier
Mt. Terror
Mt. Terra Nova
Mt. Erebus
1st Aug.
June 27.11
Cape Evans
Track of Journey from Cape Evans
to Cape Crozier -
June 27.11 to Aug. 1.11.

The active volcano Mount Erebus sketched on 13 August 1911. The days are getting longer and light is returning. Soon preparations will begin and the men will leave the safety of their hut at Cape Evans for the Pole. They will never return.

In cold conditions in April 1911, Wilson sketched the view down to the sea ice from Observation Hill, which overlooks the present-day McMurdo Base. It had been home to the Discovery Hut from his first expedition, visible on the small headland. The sketch shows his intricate colour annotations so that the later coloured version could be completed in the warmth of their hut.

lemon yellow
rose pink
bright white
Yellow light

Putting up a pyramid tent in strong winds is a difficult business, but once inside it can be made relatively snug. Here Wilson draws three men sharing a reindeer-skin sleeping bag, with their gear hanging in the apex to try to thaw it out in the warm air of the primus. These sketches are from Wilson's first expedition in 1902, but equipment was much the same when he pushed for the Pole with Scott in 1911.

The fateful view on 16 January 1912. ‘We came on a black flag’, he wrote, ‘and the Norwegians’ sledge ski and dog tracks running about NE and SW both ways.’ On the following day, Wilson and the others stood at the South Pole. In the vast landscape of emptiness, they discovered traces of a camp, paw prints of dogs, wind-torn flags, a tent. Here was the signal proof that they feared to see. The Norwegians had beaten them to it.

Authors

HUW LEWIS-JONES is a historian of exploration with a PhD from the University of Cambridge. Huw was Curator at the Scott Polar Research Institute and the National Maritime Museum in London and is now an award-winning author, who writes and lectures widely about adventure and the visual arts. He travels in the Arctic and Antarctica each year working as a polar guide, and has a fascination with wilderness environments and remote islands. His books include *Ocean Portraits*, *The Crossing of Antarctica*, *The Conquest of Everest*, which won the History Award at the Banff Mountain Festival, and most recently *Across the Arctic Ocean*.

KARI HERBERT is an author and publisher whose work has been featured widely in newspapers and magazines, including *The Sunday Times*, the *Guardian*, *Geographical* and *Traveller*. Her late father was polar explorer Sir Wally Herbert and her first book, *The Explorer's Daughter*, described her childhood growing up in an isolated community in the north of Greenland. Her latest book, *Heart of the Hero*, drew attention to the remarkable achievements of the wives of celebrated explorers. Huw and Kari are married and live by the sea in Cornwall.

Contributors

DAVID AINLEY is one of the world's leading polar ecologists. He earned a PhD in animal behaviour from Johns Hopkins University, and has now made over 35 trips to Antarctica and the Southern Ocean, working on oceanographic research vessels and at challenging survey sites. He is currently involved in ongoing studies of penguin demography at Ross Island, as well as experiments using an ocean glider and ROVs to explore cetacean and penguin foraging. For the past decade he has been trying to protect the Ross Sea from humans, most immediately the threats of industrial fishing, and his efforts were highlighted in the film *The Last Ocean*. From observations recorded within his notebooks, he has written over 120 scientific papers about the ecology of penguins, seals and whales in the Antarctic. He lives in San Francisco, California.

ALAN BEAN is, quite simply, an American legend. Famous as the lunar module pilot on the Apollo 12 mission, he also became the fourth man to set foot on the Moon. Among other achievements during his long NASA career, Bean served as Commander of the 59-day Skylab III Space Station mission in 1973. Astronaut turned artist, he is the first man to paint directly from experience of another world, and his luminous works are highly sought after by collectors. He lives in Houston, Texas.

WADE DAVIS is Professor of Anthropology and the BC Leadership Chair in Cultures and Ecosystems at Risk at the University of British Columbia. Between 1999 and 2013 he served as Explorer-in-Residence at the National Geographic Society and is currently a member of the NGS Explorers Council. Author of seventeen books, including *The Serpent and the Rainbow*, *One River*, *The Wayfinders* and *The Sacred Headwaters*, he holds degrees in anthropology and biology and received his PhD in ethnobotany, all from Harvard University. Davis was awarded the Gold Medal from the Royal Canadian Geographical Society for his contributions to anthropology and conservation and the Explorers Medal, the highest award of the Explorers Club, among many other honours. His latest book, *Into the Silence*, received the 2012 Samuel Johnson prize, the top award for literary nonfiction in the English language.

TONY FOSTER is an acclaimed British artist who for the last three decades has created a series of watercolour diaries in the world's great wildernesses. Travelling mostly on foot, by raft or canoe, through mountains and canyons, rainforests and deserts, from the Arctic to the Tropics, he takes all the painting and camping equipment he needs to create his artworks on the spot. A Fellow of the Royal Geographical Society, Foster was awarded its Cherry Kearton Medal in 2001, joining an illustrious roster of creative explorers including broadcaster David Attenborough, cartographer Bradford Washburn, and more recently celebrated photographers such as Yann Arthus-Bertrand and Sebastião Salgado. His journeys have resulted in many books and exhibitions, including *Painting at the Edge of the World*, *After Lewis and Clark* and *Sacred Places*.

ROBERT MACFARLANE is the author of a number of bestselling and award-winning books about exploration, travel and landscape including *Mountains of the Mind*, *The Wild Places*, *The Old Ways* and *Landmarks*. His work has been translated into many languages and widely adapted for film, television and radio. He is currently at work on *Underland*, a book about the lost worlds beneath our feet. He is a Fellow of Emmanuel College, Cambridge.

SIR GHILLEAN PRANCE is a celebrated botanist and ecologist, one of the seminal scientific explorers of the Amazon rainforest in modern times. Formerly Director of the Royal Botanic Gardens, Kew, he has participated in some forty expeditions, beginning with a 1963 trip to Suriname as a young researcher for the New York Botanic Garden. He is still actively involved in environmental issues, as a trustee of the Amazon Charitable Trust, a Vice-President of the Nature in Art Trust, and was instrumental in setting up Cornwall's Eden Project as its Scientific Director. The first winner of the International Cosmos Prize, Prance is the author of hundreds of scientific papers and numerous books, most recently *That Glorious Forest*, which recounts a lifetime of discovery and his abiding passion for plants.

Sketch by Griffith Taylor, geologist on Scott's *Terra Nova* Expedition, 8 February 1911, showing the typical mode of dress for venturing out into the field: notebook, camera and beard, clearly, are all part of the essential get up.

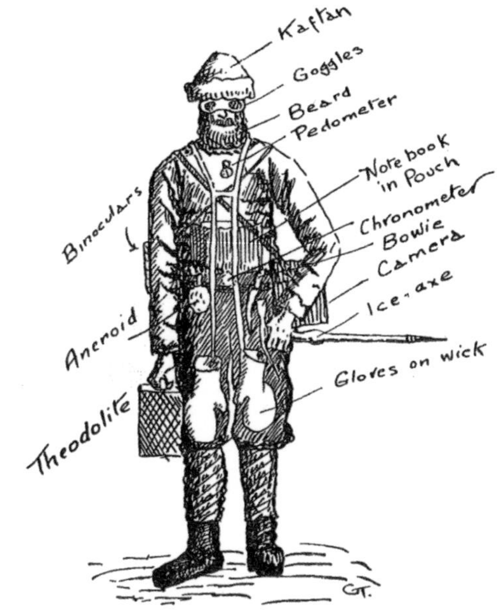

SELECTED READING

DAVID AINLEY

Ainley, David, *Breeding Biology of the Adélie Penguin* (University of California Press, 1983)
— *The Adélie Penguin: Bellwether of Climate Change* (Columbia University Press, 2002)

ROALD AMUNDSEN

Amundsen, Roald, *The North West Passage* (Constable, 1908)
— *The South Pole* (John Murray, 1912)
— *My Life as an Explorer* (Heinemann, 1927)
Kløver, Geir (ed.), *The Roald Amundsen Diaries* (Fram Museum, 2010)

JOHN JAMES AUDUBON

Audubon, John James, *Ornithological Biography* (A. Black, 1838)
— *The Birds of America* (Audubon, 1840)

JOHN AULDJO

Auldjo, John, *Narrative of an Ascent to the Summit of Mont Blanc* (Longman & Co., 1828)
— *Sketches of Vesuvius* (Longman & Co., 1833)

THOMAS BAINES

Baines, Thomas, *Explorations in South West Africa* (Longman & Co., 1864)
— *Shifts and Expedients of Camp Life, Travel, and Exploration* (Horace Cox, 1871)
Wallis, J. P. R. (ed.), *The Northern Goldfields Diaries of Thomas Baines* (Chatto & Windus, 1946)

HENRY WALTER BATES

Bates, Henry Walter, *The Naturalist on the River Amazons* (John Murray, 1863)
Crawforth, Anthony, *The Butterfly Hunter* (University of Buckingham Press, 2009)

ALAN BEAN

Bean, Alan, *Apollo: An Eyewitness Account* (Greenwich Workshop Press, 2002)
— *Painting Apollo* (Smithsonian, 2009)

LUDWIG BECKER

Darragh, Thomas (ed.), *A Letter From Australia* (Garravembi Press, 1993)
Tipping, Marjorie (ed.), *Ludwig Becker* (Melbourne University Press, 1979)

WILLIAM BEEBE

Beebe, William, *Galapagos* (Putnam, 1924)
— *The Arcturus Adventure* (Putnam, 1926)
— *Half Mile Down* (Harcourt, Brace, 1934)

GERTRUDE BELL

Bell, Gertrude, *The Desert and the Sown* (Heinemann, 1907)
— *Amurath to Amurath* (Heinemann, 1911)
The Letters of Gertrude Bell, Selected and Edited by Lady Bell (Benn, 1927)
Howell, Georgina, *Daughter of the Desert* (Macmillan, 2006)

FRANZ BOAS

Boas, Franz, *The Indian Tribes of the Lower Fraser River* (Spottiswoode, 1894)
— *Race, Language and Culture* (University of Chicago Press, 1940)
Müller-Wille, Ludger, *The Franz Boas Enigma* (Baraka Books, 2014)

CHRIS BONINGTON

Bonington, Chris, *Everest* (Penguin, 1975)
— *Mountaineer* (Baton Wicks, 1996)
— *Quest for Adventure* (Hodder & Stoughton, 1981)
— *Boundless Horizons* (Weidenfeld & Nicolson, 2000)

JAN BRANDES

Bruijn, Max de and Raben, Remco (eds), *The World of Jan Brandes, 1743–1808* (Waanders, 2004)

ADELA BRETON

Giles, Sue and Stewart, Jennifer, *The Art of Ruins* (City of Bristol Museum, 1989)
McVicker, Mary, *Adela Breton* (University of New Mexico Press, 2005)

WILLIAM BURCHELL

Burchell, William, *Travels in the Interior of Southern Africa* (Longmans, 1822)

HOWARD CARTER

Carter, Howard and Mace, A. C., *The Discovery of the Tomb of Tut-Ankh-Amen* (Cassell, 1923)
— *Tutankhamen* (Libri, 1998)
Herbert, George, Earl of Carnarvon, *Five Years' Explorations at Thebes* (Henry Frowde, 1912)
James, T. G. H., *Howard Carter* (Tauris, 2006)

BRUCE CHATWIN

Chatwin, Bruce, *In Patagonia* (Penguin, 1977)
— *The Songlines* (Viking, 1987)
Chatwin, Elizabeth and Shakespeare, Nicholas (eds), *Under the Sun* (Jonathan Cape, 2010)

JAMES COOK

Aughton, Peter, *Endeavour* (Cassell, 2002)
Beaglehole, J. C. (ed.), *The Journals of Captain James Cook on His Voyages of Discovery* (Cambridge University Press, 1955–74)
— *The Life of Captain James Cook* (Black, 1974)

WILLIAM HEATON COOPER

Cooper, W. Heaton, *The Hills of Lakeland* (Warne, 1938)
— *The Tarns of Lakeland* (Warne, 1946)
— *The Lakes* (Warne, 1966)
— *Mountain Painter* (Peters, 1984)

CHARLES DARWIN

Darwin, Charles, *Voyage of the Beagle* (Colburn, 1839)
Barlow, Nora (ed.), *Charles Darwin's Diary of the Voyage of H.M.S. 'Beagle'* (Cambridge University Press, 1933)
Hodge, Jonathan and Radick, Gregory (eds), *The Cambridge Companion to Darwin* (Cambridge University Press, 2003)
Keynes, Richard, *The Beagle Record* (Cambridge University Press, 1979)

WADE DAVIS

Davis, Wade, *The Serpent and the Rainbow* (Warner, 1985)
— *One River* (Simon & Schuster, 1996)
— *Shadows in the Sun* (Island Press, 1998)
— *Light at the Edge of the World* (Douglas & McIntyre, 2001)
— *Sacred Headwaters* (Greystone, 2012)

AMELIA EDWARDS

Edwards, Amelia, *A Thousand Miles up the Nile* (Longmans, 1877)
Rees, Joan, *Writing on the Nile* (Institute for Advanced Research, 1992)

CHARLES EVANS

Evans, Charles, *Eye on Everest* (Dobson, 1955)

RANULPH FIENNES

Fiennes, Ranulph, *Hell on Ice* (Hodder & Stoughton, 1979)
— *To the Ends of the Earth* (Hodder & Stoughton, 1983)
— *Mad, Bad and Dangerous to Know* (Hodder & Stoughton, 2007)

TONY FOSTER

Foster, Tony, *Sacred Places* (Foster Wilderness Foundation, 2015)
Robinson, Duncan and Kennedy, Robert F. (eds), *Painting at the Edge of the World* (University of Washington Press, 2008)

MARGARET FOUNTAINE

Fountaine, Margaret, *Love Among the Butterflies* (Collins, 1980)
— *Butterflies and Late Loves* (Collins, 1986)

VIVIAN FUCHS
Fuchs, Vivian and Hillary, Edmund, *The Crossing of Antarctica* (Cassell, 1958)
— *Of Ice and Men* (Nelson, 1982)

EUGENE VON GUERARD
Guerard, Eugene von, *Tinted Lithographs Illustrative of the Landscape Scenery of Victoria, New South Wales, South Australia and Tasmania* (Hamel & Ferguson, 1867)
Pullin, Ruth, *Nature Revealed* (National Gallery of Victoria, 2011)

ROBIN HANBURY-TENISON
Hanbury-Tenison, Robin, *The Rough and the Smooth* (Hale, 1969)
— *Mulu* (Weidenfeld & Nicolson, 1980)
— *Worlds Apart* (Arrow, 1984)

CHARLES TURNBULL HARRISSON
Rossiter, Heather (ed.), *Mawson's Forgotten Men* (Murdoch, 2011)

SVEN HEDIN
Hedin, Sven, *My Life As an Explorer* (Cassell, 1926)
— *Silk Road* (Routledge, 1938)
— *History of the Expedition in Asia, 1927–1935* (Elanders, 1943)

WALLY HERBERT
Herbert, Wally, *Across the Top of the World* (Longmans, 1969)
— *Hunters of the Polar North* (Time-Life Books, 1981)
— *The Noose of Laurels* (Hodder & Stoughton, 1989)
— *The Polar World* (Polarworld, 2007)
— and Lewis-Jones, Huw, *Across the Arctic Ocean* (Thames & Hudson, 2015)

THOR HEYERDAHL
Heyerdahl, Thor, *The Kon-Tiki Expedition* (Allen & Unwin, 1950)
— *Early Man and the Ocean* (Vintage, 1980)
— *Easter Island: The Mystery Solved* (Stoddart, 1989)

ED HILLARY
Hillary, Edmund, *High Adventure* (Hodder & Stoughton, 1955)
— *No Latitude for Error* (Hodder & Stoughton, 1961)
— *View from the Summit* (Doubleday, 1999)
Hunt, John, *The Ascent of Everest* (Hodder & Stoughton, 1953)

WILLIAM HODGES
Quilley, Geoff and Bonehill, John (eds), *William Hodges* (Yale University Press, 2004)
Smith, Bernard, *European Vision and the South Pacific* (Yale University Press, 1985)

HECTOR HOREAU
Horeau, Hector, *Panorama d'Egypte et de Nubie* (1841)

ALEXANDER VON HUMBOLDT
Humboldt, Alexander von, *Personal Narrative of Travels to the Equinoctial Regions of the New Continent During the Years 1799–1824* (Longman, 1822)
Helferich, Gerard, *Humboldt's Cosmos* (Gotham Books, 2004)
Wulf, Andrea, *The Invention of Nature* (John Murray, 2015)

MERIWETHER LEWIS
Devoto, Bernard (ed.), *The Journals of Lewis and Clark* (Houghton Mifflin, 1953)
Gilman, Carolyn, *Lewis and Clark* (Smithsonian, 2003)

CARL LINNAEUS
Blunt, Wilfrid, *The Compleat Naturalist* (Frances Lincoln, 2002)
Jarvis, Charles, *Order Out of Chaos* (Linnean Society of London, 2007)
Koerner, Lisbet, *Linnaeus* (Harvard University Press, 2001)
Smith, James Edward (ed.), *Lachesis Lapponica* (Cochrane, 1811)

DAVID LIVINGSTONE
Livingstone, David, *Missionary Travels and Researches in South Africa* (John Murray, 1857)
Jeal, Tim, *Livingstone* (Yale University Press, 2013)
Pettitt, Claire, *Dr Livingstone, I Presume?* (Profile, 2007)
Waller, Horace (ed.), *The Last Journals of David Livingstone in Central Africa* (John Murray, 1874)

GEORGE LOWE
Lowe, George, *Because It Is There* (Cassell, 1959)
— and Lewis-Jones, Huw, *The Conquest of Everest* (Thames & Hudson, 2013)
— and Lewis-Jones, Huw, *The Crossing of Antarctica* (Thames & Hudson, 2014)
Lewis-Jones, Huw (ed.), *Letters from Everest* (Polarworld, 2013)

ROBERT MACFARLANE
Macfarlane, Robert, *Mountains of the Mind* (Granta, 2003)
— *The Wild Places* (Granta, 2007)
— *The Old Ways* (Hamish Hamilton, 2012)
— *Landmarks* (Hamish Hamilton, 2015)

MAXIMILIAN DE WIED
Wied-Neuwied, Prince Maximilian de, *Voyage au Bresil* (Bertrand, 1822)
— *Travels in the Interior of North America* (Ackermann, 1843)

MARGARET MEE
Mee, Margaret, *Flowers of the Brazilian Rainforests* (Tryon Gallery, 1969)
— *Return to the Amazon* (Stationery Office, 1996)
Mayo, Simon, *Margaret Mee's Amazon* (Royal Botanic Gardens, 1988)

MARIA SIBYLLA MERIAN
Merian, Maria Sibylla, *The Surinam Album* (Folio Society, 2006)
Stearn, W. T., *The Wondrous Transformations of Caterpillars* (Scolar Press, 1978)
Wettengl, K. (ed.), *Maria Sibylla Merian 1647-1717* (Hatje Cantz, 1997)

JAN MORRIS
Morris, Jan, *Coronation Everest* (Faber & Faber, 1958)
— *Venice* (Faber & Faber, 1960)
— *Wales* (Viking, 1998)
— *A Writer's World* (Faber & Faber, 2004)

EDWARD LAWTON MOSS
Moss, Edward Lawton, *Shores of the Polar Sea* (M. Ward, 1878)
Appleton, Paul, *Resurrecting Dr Moss* (University of Calgary, 2008)

FRIDTJOF NANSEN
Nansen, Fridtjof, *The First Crossing of Greenland* (Longman, 1892)
— *Farthest North* (George Newnes, 1898)
Huntford, Roland, *Nansen* (Duckworth, 1997)

MARIANNE NORTH
North, Marianne, *Recollections of a Happy Life* (Macmillan, 1892)
Birkett, Dea, *Spinsters Abroad* (Blackwell, 1989)
Middleton, Dorothy, *Victorian Lady Travellers* (Routledge, 1965)

EDWARD NORTON
Norton, Edward, *The Fight for Everest* (E. Arnold & Co., 1925)
Norton, Christopher (ed.), *Everest Revealed* (History Press, 2014)

HENRY OLDFIELD
Oldfield, Henry Ambrose, *Sketches from Nipal* (W. H. Allen & Co., 1880)

JOHN LINTON PALMER
Palmer, J. Linton, 'A Visit to Easter Island, or Rapa Nui, in 1868', *The Journal of the Royal Geographical Society of London*, 40 (1870), 167–81

SYDNEY PARKINSON
Parkinson, Sydney, *Journal of a Voyage to the South Seas* (Charles Dilly, 1784)

Joppien, Rüdiger and Smith, Bernard (eds), *The Art of Captain Cook's Voyages* (Yale University Press, 1985–87)

TITIAN RAMSAY PEALE

Poesch, Jessie, *Titian Ramsay Peale, 1799–1885* (American Philosophical Society, 1961)

Wild, Peter, Barclay, Donald, and Maguire, James (eds), *Different Travellers, Different Eyes* (Texas Christian University Press, 2001)

ROBERT PEARY

Peary, Robert, *The North Pole* (Stokes, 1910)

Bryce, Robert, *Cook & Peary* (Stackpole, 1997)

Henderson, Bruce, *True North* (Norton, 2005)

Herbert, Wally, *The Noose of Laurels* (Hodder & Stoughton, 1989)

GHILLEAN PRANCE

Prance, Ghillean, *Leaves* (Thames & Hudson, 1985)

— *Rainforests of the World* (Harvill, 1998)

— *That Glorious Forest* (New York Botanical Garden, 2014)

KNUD RASMUSSEN

Rasmussen, Knud, *People of the Polar North* (Kegan Paul & Co., 1908)

—*Across Arctic America* (G. P. Putnam's, 1927)

Bown, Stephen, *White Eskimo* (Douglas & McIntyre, 2016)

PHILIP GEORG VON RECK

An Extract of the Journals of Commissary von Reck (Christian Knowledge Society, 1734)

Hvidt, Kristian (ed.), *Von Reck's Voyage* (Library of Georgia, 1980)

NICHOLAS ROERICH

Roerich, Nicholas, *Altai-Himalaya, A Travel Diary* (Frederick A. Stokes Co., 1929)

— *Heart of Asia* (Roerich Museum, 1930)

ROBERT FALCON SCOTT

Scott, Robert Falcon, *The Voyage of the Discovery* (Smith, Elder, 1905)

— *Scott's Last Expedition* (Smith, Elder, 1913)

Fiennes, Ranulph, *Captain Scott* (Hodder & Stoughton, 2003)

Jones, Max (ed.), *Journals* (Oxford University Press, 2008)

ERNEST SHACKLETON

Shackleton, Ernest, *The Heart of the Antarctic* (Heinemann, 1909)

— *South* (Heinemann, 1919)

Fisher, Margery and James, *Shackleton* (Barrie, 1957)

Hurley, Frank, *Argonauts of the South* (Putnam's, 1925)

GEOFF SOMERS

Somers, Geoff, *Antarctica* (Polarworld, forthcoming)

Steger, Will, and Bowermaster, Jon, *Crossing Antarctica* (Bantam, 1992)

JOHN HANNING SPEKE

Speke, John Hanning, *Journal of the Discovery of the Source of the Nile* (Blackwood, 1863)

— *What Led to the Discovery of the Nile* (W. Blackwood & Sons, 1864)

Maitland, Alexander, *Speke and the Discovery of the Source of the Nile* (Constable, 1971)

FREYA STARK

Stark, Freya, *Baghdad Sketches* (John Murray, 1937)

— *A Winter in Arabia* (John Murray, 1940)

— *Beyond Euphrates* (John Murray, 1951)

— *Dust in the Lion's Paw* (John Murray, 1961)

Geniesse, Jane Fletcher, *Passionate Nomad* (Chatto & Windus, 1999)

MARC AUREL STEIN

Stein, Marc Aurel, *Sand-Buried Ruins of Khotan* (Unwin, 1903)

— *Ruins of Desert Cathay* (Cambridge University Press, 2014)

Mirsky, Jeanette, *Aurel Stein Archaeological Explorer* (University of Chicago Press, 1977)

Whitfield, Susan, *Aurel Stein on the Silk Road* (British Museum, 2004)

ABEL TASMAN

Duyker, Edward (ed.), *The Discovery of New Zealand* (Tasmanian Government, 1992)

Heeres, J. E. (ed.), *Abel Janszoon Tasman's Journal of His Discovery of Van Diemen's Land and New Zealand in 1642* (Muller, 1898)

JOHN TURNBULL THOMSON

Thomson, John Turnbull, *Some Glimpses into Life in the Far East* (Richardson, 1865)

— *Glimpses into Life in Malayan Lands* (Oxford University Press, 1984)

— 'Extracts from a Journal Kept during the Performance of a Reconnaissance Survey of the Southern Districts of the Province of Otago', *The Journal of the Royal Geographical Society of London*, 28 (1858), 298–332

COLIN THUBRON

Thubron, Colin, *The Lost Heart of Asia* (Heinemann, 1994)

— *In Siberia* (Chatto & Windus, 1999)

— *Shadow of the Silk Road* (Chatto & Windus, 2006)

— *To a Mountain in Tibet* (Chatto & Windus, 2011)

ALEXANDRINE TINNE

Gladstone, Penelope, *Travels of Alexine* (John Murray, 1970)

McLoone, Margo, *Women Explorers in Africa* (Capstone Press, 2000)

Tinne, John A., *Geographical Notes of Expeditions in Central Africa by Three Dutch Ladies* (Brakell, 1864)

Willink, Robert Joost, *The Fateful Journey* (Amsterdam University Press, 2011)

OLIVIA TONGE

Gates, Barbara T., *Kindred Nature* (University of Chicago Press, 1998)

Magee, Judith, *Art of Nature* (Natural History Museum, 2009)

NAOMI UEMURA

Uemura, Naomi, and Talmadge, Eric, *Homage to Naomi Uemura* (Bungeishunju, 1991)

GODFREY VIGNE

Vigne, Godfrey Thomas, *Six Months in America* (Whittaker, Treacher, 1832)

— *A Personal Narrative of a Visit to Ghuzni* (Whittaker, Treacher, 1840)

— *Travels in Kashmir* (Colburn, 1842)

— *Travels in Mexico* (Allen, 1863)

ALFRED RUSSEL WALLACE

Wallace, Alfred Russel, *The Malay Archipelago* (Macmillan & Co., 1869)

— *Narrative of Travels on the Amazon and Rio Negro* (Lock, 1889)

Hemming, John, *Naturalists in Paradise* (Thames & Hudson, 2015)

Marchant, James (ed.), *Alfred Russel Wallace* (Cassell, 1916)

Raby, Peter, *Alfred Russel Wallace* (Chatto & Windus, 2001)

JAMES WALLIS

Wallis, James, *Captain Wallis' Most Interesting and Historical Account of New South Wales and Its Settlements* (Folio Press, 1821)

JOHN WHITE

Burrage, Henry (ed.), *Early English and French Voyages* (Scribner's, 1906)

Hulton, Paul, *America, 1585* (British Museum, 1984)

Sloan, Kim, *A New World* (British Museum, 2007)

EDWARD WILSON

Cherry-Garrard, Apsley, *The Worst Journey in the World* (Constable, 1922)

King, Harry (ed.), *Diary of the 'Terra Nova' Expedition* (Blandford, 1972)

King, Harry (ed.), *South Pole Odyssey* (Blandford, 1982)

Roberts, Brian (ed.), *Edward Wilson's Birds of the Antarctic* (Blandford, 1967)

Savours, Ann (ed.), *Diary of the 'Discovery' Expedition* (Blandford, 1966)

ILLUSTRATION CREDITS

a = above, b = below, c = centre, l = left, r = right

© David Ainley 242, 244, 245
akg-images 145, 168, 170, 171, 172, 173
Alpine Club Photo Library, London 28, 29, 30, 31
American Museum of Natural History, New York. Courtesy of the Division of Anthropology 57
American Philosophical Society, Philadelphia 2br, 4, 56, 58, 59, 150, 151, 152, 153, 222, 223, 224, 225, 226, 227
Auckland War Memorial Museum -Tāmaki Paenga Hira, Sir Edmund Hillary Archive (MS-2010-1) 132, 133
Audubon, M. R., *Audubon and his Journals* (New York: Scribner's Sons, 1897) 24
Photography Cristian Barnett 272, 273
Bates, H. W., *The Naturalist on the River Amazons* (London: John Murray, 1863) 40
© Alan Bean 146, 149
Staatsbibliothek zu Berlin 144
The Bodleian Library, University of Oxford 87 (MS Eng e3685, MS Eng e3725); Courtesy British Academy, London 260 (MS Stein 324, fol. 86), 261 (MS Stein 187)
Chris Bonington Picture Library 61
Bristol Museums, Galleries & Archives 72, 73, 74, 75
The British Library Board, London 88 (Add MS 15500, f11), 89 (Add 15500, f1), 91 (Add 27886, ff176v–177), 92 (Add 31360, f32r), 93 (Add 7085, f17), 195 (WD3223) 196 (WD3244), 197 (WD3260), 199 (WD3261), 210 (WD3317), 211 (WD3278), 212 (WD3308), 213 (WD2833), 220 (Add 9345, f14v), 221 (Add 23920, f66r, Add 23920, f71r), 306l (Add 47459, f202v); © Falcon Scott 246, 247, 248, 249 (Add 51035)
The Trustees of the British Museum, London 178, 179, 180, 181, 182, 183, 300, 301, 302, 303, 304, 305
© Bungeishunju 288
Reproduced by kind permission of the Syndics of Cambridge University Library 98, 99
Royal Library, National Library of Denmark, Copenhagen 2al, 20, 230, 231, 232, 233, 234, 235, 236, 237
Academy of Natural Sciences at Drexel University, Philadelphia. ANSP Entomology, Peale Collection 16
Dutch National Archives, The Hague 262, 264, 265 (1.11.01.01, inv. 121)
Biblioteca Nazionale Centrale, Florence 12l
Getty Images/National Geographic/Photo Sissie Brimberg 229
© Griffith Institute, University of Oxford 3al, 82, 83, 84, 85, 100, 101, 140, 141, 142, 143
Courtesy Haags Historisch Museum 274, 275, 276, 277, 278, 279
Photography Martin Hartley/Art Direction Huw Lewis-Jones: Bonington Collection 60; Prance Collection 68, 70; Heaton Cooper Studio 21, 94, 95, 96, 97; Evans Collection 102, 103; Fiennes Collection 104, 105; Fuchs Collection 17, 108, 109; Hanbury-Tenison Collection 114, 115; Herbert Collection 126, 127, 128, 129; Lowe Collection 164, 165, 166, 167; Morris Collection 184, 185; Foster Collection 200, 202, 203; Somers Collection 252, 253
© Sven Hedin Foundation, at Museum of Ethnography, Stockholm 122, 123, 124, 125
Hocken Collections, Uare Taoka o Hākena, University of Otago 268 (92/1184), 269 (92/1306), 270 (92/1311, 92/1312), 271 (92/1308)
Houghton Library, Harvard University, Cambridge, MA 25 (MS AM 21.018, MS AM 21.088), 26 (MS AM 21a recto, MS AM 21.051), 27 (MS AM 21.050), 32al (Typ 825 32.1757, seq. 12), 32ar (Typ 825 32.1757, seq.8), 32bl (Typ 825 32.1757, seq. 15), 32br (Typ 825 32.1757, seq. 16), 33 (Typ 825 32.1757, seq. 13)
Joslyn Art Museum, Omaha, Nebraska, Gift of the Enron Art Foundation, 509.NNG 169
Royal Botanic Gardens, Kew 175, 176, 177, 194, 198
Kon-Tiki Museum, Oslo 130, 131
By permission of the Linnean Society of London 154, 155, 156, 157, 158, 159
Livingstone, D., *The Last Journals of David Livingstone in Central Africa* (London: John Murray, 1874) 160
© David Livingstone Centre. From Wisnicki, A. S. (ed.) 'Livingstone's 1871 Field Diary: A Multispectral Critical Edition' (Los Angeles; UCLA Digital Library, 2011. http://livingstone.library.ucla.edu/1871diary/) 161
Museum Africa, Johannesburg 76, 77, 78, 79, 80b, 81
NASA/Johns Hopkins University Applied Physics Laboratory/Southwest Research Institute 12r
Collection of the National Geographic Society. Photo Mark Hensley 228
The Trustees of the Natural History Museum, London 35r, 36, 37, 41, 42, 43, 106, 107, 218, 219, 284, 285, 286, 287, 294, 295, 296, 297
State Library of New South Wales, Sydney 1, 90, 110, 116, 117, 118, 119, 120, 121, 134, 135, 136, 137, 138, 139, 263, 266, 267, 298, 299; Dixson Galleries 111, 112, 113
© Norton Everest Archive 2ar, 204, 205, 206, 207, 208, 209
National Library of Norway, Oslo 19ac, 22, 23, 190, 191, 192, 193
Oxford University Museum of Natural History 80a
Herbert Ponting 14
Private Collection 314
Harry Ransom Center, The University of Texas at Austin 259
Rijksmuseum, Amsterdam 10, 62, 63, 64, 65, 66, 67
Courtesy Nicholas Roerich Museum, New York 238, 239, 240, 241
Royal Anthropological Institute, London. Photographer unknown 19ar
Royal Geographical Society (with IBG), London 15, 19bl, 34, 35l, 38, 39, 52, 53, 54, 55, 162, 163, 214, 215, 216, 217, 250, 254, 255, 256, 257, 258
© Eric Saczuk 280, 283
Scott Polar Research Institute, University of Cambridge 19br, 186, 187, 188, 189, 306r, 307, 308, 309, 310, 311, 312, 313; with permission of the Hon. A Shackleton 251
© Naomi Uemura 289
State Library of Victoria, Melbourne 2bl, 3r, 44, 45, 46, 47
Victoria & Albert Museum, London 290, 292, 293
© Wildlife Conservation Society. Used by permission 48, 49, 50, 51

ACKNOWLEDGMENTS

This book has benefited hugely from the support and expertise of many individuals. From archivists, private collectors and librarians through to descendants, veteran explorers and field scientists, all have generously shared their experiences. The insights of our collaborators – David Ainley, Alan Bean, Wade Davis, Tony Foster, and Ghillean Prance – have been invaluable and we appreciate Robert Macfarlane for also lending his able pen to the project. We thank all the team at Thames & Hudson – Sarah Vernon-Hunt, Sarah Praill, Johanna Neurath and Rachel Heley; Pauline Hubner for chasing up so many of our strange image requests; and dear Colin Ridler, who was this book's first champion and without whom it might never have been made. Closer to home, our special gratitude goes to our mothers, now super grandmothers too: Dr Hilary Boyle and Lady Marie Herbert, for their love and encouragement. And most importantly to Nell, who has been very patient with her busy parents: we look forward to taking you into the wilderness with a sketchbook or two, and we hope you find as much inspiration in nature as we do.

INDEX

Numbers in *italics* refer to captions to illustrations